COMMON
COASTAL
BIRDS
of
FLORIDA
&
THE CARIBBEAN

by

David W. Nellis

Pineapple Press, Inc.

Sarasota, Florida

I dedicate this book to the memory of William Robertson Jr.,
a mentor, a friend, and an example of how to do it right.

Acknowledgments

In preparing this book I have selected materials from the huge stockpile of ornithological knowledge in the published literature and have attempted to present a broad view of the lives of the birds selected. I would like to thank the following photographers whose talent, opportunity, and resources allowed them to record pleasing and informative images to supplement my own work: Charley Caniff, whose photos reveal no limitations, Ted Cross, whose reverence I share, Jerry Gingerich, who manages to fit nature photography into an already overloaded schedule, David Lee, who has an understanding of birds, Patrick Lynch, who can focus on birds in spite of distractions, Martin Muller, who has the patience and persistence to really study a bird, Carlton Ward Jr., who has the potential for a career as a photojournalist, and Betty Wargo, who has been able to treat photography seriously while still enjoying the subjects. Busch Gardens has allowed the use of several of their photos and the staff at Everglades National Park provided photos from their archives. A. Morris, G. Lasley, and Barb Collins provided photos via stock agencies. After the book was completed, Malcolm Simons and Rich Paul reviewed the shorebird photos to ensure species accuracy. The early text was reviewed by Dr. Michael Erwin of the University of Virginia who made several suggestions that improved the manuscript.

Finally, I would like to thank my family and friends for humoring the eccentricities to which I exposed them while indulging in writing and photography.

Inquiries should be addressed to:
Pineapple Press, Inc.
P.O. Box 3889
Sarasota, Florida 34230
www.pineapplepress.com

Library of Congress Cataloging in Publication Data

Nellis, David W.
Common coastal birds of Florida and the Caribbean / David W. Nellis.
— 1st ed.
p.   cm.
Includes bibliographical references.
ISBN 1-56164-191-X (hb.). — ISBN 1-56164-196-0 (pb.)
1. Shore birds—Florida. 2. Shore birds—Caribbean Area. I. Title.

QL684.F6N48 2000
598.3'3'09759—dc21

99-42529

First Edition
10 9 8 7 6 5 4 3 2 1

Design by *osprey*design
Printed in China

Table of Contents

Introduction vii

Details of Form and Function ix

PART I. General Descriptions and Photographs 1

PART II. Species Accounts 75

	Part I	Part II
Family: Grebes (*Podicipedidae*)		
Pied-billed Grebe (*Podilymbus podiceps*	3	77
Family: Shearwater and Petrels (*Procellariidae*)		
Audubon's Shearwater (*Puffinus lherminieri*)	4	80
Family: Tropicbirds (*Phaethontidae*)		
Red-billed Tropicbird (*Phaethon aethereus*)	5	83
White-tailed Tropicbird (*Phaethon lepturus*)	6	86
Family: Boobies and Gannets (*Sulidae*)		
Brown Booby (*Sula leucogaster*)	7	89
Red-footed Booby (*Sula sula*)	8	92
Masked Booby (*Sula dactylatra*)	9	95
Family: Pelicans (*Pelecanidae*)		
Brown Pelican (*Pelecanus occidentalis*)	10	98
American White Pelican (*Pelecanus erythrorynchos*)	11	101
Family: Cormorants (*Phalacrocoracidae*)		
Double-crested Cormorant (*Phalacrocorax auritus*)	12	104
Family: Anhingas (*Anhingidae*)		
American Anhinga (*Anhinga anhinga*)	13	108
Family: Frigatebirds (*Fregatidae*)		
Magnificent Frigatebird (*Fregata magnificens*)	14	111

                                                    Part I   Part II

Family: Bitterns and Herons (*Ardeidae*)
Great Blue Heron (*Ardea herodius*) 15   114
Great Egret (*Casmerodius albus*) 16   117
Little Blue Heron (*Egretta caerulea*) 17   120
Tricolored Heron (*Egretta tricolor*) 18   124
Reddish Egret (*Egretta rufescens*) 19   128
Snowy Egret (*Egretta thula*) 20   131
Cattle Egret (*Bubulcus ibis*) 21   134
Green Heron (*Butorides virescens*) 22   138
Black-crowned Night Heron (*Nycticorax nycticorax*) 23   142
Yellow-crowned Night Heron (*Nyctanassa violaceus*) 24   145

Family: Storks (*Ciconiidae*)
Wood Stork (*Mycteria americana*) 25   148

Family: Ibises and Spoonbills (*Threskiornithidae*)
White Ibis (*Eudocimus albus*) 26   151
Glossy Ibis (*Plegadis falcinellus*) 27   155
Roseate Spoonbill (*Ajaia ajaja*) 28   158

Family: Flamingos (*Phoenicopteridae*)
Greater Flamingo (*Phenicopterus ruber*) 29   161

Family: Swans, Geese, and Ducks (*Anatidae*)
Lesser Scaup (*Aythya affinis*) 30   165
Blue-winged Teal (*Anas discors*) 31   169
White-cheeked Pintail (*Anas bahamensis*) 32   172
Red-breasted Merganser (*Mergus serrator*) 33   174

Family: Kites, Eagles, and Hawks (*Accipitridae*)
Osprey (*Pandion haliaetus*) 34   177
Swallow-tailed Kite (*Elanoides forficatus*) 35   181
Red-tailed Hawk (*Buteo jamaicensis*) 36   184
Red-shouldered Hawk (*Buteo lineatus*) 37   187

Family: Caracaras and Falcons (*Falconidae*)
American Kestrel (*Falco sparverius*) 38   190
Peregrine Falcon (*Falco peregrinus*) 39   194

Family: Rails, Gallinules, and Coots (*Rallidae*)
American Coot (*Fulica americana*) 40   198
Common Moorhen (*Gallinula chlorops*) 41   201

Part I   Part II

Family: Plovers (*Charadriidae*)
Black-bellied Plover (*Pluvialis squatarola*) 42   204
Wilson's Plover (*Charadrius wilsoni*) 43   207
Semipalmated Plover (*Charadrius semipalmatus*) 44   209
Killdeer (*Charadrius vociferus*) 45   211

Family: Oystercatchers (*Haematopodidae*)
American Oystercatcher (*Haematopus palliatus*) 46   214

Family: Stilts and Avocets (*Recurvirostridae*)
Black-necked Stilt (*Himantopus mexicanus*) 47   217
American Avocet (*Recurvirostra americana*) 48   220

Family: Sandpipers (*Scolopacidae*)
Greater Yellowlegs (*Tringa melanoleuca*) 49   223
Lesser Yellowlegs (*Tringa flavipes*) 50   225
Willet (*Catoptrophorus semipalmatus*) 51   228
Spotted Sandpiper (*Actitus macularia*) 52   231
Ruddy Turnstone (*Arenaria interpres*) 53   234
Sanderling (*Calidris alba*) 54   237
Semipalmated Sandpiper (*Calidris pusilla*) 55   240
Western Sandpiper (*Calidris mauri*) 56   243
Least Sandpiper (*Calidris minutilla*) 57   246
Stilt Sandpiper (*Calidris himantopus*) 58   249
Short-billed Dowitcher (*Limnodromus griseus*) 59   252

Family: Gulls, Terns, and Skimmers (*Laridae*)
Laughing Gull (*Larus atricilla*) 60   254
Ring-billed Gull (*Larus delawarensis*) 61   258
Caspian Tern (*Sterna caspia*) 62   261
Royal Tern (*Sterna maxima*) 63   265
Sandwich Tern (*Sterna sandvicensis*) 64   268
Roseate Tern (*Sterna dougallii*) 65   271
Least Tern (*Sterna antillarum*) 66   274
Bridled Tern (*Sterna anaethetus*) 67   277
Sooty Tern (*Sterna fuscata*) 68   280
Brown Noddy (*Anous stolidus*) 69   283
Black Skimmer (*Rynchops niger*) 70   286

Family: Cuckoos and Anis (*Cuculidae*)
Mangrove Cuckoo (*Coccyzus minor*) 71   290

Part I   *Part II*

Family: Grackles (*Icteridae*)
Boat-tailed Grackle (*Quiscalus major*) 72   293

Family: Swallows (*Hirudinidae*)
Cave Swallow (*Hirundo fulva*) 73   297

Family: Crows (*Corvidae*)
Fish Crow (*Corvus ossifragus*) 74   300

General References 303

Index 306

Introduction

This book is written for those who enjoy that precarious and ever-changing place where the sea meets the land on beaches, mangroves or rocky cliffs in south Florida and the Caribbean. Over 95 percent of the residents of Florida live within 5 miles of navigable water, and those who are lucky enough to live in the Greater or Lesser Antilles have an even closer proximity to the water. A great variety of birds have evolved to make a living at this interface. This book is intended to enhance the appreciation of the variety of forms and lifestyles of our fellow coastal residents. I have selected most of the commonly seen birds found along shorelines, and certain less abundant ones, to demonstrate the theme and variations on how birds make a living along the shoreline. All aspects of coastal birds show the influence of natural selection on a basic body plan. Beaks, feet, leg placement, plumage, and many other features have evolved over time to produce a host of specialists. I have selected closely related birds to show how each has specialized as compared with its relatives. Other birds, only distantly related, have been chosen to show the wonderful range of variation in form and function.

Longevity The lifespan of wild birds is usually determined by reading bands that have been placed on birds in the field. Some researchers have been able to conduct long-term studies in which adults and chicks are captured and banded on a seasonal basis.

Reading bands allows the construction of life tables showing duration of survival. When birds are banded, a banding report is sent to the U.S. Bird Banding Laboratory (BBL), U.S. Geological Survey, Laurel, Maryland. If someone finds a banded bird, the band asks them to report the number to the BBL, which will give them a report of when and where the bird was banded. Most maximum ages of birds have been determined by these banding records. This system leads to considerable bias toward younger birds reported. Some of the reasons are:

(1) A high mortality rate between fledging and breeding age

(2) Band loss, which increases in probability with age

(3) A population structure that has few old birds

Thus, when you find an old banded bird, you have usually found one of a group of chicks or adults banded by a researcher. This individual is one of the few members of its group that has lived to this age. It is one of the few birds that has not lost its band through accident or wear and whose band was recovered by a person who reported its number to the BBL. From the above, it can be concluded that the maximum age recorded for most birds is probably exceeded by undocumented cases in the wild.

Measurements The study of living animals is not an exact science. Physical measurements of individuals in natural populations always show some variation. Almost every characteristic we have attempted to measure shows variation. This variation is usually distributed such that most of the measurements are near the arithmetic average with increasingly fewer numbers either larger or smaller than the average. The measurements of individuals vary with season, gender, nutritional status, geographic locality, and individual genetics. Calendar dates and seasonal expectations are subject to alteration by the influences of weather and other natural events. The measurements in this book are rounded off from actual reports of researchers and should not be considered to be representative of all members of a population. When compiling data on free-living organisms, variation is the rule.

References There are truckloads of references on birds in any respectable university library. I have selected a few of the more relevant references published in professional journals to follow each species account. In an appendix, I list books that provide more general information about groups of birds. Theses, dissertations, and agency reports often contain much valuable but otherwise unpublished material, but because of the great difficulty in accessing most of this material I have omitted these categories from reference lists. People wishing to know more about these or other birds would be well served to use one of the databases available in most large libraries. A very useful series of comprehensive reports on individual bird species is available in larger libraries under the title *Birds of North America*.

Details of Form and Function

Lift and Ground Effect An aircraft flies because air passing over the curved top of the wing travels faster than air traveling in a straight path below: The faster the air moves, the less pressure it exerts, so the air pressure from below pushes up and raises the plane. The wings of an aircraft and a bird have similar dynamics. As an aircraft or bird flies within a wing-length of a fixed surface such as a runway or the ocean, the downwardly deflected air piles up, creating an area of higher pressure under the wing, providing additional lift. Pelicans and boobies glide close to the water in order to utilize ground effect to save energy. Military aircraft over water have tried to use the effect, but it requires such careful flying that it is not generally done. Birds are better pilots than humans and don't have nearly the catastrophic outcome of an error when flying very close to the water surface.

Thermoregulation Birds use several techniques to cool themselves in hot weather. The moist, highly vascularized skin in the throat and lower mouth may be vibrated in a process known as "gular" fluttering. Air moving rapidly over the surface of the pouch evaporates water from the surface and removes heat from the underlying tissue. Because of the large blood flow to the gular area, the cooling effect is transmitted throughout the body. This phenomenon is common in many species of birds but is most evident in the Pelicaniformes with their more developed gular pouches.

Sooty Terns cool themselves by dipping their feathers into water, while herons stand in water. Other cooling strategies include facing directly into the sun to reduce the cross-sectional area subject to heating, or defecating on the feet to cool them by evaporation. The most commonly used cooling technique is to rest quietly in dense shade.

Flying in Vs, Js, or Oblique Single File When large birds such as pelicans or geese fly, they push down on the air. The rebound of this compressed air produces a brief vortex. When flying in formation, each bird is offset to allow better forward vision and is critically spaced to take advantage of the lift from the upward side of the vortex with the inner wingtip. Flocks flap in unison, and when the leader begins to glide, each bird in turn behind glides also, giving the impression best described by the German word *Resonanzflug,* "resonance flying." The flock leader lacks the energy-saving lift and periodically drops back in the formation to allow another bird to take the more demanding lead position.

Pecten Many wading birds have a comblike structure (pecten) made of a series of slots in the nail of the middle toe. This pecten is used in plumage maintenance. Each heron species can be identified by the unique nature of its pecten.

DDT and Pesticides Control of pest insects by the use of DDT and other chlorinated hydrocarbon pesticides became popular after WW II. These pesticides were very effective and highly toxic to insects, while being chemically stable and retaining toxicity for long periods. The new pesticides were considered to be a miracle by farmers and were the key to many urban mosquito-control efforts. Gradually it was realized that many pesticides became concentrated through a process known as biomagnification as they moved up the food chain. As an example: if water has a pesticide concentration of 1 unit per kg, then the plants growing in the water may have 10 units. A snail feeding on the plants may further concentrate the toxin and have 100 units in its flesh. The sunfish feeding on snails may then have 1,000 units in its flesh, which is further concentrated by the bass to 10,000 units. The Osprey eating bass from pond water with very low concentrations of pesticide could nonetheless accumulate 100,000 units per kilogram.

After the sale of DDT was banned in the U.S., American companies continued to manufacture and export DDT to other countries. DDT levels in the environment have declined significantly in the past 25 years, but breakdown products such as DDE are still regularly found in human milk and in marine mammals in Antarctica. While pesticides are directly toxic to vertebrates, one of the insidious factors is that pesticides may have adverse effects on several physiological functions. Birds with low levels of DDT in their systems lay eggs with very thin shells that seldom withstand the jostling associated with incubation. Thus DDT can significantly reduce reproduction in birds without showing any overtly toxic symptoms.

Heron Feeding Techniques When fishing, herons may stand and wait for a fish to approach within striking range. They may walk slowly forward in a deliberate manner while searching for prey. When feeding on very active prey or when sighting prey, they may walk rapidly or run in pursuit. In canopy feeding, after a short run and abrupt stop, the wings are spread and brought forward over the head and neck to produce an umbrella-like shade under which the heron feeds. This shade can aid feeding in three ways: it produces a false haven for disturbed fish, it enhances the heron's vision by reducing glare on the water, and sudden shade may confuse a prey species. With open wing feeding one or both wings are extended horizontally while the heron peers about and strikes under the wing. When foot stirring, the bird rapidly scrapes or vertically pumps the foot on the substrate, then peers intently to catch disturbed prey. Hover stirring is a similar action while the bird is airborne. Herons may at times dive on prey from the air, sometimes with continued flight after submerging only the head and neck, and at other times coming to rest with the feet on the bottom.

Heron Courtship Each species of heron and egret has a unique courtship repertoire composed of theme and variations on the basic choreography. Prior to the beginning of the breeding season, North American herons molt into the finery of nuptial plumes in order to gain the attention and admiration of a potential mate. Details of the plumes vary in style with the species, but all are highly flexible and can be erected at will by the bearer. As sex hormones peak and courtship blooms, the beak and legs often take on a characteristic color. The skin at the base of the bill and around the eyes takes on vivid coloration. The male claims a territory and marks it by building a platform of sticks. He then displays with a series of short circling flights and stereotyped postures that show off his plumes. His displays often include special vocalizations. Females are attracted to this exhibition but are often initially repulsed by the highly territorial male. Persistence and posturing leads to eventual acceptance. Following a period of mutual displays and much touching, the pair bond is established and the male begins to deliver sticks to the female, who constructs the nest. Once an egg is in the nest, the unfeathered parts of the parents begin to lose their luster. Their nuptial plumes become soiled and worn by the time the young are independent.

Brood Reduction Many of the birds discussed in this book begin to incubate their clutch after the first egg is laid, with the result that the eggs hatch over a period of days. The first-hatched chick initially has no competition for the food provided by the parents and grows rapidly. Subsequent chicks are sequentially smaller and less able to compete at feeding time. Typically the smaller chicks get less food, and the disparity in size increases until the youngest chicks in the brood may starve to death. When food is abundant, all chicks may survive, but in lean years only the first chick may survive to fledge.

Distraction Displays Many ground-nesting birds use distraction displays to lure predators away from the nest. In the "injured-bird display" the bird seems to have a disabled wing, which it drags on the ground while running away from the nest, often calling loudly. Other birds alter their posture and movements to imitate a rodent dashing from one piece of cover to another. Once the predator has been led away from the nest, the injured bird or "rodent" takes flight away from the nest.

Nest Relief Nest relief is the term used when one member of a pair of birds replaces the other member of the pair incubating eggs or brooding chicks. Arriving birds show a variety of species-specific behaviors to signal the mate that they are now prepared to take over parental care. The bird on the nest may have conflicting drives between the need for incubation and the need for food or exercise, and may require some urging before departure.

Mangroves Along protected marine coasts and brackish estuaries of the tropics and subtropics, groups of trees have evolved to live in the muddy margins between upland and open water. These salt-tolerant trees, called mangroves, belong to several very different plant families whose other members are not generally salt tolerant. Mangroves share the trait of retaining their seeds, which germinate and begin development while still on the tree. Thus the term "mangrove" is not a taxonomic term but rather refers to a tree that fills a particular ecological niche.

In south Florida and the Caribbean three species of mangroves are generally common. Red mangroves with long-branched stilt roots and pencil-like fruits usually grow on the most seaward side of the coast. They are able to thrive in shallow water and may form large islandlike thickets called manglars, which originally have no dry land. But wave action often deposits sediments among red mangrove roots resulting in the gradual building of land. Mature red mangroves may reach 20 m (70 ft) in height with a trunk diameter of 1 m (3 ft). White mangroves may have modest aboveground prop roots, and when growing in water-saturated soil with no oxygen the roots send up pencil-like pneumatophores. Black mangroves, also with pneumatophores, can grow in environments with three times the concentration of salt found in seawater and are often found on the fringes of salt flats or other periodically dry salty areas. They are easily distinguished from other mangroves by the dark-green lanceolate leaves.

A fourth species called buttonwood or button mangrove, for its shoe-button-like spherical fruits, typically grows in moist, salty soil on the landward side of the three true mangroves. It is not a true mangrove because the seeds do not germinate on the tree. Many coastal birds nest in mangroves.

Ecological Niche

The nesting, feeding, roosting, and migrations of a bird reveal its role in the ecosystem and are called its ecological niche. Competition between species is such that if two species occupy the same niche at the same time, one will eventually triumph and eliminate its competitor from the area or force it into another niche. In order to occupy the coastal areas described in this book, the many different types of birds have developed special adaptations that allow them to use niches that are different from those of their competitors. Birds as similar as Little Blue Herons, Tricolored Herons, and Snowy Egrets feeding on the border of an estuary are able to partition the food resource to reduce competition. One study showed that while Little Blue Herons feed by walking slowly, Snowy Egrets also catch prey by stirring them from the bottom with their bright yellow feet, and Tricolored Herons are more inclined to chase prey. Little Blue Herons eat fish 31 to 100 mm long, marine worms, and crabs, while Snowy Egrets eat fish 18 to 30 mm long and small prawns. Tricolored Herons eat primarily fish and large prawns. Thus three medium-size herons foraging together in the same habitat consume quite different diets.

Brood Patch

In order to facilitate the transfer of heat from the incubating adult to the eggs, many species of birds develop a bare patch on the breast called a brood patch to allow direct heat transfer without the interfering insulation of feathers.

Disabled Birds

It is not uncommon to see seemingly abandoned or disabled young birds in the breeding season. These are usually birds that have left the nest before they have matured enough to show adult skills. If no parents are in evidence, it is often because they are off seeking food for the precocious chick. It is usually best for all concerned to leave the area with as little disturbance as possible and allow the parents to take care of the chick. In the rare instances when an obviously injured bird is found, it can be placed in a closed cardboard box and transported to a wildlife rehabilitation facility. Many injured birds can be rehabilitated and returned to the wild and the permanently crippled birds can become part of exhibits at zoos or receive lifetime care as part of an adopt-a-bird program. One such program is sponsored by the Audubon Society. Non-releasable birds of prey are provided with food, housing, and care at their center in Maitland, Florida.

Incubation Within a species, all the eggs require about the same length of incubation time to develop and hatch. If a parent begins to incubate when the first egg is laid, the hatchlings will all be of different ages. If food resources are limited, the parents may more easily find an array of food types for the multi-aged chicks rather than a large amount of a specific food type for uniform-aged chicks. In some species, brood reduction is common when the older and thus larger chicks out-compete their siblings for food delivered to the nest. In times of food abundance, the younger siblings may survive with resulting larger broods.

If the parent begins to incubate only when the clutch is complete, the chicks all hatch near the same time. This synchrony minimizes the time that the nest is occupied and is susceptible to predators. In species such as ducks and shorebirds in which the parents lead the chicks to suitable habitat but do not feed them, synchronous hatching is necessary to allow the entire brood to leave the nest shortly after hatching while all members of the group have similar needs and capabilities.

PART I: GENERAL DESCRIPTIONS AND PHOTOGRAPHS

Photo credits appear at the end of each caption. Use the following key for reference:

KEY:

DWN = David Nellis
MJM = Martin J. Muller
DSL = David S. Lee
TC = Theodore Cross
CW = Carlton Ward, Jr.
BW = Betty Wargo
JLG = Jerry L. Gingerich
CC = Charley Caniff
PL = Patrick Lynch
BG = Busch Gardens
NPS = National Park Service

Pied-billed Grebe

Podilymbus podiceps | **Podicipedidae Podicipediformes** | **p. 77**

DESCRIPTION With a laterally compressed, tapered body to part the water and a rounded rear to reduce drag, grebes are ideally formed for an aquatic existence. The male Pied-billed Grebe is 38 cm (15 in) long with a weight of 458 g (1 lb) and a wingspan of 62 cm (24.5 in). The female is 30 cm (11.8 in) long with a weight of about 340 g (12 oz) and a wingspan of 58 cm (22.8 in). The white bill has a central black band. The throat is black in breeding season and the bird is a drab brown-gray outside the breeding season. The plumage is thick and waterproof, and the toes

are individually lobed. With small wings and high wing loading, grebes develop the necessary high forward speed to take flight by pattering the feet on the water while frantically flapping the stubby wings. The territorial song opens with a trilling phrase lasting about 2.5 seconds followed by a series of about 9 bell-like tones. In the male, the call often terminates with a series of notes that sound like *cow*. Call duration is about 15 seconds. Duets or sequential greeting calls are common when the pair have been out of sight of each other for several minutes.

Above Top: *An adult grebe feeding a chick.* MJM

Above Middle: *Chicks closely follow the adults and sometimes ride on their backs (tucked under the wings), even for short dives.* MJM

Above Bottom: *The nest is a mound of floating vegetation.* MJM

Left: *Pied-billed Grebes are often found in water with dense vegetation.* DWN

Audubon's Shearwater

Puffinus lherminieri | **Procellariidae Procellariiformes** | **p. 80**

DESCRIPTION This family of birds, referred to as "tube-noses," is characterized by tubular nostrils located on top of the hooked bill. Almost all members of the family are pelagic seabirds usually found beyond the sight of land. The Audubon's Shearwater is 30 cm (12 in) long, weighs 200 g (7 oz), and has a wingspan of 69 cm (27 in) with dark blackish-brown upperparts, light underparts and flesh-colored legs and feet. The fluttery flight interspersed with short glides often changes direction. Shearwaters, unable to support the body on the feet, move forward on land by pushing with the feet while flapping and sliding on the breast. The voice, usually heard only at night, has been described as a ghostly emission from the underworld. A breeding colony in full voice at 2:00 A.M. is loud, eerie and inclined to induce people's superstitious thoughts. A call rendered as *capimlico-capimlico-capimlico* is reported from mated pairs in burrows.

Above: *Shearwaters are found on land only when they return to breed in traditional burrows.* DWN

Left: *The nostrils open through raised tubes on the top of the beak. Special glands near the eyes also discharge hypersaline solution through the tubes. This salt secretion helps the bird to maintain its salt balance in the absence of fresh water.* DWN

Red-billed Tropicbird

Phaethon aethereus | **Phaethontidae Pelicaniformes | p. 83**

DESCRIPTION This white, pigeon-size seabird with black wingtips is about 50 cm (20 in) long with the tail streamers extending as far behind. The adult has a barred back and a black line through the eye. The eye stripes of the juvenile are joined at the nape. Wingspan is about 1 m (40 in) with a weight of around 700 g (1.5 lbs). The sturdy, bright-red bill (yellow in juveniles) is slightly curved downward with sharp, finely serrated edges. The streamers, present only in adults, are variable in length, but the males' average 12 cm (5 in) longer than the females'. The

small, weak legs with webs between all the toes are placed far back on the body. When moving on land, they push themselves along, sliding on their breast. The long, narrow, pointed wings are used with strong, rapid wing-beats with little gliding or soaring. The gular pouch, characteristic of the order, is inconspicuous and covered with feathers. When disturbed on the nest, they emit a daunting, loud, shrill, raspy pulsating scream. A less vituperative form of this scream is given in courtship flights.

Above Top: *A pair of chicks on the nest.* DWN

Above Middle: *The long tail is evident in flight.* DWN

Above Bottom: *An adult attentively guards the chick.* DWN

Left: *The bill is a formidable weapon.* DWN

White-tailed Tropicbird

Phaethon lepturus | **Phaethontidae Pelicaniformes** | **p. 86**

DESCRIPTION When not breeding, this small but conspicuous seabird spends its life flying over the sea out of sight of land. The compact, white plumage with a satin sheen is marked with a black stripe through the eye and an interrupted black stripe on the top of each wing. Two long, narrow central tail feathers form streamers almost as long as the body. The back of immatures appears distinctly barred, while the immatures of other species appear pale gray at a distance. In flight the tail streamers are very evident. The length of the bird with the plumes is about 81 cm (32 in), and without plumes it is 38 cm (15 in). The long, narrow pointed wings have a span of

about 91 cm (36 in). Wingbeats are more rapid than with the other species of tropicbirds and produce a strong, forceful flight. Tropicbirds are unable to walk upright. They move forward on the ground by shuffling on the breast and belly while pushing with the feet and pulling against the substrate with the bill. The sturdy, slightly decurved, orange-to-yellow 5 cm (2 in) bill is sharp and finely serrated. Weight is variable by season and geographic location but averages about 333 g (11.6 oz). The voice in display flights near the nest sounds like *kek-kek-kek* and is a harsh, rasping snarl when the bird is disturbed on the nest site. At sea they give single-note contact calls. Other calls are produced in a reproductive context by adults and by chicks begging for food.

Above Top: *Very graceful in flight.* DSL

Above Middle: *Eye stripes are conspicuous.* DSL

Above Bottom: *An adult guards a chick.* DSL

Left: *A rare instance of an adult resting in the open.* DWN

Brown Booby

Sula leucogaster | **Sulidae Pelicaniformes** | **p. 89**

DESCRIPTION This medium-size bird is a dark chocolate brown with a sharply demarcated white breast and abdomen. Underneath the body, the tail is brown, and the white of the breast extends in a central bar to about half of the wing length. The slightly lighter color of the back and the upper surface of the wings and tail may be distinguished when the birds are perched nearby. The slightly decurved, conical bill is sharply serrated on the edges. As an adaptation to high-speed diving, the external nostrils are closed, but open secondarily in the roof of the mouth. The female has a wingspan of

about 150 cm (60 in), a length of 80 cm (32 in) and a weight of 1,325 g (2.9 lbs). The smaller male has a wingspan of 140 cm (56 in), a length of 76 cm (30 in) and a weight of about 1,000 g (2.2 lbs). In breeding condition, the feet and facial and gular skin of the male become a bright yellow. The equivalent female skin color increases only slightly in intensity with the breeding season. The immatures are a lighter shade of brown than the adults and have pale-brown underparts that may remain into the 3rd year of life. The flight is a regular solid wingbeat interspersed with short glides, often low over the waves. The call of the male is a high-pitched hissing whistle, and that of the female is a honk or quack. The chicks in the nest and fledged immatures have a call (similar to that of the female) described as an extended harsh quack.

Above Top: *This downy chick is beginning to show some juvenile plumage.* DWN

Above Middle: *Adults soar with ease.* DWN

Above Bottom: *A juvenile (capable of flight) in immature plumage.* DWN

Left: *The sharp, serrated bill helps to catch fish.* DWN

Red-footed Booby
Sula sula | **Sulidae Pelicaniformes** | **p. 92**

DESCRIPTION The Red-footed Booby is the smallest of the boobies, with a male length of 70 cm (27 in), a wingspan of 153 cm (60 in) and a body weight of about 900 g (2 lbs). The females average slightly larger than the males, with body weights up to 1,100 g (2.4 lbs). The body form is more delicate than that of the other boobies, with long, tapered wings and a longer tail, allowing faster and more graceful flight. The Red-footed Booby occurs in 2 color phases in the waters of the Gulf of Mexico and the Caribbean. The brown form has a brown body with white hindparts. The brilliant-white form has a black outer quarter and trailing edge of the wing, and an all-white tail that distinguishes it from the similar Masked Booby, which has a dark tail.

Both forms have brilliant-scarlet feet. The sturdy, serrated, conical bill is slightly decurved at the tip. As an adaptation to high-speed diving, the external nostrils are closed, but open secondarily in the roof of the mouth. The male develops a bright-green facial skin prior to breeding. Fledglings are brown with a light-tan belly and darker chest band. The flight is a series of strong strokes followed by a glide. If wind and wave conditions allow the use of wave-induced updraft, the glide may continue above the crest for over a mile. The most commonly heard call is an accelerating series of coarse squawks, *kark, kark, kark,* given on the final approach to a landing.

Top: *This brown-phase adult is on its typical tree nest.* DWN

Middle: *This perched bird shows the namesake red feet.* TC

Above: *In flight, the white tail and black trailing edges of the wings are distinctive.* DWN

Left: *A white-phase adult with a 12-week-old chick.* DWN

Masked Booby

Sula dactylatra | **Sulidae Pelicaniformes** | **p. 95**

DESCRIPTION The Masked Booby is the largest of the boobies with less size difference between the sexes than any of the other species. Perched, the black feathers of the folded wing produce a broad black band across the brilliant-white plumage. In flight the bird is brilliant white with a dark tail and the outer quarter and the trailing edge of the wing black. The adults range from 76 to 84 cm (30 to 33 in) in length with a wingspan of 160 to 170 cm (63 to 67 in). The body weight is slightly less than 2 kg (4.4 lbs) and is quite variable depending on nutrition. As an adaptation to high-speed diving, the

external nostrils are closed, but open secondarily in the roof of the mouth. The flight is generally more than 8 m (27 ft) above the water and is composed of strong wingbeats interspersed with short glides. Traveling groups often form diagonal flight lines. The greenish-yellow, conical bill contrasts strongly with the dark facial skin of the mask. The bright yellow eyes are placed to provide forward-looking binocular vision. The upper parts of the juveniles, including wings and tail, are dark brown; the underparts are white. The voice of the females and juveniles is a honk, often given in a series of descending pitch. The sexually mature male calls with a clear whistle that may be given in a frantic series. Transition to adult plumage is gradual, completed before the age of 3 years.

Above Top: *The eyes aim down the beak to aid in prey capture.* DWN

Above Middle: *A nest in typical habitat.* DWN

Above Bottom: *A handsome and distinctive bird in flight.* DWN

Left: *An adult with a chick near sedge habitat often used as shade by the chick.* DWN

Brown Pelican

Pelecanus occidentalis | **Pelecanidae Pelicaniformes** | **p. 98**

DESCRIPTION A large gray-brown bird with a length of 107 to 137 cm (42 to 54 in) and a wingspan of up to 2.3 m (7.5 ft). Males are larger and weigh about 3.6 kg (8 lbs), while females weigh about 3 kg (6.6 lbs). The 30 cm (12 in) bill is pearly olive gray. Below the split lower part of the bill is a conspicuous gular pouch. The adults have a white head and neck with a yellow forehead. In the breeding season, the back of the neck is cinnamon colored. Immatures are brown with white underparts. Adults are mute except in courtship displays. Flight is a series of sturdy wing-beats interspersed with short glides.

Top: *A bird in breeding color resting on the beach.* DWN

Middle: *The nest is a simple platform of twigs.* DWN

Bottom: *They often fly very close to the water surface.* CW

American White Pelican

Pelecanus erythrorynchos | **Pelecanidae Pelicaniformes | p. 101**

DESCRIPTION A huge, white goose-shaped bird with a long, sturdy bill. In the breeding season the upper bill develops a vertical plate about 1/3 of the distance from the tip; yellow feathers develop on the head, neck and chest; and the feet become bright red. In flight, the tips and trailing edges of the wings are black and the neck is folded to bring the head to rest on the shoulders. Pelicans walk with a clumsy waddle but can run surprisingly well with the wings spread for balance. They usually fly in a flock and when traveling any distance form Vs or diagonal formations. The formation flying allows each bird to take aerodynamic advantage of the bird in

front. When the leader shifts between flying and gliding, the following bird shifts and on down the line like a well-rehearsed dance group. The length is 1.3 to 1.8 m (51 to 71 in), the wingspan is 244 to 290 cm (8 to 9 ft) and the weight 5 to 9 kg (11 to 20 lbs). Males are larger than females in all measurements. The voice is seldom heard except for a series of grunts in hostile or sexual context in the colony.

Above Top: *They often swim in formation when chasing schools of fish.* DWN

Above Middle: *This species of pelican captures all its prey with head thrusts while floating on the surface.* DWN

Above Bottom: *The black wing edges contrast strongly with the rest of the plumage in flight.* BW

Left: *In breeding condition the upper bill develops a vertical plate.* DWN

Double-crested Cormorant

Phalacrocorax auritus | **Phalacrocoracidae Pelicaniformes** | **p. 104**

DESCRIPTION This glossy black bird about 80 cm (32 in) long has duck-like legs and feet mounted far aft on the body, averaging about 1,900 g (4.2 lbs) with a wingspan of about 137 cm (54 in). Small, earlike tufts of feathers present on each side of the head in breeding plumage account for the name. Males average larger than females. The feathers on the back and the folded wings have a metallic bluish-to-greenish sheen, and the darker margins produce a scaly appearance. The emerald-green eye, surrounded by an orange facial skin, is covered with a bright-blue eyelid. The skin of the face and gular pouch is orange. The sturdy, hooked bill is laterally flattened with the nostrils closed. An insulating layer of waterproof, down-like feathers near the skin traps air and helps reduce heat loss when the birds are diving in cold water. They must paddle strongly with the feet to remain submerged. They

fly with continuous, strong, rapid wingbeats and show a distinct crook in the extended neck when airborne. Vocalizations include a grunting alarm call and an *ok-ok-ok* call on the territory. They often swim with the head inclined upward at about 20 degrees above the horizontal and may submerge until only the head and neck appear above water. When swimming underwater they use both of the totally webbed feet simultaneously in a rowing motion, but when swimming on the surface they paddle with alternate feet. After swimming they usually sit with the wings spread until they dry. They can perch on very small branches and overhead utility wires. Perched, they assume an upright posture with the neck folded into an S and rested on the shoulders.

Above Top: *Feather patterns seem almost scalelike.* DWN

Above Middle: *Tufts of feathers on the head contribute to the name.* DWN

Above Bottom: *They have a throat-pouch, as do other members of the order.* DWN

Left: *They can balance on precarious perches.* DWN

American Anhinga

Anhinga anhinga | **Anhingidae Pelicaniformes** | **p. 108**

DESCRIPTION A slim waterbird with a very narrow head and neck; a long, terminally banded tail; and an 80 mm (3 in), narrow, sharp, spear-shaped bill with sharp serrations on the cutting

edges. The adults are 86 cm (34 in) long and weigh about 1,260 g (2.8 lbs) with a wingspan of 120 cm (47 in). Males average slightly larger than females. The male is glossy black with an erectile crest on the hindneck and is marked on the back with feathers having silvery-white streaks. Head, neck and chest of the female are brown. A series of rapid wing strokes alternating with short glides is the normal flight habit. The 24 cm (9.4 in) turkeylike tail contributes to lift in soaring flights in thermals and aids in maneuvering in flights through vegetation. Normally the dull-orange gular skin becomes black, and a bright-blue eye ring develops at the peak of courtship. The plumage is not waterproof and becomes saturated to the skin soon after entering the water. They often swim with only the head and neck out of water and

may need to paddle the feet to prevent sinking. After swimming they usually climb out onto rocks or logs before taking flight by diving off a perch. They can take off laboriously from open water but only rarely do so. They are skilled at landing on small or springy perches. They usually enter the water by slipping in quietly from a perch and seldom make belly landings from flight. Flight is with strong, rapid wingbeats interspersed with short glides. The long, fanned tail and long, thin extended neck aid in identification when in flight. The similar Double-crested Cormorant flies with continuous wingbeats and rarely glides. Anhingas walk rarely, and when they do it is with a clumsy waddle. Anhingas may make repetitive rattling or clicking calls when on the nesting territory.

Top: *Young anhingas (still in the downy phase) on the nest.* DWN

Above: *Anhingas stab their prey.* DWN

Left: *A drying anhinga is a work of art.* DWN

Magnificent Frigatebird

Fregata magnificens | **Fregatidae Pelicaniformes | p. 111**

DESCRIPTION The adult Magnificent Frigatebird weighs about 1,500 g (3.3 lbs), with the male only slightly smaller than the female. The length is 95 to 110 cm (37 to 43 in) and the wingspan 2.15 to 2.45 m (7 to 8 ft). The small feet are only partially webbed but have strong nails to grip perches. In flight, the Magnificent Frigatebird appears as a short-necked bird with long wings held

bent at the wrist, providing a silhouette of an open W. The tail is deeply forked but may be held closed. Near the breeding season, when the black male is in flight (or perched near the breeding colony) he may inflate his gular (throat) pouch to a large crim-son balloon with black speckles. The female has a white breast, and the immatures of both sexes have white heads, necks and underparts. The most distinctive characteristic of frigatebirds is their expert-ise in flight. The long narrow wings, proportion-ally larger pectoral muscles, and light hollow bones help these birds demonstrate a speed and dexterity in flight that is beautiful to behold. A frigate may circle at an altitude of several hundred feet, swoop down to pluck a morsel from the sea surface, and return to its original elevation, all without flapping once. When the frigate is trying to steal the catch of another seabird, its power dives, swoops, and loops make the otherwise skillful flight of the victim seem clumsy, awkward, and hopeless.

Above Top: *A male in flight with inflated pouch.* DWN

Above Bottom: *Females have a white breast.* DWN

Left: *Immature bird (character-ized by white head) on typical nest site on top of a shrub.* DWN

Great Blue Heron

Ardea herodias | **Ardeidae Ciconiiformes** | **p. 114**

DESCRIPTION This is the largest heron in North and South America. The adults range from 100 to 135 cm (40 to 53 in) in length with a wingspan of 179 cm (70 in). The 13.5 cm (5.3 in)-long, sturdy, slate-colored bill tapers evenly to a sharp point with the lower mandible showing a yellowish cast. The weight ranges from 2.1 to 2.5 k (4.6 to 5.5 lbs). Standing erect, it is about 1 m (3 ft) tall. The male is slightly larger than the female. The wings, back and sides of the neck are slate gray with the primaries slightly darker. The front of the neck is streaked with black, white and rusty brown. The top of the head is white with a broad, black band ending in a plume on each side. The top of the head is all black in immatures and they have a more brownish plumage. The Great White Heron of Florida and the

Caribbean is considered to be a color variation and sometimes mates with Great Blue Herons, producing a morph formerly referred to as "Wurdemann's Heron" south of the Everglades. When in flight the Great Blue Heron's legs are extended straight behind the body and the neck is folded into an S resting on the shoulders. The wingbeats are deep and slow at the rate of slightly more than 2 per second. A harsh *frawnk* is the commonly heard voice of this bird when it is disturbed and has just taken flight or when it is aggressively approaching another heron. A series of clucks and other sounds may be given when the bird is feeding near other herons or when it is at the breeding colony.

Above Top: *A characteristic heron hunting ground near thick vegetation with a lurking alligator.* DWN

Above Middle: *The heavy bill (here showing courtship colors) identifies a Great Blue Heron.* DWN

Far Left: *A Great Blue Heron hunting on the beach.* DWN

Left: *A white-phase Great Blue Heron.* DWN

Great Egret
Casmerodius albus | **Ardeidae Ciconiiformes** | **p. 117**

DESCRIPTION A slender, sleekly shaped white bird 95 cm (38 in) tall with a wingspan of 150 cm (4.5 ft) and an average weight of 1 kg (2.2 lbs). The bill is yellow, and the legs and feet are black. The bare skin between the beak and the eye is dull yellow-green but becomes bright green during the breeding season. A dark line extends from the gape of the mouth past the eye, and the neck has an exaggerated kink. When the egret is in breeding condition the lacy nuptial plumes extend from the lower back to as much as 30 cm (1 ft) beyond the tail. The flight

is strong and deliberate with the neck folded back in the shoulders and the legs extended behind. When landing, the forward momentum is dissipated with a flair of the wings before a precise and delicate landing. The voice is a low-pitched *kwaak* given when the bird is disturbed or in antagonistic encounters. A repeated *cuk-cuk-cuk* may be given in lower-level antagonistic interactions. The similar white morph of the Great Blue Heron has a more massive head and bill and lighter-colored legs.

Above Top: *A plumed adult catches a fish.* DWN

Above Middle: *Breeding colors add interest while courting.* DWN

Above Bottom: *A courtship display showing the plumes.* JLG

Left: *Scruffy-looking chicks on a typical nest platform of twigs.* JLG

Little Blue Heron

Egretta caerulea | **Ardeidae Ciconiiformes** | **p. 120**

DESCRIPTION This small, slate-blue heron averages about 70 cm (28 in) long with a wingspan of 84 to 100 cm (33 to 40 in). The males average 370 g (13.2 oz), and the smaller females 320 g (11.4 oz). The neck and head are reddish brown and the legs are grayish green. The bill is light gray at the base with a black tip. In the breeding season they develop lanceolate plumes on the back and crest rather than the open fila-mentous plumes character-istic of other members of the genus. The young are white at fledging and remain so for the 1st year. When white, they may be

distinguished from the other small white herons by the black-tipped gray bill, lack of yellow on the facial skin, and greenish legs. They molt through a piebald intermediate stage to the adult plumage although some individuals may still have traces of white when breeding in the 2nd spring. Adults emit a *skaa* call when in agonistic encounters with con-specifics or others. The other calls, such as the *unh* used by the male and *eh-oo-ah-eh-eh* used by both sexes as a greeting, are heard only in breeding season. The young produce a sibi-lant squealing *see-see-see* when begging for food.

Above Top: *Crayfish are a favorite food item.* DWN

Above Middle: *The crest can be erected at will as it is here while being scratched.* DWN

Above Bottom: *Immatures show a piebald plumage when molting.* JLG

Left: *A heron lurking in typical habitat.* DWN

Tricolored Heron
Egretta tricolor | **Ardeidae Ciconiiformes** | **p. 124**

DESCRIPTION This medium-size, gray heron has a white breast and posterior underparts. The bill and neck are long and thin with a white throat and rufous-bordered line down the foreneck. The beak, facial skin, legs and feet are yellow. In the breeding season the skin near the eyes becomes blue and the iris bright magenta. The bird develops a white crest, which is

erected in displays, a maroon area at the base of the neck, and buff plumes on the lower back. The adult is 50 to 76 cm (20 to 30 in) long with a wingspan of 90 cm (35 in). The average male weight is 415 g (15 oz) and that of the female is 334 g (12 oz). The head and neck of juveniles are chestnut colored rather than the gray of those of adults. The alarm call is a coarse guttural *guarr.* Most other calls are given in a courtship context on the breeding territory.

Top: The crest is erected as part of a breeding display. JLG

Middle: An adult with crest in normal position. DWN

Bottom Left: The long beak is an effective hunting tool. DWN

Below: A juvenile capable of flight. DWN

Reddish Egret

Egretta rufescens | **Ardeidae Ciconiiformes** | **p. 128**

DESCRIPTION The Reddish Egret is a medium-size heron 75 cm (29 in) in length with a wingspan of 120 cm (47 in) and a weight of 450 g (1 lb). There are 2 color phases, the nominate form is dark blue-gray on the back, wings, tail and abdomen with a reddish-brown head and neck. The plumage of the white phase is completely white. The percentage of white birds in the population varies from less than 4% to over 89% depending on locality. Both forms have black legs and a flesh-colored beak (dusky in winter), the tip of which is black. They have shaggy, lanceolate (lance-head-shaped) plumes on the head, neck, back and breast. In courtship the base of the bill becomes bright coral pink and the skin around the eyes a turquoise blue. Males are slightly larger than females. The Reddish Egret can be distinguished from the immature Little Blue Heron, which has yellowish legs, the Snowy Egret, which has a black bill with yellow feet, and the Cattle Egret, which has a yellow bill and yellowish legs. Flight is strong and rapid, with the head and neck retracted over the shoulders. For short flights at slow speed, the head and neck are fully extended forward. Feeding movements are light, graceful and varied and are often compared to a dance or alternatively to a stumbling drunk. The bird may seem frantic at times when prey is abundant but elusive. This egret has a clear, buglelike call while feeding. A startled bird often gives a *raah* or *crog* note when taking flight. Various expressive croakings are made in the breeding colony, and a booming, raspy call is used in courtship.

Above Top: *A shaggy rufous head and neck are the source of the common name.* TC

Above Middle: *The white-phase bird, here in breeding display, is relatively scarce.* TC

Above Bottom: *Neck and legs are fully extended for landing approach.* TC

Below: *An adult feeding scruffy-looking offspring.* TC

Snowy Egret
Egretta thula | **Ardeidae Ciconiiformes** | **p. 131**

DESCRIPTION This is a delicate, medium-size white heron 60 cm (24 in) in length with a weight of 370 g (13 oz) and a wingspan of 1 m (39 in). The legs and bill are black while the feet and lores (the unfeathered area near the beak and eyes) are bright yellow. Immatures have green legs. After the prebreeding molt in January or February, exquisite, conspicuous, lacy, recurved plumes grow on the back and straight ones on the head and neck; the lores then become pinkish red and the toes orange-red. The crest is often raised when the bird is alarmed, in aggressive situations and when landing. Flight is strong, direct and often close to the water surface with the yellow feet extended behind. This egret is quite vocal when feeding and breeding. On the feeding grounds a harsh *ahh* may be uttered when the bird is disturbed by a predator or when another Snowy Egret approaches too closely.

Above Top: *Adults add material to the nest throughout incubation and chick rearing.* DWN

Above Middle: *They prefer to fish in calm water.* DWN

Above Bottom: *The yellow feet help identify this egret.* DWN

Left: *The crest and plumes can be erected to display at will. The lacy plumes used in women's fashion led to the harvesting of thousands of egrets.* TC

Cattle Egret

Bubulcus ibis | **Ardeidae Ciconiiformes | p. 134**

DESCRIPTION This medium-size white heron has a length of 50 cm (20 in), a weight of 400 g (14 oz) and a wingspan of 90 cm (35 in). This is the only egret regularly seen feeding in uplands. Males average slightly larger than females. The legs are greenish black, and the sturdy beak is lemon yellow. When roosting they usually assume a hunched position, and when actively feeding they show shorter legs and a thicker neck than those of other, similar herons. In breeding condition they develop orange-buff plumes on the foreneck, forehead to nape and lower back. In the peak of breeding condition the legs, bill and iris become bright reddish orange. Cattle egrets are relatively silent when away from the breeding colony. In the breeding colony 9 different calls have been classified. In flight the neck is folded on the shoulders and the feet extended behind as with other herons.

Top: *Full breeding colors are shown in the spring.* BW

Above: *Fights are common in the colony early in the breeding season.* TC

Left: *Erected plumes are part of courtship displays.* JLG

Green Heron

Butorides striatus | **Ardeidae Ciconiiformes** | **p. 138**

DESCRIPTION The Green Heron is a small, chunky heron 41 to 46 cm (16 to 18 in) long with a glossy greenish-black back and wings. A large, dark crest can be erected as an aggressive or courtship display. An adult bird weighs about 240 g (8.5 oz) with a wingspan is 66 cm (26 in) The wings are also black with a greenish or bluish cast. The upper mandible is brownish black, and the lower mandible is dusky green with yellowish at the base. The bare skin at the base of the bill and around the eyes is a dull yellowish green. The neck is rufous with a buff-white streak

beginning under the chin and extending down to the breast. The underparts are gray. The result is a camouflaged appearance in the Green Heron's normal habitat. In the breeding season the skin in the face becomes bluish black, the bill becomes glossy black; and the legs bright orange-red. The male is slightly larger than the female in some populations and smaller in others. When flying casually, the wingbeat is a slow and steady 2.8 strokes per second, but it may increase by 30% or more when the bird is alarmed. The call is a surprisingly loud *skeow* given when the heron is in flight and when alarmed. When disturbed on the nest or when feeding, it gives a *kuk-kuk-kuk* call, or when highly aroused, an aggressive *raaah-raaah*.

Above Top: *They are often seen resting or lurking in mangroves.* DWN

Above Middle: *Food is often minnows caught in shallow water.* DWN

Above Bottom: *The neck is extended in an alert posture.* DWN

Left: *About to strike at a fish from a perch over the water.* DWN

Black-crowned Night Heron

Nycticorax nycticorax | **Ardeidae Ciconiiformes** | **p. 142**

DESCRIPTION A sturdy heron 61 cm (24 in) long weighing 600 to 1,000g (1.3 to 2.2 lbs) with a wingspan of 108 cm (42 in). The crown and back are black, the eyes red, wings and tail are gray and underparts are whitish. Two or 3 narrow, white 180 mm (7 in) nuptial plumes, erected only in reproductive displays, extend from the nape down to the back. The stout 8 cm (3 in) bill is slightly decurved and serrated. The tips of the

toes extend beyond the tail in the strong stable flight. Except when preparing to strike prey, the neck is folded so that the head seems to rest on the shoulders. The voice is a series of barklike *quocks* typically heard at night but also given immediately after being forced into flight or startled while in flight. Similar sounds at lower intensity are given in nest relief, copulation and food provisioning.

Above Top: *The immature is brown with fawn speckles and has a yellow eye.* DWN

Above Bottom: *Immatures are well camouflaged with streaks on the breast.* JLG

Left: *Adults have a black crown and are seldom active by day.* JLG

Yellow-crowned Night Heron
Nyctanassa violacea | **Ardeidae Ciconiiformes** | **p. 145**

DESCRIPTION This is a medium-size, dark-bodied heron about 62 cm (24 in) long, weighing about 725 g (1.6 lbs) with a wingspan of 108 cm (42 in). Males average about 10% larger than females. The head and throat are black with orange-red eyes and a white cheek patch broader behind the eye. The forehead is yellowish with the crown and crest cream to tawny. In breeding season both sexes produce 20 cm (8 in), narrow, white nuptial plumes, which rest along the contours of back and neck except when erected in reproductive displays. The 71 mm (2.8 in) bill is thick and sturdy and tapers over its entire length to a sharp point. The neck and body are dark blue-gray. Feathers of the back and wing coverts have dark

centers and light-gray edges, producing a scaly appearance. Juveniles are drab olive brown with fine, light-buff spots and brown-streaked white underparts. They acquire their full adult plumage at about 30 months of age. The pattern of both the juvenile and adult make them very inconspicuous when moving about by day in deep shade or at night in more open habitat. The more upright posture with neck extended vertically aids in distinguishing them from the similar Black-crowned Night Heron. The typical voice is a loud *caup* or *quok* often given when in flight after being disturbed. It is also given as an alarm call in flight when detecting a threat such as a predator or fisherman on a beach. The wingbeat is strong and regular, and in flight the feet are extended beyond the tail.

Above Top: *Crabs are broken apart before being swallowed.* DWN

Above Bottom: *The smoky gray color helps conceal them in the shadows.* DWN

Left: *The neck is extended in an alert posture.* DWN

Wood Stork

Mycteria americana | **Ciconiidae Ciconiiformes** | **p. 148**

DESCRIPTION These large, white wading birds with black wingtips, black trailing edges of wings and black tail are conspicuous in the field. They are about 1 m (40 in) long weighing 2 to 3 kg (4.4 to 6.6 lbs) with a wingspan of 150 cm (60 in). Males are larger than females. Naked, black wrinkled skin covers the head and upper neck except for a horny plate that covers the forehead at the base of the bill. The sturdy, tapered beak is about 22 cm (8.7 in) long and 5 cm (2 in) wide at the base with a slight downward curve at the tip. They walk in a stately manner and do not hop. When space is available, they run into the wind to aid takeoff. In flight the head and neck are stretched forward and the legs extend back beyond the tail. When moving over long distances they commonly use ther-

mals to soar over 1,000 m (3,280 ft) in altitude then glide for long distances before again seeking a lift by additional thermals. They often travel in small flocks arrayed in Vs, Js or diagonal lines. When returning to the colony from distant flights they may descend from altitude by a downward gliding spiral or a steep acrobatic dive. Short-distance flights typically have 8 to 10 flaps followed by short glides. The deep, strong wingbeats produce an audible whoosh. When at rest they often stand solemnly on 1 leg and withdraw the neck to rest on the shoulders while the beak rests on the breast feathers. Wood Storks rarely vocalize but give a deep croak when disturbed and produce a hisslike *fizz* in the nesting colony.

Above Top: *They may gather in large numbers when prey is concentrated by drought.* DWN

Above Bottom: *The beak is an effective forceps for removing fish from drying pools, and the feather-less head allows for easier cleanup after feeding in mud.* JLG

Left: *A large and striking bird in flight.* CC

White Ibis

Eudocimus ruber (albus) | **Threskiornithidae Ciconiiformes** | **p. 151**

DESCRIPTION This bird is a medium-size ibis 56 to 68 cm (22 to 27 in) in length with pure-white plumage except for black wingtips. The adults weigh 750 to 1,000 g (26 to 35 oz) and have a wingspan of 1 m (39 in). The 15 cm (6 in) thin, orange-red, decurved bill with a dark tip is conspicuous. The facial skin, bill, and legs are pink. They become bright red, and the distal part of the bill becomes black during courtship, but the colors fade soon thereafter. At close range its blue iris strongly contrasts with the red facial skin. The immature bird is dirty brown with white underparts. In flight the bird's black wingtips and fully extended neck are distinctive. White Ibises use rapid wingbeats at 3.3 per second alternating with glides on the same flight

path. When in a flock, they travel in V formation or in diagonal skeins. To allow long glides to distant feeding sites they may soar to over 1,000 m (3,280 ft) when suitable updrafts are present. The Scarlet Ibis, a subspecies more predominant in South America, has genetically controlled scarlet plumage produced by dietary carotenoids. The White Ibis sometimes interbreeds with the Scarlet Ibis when they occur together, usually producing salmon-colored descendants. The juveniles of both forms are brown with white underparts. The plumage of the similar Glossy Ibis is all dark brown. When disturbed or in flight White Ibises give a honklike *hunk-hunk-hunk*. When feeding in a flock they often produce a *huu-huu-huu* contact call.

Above Top: *The brown immatures gradually molt into adult plumage.* JLG

Above Middle: *The scarlet Ibis is common in Latin America.* DWN

Above Bottom: *Feeding is often in mud and shallow water.* DWN

Left: *Adults in flight are easily identified.* CW

Glossy Ibis

Plegadis falcinellus | **Threskionithidae Ciconiiformes** | **p. 155**

DESCRIPTION Although the Glossy Ibis appears completely black at a distance, the head, neck, back, wing, rump and tail are chestnut brown with a metallic-green or -purple sheen seen best in sunlight. The facial skin of the Glossy Ibis is bluish. The long, slender, gray-brown bill is curved from base to tip. The male is proportionately larger than the female in weight and body measurements with little overlap between the sexes. Males average 63.5 cm (25 in) in length and females 55.3 cm (21 in). Wingspan is about 92 cm (3 ft), and the adult weighs from 500 to 800 g (18 to 28 oz). The head and neck of the young are streaked with white. The underparts are dark and the plumage is a dark, dusky green lacking the gloss of the adult. Glossy Ibises fly in Vs or in diagonal skeins with alternating rapid wingbeats and short glides. Soaring birds often form cylindrical groups as they use the lift of thermals to gain an altitude of more than a mile over the colony. In flight, the dark appearance; curved bill; and outstretched drooping neck, head and legs make them easy to identify. The voice has been described as a sheeplike bleating grunt, *ka-onk*. A contact call while feeding is a low *kruk-kruk* or *huu-huu-huu*. A soft crooning sound is produced in courtship and when the bird approaches the nest.

Above Top: *The long beak allows them to probe deeply for prey.* DWN

Above Middle: *The nostrils located at the base of the beak allow them to probe in shallow water or mud while still breathing.* DWN

Above Bottom: *The plumage makes the bird inconspicuous, but is iridescent in strong sunlight.* JLG

Left: *Feeding is often among shallow, emergent vegetation.* BW

Roseate Spoonbill

Ajaia ajaja | **Threskiornithidae Ciconiiformes** | **p. 158**

DESCRIPTION A vivid-pink wading bird standing about 80 cm (32 in) tall and weighing about 1.5 kg (3.3 lbs). The wingspan is 120 to 130 cm (47 to 51 in) with the males somewhat larger than the females. Perched or wading, the adult is easily identified by the black, flattened, spoon-shaped bill; pink wings and underparts; white back and neck; and a carmine drip on the shoulders and rump and a patch on the lower neck. The head is bald and greenish, the tail is tawny buff to orange, and the

legs are ruby red. Immatures are white with pink tinges. The neck and legs are fully extended in flight, and flight mode alternates between flapping and gliding. Flocks often fly in Vs or diagonal lines. The voice is a low croaking grunt *uh-uh-uh* used when feeding with other birds. When apprehensive they may produce a rapidly repeated *huh-huh-huh*. When in courtship or near their nests, they may produce bill rattling or low clucking and cackling sounds.

Above Top: *The spatulate beak is used to feel for food in muddy water.* DWN

Above Middle: *Roseate Spoonbills are often found with other wading birds.* DWN

Above Bottom: *Nestling spoonbills gradually develop the adult beak shape.* TC

Left: *A carmine "drip" mark is present at the point of the shoulder.* DWN

Greater Flamingo

Phoenicopterus ruber | **Phoenicopteridae Phoenicopteriformes** | **p. 161**

DESCRIPTION This bright-pink, long-legged bird is 120 to 145 cm (47 to 57 in) long, weighs 2,100 to 4,100 g (4.6 to 9 lbs) and has a wingspan of 140 to 165 cm (55 to 65 in). When standing, they are just over 1.5 m (5 ft) tall. Males are taller and heavier and have longer legs than females. The wingtips, outer flight feathers and the tip of bill are black and the legs are pink. The webbed toes allow them to walk on soft bottoms and swim when needed. The large, thick bill is bent sharply downward at the midpoint. Juvenile plumage is gray-brown. Immatures are almost white and develop

increasing amounts of pink until the adult plumage is attained at about the age of 3. The flight, with neck and feet extended, has strong wing-beats somewhat faster than those of a Great Blue Heron and sometimes interspersed with short glides. The calls are varied from several gooselike calls when flying in a flock to a low gabbling conversational contact call, *kuk-kuk-kuk,* when feeding in a group. In the early stages of pair formation the male continuously produces a *cak-cak,* which is answered by the female with an *eep-eep.*

Above Top: *Strolling flamingos are evocative of the tropics.* PL

Above Middle: *There is continuous bickering in nesting colonies.* BG

Above Bottom: *Flamingos deposit a single egg on the apex of a volcano-shaped mound of mud.* DWN

Left: *Newly hatched chicks do not yet have the unusual adult beak shape.* BG

Lesser Scaup

Aythya affinis | **Anatidae Anseriformes** | **p. 165**

DESCRIPTION The Lesser Scaup is a small, compact black-and-white diving duck 43 cm (17 in) long. The males average 850 g (30 oz). The smaller females average 790 g (28 oz). Wingspan ranges from 60 to 84 cm (24 to 33 in). The male has a purple, iridescent black head, neck and breast that end abruptly when meeting the darkly vermiculated white back and white belly. Females are brown with a white patch at the base of the beak. The bill is pale bluish with a very dark nail, and the eyes are bright yellow. In flight, a

white patch is evident on the secondary feathers of both sexes. They run across the surface of the water before taking flight. They fly in irregular compact flocks that maneuver abruptly like squadrons of combat aircraft. When migrating, they fly in Vs or in diagonal lines. They are generally silent on the wintering grounds except for a loud *scaup* alarm call. In courtship, the male may accompany various displays with a *whew* or *whee-ooo.*

Above Top: *Scaup float high in the water.* BW

Above Middle: *Scaup often avoid predators by maintaining a distance from shore.* DWN

Above Bottom: *The white patch at the base of the beak helps identify the female.* DWN

Left: *The male is distinctly marked.* DWN

Blue-winged Teal

Anas discors | **Anatidae Anseriformes** | **p. 169**

DESCRIPTION Both sexes of this 40 cm (16 in) mottled brown duck have similar nonbreeding plumage and can be distinguished from other small ducks in flight because both sexes show a blue forewing with a green patch of color (speculum) and a white underwing. The speculum of the male is iridescent, while that of the female is dull. When swimming, standing or sitting on land the forewing and speculum are not visible. From January to March, the male has a dark iridescent head with a white crescent in front of the eye, a brown back and a dark-brown, dappled buffy breast. The female is a dull-brown duck with a dark crown, a lighter eyebrow, a dark line through

the eye and a buff patch at the base of the bill. They take off from the water with a direct leap into the air. The teal's weight tends to be highest on the wintering ground and lowest at the end of the reproductive season, with males weighing an average of 450 g (1 lb) and having a 65 cm (25 in) wingspan, and females weighing 380 g (13.3 oz) and having a 56 cm (22 in) wingspan. Feeding males sometimes have a *peep-peep* contact call when feeding, but the females only rarely vocalize when feeding—their call is a quack. During the breeding period the female has a high-pitched quack, and the male calls with a high-pitched *see*.

Above Top: *The sexes have different plumage in the breeding season.* JLG
Above Middle: *Feeding takes place in shallow water.* DWN
Above Bottom: *Teal often aggregate in large flocks.* DWN
Left: *A male in breeding plumage.* DWN

White-cheeked Pintail

Anas bahamensis | **Anatidae Anseriformes** | **p. 172**

DESCRIPTION This small, slim, gray-brown, speckled duck is 43 cm (17 in) long with a weight of 500 g (1.1 lbs). The cheeks below the eye, throat, and foreneck are white. The bill is blue-gray with a red patch (more vivid in the male) at the base. The breast and underparts are brown with black spots becoming larger posteriorly. In flight the white cheeks, bright-red base of the bill, and tan-bordered green speculum are distinctive. A narrow, black bar separates the trailing edge of the speculum from the buff border. The subspecies in the Galapagos Islands is less distinctly colored, while the subspecies in southeast South America is larger and darker. The voice of the male is a soft, squeaky, whistled *whee*, while the female has a high-pitched quack. In small, undisturbed gatherings the vocabulary is quite extensive.

Above Top: *The ducklings are yellow with chocolate markings.* DWN

Above Middle: *In an alert posture, the white cheeks are evident.* DWN

Above Bottom: *The eggs are deposited in a very well hidden nest at some distance from the water.* DWN

Left: *At close range they are very colorful.* DWN

Red-breasted Merganser

Mergus serrator | **Anatidae Anseriformes** | **p. 174**

DESCRIPTION This duck is highly specialized for the capture and consumption of fish. It has a long, slim body 56 cm (22 in) in length with a weight of 1.2 kg (2.6 lbs) for the male and 1 kg (2.2 lbs) for the female. They have a red eye; a ragged crest; a slim, sharply serrated,

carmine beak, and a wingspan of 86 cm (34 in). They float low in the water and usually use a long surface run to take flight, but if frightened, they are capable of direct lift-off from the water. In breeding condition the male has a dark metallic-

green head; red beak; incomplete white collar; brown-streaked, red-orange breast; light-gray flanks with darker, finely vermiculated markings; and black back. The grayish body of the smaller female merges gradually with the brownish head and pale throat. The wispy, ragged crest is smaller than that of the male and is sometimes slicked down to become almost undetectable. In the summer the male and female have a rusty-colored head and grayish body. Both sexes show a white patch on the inner part of the trailing edge of the wing when in flight. They are generally silent in winter but may produce a *rark* when flying and harsh croaks or a *yeow* in the breeding season. They are usually found in small groups. Because they walk with considerable awkwardness, when resting on land they seldom venture far from water.

Top: *The shaggy dark green head and white collar identify the less commonly seen male.* JLG

Left: *The narrow saw-edged bill of the female is distinctive.* TC

Osprey

Pandion haliaetus | **Pandionidae Falconiformes | p. 177**

DESCRIPTION The Osprey is an easy-to-identify, large hawk with a dark band from the beak through eye and down the neck. The back and tail are dark brown. The head, neck and underparts are white. The long, narrow wings are generally held slightly bent to produce a V-shaped silhouette. The brow ridges of many other raptors are absent in the Osprey. Males are 55 cm (22 in) in length with a weight of 1,400 g (3 lbs) and a wingspan of 150 cm (59 in). The larger females average about 58 cm (22.8 in) in length with a weight of 1,800 g (4 lbs) and a wingspan of 165 cm (65 in).

In flight from below they are white with a dark patch at the bend of the wings. The flight is with strong wingbeats over a small arc interspersed with short glides. They often hover when a fish is sighted, then dive when the prey is in a vulnerable position. The voice is a series of short, high-pitched whistles with an average of 14 syllables lasting 2 to 6 seconds. This call if often given in a more prolonged manner near the nesting area or after the bird catches a fish. An *ick-ick-ick* alarm call is given when the nest is perceived to be in danger of predation.

Above Top: *Ospreys often use standing dead trees to roost and nest.* JLG

Above Middle: *Fish are dismembered while the bird perches on a dead branch.* DWN

Above Bottom: *A dark stripe through the eye on the white head helps identify an Osprey.* BG

Left: *Ospreys usually fly with a crook in their wings.* TC

Swallow-tailed Kite

Elanoides forficatus | **Accipitridae Falconiformes | p. 181**

DESCRIPTION The Swallow-tailed Kite is an elegant raptor with black-and-white plumage, long, tapering wings and a very mobile, deeply forked tail. They average about 58 cm (23 in) in length and weigh 465 g (1 lb) with a wingspan of 1.3 m (51 in). From below, the head and underside of the bird are white with black trailing edges of wings, wingtips and tail. From above, the black wings and back sometimes show a blue-green metallic sheen and

contrast strongly with the white head and neck. Absence of a supraorbital ridge gives them a visage more like a pigeon than the usual stern face of a hawk. The sexes are similar in size and plumage, but juveniles up to about 1 year of age can be distinguished by a shorter tail. In flight the silhouette with narrow, pointed, down-curved wings is distinguishable from those of soaring hawks and vultures. The tail is rotated and adjusted constantly to

produce a graceful and acrobatic soaring flight. They sometimes hunt and roost in small groups. The adults make a *klee-klee-klee* call with the approach of predators or toward other Swallow-tailed Kites when establishing a nesting territory. The *tew-whee* is given during courtship, after copulation and as a greeting to a mate. The *eep* call is used by the female to solicit copulation or courtship feeding and by the young to beg for food.

Above: *The kite in flight is always an attractive sight.* DWN

Left: *The rounded head gives them a less formidable appearance than most raptors.* NPS

Red-tailed Hawk

Buteo jamaicensis | **Accipitridae Falconiformes** | **p. 184**

DESCRIPTION This is a large, sturdy hawk with broad, rounded wings and dark upper side of the body. The upper side of the tail shows distinct red with a terminal black band. From below, the plumage is light with a dark abdominal band and dark rims on the wings. The males average about 50 cm (20 in) in length with a wingspread of 114 cm (45 in) and a weight of 900 g (2 lbs). The larger females are about 58 cm (23 in) long with a wingspread of 122 cm (48 in) and a weight of 1,150 g (2.5 lbs). Dark individuals are very common in some western parts of the range, and albinos have been recorded. The voice is a hoarse piercing scream, *keeaar*, descending in pitch over 2 or 3 seconds. The call varies considerably with age, gender and circumstances.

Above Top: *The broad wings allow a soaring flight.* BW

Above Bottom: *The red dorsal side of the tail gives this hawk its name.* JLG

Left: *Large, forward-facing eyes help produce an acute vision for spotting rodents at a distance. The heavy, hooked bill is used to dismember larger prey.* DWN

Red-shouldered Hawk

Buteo lineatus | **Accipitridae Falconiformes** | **p. 187**

DESCRIPTION The Red-shouldered Hawk is about the size of a crow with a length from 43 to 61 cm (17 to 24 in) weighing 475 to 775 g (1 to 1.7 lbs). The back and wings are black with white checks, and each shoulder has a reddish patch. (This red shoulder is not always evident.) Underparts are barred with brown, russet and white from the throat to the tail. The tail is black with three equal-spaced white bars and a white tip. The wings show a translucent patch from underneath in flight. Females are generally larger than males in length and weight, but large males may overlap the measurements of small females. Males average 550 g (1.2 lbs) with a wingspread of 96 cm (38 in), and females average 700 g (1.5 lbs) with a wingspan of 114 cm (45 in). Seven calls have been recognized, with the most common being a *kee-aah* or *kee-you,* which announces the territory and is used as an alarm call. When particularly excited or alarmed they may give one or a series of *kip* calls. Most of the other calls are related to reproductive activity.

Above Top: *The rufous shoulders are the source of the common name.* DWN

Above Middle: *Some individuals show distinct barring on the underside.* DWN

Above Bottom: *Much hunting is done while perched alertly on a vantage point.* DWN

Left: *Black and white checks on the back and wings help in identification.* PL

American Kestrel

Falco sparverius | **Falconidae Falconiformes** | **p. 190**

DESCRIPTION The smallest of the American hawks, this kestrel has 2 facial stripes on the side of the head and a dark-russet back. The male has slate-blue wings and crown, buff underparts, and rufous back and tail with a terminal black band. They are 24 cm (9.5 in) long with a weight of 114 g (4 oz) and a wingspread 53 cm (21 in). The female has a chestnut-colored crown and wings, buff underparts barred by darker browns and a tail with multiple bars. They are

27 cm (10.5 in) long with a weight of 147 g (5.2 oz) and a wingspan of 59 cm (23.2 in). Wingbeats are deep and rapid. They frequently pump their tail after landing on a perch. The commonly heard voice is a penetrating *killi-killi-killi*. A whine is used by adults to solicit courtship feeding and copulation and by the young to beg for food. The chitter is used between the sexes to signal friendly intent of an approach.

Above Top: *Males have a slate-colored crown and wings.* DWN

Above Middle: *Prey is always captured with the talons.* DWN

Above Bottom: *Kestrels swoop dramatically at their prey.* BW

Left: *Kestrels often perch while scanning their territory for prey.* DWN

Peregrine Falcon

Falco peregrinus | **Falconidae Falconiformes** | **p. 194**

DESCRIPTION This large, handsome, sturdy raptor is 35 to 50 cm (13.8 to 20 in) in length with a dark-slate back, white to rufous underparts with variable bars or spots, and a prominent mustache or mask extending from the joint of the beak past and below the eye. The legs, feet, and eye ring are yellow, sometimes with an orange tint. The long, pointed wings extend beyond the tail when the falcon is perched and have a span of 1.1 m (45 in) in flight. Males average 700 g (1.5 lbs) and females 1,000 g (2.2 lbs). The size difference is not consistent enough to determine the gender of birds in the wild. There are considerable variations in average size among geographic subspecies with the largest in the Pacific Northwest. The lightest-colored races are found in African and Asian deserts, with the darkest in the Old World tropics and Tierra del Fuego. Peregrine Falcons are generally silent except when interacting with family members or threatening an intruder with a staccato *cack-cack-cack*. Females and chicks may utter a wailing treble whine when begging for food.

Above: *The streamlined head contributes to the high flight speed attained by these falcons.* DWN

Left: *The color pattern suggests the falcon has a dark helmet.* DWN

American Coot
Fulica americana | **Rallidae Gruiformes** | **p. 198**

DESCRIPTION Coots are small, dark ducklike birds with a tapered silhouette; they commonly bob their heads in synchrony with foot strokes when they swim. The plumage is black on the head and neck with a slight blue or green gloss. The balance of the body is various shades of dark gray. The chickenlike bill is white with a chestnut-colored ring near the end, and the coot has a chest-nut-colored shield on the forehead. The feathers under the tail are white. Green legs end in broadly lobed toes that provide powerful propulsion when the coot is on the surface and underwater. The American Coot is 38 cm (15 in) long with a wingspan of 65 cm (26 in). The males are larger than the females and weigh 742 g (26 oz), compared with the female weight of 560 g (20 oz). When taking flight they patter

across the surface of the water to gain speed before becoming airborne. When the coot is in flight, the head and neck are extended forward and the feet protrude beyond the tail. Juveniles are paler with a duller plumage than that of adults. The most commonly heard coot call is a sharp *kak* or *crek*. The alarm call is a *puhlk* in the male and *poonk* in the female. When showing nervous tension the male may give a *puhk-cowah* and the female a *cooah*. They make vari-ous other squawks, cackles, clucks and croaks. The Caribbean Coot (*Fulica caribaea*) is similar in appear-ance and habits but has a large white shield extending from the beak to the crown. Some authors have deter-mined that the Caribbean Coot is simply a color variation of the American Coot.

Above Top: *The lobed toes are a distinctive feature of coots.* DWN

Above Bottom: *Coots eat tender aquatic vegetation.* DWN

Left: *The dark ring on the bill tip is seen on close observation.* DWN

Common Moorhen

Gallinula chlorops | **Rallidae Gruiformes** | **p. 201**

DESCRIPTION This is a slate-black, chickenlike bird of marshy shores with a yellow-tipped red beak and a red frontal shield. The male Common Moorhen is 34 cm (13.4 in) long with an average weight of 339 g (12 oz) and a wingspan of 53 cm (21 in). The average weight of the female is 271 g (9.5 oz) with a length of 32 cm (12.6 in) and a wingspan of 51 cm (20 in). Careful body measurements of the males, which are larger, can distinguish them from females. The dark olive-brown of the back and wing has a sheen in sunlight. A horizontal white line is often exposed on the flanks when the bird is perched or swimming. A white patch of feathers under the tail on each side is often visible as the tail is flicked. Legs and toes are yellow to yellow-green. The long, slender toes are neither webbed

nor lobed but are very effective in distributing the weight broadly over lily-pads and other floating aquatic vegetation. In immatures the beak and shield are gray-green with a yellow tip. The calls are many and various, with the most commonly heard being a *kik-kik-kik* or *kek-kek-kek* of a courting male or of either bird when alarmed. An explosive *kup* may emanate from thick cover if disturbance is perceived. A soft clucking, often repeated, is a contact call given by the male in early courtship and is later given near the nest or female; both adults use it to call chicks. They swim and climb well but generally do not dive except to evade predators. When the bird is swimming, the head nods with each push of the feet. For short flights the legs are left dangling and the wings are flapped frantically. On longer flights the head and neck are extended forward and the feet are extended aft beyond the tail.

Top: *Chicks have a bright red crown seen through sparse down.* DWN

Middle: *They sometimes feed on submerged vegetation in open water.* CW

Left: *The nest is often built on a tangle of vegetation over water.* BW

Black-bellied Plover

Pluvialis squatarola | **Charadriidae Charadriiformes** | **p. 204**

DESCRIPTION The Black-bellied Plover is a sturdy shorebird with a heavy head, neck, and beak and a length of 30 cm (12 in), a weight of 280 g (10 oz), and a wingspan of 60 cm (24 in). The name "gray plover" applied to this bird in Europe is earned by the plain gray-brown plumage worn in the winter. In the spring breeding plumage the breast, chin, and throat are black in the male and

have an intermix of white in the female; the back is orange-brown with white speckles; the wings have a white stripe and lining; the crown, hindneck and rump are white; and a patch of black feathers in the wing-pit is evident in flight. The flight is swift and power-ful. The whistling contact call (*quee-u-eee* or *plee-uu*) given in flight can be heard on the seashore by day and night.

Above Top: *Feeding is often among sparse wetland vegetation.* BW

Above Middle: *Black-bellied plovers often feed on invertebrates captured in shallow water. The winter plumage is less distinctive, but the heavy bill and black under the wings aid in identification.* DWN

Left: *The adult in full breeding colors is easily identified.* DWN

Wilson's Plover

Charadrius wilsoni | **Charadriidae Charadriiformes** | **p. 207**

DESCRIPTION The Wilson's Plover is a shorebird 20 cm (8 in) long with a weight of 57 g (2 oz) and a wingspan of 38 cm (15 in). The birds have a sturdy, black bill more than half the length of the head, a white forehead extending as a white eyebrow, and a broad band at the base of the neck that is brown in females and black in breeding males. The back is grayish brown speckled with white, and the legs are pinkish. When the plover is seen in flight from below, the wing and belly are white. Seen from above, the wing is dark with a short, white bar. The call is a shrill *wheet* or *whit* and more rarely, when the bird is alarmed, *quit-it*.

Above: *The band across the chest is darker in the male Wilson's Plover.* DWN

Left: *Wilson's Plovers feed on small marine and shoreline invertebrates, but must dismember some (such as this crab) before swallowing.* JLG

Semipalmated Plover

Charadrius semipalmatus | **Charadriidae Charadriiformes** | **p. 209**

DESCRIPTION The Semipalmated Plover is a small shorebird about 18 cm (7 in) long and weighs an average of 42 g (1.5 oz) with a white neck band above a thick dark collar at the base of the neck. The forehead has a white blaze with a black band above and below connecting and extending behind the eye. The chin, nape and underparts are white. The balance of the upper surface is grayish brown. In winter, the black on the head and collar are replaced with gray-brown. The short beak is light orange with a black tip in breeding plumage, and black in winter plumage. The legs are yellowish orange, and the 3 front toes are partially webbed—hence the name "Semipalmated." The males are slightly larger than the females but not significantly so. In flight the wing is white underneath with a long white bar on the upper surface. When disturbed, the voice is an ascending whistle *tee-wee,* but may be only the last syllable. The complex song on the breeding grounds is a short accelerating series of notes that become a chuckle, then end with a descending yelp.

Above: *A dark collar with white undersides and dark brown upper parts help identify the Semipalmated Plover while it is skittering up and down the beach.* JLG

Left: *This adult is about to leave the camouflaged eggs and chick.* TC

Killdeer

Charadrius vociferus | **Charadriidae Charadriiformes** | **p. 211**

DESCRIPTION The Killdeer is a large, 25 cm (10 in) plover with a wing-spread of 60 cm (23 in), a weight of 90 g (3 oz), and 2 black bands across the white chest. The long tail extends beyond the tips of the folded wings. A black band continues the line of the beak below the eye, separating the white neck from the white forehead. A white streak above the eye continues about 2 diameters behind the eye. The upperparts are brown with rufous fringes on the feathers. The short bill is

thin and black, and the legs are flesh colored. The lower back and rump are a bright, tawny brown. In flight from above, the long wings show a white bar, a rufous rump and tapered tail. From below, it is a white bird with the 2 black bands on the chest and gray tips on the primary wing feathers. The chicks initially have only a single bar on the chest. The voice is the onomatopoetic, loud, shrill *kill-deer,* which is frequently repeated; a rising *dee-ee;* and a low trill.

Above Top: *The cryptic coloration of the chicks helps them avoid predators.* JLG

Above Middle: *Killdeers are hard to see when incubating on a rocky field.* TC

Above Bottom: *3 or 4 eggs are laid in a simple depression.* NPS

Left: *Young chicks are carefully attended.* JLG

American Oystercatcher

Haematopus palliatus | **Haematopodidae Charadriiformes** | **p. 214**

DESCRIPTION This shorebird is 42 to 47 cm (17 to 18.5 in) long, weighs about 600 g (21 oz) and is easily identified by the large, knifelike orange-red bill; black head and neck; dark-brown back and white breast and flanks. The underparts are white and the legs pink. Immatures have a dull pink back and gray legs. In flight with the deep, rapid wingbeats, the white wing stripe and white rump are conspicu-ous. Females average about 15% larger than males, with longer bills and wings and greater body weight. The whistled *weep* or *kleep* call is most often heard as a series in flight after a bird has been flushed from the shoreline. The call may also be given as a bisyllabic *klee-eep*. Adults walk or fly to evade predators and seldom swim or dive.

Above Top: *The red-rimmed yellow eye stands out from the black plumage of the head.* JLG

Above Middle: *The long, brightly colored bill and black and white plumage make it easy to identify this large shorebird.* DWN

Above Bottom: *The coquina, a small but abundant clam, is some-times eaten in great numbers.* DWN

Left: *Oystercatchers may probe in the sand for marine invertebrates.* DWN

Black-necked Stilt

Himantopus mexicanus | **Recurvirostridae Charadriiformes** | **p. 217**

DESCRIPTION The Black-necked Stilt is a slim, 38 cm-tall (15 in), white wader with black wings, crown and nape of neck extending to the scapula. The very long, thin legs are pinkish red and without a hind toe but webbed fully between the outer toes and partially between the inner toes. The neck is long, and the thin, straight, needle-sharp, forceps-like black beak is about 1.3 times the length of the head—6.3 cm (2.5 in). The eye is dark red.

The males are smaller, with a weight of 152 g (5.3 oz) compared with a weight of 177 g (6.2 oz) for females. When seen in flight from below, the bird's white neck, breast and belly contrast with its solid-black wings. When seen from above, it appears to be a black bird with white back and rump. Its flight seems swift and effortless on long, pointed wings, with neck and legs extended. The voice is a sharp *yip-yip-yip* or *kek-kek-kek.*

Above Top: *The dark upperparts and white underparts produce a strong contrast.* JLG

Above Middle: *The white body and black wings contrast sharply when it flies overhead.* BW

Above Bottom: *Stilt chicks are able to run about and feed themselves soon after hatching.* BW

Left: *The thin, straight bill is ideal for plucking invertebrates from the mud.* DWN

American Avocet

Recurvirostra americana | **Recurvirostridae Charadriiformes** | **p. 220**

DESCRIPTION The American Avocet is a large, white shorebird with broad black stripes on the wing and back and a wingspan of about 90 cm (35 in). It is 45 cm (17.5 in) long, with very long blue-gray legs, a

long neck and a long, upwardly curved 9-m (3.6 in) black bill. Males have longer, straighter bills than those of females, which are shorter with a more pronounced upward curve. The first feathers on the wing and the smaller feathers covering them are black, giving a black-tipped wing in flight. Two bold, black stripes on the back are conspicuous when viewed from above. The molt to breeding plumage takes place from January to March when the head and neck become orange-brown, shading into the white breast and back

plumage. In the late summer, the orange plumage is replaced with very pale gray. Males average 323 g (11.4 oz) and females 310 g (10.9 oz), but considering the wide variation and overlap in body measurements in both sexes, neither gender is consistently larger. The wingbeat is 43 beats per minute, with strong deep strokes. They may stand, sleep, take off or land using only 1 leg. In flight the head and legs are extended fore and aft. The penetrating alarm call is a disyllabic *plee-eek, kleet* or *kluit,* which is given in a less vociferous manner as a contact call between members of a flock or parents calling young.

Top: *Avocets usually feed in shallow water.* DWN

Left: *The upward curve of the beak and the strongly contrasting plumage identify this bird.* TC

Greater Yellowlegs

Tringa melanoleuca | **Scolopacidae Charadriiformes** | **p. 223**

DESCRIPTION A tall, 35 cm (14 in) gray-brown shorebird with fine gray, white and black checkering on the back, a weight of about 170 g (6.7 oz) and a wingspan of 72 cm (28 in). The dusky-brown streaks on the crown and back of neck become arrowhead shaped on the front of neck and the sides. The long, robust bill, 1.5 times as long as the head, is black on the tip, grading to brown at the base and may curve slightly upward. The legs are bright yellow. The hind toe is well developed, and webbing is present at the base of the middle and outer toes. In breeding plumage, the head and neck are very heavily streaked with dark brown while the back and

wings have more distinctive checkering. In flight the tail coverts show as a square white patch before the barred tip. The toes extend beyond the tail in flight. The females are larger than the males, but the difference is slight and there is a large overlap in values between the sexes. They have a very deliberate wingbeat and often a long slow glide before landing. The call is a ringing series of 3 or more *teu* or *wheu* notes. It may be distinguished from the very similar Lesser Yellowlegs by a longer bill, thicker leg joints and a nostril opening in the beak that is 1 nostril length from the base of the beak. If individuals of the 2 species stand side by side, the size difference is distinctive.

Top: *Feeding is usually in water or wet mud.* JLG

Middle: *They are very alert for predators.* JLG

Left: *The bright yellow legs obviously give the bird its name.* JLG

Lesser Yellowlegs
Tringa flavipes | **Scolopacidae Charadriiformes** | **p. 225**

DESCRIPTION A medium-size gray-brown shorebird with bright-yellow legs in the breeding season that may sometimes be more orange. The hind toe is well developed, and webbing is present at the base of the middle and outer toes. The back has fine gray, white and black checkering, and the body length is 28 cm (11 in). They average about 80 g (2.8 oz) in weight with a wingspan of 61 cm (24 in). The wings of females average longer than those of males. The pointed, slim straight bill is black on the tip grading to brown at the base and is about 3.8 cm (1.4 in) long and 1.0 to 1.3 times as long as the head. In the field the bill appears as long as the head. In breeding plumage the head and neck are very heavily streaked with dark brown, while the back and wings have more distinctive checkering. The wingbeats in flight are slow and elastic, but the bird has the capacity for high-speed zigzag flight when frightened. In flight the tail coverts show as a square white patch and the toes extend beyond the tail. The call is a *tu, yew, tew* or *wheo* given once or twice. They may bob the head and tail when walking. The Lesser Yellowlegs may be distinguished from the very similar Greater Yellowlegs by a shorter, slimmer bill, thinner leg joints and a nostril opening that begins at the base of the beak. If the 2 species can be compared side by side, the size difference is distinctive.

Above: *They may feed in shallow water.* TC

Left: *The Lesser Yellowlegs is calling and displaying.* JLG

Willet

Catoptrophorus semipalmatus | **Scolopacidae Charadriiformes** | **p. 228**

DESCRIPTION The Willet is a large 35 cm (14 in) sandpiper with a straight, heavy black bill. The females average heavier, 301 g (11 oz), than the males, 273 g (9.7 oz), in the spring. Winter birds weigh about 25% less. The laterally compressed bill averages 5.8 cm (2.3 in) in length for both sexes, and the wingspan is about 71 cm (28 in). Willets are a drab, speckled bird when on the ground but become conspicuous in flight. From above they show black-tipped gray wings with a bold white stripe. From below in flight the black wings with a white stripe contrast strongly

with the body. The upper parts of the adult in fall and winter are brownish gray with lighter fringes on the feathers. The underparts are white with grayish on the breast and flanks. In breeding plumage the back becomes more boldly marked with brown and black, and in the eastern race, the neck, breast and flanks become heavily streaked and barred. They have a pale eye ring and a white eyebrow. The long, thick bluish-gray legs have a hind toe and webs between all the front toes. The alarm call is a repeated *kip-kip* or *yip-yip* that increases in frequency and volume as the threat increases. In the breeding season the call is a strident, onomatopoetic *pill-will-willet* or a descending *kay-ee*.

Above Top: *The nests are sometimes carefully concealed in dense vegetation.* DWN

Above Middle: *The wing markings are conspicuous in flight.* CW

Above Bottom: *They are often in flocks.* CW

Left: *The winter plumage tends to be shades of gray, darker above and lighter below.* DWN

Spotted Sandpiper
Actitus macularia | **Scolopacidae Charadriiformes | p. 231**

DESCRIPTION This small 20 cm (8 in), 40 g (1.4 oz) sandpiper is gray-brown above with a tail that extends slightly beyond the folded wings. The wingspan is 38 cm (15 in). It has short legs with only the outer and middle toes webbed at the base. The stout bill is about the length of the head and often droops slightly. A dark line through the eye contrasts with a white eyebrow. In winter the upper parts are gray and the under-parts are white with spots, but in breeding plumage they have bold, round spots below and the bill and legs become bright pink or yellow.

Females weigh 20% to 25% more than the males, but invest so much of their physical reserves in multiple clutches of eggs that they weigh considerably less than the males at the end of the nesting season. In flight the Spotted Sandpiper shows a conspicuous white wing stripe and a round-tipped tail with black-barred, white outer feathers. It alternates quick, shallow wingbeats (halting abruptly just below the horizontal) with soaring low over the water on stiffly bowed wings. A solitary feeder, it teeters and tips up its tail at almost every step. The voice is a rising series of *peet* or *peet-weet* notes.

Below: *The spotted sandpiper has white undersides in winter plumage and develops the distinct spots in late spring and summer.*
JLG

Ruddy Turnstone

Arenaria interpres | **Scolopacidae Charadriiformes** | **p. 234**

DESCRIPTION This small, 23 cm (9 in), chunky shorebird, with a wingspan of 44 cm (17.5 in) has a short neck; a short, wedge-shaped slightly upturned bill; and short, sturdy orange-red legs with no webbing between the toes. In breeding plumage it has a sharply patterned black-and-white head, rusty upperparts, a white belly and a black bib. In the winter the plumage is less distinct with a brown head, buff throat and gray-brown bib. The females have slightly larger body measurements than the males and weigh about 120 g (4.2 oz). The males weigh about 110 g (3.9 oz). In flight the

top view gives bold stripes, and blocks and bands of black, white and rust. From below it is white with a black bib and tail band. The wingspan is about 54 cm (21 in). The voice is a *trik-tuk-tuk-tuk* or a low *kut-kut-kut* as a contact call while feeding. When flushed, the bird may call *kuu* or *kik-ik*. The flight is strong with stiff shallow wingbeats. When in a flock on the wintering grounds, they fly in very tight groups, but they migrate in straggling lines.

Above Top: *Ruddy Turnstones often flip over shells and small stones to reveal invertebrate food species.* JLG

Above Middle: *Turnstones often scuttle about with a distinctive hunched-over posture.* DWN

Above Bottom: *Digging in windrows of seaweed is a favorite foraging technique.* DWN

Left: *A Ruddy Turnstone on its nest among lichens.* TC

Sanderling

Calidris alba | **Scolopacidae Charadriiformes** | **p. 237**

DESCRIPTION

Sanderlings in winter plumage are small, light-gray shorebirds 20 cm (8 in) long, weighing about 54 g (1.9 oz) and having white eyebrows and underparts. The straight, black tapered bill is 25 cm (1 in) long. The wingspread is about 38 cm (15 in). In flight they have a bold, white wing stripe and a black patch at the bend of the wing. They often fly in compact, coordinated

flocks near the surface of the sea or the shore. They also forage and roost in close proximity to each other. In breeding plumage the head, neck and upper breast are rufous and spotted with black, and the feathers on the back have rufous edging. Sanderlings do not have a hind toe, but the front toes have narrow marginal webs that allow them to swim well. Their call while in flight is a distinct *kip, twit, twick* or *quit.*

Above Top: *Sanderlings often feed in unison as they follow receding waves.* DWN

Above Middle: *They appear to be in constant motion as they dash up and down the beach while feeding.* DWN

Above Bottom: *Even on an otherwise deserted beach, Sanderlings often stay close together.* TC

Left: *Large flocks sometimes gather in suitable shallow habitats.* DWN

Semipalmated Sandpiper

Calidris pusilla | **Scolopacidae Charadriiformes** | **p. 240**

DESCRIPTION This small sandpiper is about 15 cm (6 in) long with a weight of about 25 g (1 oz) and a wingspan of 35 cm (14 in). These sandpipers have a short, sturdy black bill sometimes slightly downcurved at the tip, a light stripe above the eye, and black legs with small webs between the toes. In the fall and winter they are an irregular brownish gray on the crown, nape and back; have grayish white on the throat, breast and abdomen; and have a black tail. In breeding plumage the feathers on the back are dark centered with buff borders. In flight, usually low over the water, pointed wings are narrow and straight with a distinct white wing bar. The central rump and tail are black. The most common call is an unobtrusive *chert* or *cherk* that becomes softer when used in the twittering of a foraging group. A variety of special calls are given on the breeding grounds. This bird is notoriously similar to several other small sandpipers, especially the Western Sandpiper.

Below: *This Semipalmated Sandpiper (being held by a biologist) is in breeding plumage.* NPS

Western Sandpiper

Calidris mauri | **Scolopacidae Charadriiformes | p. 243**

DESCRIPTION The Western Sandpiper is often one of the small peeps on the beach. It is 16 cm (6.2 in) long with a wingspan of 36 cm (14 in) and an average weight of 26 g (1 oz). In breeding plumage these sandpipers have reddish crown, cheek patch and scapular feathers. The long, black slightly decurved beak is 2.5 to 3 times the distance from the base of the beak to the eyes. Females average slightly larger than males. Female beaks are generally more than 24.8 mm (1 in) in length and males' less than 24.2 mm (.95 in). The Western Sandpiper is very similar in appearance to the Semipalmated Sandpiper, but some studies have shown that the length-to-width ratio of the bill is diagnostic for some specimens and that a series of 22 body measurements correctly identify 88% of the specimens. With poor lighting or at some distance, identification is almost always in doubt. The flight note has been described a *bleet, cheerp, kreep* or *chir-eep.* The call is given by both sexes when flying, resting in a flock or when disturbed.

Below: *This Western Sandpiper is seen trotting along its typical open beach habitat.* © (A. Morris)/VIREO

Least Sandpiper

Calidris minutilla | **Scolopacidae Charadriiformes | p. 246**

DESCRIPTION The smallest of the shorebirds, it has a length of 14 cm (5.5 in), a wingspan of 28 cm (11 in) and a weight of 24 g (0.86 oz). The black, 18 mm (0.7 in) bill tapers to a fine point. The head is dark with a line over the eye, and the bird has a dark, slender bill and white belly and undertail coverts. The breast is buff gray with streaked sides. The pale-green to yellow-green legs help distinguish it from the similar Semipalmated Sandpiper. The contact call when the bird is flying in the nonbreeding season is a *wheet-wheet-wheet*.

Left: *The Least Sandpiper uses a variety of open wetland habitats to seek its prey of crustaceans, mollusks, and insects.* NPS

Stilt Sandpiper
Calidris himantopus | **Scolopacidae Charadriiformes | p. 249**

DESCRIPTION A medium-size shorebird 20 cm (8 in) long with a wingspan of 40 cm (15.7 in) with dull-greenish legs and a long, sturdy bill curved slightly down at the outer third, and laterally expanded at the tip. During the bird's strong, powerful flight, the bill and feet, extended perpendicular to the long wings, give the impression of a cross. The toes and lower part of the leg extend beyond the tail tip when the bird is in flight. In the fall and winter, the feathers of the back are ash gray with lighter edges. The underparts are white, with gray streaks on the neck and breast. A dark stripe in front of the eye contrasts with a white patch over the eye. In breeding plumage, the head has a broad, rufous band; the black dorsal feathers are rufous edged; the upper neck and breast are streaked

with brown; and the underpart barring is brownish in females and closer to black in males. The lower breast, belly and undertail are strongly barred. The wing, bill and other measurements of females average slightly longer than those of males, and in the breeding season the female averages 61 g (2.1 oz), compared with the male's average of 54 g (1.9 oz). For all practical purposes the genders cannot be separated by field observation. The voice is usually a trilled *grrt, kirrt* or *querp,* sometimes ending with a short chatter. A varied series of calls are given to designate territory and threaten intruders. A soft *weet* is given by the parents as a contact call to the chicks hiding from a predator.

Above: *The comparatively long legs of the Stilt Sandpiper are an obvious source for its name.* Barb Collins

Left: *The cryptic patterns on the chicks help conceal them from predators.* TC

Short-billed Dowitcher

Limnodromus griseus | **Scolopacidae Charadriiformes** | **p. 252**

DESCRIPTION The Short-billed Dowitcher is a long-billed shorebird 28 cm (11 in) long with a dark-gray back, light-gray barred breast, and white underparts; the bird weighs 110 g (3.8 oz) and has a wingspan of 48 cm (19 in). The beak ranges from 51 to 68 mm (2 to 2.6 in) with an average of about 60 mm (2.4 in) and is about twice the length of the head. Beak lengths of Short-billed and Long-billed Dowitchers of both sexes overlap considerably. A white streak extends from the beak to back above the eye, and a black streak extends from the beak to the eye and beyond. The streaks separate the darker crown from the lighter cheeks. A white rump patch that is conspicuous in flight extends well up on the back.

Males on average are smaller than females, but due to overlap of range of measurements, size is not diagnostic of gender. In breeding plumage the breast and head become reddish brown with no spotting on the Short-billed, but dark spotting on the neck and breast of the Long-billed Dowitcher. The Short-billed Dowitcher has a whistling 3-note call, *tu-tu-tu,* that can be used to separate it from the very similar Long-billed Dowitcher, which has a single, thin *keek* call. The white or tan bars on the tail of the Short-billed Dowitcher tend to be wider than the black bars, while the opposite is true of the tail of the Long-billed Dowitcher.

Above: *This Short-billed Dowitcher is displaying in full breeding plumage.* TC

Left: *The Short-billed Dowitcher probes in sandy beaches, wetland mud, and marshes for invertebrate prey.* DWN

Laughing Gull

Larus atricilla | **Laridae Charadriiformes** | **p. 254**

DESCRIPTION This is a medium-size gull 40 to 46 cm (16 to 18 in) long with a wingspan of 104 cm (41 in), a black head and wingtips, a dark-gray back and a white neck, breast and tail. Narrow crescents of white feathers accent the eyes. The males are slightly larger, with an average weight of 249 g (9 oz), compared with the 224 g (8 oz) average weight of females. The bill and legs are dark red in the breeding season but black in the winter when the head becomes a mottled gray. The calls of the very vocal

Laughing Gull have been studied in much detail. The onomatopoetic *ha-ha-ha* carries very well and typifies the auditory ambiance of many harbors. The alarm call, a repeated *kut-kut-kut,* is one of the many calls described in detail in ornithological journals. The delicate, agile flight allows dipping to pluck small fish from schools near the surface and snatching morsels exposed by working tractors in agricultural fields and by heavy equipment in landfills. They often soar on thermals.

Above Top: *The black hood is characteristic in the breeding season.* DWN

Above Middle: *Laughing Gulls are often found around marinas and other works of man.* CW

Above Bottom: *Gull chicks are mobile and able to run soon after hatching, but young ones usually crouch and hide when disturbed.* DWN

Left: *The flight is light and skilled.* DWN

Ring-billed Gull

Larus delawarensis | **Laridae Charadriiformes** | **p. 258**

DESCRIPTION This gull has a dove-shaped head, gray back and upper wings, black wingtips with conspicuous white spots and a wingspan of 138 cm (54 in). From below in flight they are white with spotted black wingtips. Males are 50 cm (20 in) long and weigh about 550 g (19 oz); females are 47 mm (18.5 in) long and weigh 470 g (16.5 oz). Skeletal measurements of males average 6% longer than those of females. The legs are yellow-green. The yellow 4.2 cm (1.6 in) bill has a black band just before the decurved, yellow-white tip. The most commonly heard call is a

kakakak or *uk-uk-uk*, given when the gull is disturbed by the approach of a predator, or a high-pitched *kee-ow*, along with other complex calls and variations.

Above Top: *The spread tail increases lift and allows slower flight.* JLG

Above Middle: *They spend much of the day perched in small flocks, often on or near the works of man.* CW

Left: *The plumage is maintained by frequent, careful preening.* DWN

Below: *They soar and hover with skill in windy weather.* CW

Caspian Tern

Sterna caspia | **Laridae Charadriiformes** | **p. 261**

DESCRIPTION The Caspian is the largest of the terns with a length of 52 cm (20 in), a weight of 700 g (1.5 lbs) and a wingspan of 134 cm (53 in). Males tend to be larger than females. Outside the breeding season the smooth black cap becomes flecked with white and the 7 cm (2.8 in) red-orange beak has a black tip. In the breeding season the beak becomes coral red with a black band at the end. In flight they have a slightly forked tail and dark-gray undersurface of primary feathers. Immatures retain the white flecks in the cap until the birds attain breed-ing plumage. The contact call is a loud, harsh *kraaa* or *r-rau*, similar to that of the gray heron, which becomes a series of barks, *ra-ra-ra,* as an alarm call. Also regularly heard at breeding colonies is a female begging and a call advertising the delivery of fish.

Above: *Parents closely attend newly hatched chicks.* TC

Left: *Nesting is typically in very dense colonies, commonly with other seabirds such as Sandwich Terns.* TC

Royal Tern
Sterna maxima | **Laridae Charadriiformes** | **p. 265**

DESCRIPTION This large, crested tern with a daggerlike, 6 cm (2.4 in) orange bill has a deeply forked tail and a black crest. From above and when the tern is perched, the back and top of wings are light gray, and the balance of the plumage is white. During incubation and chick rearing the forward part of the crest becomes white with white speckling in much of the remaining black cap; the beak becomes a more pale orange or even yellow after breeding. The average length is 48 cm (19 in) with a weight of 400 g (14 oz) and a wingspan of 130 cm (51 in). Males average larger than

females, but there are overlaps between the sexes in most measurements. The graceful wingbeats are deep and powerful. The typical voice is a deep *krryuk*, and the alarm call is *keet-keet*. Several other similarly structured calls are associated with reproductive activities.

Above Top: *Royal Terns are very vocal in the breeding colony.* DWN

Above Middle: *Nests are placed close together in breeding colonies.* DWN

Below: *The flight is strong and controlled.* DWN

Sandwich Tern

Sterna sandvicensis | **Laridae Charadriiformes** | **p. 268**

DESCRIPTION This medium-sized crested tern has a black cap, light gray back, white underparts and dark-tipped wings extending beyond the tail when it is perched. The terns are 40 cm (16 in) long with a weight of about 250 g (9 oz) and a wingspan of 90 cm (35 in). The 14 cm (5.5 in) tail has a 9 cm (3.5 in) fork. The narrow black bill with a yellow tip is 5.5 cm (2 in) long. In the winter the forehead is white and merges into the black,

speckled crest. Immatures are mottled. The contact call in flight is a *kireet,* with repeated *krik, krik* as an alarm call at the colony. Juveniles beg with a *chee-chee-chee.*

Above Top: *Sandwich Terns have an airy flight.* DWN

Above Middle: *Sandwich Terns nest in dense colonies, often with Royal Terns.* DWN

Left: *The yellow-tipped black beak is distinctive.* DWN

Below: *Sandwich Terns develop a white forehead in winter plumage.* DWN

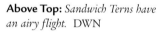
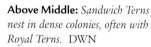
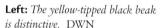

Roseate Tern

Sterna dougallii | **Laridae Charadriiformes** | **p. 271**

DESCRIPTION Roseate Terns have a black cap, pearl-gray back and wings, white underside and deeply forked tail with the outer feathers forming streamers 15 to 20 cm (6 to 8 in) long. The slim, black bill with a red base and narrow, decurved tip is 3.8 cm (1.5 in) long. The bill of Caribbean individuals is commonly red for 2/3 or more of its length. Body length is 35 cm (14 in), weight is 110 g (3.8 oz) and wingspan is 76 cm (30 in). The flight is light and

graceful with shallow, rapid wingstrokes. When the tern is perched, the tail extends considerably beyond the wings. The voice is a *chew-ik* and when alarmed a *kraak* in addition to other calls between mates and offspring.

Above Top: *This delicate tern flies in a lively and graceful manner.* DWN

Above Middle: *Roseate Tern chicks can hide effectively.* DWN

Left: *Airspace is often very congested over nesting colonies.* DWN

Below: *In the Caribbean, flocks often choose small, rocky islands for their colonial nest sites.* DWN

Least Tern

Sterna antillarum | **Laridae Charadriiformes** | **p. 274**

DESCRIPTION This delicate little tern is 22 cm (9 in) long with a black cap, white forehead and gray mantle. Least Terns have a bright-yellow bill with a black tip in the spring and summer. Adults have a wingspan of 51 cm (20 in) and weigh about 48 g (1.7 oz), depending on reproductive and nutritional state. In the fall and winter they lose the black cap, leaving only a dark line behind the eye while the bill and legs are dark. The light, graceful strong flight often includes acrobatic maneuvers. The considerable array of vocalizations of Least Terns includes an alarm call, *zreeep*, which is

mixed with staccato *tsip* or *kit*, and may escalate to a growling *krowk* at the closest approach in an aggressive dive. At colonies a contact call is made by males bringing fish to the nest; it is also a summons call by the parents to the chicks and a begging call by the chicks.

Above Top: *This tiny tern has a light and bouncy flight.* DWN

Above Middle: *The speckled and splotched eggs are laid in a slight depression.* CC

Left: *Chicks are mobile and seek nearby cover soon after hatching.* CC

Below: *Entire colonies nest in the open on beaches or other cleared areas.* CC

Bridled Tern

Sterna anaethetus | **Laridae Charadriiformes** | **p. 277**

DESCRIPTION The Bridled Tern has a dark back, white to clouded underparts and a white forehead that extends several diameters past the eye. A dark line extends from the bill through the eye to the nape. A light-gray band separates the dark back from the black head. Adults are about 31 cm (12 in) long with a wingspan of 79 cm (31 in) and a weight of 130 g (4.7 oz). Males are slightly larger than females and have longer wings and beaks. First-winter birds have a crown streaked with white. The flight on long, narrow pointed wings and deeply forked tail is

considered to be the most graceful of the terns; there is a rising and falling of the body in response to the wingbeats. They seldom venture more than 50 m (164 ft) above the water surface. Varied calls include a yapping alarm call (*wep-wep*), an angry growl (*grrr*) given toward conspecifics, and a tremulous *hrrr* commonly given by males as an advertising call. Fishing birds may give a *kit* or *kee-yarr*. The similar Sooty Tern is 10% larger than the Bridled Tern and has longer wings and a white bar from the forehead that extends only to the eye.

Above Top: *They often pause in flight before diving to capture small prey.* DWN

Above Middle: *Bridled Terns may travel far offshore in small flocks to feed.* DWN

Left: *The white forehead band extending past the eye helps identify the Bridled Tern. They often perch on a rock before walking to the concealed nest.* DWN

Sooty Tern

Sterna fuscata | **Laridae Charadriiformes** | **p. 280**

DESCRIPTION The Sooty Tern is dark as seen from above and white as seen from below. It has a white forehead extending back to the eye and a black line from the bill to the eye. The crown, nape and back are all dark. The beak, feet and legs are black. They are about 36 cm (14 in) long with a weight of about 190 g (6.7 oz). The long, pointed wings have a

span of 88 cm (35 in), and the tail is deeply forked with white outer feathers. The distinctive voice has been described as *ker-wacki-wack*. They also produce variations of other typical tern calls.

Above Top: *The white forehead extends only to the eye in Sooty Terns.* DWN

Above Middle: *The fine detail of the feathers is evident when they flare for landing.* DWN

Left: *The entire colony becomes alert at the slightest disturbance.* DWN

Below: *Sooty Terns may aggregate in breeding colonies of over 100,000 birds.* DWN

Brown Noddy
Anous stolidus | **Laridae Charadriiformes** | **p. 283**

DESCRIPTION This dark-brown, ternlike bird is about 42.5 cm (17 in) long. The white forehead contrasts with the black bill and gradually becomes more grayish on the back of the crown before blending gradually with the brown feathers of the nape. The inside of the open mouth is a conspicuous orange-red. Females have smaller body measurements than the males and a weight of 167 g (6 oz), as compared with 178 g (6.4 oz) for males. Brown Noddies have a broad vari-

ety of calls and displays. The adult calls are a series of different, harsh, low-frequency calls commonly used in antagonistic or reproductive encounters. The most commonly heard call is a growling *caw* given at the closest approach when diving at a predator. Brown Noddies travel over the sea with shallow, gull-like wingbeats sometimes giving a *kark* contact call.

Above Top: *The neck is extended in an alert posture.* DWN

Above Middle: *The chicks stay on the precarious nest until ready to fly.* DWN

Above Bottom: *The nest on a bare, rocky ledge is composed of a few added shells or pebbles.* DWN

Left: *The light forehead blends gradually into the fine, dark chocolate body color.* DWN

Black Skimmer

Rynchops niger | **Laridae Charadriiformes** | **p. 286**

DESCRIPTION The skimmer has a ternlike body shape with black upperparts and white forehead, cheeks and underparts. The most distinctive feature is the laterally compressed bill 6.5 cm (2.5 in), bright red at the base and black at the tip with the lower mandible longer than the upper. When closed, the knifelike edge of the lower mandible rests in a slot in the upper. The feet are reddish orange. A large pupil that contracts to a vertical slit in bright light is probably an adaptation to enhance vision while feeding at night. The adult bird is 46 cm (18 in) long with long, narrow pointed wings with a span

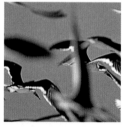

of 112 cm (44 in). The male is about 25% larger—365 g (12.8 oz)—than the female at 265 g (9.3 oz). In flight the white underwings alternate with the black wing coverts to provide an alternating black-and-white pattern. Skimmers often synchronize their movements when skimming or traveling in flocks. When the bird is skimming, the wingbeats are rapid and remain above the horizontal; when it is not feeding, its flight is similar to that of a large tern. The voice is a sharp bark, singly or in a series, by day or night.

Above Top: *Skimmers nest in a depression scraped in the beach.* CC

Above Middle: *Skimmers often gather in large flocks.* DWN

Above Bottom: *Skimmers feed by slicing the lower bill through shallow water until a fish is contacted.* JLG

Left: *The lower mandible is much longer than the upper.* DWN

Mangrove Cuckoo

Coccyzus minor | **Cuculidae Cuculiformes** | **p. 290**

DESCRIPTION This quietly elegant bird gives the impression of an aristocratic lady departing for a night at the opera. The length is 30 cm (11.8 in) and weight is about 70 g (2.5 oz). The crown, nape and mantle are gray-brown. A black mask extends from the upper mandible through the eye to about 3 eye diameters past the eye. With a sharp demarcation, the chin, throat and upper breast are gray to buff that grades into cinnamon on the belly and flanks. Both sexes keep identical plumage throughout the year. The beak is 2 cm (0.8 in) long and curved, with a slight hook on the end. The toes of each foot are arranged in pairs—the 2 outer toes point backward and the 2 inner toes point forward. The upper mandible is dark and the lower is yellow. The long, black tail feathers are graded in length, making their terminal white tips appear as 3 pairs of spots. The flight is several firm and direct flaps followed by short glides, seldom above the canopy or for any great distance. The typical voice is a *gow-gow-gow* or *ahrr-ahrr-ahrr* descending in pitch and frequency as it is repeated 8 to 25 times. Various clucks and chuckles are made at a much lower volume. They are more often heard than seen.

Above: *Cryptic coloration and a propensity for creeping through thickets make the cuckoo hard to discover.* DWN

Left: *The fine and subtle plumage can only be appreciated when seen at close range.* DWN

Boat-tailed Grackle

Quiscalus major | **Icteridae Passeriformes** | **p. 293**

DESCRIPTION The male and female look quite dissimilar and often segregate into single-gender flocks by day but are usually found together in small roosting flocks at night. Males have shiny black plumage with a metallic-blue sheen on the head and neck grading into a blue-green to purple sheen on the back and breast. They are 42 cm (16.5 in) long, weigh 200 g (7 oz) and have a wingspan of 56 cm (22 in). They often fluff the head feathers in breeding season, giving them a thick-headed appearance. Females have cinnamon-brown upperparts with a buff breast; they are 33 cm

(13 in) long, weigh 110 g (3.8 oz) and have a wingspan of 41 cm (16 in). The iris is brown, and the tail feathers of both sexes form a deep V similar to the bow of a boat. The vocal array is complex with at least 10 different calls characterized as clicks, chips, churrs, quees, and a guttural rattle. These calls vary among individuals and may be combined in a complex array to make up the song. The commonest calls are *jeeb-jeeb-jeeb* and *tireet*. The similar but smaller Common Grackle is also found in Florida and can be distinguished by its pale-yellow or white iris and its *tchack* or *shkleet* calls. Males are 35 cm (14 in) long and have bright-yellow eyes and glossy, black plumage with a metallic-purple sheen. Females are smaller and less glossy.

Above Top: *The male has a glossy, iridescent black plumage.* PL

Above Middle: *Grackles have a great range of calls.* DWN

Above Bottom: *Males often display from an exposed perch.* DWN

Left: *Feeding is in a great variety of habitats, including shallow water.* JLG

Cave Swallow

Hirundo fulva | **Hirudinidae Passeriformes** | **p. 297**

DESCRIPTION A medium-size 13 cm (5 in) swallow weighing about 24 g (0.8 oz) with dark wings, tail, and crown. The throat is buff, the rump rusty, the forehead dark cinnamon, and the underparts dull white washed with buff. The similar cliff swallow has a buff forehead and a chestnut chin and throat. Juvenile Cave Swallows are very similar in appearance to juvenile cliff swallows. In flight the Cave Swallow's tail is only slightly notched, allowing easy distinction from the deeply notched tail of the barn swallow. The flight has deep, strong wingbeats interspersed with short glides. Five major types of vocalizations have been reported: a *che* given as a response to another bird flying near the nest or in the presence of a threat, such as a predator in the area; 3 different types of chattering; and a song composed of several highly variable elements, including a complex melodic warble. The entire song takes 3 to 4 seconds to complete.

Below: *The nests are built of mud stuck to rock walls near the mouths of caves.*
©(G. Lasley)/VIREO

Fish Crow

Corvus ossifragus | **Corvidae Passeriformes** | **p. 300**

DESCRIPTION Crows are large birds with glossy, black plumage; tapered, sturdy bills; and strong feet. Fish Crows are 45 cm (18 in) long, weigh 400 g (14 oz) and have a wingspread of 91 cm (36 in). When foraging on the ground they walk with an easy but deliberate gait. In flight the rowing wingbeats are deep and strong. When wind or updrafts allow it, Fish Crows are inclined to soar and indulge in seemingly play-

ful aerobatic maneuvers. They are usually found near water. The voice is a short, hoarse, nasal, coughing *ca, cahr* or a 2-note *ca-ha* or *aw-uk*. The similar American Crow *(C. brachyrynchos)* is slightly larger with a broader, more drawn-out caw and is more likely to be found away from the coast.

Above Top: *Fish Crows often take advantage of man's activities.* JLG

Above Middle: *The strong bill allows the crow to break up items too large to swallow.* JLG

Above Bottom: *Crows commonly forage for worms and insects on lawns.* DWN

Left: *Crows carry a great variety of food items to the nest when raising chicks.* CW

PART II. SPECIES ACCOUNTS

Pied-billed Grebe

Podilymbus podiceps | Podicipedidae Podicipediformes | p. 3

DISTRIBUTION The genus *Podilymbus* had 2 species, but the Lake Atitlan Grebe of Guatemala, *P. gigas,* recently became extinct due to lakeside resort development and introduction of a large exotic predatory fish that competed with grebes and ate their chicks. The northern subspecies of the Pied-billed Grebe, *P. p. podiceps,* nests from British Columbia across the Canadian provinces to Nova Scotia and south to Panama. The Caribbean race, *P. p. antillarum,* is resident in the Antilles; and the South American race, *P. p. antarctica,* nests from Panama south to Chile and Argentina except at elevations above 3,100 m (10,000 ft).

FOOD AND FEEDING HABITS

Pied-billed Grebes feed in shallow, calm water such as marshes, ponds, lakes, slow rivers or protected estuaries. They often feed among thick stands of rooted and emergent aquatic vegetation and freely forage under mats of water hyacinth. The diet is greatly influenced by prey availability. The main food items are aquatic insects, the larvae of dragonflies and beetles, shrimp, crabs, snails, clams, and frogs and tadpoles. They are particularly fond of crayfish and break off the large claws before swallowing the animal tailfirst. Leeches sometimes make up the preponderance of the diet in the breeding season. Small, heavy-bodied fish with spines and armor such as catfish and carp are regularly consumed after the spines are broken off. Feeding is exclusively underwater and may include paddling the feet at the bottom to flush prey into the open. Surface dives begin as a forward lunge at a downward angle. When a deep dive is intended, a small hop at the water surface is followed by a more vertical descent. Dive duration averages about 8 seconds and rarely exceeds 30 seconds in duration or 20 m (65 ft) in depth or 12 m (40 ft) in horizontal distance. Foraging grebes may feed mutualistically with herons and egrets when each species flushes prey toward other feeding birds. Grebes consume their own molted feathers and eventually regurgitate them as pellets combined with indigestible prey residue. Many types of birds regurgitate indigestible food as pellets, but in the case of grebes the feathers and vegetable matter in the diet seem to pack around the sharp fish bones making them easier to regurgitate.

REPRODUCTION A pair of grebes builds a well-camouflaged nest in a secluded spot near the edge of a body of water. They commonly nest in fresh water but will build the nest in brackish or salt water when habitat is suitable.

Seasonality Grebes in temperate areas nest in the spring and summer. In the tropics they may nest in any month.

Courtship Grebes form monogamous pair bonds within a season after lengthy and varied courtship displays. Pairs call together in duets and are often answered in duets from grebes on nearby territories. Copulation is usually on the nest.

Territoriality Grebes breed as solitary pairs and do not aggregate. The male defends an area with a radius of 20 to 100 m (66 to 328 ft) around the nest.

Ponds of 4 ha (10 acres) or less accommodate only 1 nesting pair.

Nest and Nest Site The nest is a platform of floating aquatic vegetation anchored to emergent bulrushes, cattails, or other concealing vegetation in an average water depth of 64 cm (25 in) or less but near broad channels of deeper, open water. Typical vegetation at the nest site includes cattails, bur reeds, reeds, and reed grass. Edges of emergent vegetation exposed to wave action are generally avoided.

Eggs The clutch of 5 to 9 bluish-white eggs laid on a daily basis quickly becomes brown stained. The eggs measure 44 by 30 mm (1.7 by 1.2 in) and weigh about 22 g (0.8 oz). The development of bird eggs produces water by metabolic processes, and the eggs lose about 15% of their original weight by water vapor diffusion into the surrounding atmosphere during the incubation period. Loss of water by diffusion through the shell is a critical component of the development of the embryo in the egg and is difficult to attain in the hot, wet nest environment. To allow adequate moisture loss, Pied-billed Grebe eggs have about 3 times as many pores as other bird eggs. Hatching success averages about 85%. Replacement clutches are normal for failed nests, and multiple broods may be raised in a single breeding season.

Incubation Both sexes have brood patches and participate in incubation after the 2nd egg is laid. Parents cover the eggs with nest material before departing from the nest. After a full clutch is present in the nest, the parents incubate the eggs 90% of the time but attentiveness declines late in the incubation cycle. Incubation is 21 to 27 days, and hatching may be within 3 days or spread over more than a week. After a few chicks hatch, the parents are often negligent in incubation duties, leading to an exaggerated hatching span.

Fledging Chicks are grey-black and have 4 white stripes on the head, and pale underparts. Hatching is asynchronous, and when all the eggs have hatched, the newly hatched chicks leave the nest, climb onto the adult's back, and shelter between the wing and the feathers of the back. One parent serves as a floating nest while the other parent dives for food, but the parent with chicks aboard may dive for short periods. The range of ages and sizes of chicks allows the parents to forage more efficiently on a wide range of prey sizes and types. In times of food scarcity the smaller chicks often die. Parents perform extensive distraction displays in the presence of predators with kicking and flapping about in open water. Fledging is at 35 days. Mortality is about 37% of hatched young, with an average 2.6 young fledged per nest.

Age at First Breeding First breeding attempts have been recorded at 13 months, but adult plumage and full breeding competence is not usually attained until the 2nd year.

BEHAVIOR Movement underwater is by simultaneous strong strokes of the feet for a top speed of 7.2 kph (4.5 mph). Grebes have an amazing capability to alter their specific gravity to float as high on the water as a duck or to float submerged with only the head and neck above water. The primary buoyancy control is the amount of air retained in the lungs, but grebes can also fluff or compress the body feathers to trap variable amounts of air.

MIGRATION The grebes at the extreme north and south of the breeding range move toward the equator to avoid freezing winter temperatures. Migration flights are usually at night and end abruptly at dawn in a landing on the first available water. The migration of northern-nesting birds adds considerably to grebe populations in Florida and the Caribbean from September to April.

PREDATORS By sleeking their feathers and increasing their specific gravity, grebes can sink quietly out of sight or kick water into the air in a powered crash drive. They then often swim away underwater in an unexpected direction to avoid the attentions of a terrestrial predator. The eggs are taken by raccoons, mink, crows, gulls, coots, and snakes. The chicks are taken by water moccasins, snapping turtles, predatory fish such as pike, and largemouth bass. The adults are eaten by eagles, hawks, owls, alligators, and snapping turtles.

CONSERVATION ISSUES Grebe skin with thick insulating feathers, known as grebe-fur, was in high demand by the millinery trade in the 19th century to make ladies' coats and capes. The Migratory Bird Treaty Act of 1918 brought protection to grebes and many other birds. Pied-billed Grebes are not usually hunted today, but in some tropical countries the eggs are collected for sale. Over half of the wetlands in the United States have been destroyed since the European colonization. Grebe populations have declined with this habitat loss.

NOTES The genus name is derived from the Latin *podiceps* (rump) and the Greek *kolymbos* (a diving bird). The species name is from the Latin referring to the legs that are set to the rear of the body. It is also known as didapper, hell diver, and water witch in English; *zampullín picogrueso* or *macá picopinto* in Spanish and *grèbe à bec bigarré* or *grèbe à bec cerclé* in French.

SUGGESTED ADDITIONAL READING

Davis, T.A., M.F. Platter-Reiger, and R.A. Ackerman. 1984. Incubation water loss by Pied-billed Grebe eggs: Adaptation to a hot wet nest. *Physiol Zool*, 57:384–391.

Muller, M.J. and R.W. Storer. 1999. Pied-billed Grebe (*Podilymbus podiceps*). In A.Poole and F. Gill (eds.), *The Birds of North America No. 410*. Philadelphia: The Birds of North America, Inc.

Audubon's Shearwater
Puffinus lherminieri | **Procellariidae Procellariiformes | p. 4**

DISTRIBUTION This genus with 20 species is found worldwide over temperate and tropical oceans. Audubon's Shearwater has a patchy distribution over the world's tropical oceans. It is usually found in areas of ocean upwellings near islands. This species has been divided into 10 subspecies with *P. l. lherminieri* nesting in Bermuda, the Bahamas, the Lesser Antilles, and small islands in the Greater Antilles. They are regularly seen feeding over the Gulf Stream from Florida to North Carolina in the summer months.

FOOD AND FEEDING HABITS
Squid is the primary food, supplemented by flying fish and other small fish forced to the surface by tuna and other predators. Planktonic larvae of fish, crustaceans, cephalopods, and other invertebrates are a regular part of the shearwaters' diet, and they may follow fishing and shrimp boats to feed on discarded noncommercial fish and offal. They dive from the air or the surface of the sea to pursue their prey underwater, using the partly folded wings in a rowing motion for propulsion. They may also patter the feet on the water and seize food from near the surface while in flight. Swimming shearwaters may submerge their heads to look for prey, then pursue it underwater. They often seek prey by swimming near floating rafts of sargassum weed.

REPRODUCTION
Shearwaters only come to land to lay their eggs and raise their chicks.

Seasonality In the Antilles, pairs begin to occupy their burrows from November to February and typically have eggs by mid-March, which hatch in early May. Audubon's Shearwaters in the Galapagos have been found nesting in all months, and individual birds have been found to have a breeding cycle of 9 months.

Courtship Groups of shearwaters may be seen to wheel and circle near the nesting holes early in the courtship. Pairs will often sit together in a nest site at night while calling and grooming each other. Much of the courtship has not been recorded because it takes place at night in remote areas. Pair bonds typically last for multiple years.

Territoriality The nest burrow is the territory that is usually used in succeeding seasons by the same pair. When 1 member of a pair is lost, the remaining bird is joined by a new mate in the established hole. Burrows are often near others in colonies.

Nest and Nest Site The nest is commonly in a burrow in sand or soil and less commonly in a rock crevice from near sea level to several hundred feet above the sea. Shearwaters arrive and depart from the nest burrows primarily at night. Pairs with unsuccessful nests do not renest but do breed again within 6 to 8 months. A single nest site may be used alternately by 2 pairs that are out of synchrony. Tropicbirds may compete for nest holes and evict shearwaters.

Eggs The single, smooth white egg measures 53 by 36 mm (2.1 by 1.4 in) and weighs about 35 g (1.25 oz). The egg constitutes about 18% of the weight of the female. Lost eggs are not replaced in the same breeding cycle.

Incubation Parents take turns at the 3- to 10-day unrelieved incubation periods as soon as the egg is laid. Although 6 g of body weight is lost per day while incubating, most of the loss is regained in the subsequent feeding period. The egg hatches after about 51 days of incubation. Hatching may be delayed as much as an additional 2 weeks with inattentive incubation.

Fledging The chick hatches with gray down upperparts and white underparts. It is brooded for the first 3 or 4 days after hatching, then it is accompanied by an adult for a few more days before being left alone in the burrow during daylight hours. The chick is fed once nightly and gains weight rapidly, until at 30 days it weighs as much as an adult but is still covered with soft dusky-gray down. The feathers begin to show at 45 days and are fully erupted at 55 days, with some down persisting until about 63 days. At about 69 days of age the chick, weighing considerably more than an adult, is abandoned by both parents. The chick begins to lose weight, and 3 to 5 days later at the age of about 72 days it emerges from the burrow, exercises its wings on a promontory at about 5 beats per second, and takes its 1st flight toward the sea. The development rate is variable, depending on food supply, with fledging age ranging from 62 to 100 days.

Age at First Breeding Audubon's Shearwaters begin to breed successfully at age 8.

BEHAVIOR Audubon's Shearwater is most often seen as a solitary individual at sea, but small flocks may aggregate when currents or other factors produce concentrations of prey items. They may rest on the water in dense flocks. A population in the Galápagos has become diurnal, presumably as an adaptation to avoid the predation of owls.

MIGRATION Postbreeding dispersal sometimes takes birds thousands of miles from nesting islands, but seasonal migration does not exist.

PREDATORS Rats and mongooses may attack the chicks in the burrow. Several types of owls take the adults near the nest. Cats introduced to nesting islands often wreak havoc on local populations.

LONGEVITY The oldest banded bird recovered was 19 years of age, but 95% annual survival of adults has been recorded. Abrasion and loss of bands in the burrow is significant and probably accounts for the fewer number of older birds recorded.

CONSERVATION ISSUES Due to the high fat content and tender flesh of the nestlings, they have historically been collected and marketed as salted and dried, smoked, or fresh fowl. Shearwater chicks are still collected and sold in local markets in several parts of the world. Small colonies of shearwaters with infrequent nocturnal nest visits and offshore feeding often go undetected by predators and local human harvesters.

NOTES The genus name is a Latinized form of the old English originally applied to the dried carcass of a nestling. The name was applied erroneously to shearwaters, which where considered to be a type of puffin. The species name honors Dr. Felix-Louis l'Herminier, a French naturalist. The common name honors John James Audubon, a pioneering American ornithologist and artist. Other common names are diablotin, pimlico, wedrego, and dusky shearwater. The name is *pardela de Audubon* and *pampero* in Spanish, and *puffin obscur* or *puffin d'Audubon* in French.

SUGGESTED ADDITIONAL READING

Harris, M.P. 1969. Food as a factor controlling the breeding of *Puffinus lherminieri*. *Ibis*, 111:139–156.

Snow, D.W. 1965. The breeding of Audubon's Shearwater (*Puffinus l'herminieri*) in the Galápagos. *Auk*, 82:591–597.

Red-billed Tropicbird

Phaethon aethereus | Phaethontidae Pelicaniformes | p. 5

DISTRIBUTION The family has 1 genus with 3 species that fish in all the tropical seas. The Red-tailed Tropicbird (*P. rubricauda),* named for its red streamers, is found over the tropical and subtropical Pacific and Indian Oceans. The White-tailed Tropicbird (*P. lepturus)* is found in the subtropical and tropical Atlantic, Pacific, and Indian Oceans. The Red-billed Tropicbird has been divided into 3 subspecies, of which *P. a. indicus* is found in the Red Sea, Persian Gulf, and Arabian sea; *P. a. aethereus* on Ascension, St. Helena, and Fernando Noronha Islands; and *P. a. mesonauta* on the Cape Verdes, West Indies, and eastern Pacific Ocean from the Gulf of California to Lima, Peru. In the U.S. it is seen near the Gulf Stream off the East Coast and sporadically in the Gulf of Mexico. They breed on many small Caribbean islands.

FOOD AND FEEDING HABITS Tropicbirds are continuously pelagic except when breeding. They eat mostly flying fish and squid taken by plunge-diving from heights of as much as 25 m (80 ft), but occasionally they catch flying fish in the air. Food items recovered at the nest include flying fish, blennies, and squid. Chicks are generally fed small prey items less than 6 cm (2.4 in), but larger chicks may be fed flying fish up to 30 cm (12 in) long. Foraging birds often hover for short periods before diving. A series of air sacs under the skin in the forward part of the body helps cushion the impact of high-speed dives into the sea to a depth of 2 m (6 ft).

Feeding is usually solitary and tends to be crepuscular. Red-billed Tropicbirds may join groups of shearwaters or Sooty Terns over shoals of bait-size fish forced to the surface by predators. Prey is held crosswise in the beak and swallowed after surfacing.

REPRODUCTION Red-billed Tropicbirds nest in loose groups in holes and crevices in cliffs, and under rocks on small isolated islands.

Seasonality Most nesting is from December to March, but because of an irregular and prolonged breeding season, active nests have been found in every month. Many pairs seem to lay at less than 12-month intervals.

Courtship In courtship, groups of 2 to 10 birds circle in loose groups within several hundred meters (yards) of potential nest sites. Pairs or trios may perform astonishing, synchronized aerobatic maneuvers with glides, dives, and zigzags. They often singly or simultaneously utter their pulsing call. Many pairs remain together in succeeding years.

Territoriality Red-billed Tropicbirds will peck and bite ferociously to defend suitable nest sites. Bloody battles with shrieking, pecking, and biting may continue for several hours, and mortality has been reported. Individuals show considerable fidelity to nest sites, and long-term pairs almost always nest repeatedly in the same crevice. In courtship, when they are incubating, or when feeding a chick in the nest, they usually make repeated approaches to the nest site and poise as though landing, then turn and fly about the vicinity before repeating the maneuver.

Nest and Nest Site The nest is typically in a crevice or shaded ledge on a cliff face above the sea, but may be under boulders at the top of a plateau or on cliffs over 3 km (2 mi) from the sea. Both adults may contribute to scraping out a nest site but do not add material. On a hard surface the nest is in a depression with no added material. Red-billed Tropicbirds may displace less aggressive seabirds such as White-tailed Tropicbirds, shearwaters, and petrels from desirable nest sites. Instances have been recorded in which Red-billed Tropicbirds have displaced White-tailed parents but failed to destroy their eggs and thus reared White-tailed chicks.

Eggs The single buff to reddish-brown egg covered with brown blotches and smears measures 45 by 60 mm (1.8 by 2.4 in) and weighs about 67 g (2.3 oz). The egg is about 10% of a female's weight. Replacement eggs may be laid if the loss is early in the breeding cycle.

Incubation Incubation in Red-billed Tropicbirds is 42 to 44 days, with each member of the pair incubating for several uninterrupted days at a time. More feather wear indicates the female probably spends more time incubating.

Fledging The newly hatched chick has silky pale-gray down and is continuously brooded for 3 to 5 days until it can thermoregulate, then with decreasing frequency and duration. The chicks gain weight slowly and adjust their rate of growth depending on the food calories delivered by the adults. In times of plenty, chicks store considerable energy as body fat. The chicks reach adult weight about halfway through their nestling stage. They then gain additional weight until the adults cease feeding them at 70 to 90 days of age. The young then lose weight and strengthen the flight muscles before fledging about a week or 10 days later. Nest success is quite variable, with an average of about 1 fledged offspring per 2 nesting attempts. Chicks are susceptible to avian pox infections that may be fatal. Nest success may exceed 90% in good years or decline to near zero due to food scarcity or heavy predation.

Age at First Breeding Adult plumage and bill coloring are reached at 2 to 3 years; breeding usually begins at age 5, but a 3-year-old bird has been found on a nest.

BEHAVIOR Tropicbirds have waterproof plumage and float buoyantly on calm seas with the tail raised clear of the water. After resting on the sea, they lift lightly into the air. Tropicbirds cannot walk on land but push themselves along on the breast. Takeoff from land requires considerable effort unless the individual dives from the nest entrance on a cliff face. When traveling over the open ocean, they have attained a flight speed measured at 44 kph (27 mph).

MIGRATION There is no consistent migration, but both adults and juveniles disperse widely outside the breeding season.

PREDATORS Tropicbird adults seem to have few natural predators of significance, but Peregrine Falcons learn to detect tropicbird nests and may devastate both chicks and adults in breeding cavities. Dogs, cats, and rats attack adults on the nest. Rats and various crabs eat the hatchlings.

LONGEVITY The oldest recovered banded bird was 16 years old, but band loss is a problem due to abrasion associated with shuffling about on land.

CONSERVATION ISSUES The greatest potential threat to tropicbirds is the introduction of rats, cats, mongooses, or other predatory mammals to nesting islands. Food abundance and nest site availability seem to be the major population-limiting factors. World estimates of population trends are less than satisfactory due to the dispersed nature of feeding areas and generally inaccessible nest sites.

NOTES The genus is named for *Phaëton* (from Greek mythology) who was allowed to drive the chariot of the sun for 1 day. The species name is from the Greek *aitherios* (upper air or heaven) for its ethereal plumage and graceful flight. In English it is also called bosun-bird, in reference to its call sounding somewhat like a bosun's pipe, and longtail or marlinspike in obvious reference to the long tail streamers. In Spanish it is *chirre de pico colorado, rabijunco etéreo, rabijunco pico rojo, rabijunco piquirrojo* or *rabijunco común*. In French it is *phaéton à bec rouge, paille en queue éthérée* or *flèche en cul*.

SUGGESTED ADDITIONAL READING

Diamond, A.W. 1975. The biology of tropicbirds at Aldabra atoll, Indian Ocean. *Auk*, 92:16–39.

Nelson, J.B. 1983. Contrasts in breeding strategies between some tropical and temperate marine pelecaniformes. *Studies in Avian Biology*, 8:95–114.

Stonehouse, B. 1962. Tropicbirds (genus *Phaethon*) of Ascension Island. *Ibis*, 112:124–259.

White-tailed Tropicbird
Phaethon lepturus | Phaethontidae Pelicaniformes | p. 6

DISTRIBUTION The family has 1 genus with 3 species that fish in all the tropical seas. The Red-tailed Tropicbird (*P. rubricauda),* named for its red, streaming tail feathers, is found over the tropical and subtropical Pacific and Indian Oceans. The Red-billed Tropicbird (*P. aethereus)* is found in the tropical Atlantic and Pacific Oceans, the Red Sea and the Gulf of Aden. The White-tailed is the smallest tropicbird and is found in the subtropical and tropical Atlantic, Indian, and western and central Pacific Oceans. They are absent from the eastern Pacific. Five geographic subspecies have been named, with *P. l. ascensionensis* on Ascension and equatorial Atlantic islands, *P. l. lepturus* on islands in the Indian Ocean, *P. l. dorotheae* on Hawaii and the southwest Pacific islands, and *P. l. fulvus* (the apricot-colored form), which breeds on Christmas Island. *P. l. catesbyi* nests on Bermuda and the Bahamas and in the Caribbean. They are regularly seen in the Sargasso Sea while pelagic and may gather in small groups hundreds of kilometers from land to feed on schools of small fish forced to the surface by tuna.

FOOD AND FEEDING HABITS
White-tailed Tropicbirds feed at sea out of sight of land. The major food items are flying fish, ommastrephid squid, and surface-feeding fish. Prey is generally 4 to 12 cm (1.6 to 4.7 in) in length with a weight of 3 to 79 g (0.1 to 2.8 oz). Individual prey items up to 18% of the tropicbird's body weight have been recorded. Feeding is often at dawn and dusk to catch squid that surface only at low light levels. They catch their prey by plunge-diving from 20 m (65 ft), often correcting their dive en route to compensate for prey movement. They regularly snatch flying fish out of the air. Prey is swallowed underwater or at the surface, and never carried in the bill while flying. Adults can fly with prey loads of up to 30% of their body weight. Nesting tropicbirds have been followed as far as 89 km (55 mi) from the burrow to feed in deep ocean waters. Calculations show they can travel 315 km (195 mi) in the average 6.7 hours between chick feedings. They are attracted to feeding frenzies and will join petrels, shearwaters, terns, boobies, and noddies feeding on schools of bait chased to the surface by feeding tuna.

REPRODUCTION
White-tailed Tropicbirds nest in a variety of habitats that provide an enclosure and overhead cover for eggs and chicks.

Seasonality Eggs are present in every month in some populations, but in Bermuda, the Bahamas, and the Caribbean, nesting is in the spring and summer months. Individual pairs in the Seychelles in the Indian Ocean average 273 days between breeding attempts and may breed sooner with prior nest failure.

Courtship Most courtship behavior is in the form of aerial displays, with pairs or small groups flying over the water in large circles in front of the nest sites. Tandem flight with glides and zigzags are common early in the morning. In more advanced courtship they may show vertical tandem flight with the upper bird depressing its tail to touch the bird below. The wings are lifted high over the back with wingstrokes ending at the horizontal in tandem flight associated with courtship. Copulation takes place on the nest site. Pairs are monogamous, with a pair bond that usually continues until 1 mate is lost.

Territoriality The nesting burrow or crevice comprises the entire territory and is usually occupied in successive breeding cycles by the same pair of tropicbirds. The nest may be solitary or in dispersed colonies with nearest-neighbor distance less than a meter (yard) if suitable sites are present. Fierce battles over nest sites sometimes ensue with injuries and permanent scarring.

Nest and Nest Site The nest scrape is preferentially placed in caves, crevices and holes opening onto inaccessible cliff faces. No nesting material is added to the scrape, which is usually 80% or more enclosed by rock. Deep shadows seem to be one of the criteria for nest site selection. Nests are almost invariably partially enclosed by and under cover of rock that provides protection from the intense tropical sun. Those nests that are exposed to the sun have a much lower success rate than those in constant shade. They will also use holes in trees, shallow excavations under vegetation, and snug spots underneath overhangs. There is some competition between them and with Red-billed Tropicbirds in areas with limited nest sites. Two pairs of White-tailed Tropicbirds may successively occupy a single nest site.

Eggs The single, beige, 40 g (1.4 oz) egg in the clutch measures 54 by 39 mm (2.1 by 1.5 in) and is splotched with chestnut, chocolate, and purplish-red colors. The egg makes up 10% or more of the weight of the female. Lost eggs are replaced by renesting in about 20% of the nests, with most birds relaying to replace nests lost in the early stage of incubation. A minimum of 17 days is required to produce a new egg after nest loss.

Incubation Both parents participate in the incubation period of 41 days. Each parent may remain incubating on the nest for 3 to 13 days before nest relief from the foraging member of the pair. The incubating bird may lose up to 20% of its body weight on long incubation periods. A 48% hatch rate has been recorded. Replacement eggs have been recorded 6 or 7 weeks after the loss of eggs or small chicks. The parents soar and wheel for several hundred meters (yards) in front of the nest hole and make many abortive landing attempts before entering the nest, even when eggs or chicks are present in the nest.

Fledging Hatchlings are covered with a thick, grayish down and are brooded almost continuously for the first 10 days. Due to the patchy nature of the food resource, each adult may deliver food as infrequently as every 1 to 3 days. Chicks grow slowly and develop body fat as a hedge against periodic food shortages. Fishing in deep ocean waters with low prey density taxes the reserves of the adults, who experience a weight loss while chicks are in their most rapid growth phase. Juvenile plumage begins to show by 16 days and is completed by 62 days of age. Chicks accumulate considerable stores of fat in the last 2 weeks in the nest and typically weigh 25% more than breeding adults. The adults abandon the chick, which then exercises and loses weight before fledging at approximately adult weight. Fledging ranges from 67 to 89 days and averages 76 days. Fledging success has been reported as 63% of hatched eggs and 30% of all eggs laid. **Age at First Breeding** Tropicbirds begin breeding after attaining adult plumage in their 4th year.

BEHAVIOR White-tailed Tropicbirds are usually solitary or in pairs when encountered away from nesting areas. Travel speed between nest and feeding areas has been recorded as 44 kph (27 mph). While other seabirds are known to fly for long periods by soaring flight, tropicbirds remain airborne for long periods with flapping flight and only short glides. They rest buoyantly on the sea holding the plumes arched above the water.

MIGRATION Outside of the breeding season, White-tailed Tropicbirds roam deep ocean water over 1,000 km (620 mi) from possible nesting colonies and often wander into temperate waters.

PREDATORS Some Peregrine Falcons have learned to walk into nesting caves to eat the chicks and adults. Dogs, cats, mongooses, and rats attack adults on the nest. Introduced rats and various crabs eat the hatchlings.

LONGEVITY There is no published record of recovery of banded Whitetailed Tropicbirds away from the nesting hole, but they probably have a potential life span exceeding 15 years.

CONSERVATION ISSUES Nest sites seem to be the primary population-limiting factor, and tropicbirds seem receptive to enhanced and manmade sites. Reproductive efforts could be aided by local groups' constructing and maintaining nest sites. The greatest threat to tropicbirds is the introduction of rats or other predatory mammals to nesting islands.

NOTES The genus name is from the Greek *Phaethon* (sun god). The species name is from the Greek *leptos* (slender) and *oura* (tail), referring to the thin, trailing tail feathers. In English they are also known as boatswain bird, scissortail, longtail, and yellow-billed tropicbird; in Spanish as *rabi-junco, caracolera* or *chirre de altura;* and in French as *paille en queue,* or *phaéton à bec jaune.* Columbus' sighting of a tropicbird in the middle of the Atlantic led him to the erroneous assumption that he was nearing land.

SUGGESTED ADDITIONAL READING

Lee, D.S. and M. Walsh-McGehee. 1998. White-tailed Tropicbird (*Phaethon lepturus*). In A. Poole and F. Gill (eds.), *The Birds of North America. No. 353.* Philadelphia: The Birds of North America, Inc.

Pennycuick, C.J., F.C. Schaffner, M.R. Fuller, H.H. Obrecht III, and L. Sternberg. 1990. Foraging flights of the White-tailed Tropicbird (*Phaethon lepturus*) radiotracking and double labeled water. *Colon Waterbirds,* 13:96–102.

Brown Booby

Sula leucogaster | Sulidae Pelicaniformes | p. 7

DISTRIBUTION This genus with 7 species is found worldwide foraging pelagically over ice-free ocean waters. The Brown Booby is found worldwide in tropical oceans but is quite rare between the Seychelles and the coast of Africa in the Indian Ocean. Several geographic subspecies have been recognized, with *S. l. leucogaster* occurring in the Caribbean and tropical Atlantic, *S. l. brewsteri* in the Gulf of California and the western Pacific, and *S. l. plotus* in the Central and Western Pacific and Indian Ocean. The validity and exact distribution of several other subspecies are still being debated.

FOOD AND FEEDING HABITS Brown Boobies feed on flying fish, ballyhoo, half-beak, squid, needlefish, mullet, scad, anchovy, immature tuna, and other fish living near the surface of the sea. The feeding behavior is quite varied and is adapted to the conditions of the moment. Hunting boobies look ahead and only slightly downward—but may hover into the wind with the beak pointed straight down—when closely studying a potential prey item. Although they are most commonly seen feeding in solitude or small groups, they maintain a constant vigil and eagerly join distant aggregations of other seabirds diving on shoals of small fish chased to the surface by predators such as tuna or jacks. In dense schools of small fish, Brown Boobies may float on the water surface and submerge the head to catch inattentive prey. They may also wait as a group on an available perching site such as a rocky peninsula while waiting for gulls, terns, and pelicans to locate a school of surfaced prey. Brown Boobies commonly accompany ships and seem adept at catching updrafts created by the wind and ships' movement. The flying fish set in flight by a ship's passage or by larger predators are often caught in the air.

When feeding offshore in very clear water, plunge-dives from 20 m (65 ft) in altitude may allow the capture of prey more than 2 m (6 ft) deep. When feeding on prey species that normally swim within less than a meter (3 ft) of the surface, a more oblique dive may be used. An extreme form of this dive may be seen when a school of small fish is driven to the surface by predators. In this dive almost parallel to the surface of the water, most of the forward speed of the bird is maintained and the flight path continues as though the bird has ricocheted from the surface. When dense schools of small fish are present, the Brown Booby may rest on the surface of the water and submerge its head to peer around and jab at individual fish that come into range or even swim after them using both wings and feet for propulsion. After a successful feeding frenzy, the boobies may gather in a sociable raft or rest as a group on a nearby rock. Coordinated daily flights of small groups to a distant favored feeding area may be regularly observed from nesting colonies. These small groups fly in a V formation less than 1 m (3 ft) above the water surface and thus take advantage of the group aerodynamics practiced by geese and the ground effect of the water surface, producing more lift. Boobies return to the nesting colony at all hours of the night, suggesting they probably also actively feed at night.

REPRODUCTION

This booby tends to nest in small colonies on isolated oceanic islands but may form colonies of thousands of pairs when food resources and habitat allow. It may also breed successfully in small groups or as isolated pairs. The earliest recorded age of 1st breeding is 3 years, but 4 or 5 years is more common.

Seasonality Individual colonies show seasonal peaks of nesting activity. With some colonies the peak shifts seasonally over a several-year period. Caribbean colonies usually have a few out-of-phase pairs nesting in every month.

Courtship Once in possession of a territory, a male advertises for a mate with a distinct upright posture called sky-pointing. The actual courtship and pair bonding include a series of stereotyped behaviors including beak contacts and mutual preening. Pairs tend to stay together for multiple years, but careful studies show that remating upon disappearance of a mate is usual. Divorces, bigamy and various other complex associations have been recorded.

Territoriality Brown Boobies fly over a potential nest site and land on it with increasing frequency as the territory is claimed. They may fight vigorously by jabbing with the beak and flailing with the wings to claim and maintain a breeding territory. Considerable fidelity is shown to exactly the same spot for the same pair nesting in successive years.

Nest and Nest Site The rudimentary nest is always on the ground. An acceptable nest site may be on a cliff ledge, on steep rocky terrain, among or beneath vegetation, or on bare sandy cays. The nest is a depression loosely lined with vegetation (either plucked nearby or recovered floating in the sea), feathers, shell fragments, and various marine flotsam.

Eggs The normal clutch is 2 (rarely 3) relatively elongate eggs 6.1 cm (2.4 in) in length by 4.2 cm (1.6 in) wide, weighing 55 g (2 oz). The chalky-white surface over a light-bluish or greenish shell quickly becomes scratched and stained. The 2nd egg is deposited about 5 days after the 1st. The eggs make up about 8% of the female's weight.

Incubation The incubation period is about 43 days and is shared by both sexes. Adults lack brood patches, and transfer incubation heat to the eggs from the webs of the feet. The birds exchange incubation duties every 1 to 40 hours, depending on availability and proximity of food. The 2nd egg hatches about 5 days after the 1st. If both eggs successfully hatch, the larger chick eventually evicts the smaller from the nest. Although I have seen 2 chicks coexist in a nest for as long as 4 weeks, I do not know of any record of 2 chicks being raised to fledging together in the same nest.

Fledging The newly hatched chick is naked and gray and will die in a short time if a parent is not present to shade it from the sun. In cool weather, a chick is incubated on the webs of the feet. Within 2 weeks it develops a coat of white, fluffy down. At 4 weeks it is about half the size of an adult and has the ability to thermoregulate. The dark primary feathers become conspicuous at 7 weeks, followed by the balance of the juvenile plumage allowing 1st flight at around 100 days of age, or later in cases of food shortage. The parents continue to feed the young for 30 to 260 days.

Age at first breeding A few birds breed at 3 years of age, but most are 4 or 5 years old before they raise a chick.

BEHAVIOR Gular fluttering and panting are commonly used for cooling on clear hot days with no breeze. The young exhibit chattering of the mandibles along with a squawking *ark* call as part of their threat display to intruders.

MIGRATION Juveniles commonly disperse widely but not in any ordered direction that could be called migration. One 21-month-old bird was found 5,750 km (3,564 mi) from its natal island. When not breeding, adult Brown Boobies may be found hundreds of miles from the nearest land. They have been seen soaring in apparently complete control in hurricanes.

LONGEVITY The maximum band recovery age is 24 years, 7 months, but that is almost certainly exceeded in the wild.

CONSERVATION ISSUES As with other species in the genus, significant population declines have been associated with European exploration and colonization. The introduction of rats, cats, goats, and pigs caused the elimination of some breeding colonies and the severe reduction of others. Humans have contributed further to the population decline with military actions and by using boobies for food. The inclination to nest on isolated islands too small for sustained habitation has allowed the species to continue to occupy most of its historic range.

NOTES The genus name is the Norwegian name for the Gannet. The species name is from the Greek *leuco* (white) and *gaster* (stomach). The Brown Booby, *S. leucogaster,* has also been referred to synonymously in the literature as belonging in the genera *Pelecanus* and *Dysporus,* with many species names that are now relegated to synonymy or subspecies status. In English it is also called by various local names including brown gannet, common booby, white-bellied booby, and Atlantic booby. In Spanish it is called *alcatraz, boba prieta* and *bubi chalec,* and in French it is *le fou de Cayenne, le fou commun, fou brun* and *le petit fou.*

SUGGESTED ADDITIONAL READING

Dorward, D.F. 1962. Behavior of boobies *Sula* spp. *Ibis,* 103b:231–234.

Nelson, J.B. 1978. *The Sulidae.* Oxford, U.K.: Oxford U. Press.

Simmons, K. E. L. 1967. Ecological adaptations in the life history of the Brown Booby at Ascension Island. *Living Bird,* 6:187–212

Woodward, P.W. 1972. The natural history of Kure Atoll, northwestern Hawaiian Islands. *Atoll Res Bull,* 164:1–318.

Red-footed Booby
Sula sula | **Sulidae Pelicaniformes** | **p. 8**

DISTRIBUTION This genus with 7 species is found worldwide foraging pelagically over ice-free ocean waters. Boobies are found worldwide in tropical ocean settings. Several geographic subspecies have been recognized, with *S. s. sula* occurring in the Caribbean and tropical Atlantic. The subspecific taxonomy of a species in which several color forms are present and interbreed in most populations is much too complex to discuss here, particularly when based on plumage characteristics. Modern genetic techniques combined with intense analysis of body measurements will eventually be able to define the subspecies.

FOOD AND FEEDING HABITS Red-footed Boobies feed on flying fish, squid, snake-mackerel, ballyhoo, needlefish, and other fish living near the surface of the sea in deep-blue ocean water out of sight of land. This booby has proportionally larger eyes than the other boobies, and often hunts for squid in low light conditions. Typical feeding is an arrow-like vertical plunge from 4 to 8 m (13 to 27 ft) above the water. The momentum allows the birds to penetrate 2 to 4 m (6 to 13 ft) or more beneath the surface, but on many dives they swim deeper and have been recorded at a depth of 9.6 m (31 ft). When the prey fish are very near the surface, the dives become more oblique. Boobies may capture flying fish in the air. When dense schools of small fish are present at the surface, the Red-footed Booby may rest on the surface of the water and submerge its head to peer around and grab individual fish that come into range. Prey is always swallowed before the bird takes flight. Although boobies are most commonly seen feeding in solitude or small groups, they maintain a constant vigil and eagerly join distant aggregations of other boobies, shearwaters, petrels, Sooty Terns, and Brown Noddies that are diving on shoals of small fish chased to the surface by schools of predators such as tuna, dolphin, or jacks. They may feed at any time of day or night and return to the colony from as far as 150 km (93 mi), arriving many hours after sundown. Studies have shown that individuals returning to the colony after dark have a much lower probability of having their food stolen by frigatebirds. How they navigate back to their home island over the open sea at night is a mystery. Returning to the colony at night, at elevations above 300 m (1,000 ft) or in flocks helps reduce food piracy by frigatebirds.

REPRODUCTION This booby tends to nest in colonies on isolated oceanic islands and may form colonies of as many as 10,000 pairs when food resources and habitat allow. It may also breed successfully in small groups or as single pairs.

Seasonality Local populations of Red-footed Boobies nest seasonally, but over their wide distribution, nests with eggs may be found in every month.

Courtship The male selects the breeding territory and advertises it by repeatedly taking off and landing, then engaging in territorial display postures. Nest building is a significant part of courtship, with the male providing most of the material and the female placing most of the components. Male offerings of nest material sustain the pair bond and continue after the egg is laid. Once nest construction begins, 1 member of the pair is usually present at all times to protect the nest components from pilfering by frigates and other boobies. Pairs tend to stay together for multiple years, but remating upon disappearance of a mate is usual. Divorces, bigamy and various other complex associations have been recorded.

Territoriality The territory extends about as far as a bird can reach beyond the nest. It is maintained by jabbing or squawking at an intruder. In extreme instances a booby may flail his wings and grasp the beak of the intruder. About half of the breeding pairs show nesting fidelity to exactly the same spot in successive years if it has not been destroyed or occupied by other birds.

Nest and Nest Site The Red-footed Booby prefers to nest on the top of trees or shrubs such as large red or black mangroves, fig, gumbo limbo, beach heliotrope, beach magnolia, or various species of *Cordia*. Nests are also built on rock pillars and elevated man-made structures, sometimes inland over 3 km (2 mi) and at an elevation of 700 m (2,300 ft). The nest is built of sticks and lined with twigs and leaves. A new nest is built each year if the old nest is destroyed by the activities of the chick or in subsequent storms.

Eggs The normal clutch is a relatively elongate egg 6.2 cm (2.4 in) long by 4.1 cm (1.6 in) wide, weighing 51 g (2 oz) and making up about 5% of the female's mass. The light-blue shell is covered with a smooth, chalky-white surface that quickly becomes scratched. Replacement laying of a lost egg is common.

Incubation The incubation period is about 45 days and is shared between the sexes. The webs of the feet resting on the eggs provide the heat for incubation. Exchange of incubation duties varies from 1 to 48 hours, depending on availability and proximity of food. In very hot weather the adult may stand and produce shade for the egg.

Fledging The newly hatched chick is naked and gray and is brooded continuously by resting on adult feet for the first 10 days of life. In clear, hot weather the chick will die in a short time if a parent is not present to shade it from the sun. Within 2 weeks it is covered with a coat of white, fluffy down, which allows it to control its body temperature. At 4 weeks the down becomes longer and denser, and the chick, about half the size of an adult, has the ability to thermoregulate. The dark primary feathers become conspicuous at 7 weeks and are followed by the balance of the juvenile plumage. Tufts of down are still visible on the head when the first flight occurs, variably depending on food availability, at about the 15th week. With diminishing frequency, the fledgling returns to the nest site for feeding for another 1 to 6 months.

Age at first breeding Two-year-old birds have been recorded breeding, but most birds are 3 or 4 years old when they first breed.

BEHAVIOR Red-footed Boobies prefer to fly in a modest wind to take advantage of the updrafts as the wind flows over ocean waves. They may also land on the superstructure of ships to use them as a moving vantage point. On clear, hot days with no breeze, gular fluttering and panting are commonly used to maintain the normal body temperature of 40.9 degrees C (105 degrees F). The flight speed over water has been recorded as 46 kph (29 mph). Adults and chicks may dangle the head and limp neck over the side of the nest when sleeping. Individual distance while roosting is commonly as close as 6 to15 cm (2 to 6 in).

MIGRATION These boobies are not migratory in the traditional sense of seasonal ebb and flow of populations. Outside the breeding season, feeding flocks have been seen hundreds of miles from land, and juveniles may disperse widely and make up the majority of banded birds recovered on non-natal islands. The adults breed in successive years on the same island and often roost on nesting trees outside breeding seasons.

PREDATORS In its undisturbed habitat the Red-footed Booby is seldom exposed to predation except for the few unlucky ones eaten by predatory fish. The introduction of rats, cats, goats, and pigs has caused the elimination of some breeding colonies and the severe reduction of many others.

LONGEVITY Once the bird has matured to breeding status the annual survival rate is probably in excess of 90%. The oldest recovered banded bird was 23 years of age.

CONSERVATION ISSUES As with the other species in the genus, there have been significant population declines worldwide associated with European exploration and colonization. In spite of the bird and its eggs being taken for food by people in the Caribbean and some Pacific Islands, its inclination to nest on small, isolated islands uninhabited by people has allowed the species to continue to occupy most of its historic range, with a total world population of approximately 300,000. Some colonies such as the one in the Cayman Islands have provided a focus of interest for ecotourism.

NOTES The Red-footed Booby (*S. sula*) has also been referred to synonymously in the literature as being in the genus *Pelecanus* and *Dysporus,* with species names *piscator, rubripes* and others that are now relegated to synonymy. The genus and species names are the Norwegian name for the gannet. In English it is also called by various local names including red-legged gannet, white booby, white-tailed booby, tree booby, and bush gannet. In Spanish it is *pájaro bobo* and *pájaro bobo blanco*; and in French, *fou à pieds rouges, fou blanc* or *le petit fou brun.*

SUGGESTED ADDITIONAL READING

Balance, L.T. 1995. Flight energetics of free-ranging Red-footed Boobies. *Physiological Zoology,* 68:887–914.

Nelson, J.B. 1969. The breeding behavior of the Red-footed Booby *Sula sula. Ibis,* 111:357–385.

Schreiber, E.A., R.W. Schreiber and G.A. Schenk. 1996. Red-footed Booby (*Sula sula*). In A. Poole and F. Gill (eds.), *The Birds of North America. No. 241.* Philadelphia: The Birds of North America, Inc.

Masked Booby
Sula dactylatra | Sulidae Pelicaniformes | p. 9

DISTRIBUTION This genus with 7 species is found worldwide. In cool waters the North Atlantic Gannet; the African (Cape) Gannet; and the Australian Gannet. The other 4 (boobies) live and breed in tropical waters. The species is divided into several geographically distinct races, including: *S. d. dactylatra* (Caribbean and tropical Atlantic); *S. d. california* (Pacific coast of Mexico); *S. d. granti* (Galápagos and eastern tropical Pacific); *S. d. personata* (central and western Pacific); and *S. d. melanops* (western Indian Ocean).

FOOD AND FEEDING HABITS This pelagic booby may fish over 1,000 km (620 mi) from land, with daily round trips of 150 km (93 mi) from the nesting colony. Although out of sight of land, the birds often congregate to feed over shallow banks or the summits of seamounts with higher fish concentrations. They typically dive steeply at high speed from heights as great as 100 m (328 ft) but more usually from 15 to 35 m (50 to 115 ft). Air sacs under the skin of the neck and breast protect them from high-speed impact with the water. The plunge-dive allows them to penetrate rapidly in excess of 3 m (10 ft) into the sea in pursuit of prey. The prey are grasped and swallowed before the booby resumes flight. Boobies often submerge their heads and peer about when resting near a surfaced school of fish. When 1 bird dives, other birds within sight rapidly converge to take advantage of the schools of prey forced to the surface by tuna and other large predators. They feed primarily on flying fish, jacks, scad, skippers, anchovies, sardines and squid captured far from land. When the sardine numbers decrease due to an El Niño event, the primary food species shifts to flying fish. Boobies also feed on mullet and coronetfish. Prey has been recorded from 4 to 41 cm (1.6 to 16 in). Diving flocks of Masked Boobies are often used by fishermen to locate schools of tuna. They are frequent victims of frigatebird piracy.

REPRODUCTION The low density and widely scattered nature of the prey lead to long absences with a low feeding rate and a slow growth rate. Reproductive success is strongly related to food availability, and El Niño events may cause massive reproductive failure. **Seasonality** Masked Boobies may lay eggs in any month in the Caribbean, but most laying is between March and September. There is synchrony within a colony, but with a few pairs out of phase. Peak laying dates vary and may occur in other than a 12-month cycle. **Courtship** Individual birds generally return to the same island and nest in the vicinity of the prior nest site. After a male claims a territory, he advertises for females by stretching his neck, pointing his bill vertically, and whistling. The pair bonds are monogamous and DNA analysis shows no evidence of extra-pair copulation or egg dumping. About two thirds of the breeding birds in a colony pair with the same mate on the same nest site in a subsequent year. **Territoriality** Masked Boobies congregate in colonies but the nesting density may vary from 200 sq m (2,140 sq ft) to less than 4 sq m (43 sq ft) per nest. Even when dispersed, the distribution is clumped, with a nearest neighbor usually within 30 m (100 ft). Territorial inclinations are indicated by a special landing posture with the wings held in a V over the back. The territory is defended by calling, head shaking, and posturing. Fighting (jabbing and wing-flailing; interlocking of bills and pushing) is sometimes observed. Territory defended during courtship shrinks to a quarter or less of the previous size when an egg is deposited. When nesting on the same island with Brown Boobies, they form segregated colonies. Masked Boobies are dominant in interspecific squabbles.

Nest and Nest Site This booby is adaptable to nesting opportunities on undisturbed islands. It may construct its nest scrape on open sand, soil, or a rock depression, but also mats of recumbent herbaceous vegetation, between clumps of sedges, or under shrubs. In trade winds areas, nests are on the windward side of the island or near a cliff edge, aiding takeoff. Males may gather sticks, bones, pebbles, shells or feathers to deposit at the nest site, but none of this seems to have any structural significance.

Eggs The blue egg has a chalky-white coating when laid. The toenails and beaks of incubating birds scratch and chip the surface allowing the blue to show. Later the chalky surface becomes stained and discolored. Two eggs are the normal clutch size, the 2nd egg (laid about 5 or 6 days later) being smaller than the 1st. A typical egg weighs between 50 and 85 g (2 to 3 oz) when fresh and is 65 mm (2.6 in) long by 46 mm (1.8 in) in diameter. It

is about 3.5% of the female's weight.

Incubation Both parents share incubation duties after the 1st egg is deposited. Heat is transmitted by the webs of the feet. The incubation period averages about 43 days. The 2nd egg hatches an average of 5.4 days after the 1st. Hatching success averages about 50%. Incubation shifts (about a day in length) may be a few hours when food is available, or several days when foraging is difficult. The newly hatched chicks are brooded almost continuously until they develop a full coat of down to protect them from the sun. On hot days, the adults often pant and flutter the gular skin.

Fledging The newly hatched chick is naked with pinkish-gray skin. In nests with 2 chicks, the larger chick evicts the smaller, causing its death by overheating, chilling, or starvation. When the 1st egg fails to hatch or the 1st hatchling dies, the 2nd chick commonly survives. In rare situations where both chicks coexist for several weeks, the surviving older chick shows delayed development as a result of sharing food with a sibling. The 2nd egg acts as insurance, with the 2nd chick surviving in 19% of the nests. By 3 weeks of age the hatchling is covered with short, white down, with fully developed fluffy white down at 5 weeks and sufficient thermoregulatory capability to be left on its own as both parents forage at sea. At 15 weeks the last of the down is shed, leaving the juvenile plumage. The 1st sustained flight occurs at about 17 weeks. The juvenile returns to the nest each afternoon for 4 to 8 weeks where it is fed by its parents until it learns to fish. It then disappears from the colony and leads a nomadic life until it returns to breed. The availability of prey is the major limiting factor in the reproductive success of this booby. In the Caribbean it is common for only 1 nest out of 3 to produce a viable juvenile. Shifts in ocean currents may alter the distribution of prey so that entire colonies of breeding adults abandon eggs and chicks in order to seek distant food sources.

Age at First Breeding A few Masked Boobies have been recorded as breeding in their 3rd year, but most do not reproduce until the 4th or even 5th year of life.

BEHAVIOR The individual distance for resting birds away from the breeding territory is less than 50 cm (20 in). Sustained flight speed across open water is in excess of 39 kph (24 mph).

MIGRATION Booby life does not involve migration, although wide dispersal is common in juveniles. Adults may leave the nesting island for months between breeding cycles and roost on other islands or rocks over 1,000 km (620 mi) away. Most colonies have some adults present in every month.

PREDATORS Humans sometimes harvest eggs and chicks, but the adult birds have few predators to deal with other than the rare instances of being eaten by a shark. Raptors and frigatebirds take untended chicks.

LONGEVITY Examination of recovery records of banded birds indicates a potential life expectancy of at least 25 years, with some birds reaching 30. The annual mortality of adult birds is estimated to be 6 percent of the population.

CONSERVATION ISSUES Ecotourism visits to colonies are well tolerated. The discontinued Pacific drift-net fishery was a significant source of mortality in the past. Eggs, chicks, and nesting habitat may be destroyed on islands with rats, cats, goats, or pigs. An experiment to establish Masked Booby populations on islands with suitable habitat was performed using 2nd eggs removed from active nests. When Masked Booby eggs are placed in nests on islands exclusively inhabited by Brown Boobies, the eggs are incubated and hatchlings raised by the Brown Boobies. When mature, the Masked Boobies return to the island to pair with other Masked Boobies and start a new colony.

NOTES The Masked Booby (*Sula dactylatra*) has also been placed in the genera *Parasula, Dysporous* and *Pelecanus,* with specific names of *bassana, cyanops, elegans, melaanops, nigrodactyla, personata* and *piscator.* The genus name is the Norwegian word for gannet. The species name is from the Greek *daktulos* (finger) and the Latin *ater* (black) in reference to the black primary wing feathers. In English it is also called white booby, blue-faced booby, whistling booby, and lark; in Spanish it is called *piquero blanco, piquero enmascarado,* and *boba de cara azul;* and in French *fou generau or fou masqué.*

SUGGESTED ADDITIONAL READING

Anderson, D.J. 1993. Masked Booby (*Sula dactylatra*). In A. Pool and F. Gill (eds.), *The Birds of North America.* No. 73. Philadelphia: The Birds of North America, Inc.

Kepler, C. 1969. The breeding biology of the Blue-faced Booby (*Sula dactylatra personata*) on Green Island, Kure. *Publications Nuttall Orn Club,* 8:1–97.

Brown Pelican

Pelecanus occidentalis | Pelecanidae Pelicaniformes | p. 10

DISTRIBUTION This family with 1 genus of 8 species is found worldwide foraging in warm shallow waters. The Brown Pelican breeds on both coasts of Baja California, the Galápagos, and the west coast of South America. They also breed from Maryland to Florida and along the Gulf coast to Texas. They breed on the Antilles from Cuba to Barbuda and along the Caribbean Coast of South America. Several subspecies have been recognized.

FOOD AND FEEDING HABITS

Brown Pelicans are almost exclusively marine and are the only pelican that plunge-dives for food. Their vision is excellent in air but very poor underwater, so they must target their prey carefully before impact with the water. They feed by diving into schools of fish from an elevation 1 to 20 m (3 to 66 ft). At the water surface the 2 halves of the lower jaw bow out forming a scoop with the gular pouch which engulfs up to 10 l (10.5 qts) of water. If they have calculated correctly, the water will contain fish. Most fishing is in shallow coastal waters, but they have been seen diving on aggregations of bait-size fish 20 miles or more offshore and rarely in freshwater lakes and streams. Pelicans may dive singly, but in flocks they often dive sequentially with great precision. The 1st dive drives the school of fish forward to intersect the dive of the following bird and so on for 6 to 8 birds. The timing and spacing of the impact of the birds with the water is like a well-rehearsed military maneuver. The prey may be as small as 2 or 3 cm or as large as 30 cm.

With the smaller fish, which aggregate in dense schools, many individuals may be captured on a single dive. In Florida the diet is composed of many species of small shallow-water fish that might be scooped up incidentally or added to the diet opportunistically. Underwater observation at feeding sites in the Virgin Islands shows the diet to be composed almost exclusively of herring and fry schools forced to the surface by predatory fish. Examination of stomachs in the Netherlands Antilles showed herring, anchovies, sardines, and fry. Scavenging of bycatch and offal from commercial fishing operations and begging at piers and marinas contribute significantly to the diet of some individuals. Although gulls and several other birds steal food from the beaks of pelicans, pelicans have also been seen to steal food from other birds in rare instances. The salt gland of the Brown Pelican can excrete high concentrations of salt, which enables the pelican to drink seawater.

REPRODUCTION Brown Pelicans nest in colonies of 10 to 500 pairs that usually form on small, predator-free islands.

Seasonality The nesting season for pelicans in a temperate climate is in the spring and summer. The breeding season is progressively earlier for southern populations. In the tropics where seasonal climatic factors have little influence, eggs may be found in any month and nearby nesting colonies may be completely out of phase with each other. Some data indicate that the breeding cycle in the tropics is 8 to

10 months long, resulting in a progression of breeding seasons.

Courtship The male selects the nest site prior to developing a pair bond. The major courtship displays with the head swaying, turning, bowing and upright are performed by both sexes on the proposed nest site. The latter two displays may be accompanied by a low *raaa* call. The male presents nesting materials to the female as part of pair-bonding and nest-building ceremonies. Pelicans are monogamous within a breeding season but choose new partners in succeeding seasons.

Territoriality Nesting territories are clumped, and individual nests may be within 1 m (3 ft) of neighbors.

Nest and Nest Site The flimsy but bulky nest may be on the ground, on tangles of vines, on shrubs, or on the tops of trees. Trees used in nesting colonies include gumbo limbo, Australian pine, black mangrove, red mangrove, seagrape, and ficus of several species. The 1st egg is laid about 3 days after the nest is complete, and the balance of the clutch is laid within 4 to 6 days.

Eggs The normal clutch is 2 or 3 eggs with an average of 2.6 eggs per nest. An egg measures about 46 mm by 73 mm (1.8 by 2.9 in) and weighs about 95 g (3.3 oz). Renesting may occur if eggs are lost from a nest started early in the season.

Incubation Incubation begins with the 1st egg, and hatching begins about 30 days later. The hatching success is variable but averages about 70% of eggs laid.

Fledging Chicks weigh about 60 g (2.1 oz) at hatching. The skin of the naked pinkish-gray hatchling darkens to black by about the 9th day and is lightly covered with white down by the 10th day. Down is fully developed by 20 days. Some juvenile feathers appear at 30 days, and most are in place with some down still evident at 70 days. Juveniles begin to fly at about 11 weeks of age. Adult plumage is attained by age 3. Fledging success may be as high as 100% for the 1st-hatched chick, 60% for the 2nd chick and 6% for the 3rd chick. An average of about 1 juvenile is produced per pair per year.

Age at First Breeding Brown Pelicans have been recorded as attempting to breed in juvenile plumage as early as 2 years of age, but 3 or, more frequently, 4 years pass before they successfully reproduce.

BEHAVIOR Wing flap rate between glides has been recorded at 2.4 flaps per second. Roosting and loafing are often on sandbars or the tops of mangroves. Individual distance between perched birds is less than 1 m (3 ft) and may be as little as 15 cm (6 in).

MIGRATION Northern populations of Brown Pelicans regularly move south for the winter but are not recorded as traveling in large, organized flocks.

PREDATORS Fish Crows and other avian predators have been known to destroy pelican eggs. Raccoons eat the chicks and hatchlings when they can get at them. Bobcats rarely take pelican chicks or disabled adults.

LONGEVITY A pelican banded as an immature lived more than 19 years in the wild. In captivity, Brown Pelicans have lived more than 31 years.

CONSERVATION ISSUES In the 1950s and 1960s pesticides in general and DDT in particular accumulated through the food chain and altered the physiology of pelicans, causing the deposition of eggs with thin shells which did not withstand the rigors of incubation. The high percentage loss of eggs resulted in a serious population decline in eastern Brown Pelicans and a decline from 40,000 to virtual extirpation of the species in Louisiana. The Brown Pelican was listed as an endangered species in 1970, and the use of DDT was banned in 1972. The decreased use of DDT and other virulent pesticides has resulted in population recovery sufficient to be removed from the endangered species list from North Carolina to Alabama in 1987. The California Brown Pelican remains threatened. Pelican populations are still adversely influenced by human disturbance at nest sites and by oil spills. Pelicans take hooks and lures of fishermen. Irresponsible individuals merely cut the line to release the bird, but the dangling monofilament line is a lingering death sentence when it becomes entangled with vegetation at the colony site. The line draped between branches continues to entangle and kill other pelicans.

NOTES The genus name is from the Greek *pelekan,* the original name for this bird. The species name is Latin meaning "western." The English common name is consistent throughout the range. In Spanish it is called *alcatraz, pelícano pardo* or *pelícano moreno,* and in French, *pélican brun.*

SUGGESTED ADDITIONAL READING

Anderson, D.W. 1988. Dose-response relationship between human disturbance and Brown Pelican breeding success. *Wildlife Soc Bull,* 16:339–345.

Schreiber, R.W. 1976. Growth and development of nestling Brown Pelicans. *Bird Banding,* 47:19–39.

Schreiber, R.W., G.E. Woolfenden, and W. Curtsinger. 1975. Prey capture by the Brown Pelican. *Auk,* 92:649–654.

American White Pelican
Pelecanus erythrorynchos | **Pelecanidae Pelicaniformes** | **p. 11**

DISTRIBUTION This family has 1 genus with 8 species and is found worldwide foraging in shallow waters. This species breeds in western Canada and the northwestern U.S. They move south in the winter to southern California, the Gulf of California, and the Gulf of Mexico from the Gulf of Campeche along the Gulf coast east to Florida, with a few wandering as far east as Puerto Rico. A few birds decline to participate in the spring migration and remain in Texas or Mexico to breed.

FOOD AND FEEDING HABITS

The diet is composed almost entirely of fish caught by dipping the bill into the water and scooping the prey into the pouch. These pelicans never catch fish by diving from flight, as Brown Pelicans do. Most prey is less than half of the bill length. Sluggish bottom fish average somewhat larger. The diet in fresh water is composed of 54% carp, as well as chub, suckers, bullheads, and occasional sport fish such as trout and largemouth bass. Salamanders, frogs, and crayfish are eaten when encountered in open water. Pelicans may feed alone, but usually they feed in a coordinated flock. The flock forms a floating line which thrashes the water with wing beating and bill dipping that drives prey toward shore for easier capture. Bill dipping may become synchronized, and 2 groups may herd prey to each other. Prey capture rate is highest with coordinated flocks. They feed in association with—and pirate food from—Double-crested Cormorants, other pelicans, Great

Blue Herons and gulls. Food items for feeding the young are swallowed and never carried in the pouch. These pelicans have been recorded traveling 200 to 300 k (125 to 186 mi) on foraging flights.

REPRODUCTION

These highly social birds feed, rest, and travel together and nest in dense colonies. Reproduction events within colonies are synchronous. Subcolonies often develop in which groups of birds may be separated from the rest of the colony by space or time.

Seasonality Seasonality of nesting is determined by temperature and the melting of ice on feeding areas. Initiation of new colonies may extend over a 3-month period.

Courtship Courtship begins on the breeding grounds and proceeds quite rapidly to pair formation. It begins with short circling flights over the colony. The prospective pairs may parade in the colony in single file with a strutting walk while maintaining the heads erect and bills pointed down. Both sexes bow, with variations depending on circumstances. A head-swaying display in which the head is moved in a horizontal figure 8 is often presented in late courtship. Pairs are generally monogamous within the season but of unknown fidelity in subsequent seasons.

Territoriality There is some data showing fidelity to a breeding area, but the same nest site is not reused. The courting male may jab and bill-snap, grasp the bill of rivals, or lunge with the bill open. The nesting territory is the area within reach of the adult when sitting in the center of the nest, so nest centers average 60 cm (24 in) apart. The birds actively defend the territory against gulls but allow Double-crested Cormorants to nest within and near the colony.

Nest and Nest Site The colony is usually situated on an isolated island in a freshwater lake and often shifts nesting areas to utilize temporarily rich food supplies. Most colonies average fewer than 50 nests, but some colonies have more than 175 nests. These birds nest on the ground in the open or under spruce, fir, poplar, or willow. The nest is a scrape with a 20 cm (8 in) tall rim of soil, gravel, and vegetation raked from the periphery with the bill.

Eggs The 2 chalky-white, rough-surfaced eggs measuring 90 mm long by 57 mm wide (3.5 by 2.2 in) and weighing about 150 g (5.3 oz) are laid at 2- or 3-day intervals about 4 or 5 days after nest building begins.

Incubation Incubation begins when the 1st egg is laid. Eggs are placed under the large webs of the feet; thus it is impossible to incubate more than a 2-egg clutch. The colony may desert the nesting site if disturbed early in the nesting period. Later in the incubation period, the adults are less inclined to fish and remain nearby when disturbed. The incubating parent may turn its back on the sun in hot weather and spread its wings to shade the eggs or newly hatched chicks. One parent guards the nest while the other is away feeding. The incubation period is about 30 days, with eggs sequentially hatching 2 or more days apart.

Fledging The 110 g (4 oz) hatchling is naked and orange but develops a full coat of down by the end of the 1st week. The conflict between siblings at hatching is intense, with the 1st-hatched chick driving the smaller sibling from the nest by pecking and biting at the head and neck, or monopolizing the food supply brought to the nest. The 2nd chick survives less than 10% of the time unless something happens to its older sibling. Most of the loss of 2nd chicks is before the 2nd week of age. The 2nd chick acts as insurance that is only utilized when the 1st egg is preyed upon or the older sibling dies. Young are often heat stressed and cool themselves by resting in the shade of a parent, gular fluttering, wetting their down in nearby water, or swimming to radiate heat through the feet. The chick can crawl about at 2 weeks of age, walk at 3 weeks, and swim at 4 weeks. When the parents begin to leave the nest unattended, the nonflying young form close contact social groups or crèches. The chick makes its 1st flights at about 9 or 10 weeks and shortly thereafter leaves the colony for feeding grounds with the parents. Overall nest success averages .85 young per nest. Younger, later nesting pairs have significantly lower nest success.

Age at First Breeding The age of 1st breeding is 3 or 4 years.

BEHAVIOR White Pelicans often soar, using the energy of thermal updrafts in the middle part of the day, to gain altitude for journeys to and from the feeding site, then readjust their wings to circle down to the destination. When no thermals are available they fly close to the water to take advantage of the aerodynamic lift from ground effect. They often roost in flocks on exposed sandbars with an individual distance of less than a meter. When flying in formation, they may maintain a synchronous wingbeat of about 170 strokes per minute and a distance of less than 2 m (6.6 ft) from each other for long distances. Flocks travel at about 50 kph (31 mph).

MIGRATION Migration is often in flocks of up to 180 individuals flying in formation and stopping at night to feed and rest. They winter south of a line showing a mean January temperature above 40° F. Their journey north is sometimes faster than the seasonal change, with the result that they sometimes arrive at the breeding grounds when most feeding habitat is still covered with ice.

PREDATORS Ravens, crows, and large gulls eat the eggs if untended. Foxes and coyotes take eggs, young and, more rarely, adults if they gain access to nesting islands by low water or late winter ice. Bald Eagles and Great Horned Owls may prey on the young chicks.

LONGEVITY The maximum reported lifespan of banded birds living in the wild is 26.4 years.

CONSERVATION ISSUES Rachel Carson and others published findings that many species of birds, including American White Pelicans, high in the food chain produced thin-shelled eggs as a result of accumulating DDT from the environment. A long-term population decline was reversed around 1970 through a reduction in the use of the most damaging chlorinated hydrocarbon pesticides and an increase in colony protection. Numbers seem to be increasing at an average of 5.3% per year in recent years. The species is very susceptible to direct human disturbance and loss of wetland habitat.

NOTES The genus name is from the Greek *pelekan,* the original name for this bird. The species name is from the Greek *erythros* (red) and *rhunkos* (beak), referring to the reddish tints of the beak when the birds are in breeding condition. In English, this bird has also been called rough-billed pelican, in Spanish, *pelícano Norteamericano* or *pelicano blanco* and in French, *pélican blanc d'Amérique* or *pélican à bec rouge.*

SUGGESTED ADDITIONAL READING
Evans, R.M. and F.L. Knopf. 1993. American White Pelican (*Pelecanus erythrorhynchos*). In A. Poole and F. Gill (eds.), *The Birds of North America. No. 57.* Philadelphia: The Birds of North America Inc.

McMahon, B. F. and R. M. Evans. 1992. Foraging strategies of American White Pelicans. *Behaviour,* 120:69–89.

Double-crested Cormorant

Phalacrocorax auritus | Phalacrocoracidae Pelicaniformes | p. 12

DISTRIBUTION This genus with 28 species is found worldwide foraging in tropical and temperate marine and freshwater ecosystems. The Double-crested Cormorant is widespread and has been divided into 4 subspecies: *P. a. cincinatus* from the Aleutian Islands to the Alexander Archipelago; *P. a. albociliatus* from Vancouver Island to the Gulf of California; *P. a. auritus* from the Gulf of St. Lawrence to Virginia and the Great Salt Lake of Utah; and *P. a. floridanus* found from North Carolina south through Florida to Cuba. It is uncommon in the balance of the West Indies. The insulating layer of waterproof feathers next to the skin allows the winter range to extend as far north as Maine and the Great Lakes on ice-free water.

FOOD AND FEEDING HABITS

Cormorants eat fish, which they capture by swimming rapidly after them underwater, and may feed as individuals or cooperatively in flocks. Even when they sight fish from the air, they land before diving after them. They surface to swallow their prey. Dives may last as long as 70 seconds and go deeper than 18 m (60 ft) but are more commonly less than 30 seconds and shallower than 6 m (20 ft) with extensive surface swimming between dives. They have been shown experimentally to be able to alter the shape of the eye lens with ciliary muscles to allow acute vision in both air and water. In clear water they swim at the surface and submerge their heads, seeming to peer around looking for prey. In marine ecosystems they fish in bays,

estuaries, mangrove-lined creeks, and along rocky shorelines or coastal barrier islands. They use perches that allow drying the plumage and are seldom found in rough water or far from a shore. Cormorants are adaptable, opportunistic, and attracted to high concentrations of prey, resulting in their having a diet which varies greatly on a regional basis. They seldom travel more than 10 miles from roosts to feed. Food items include schooling herring, sardines, capelin, and mullet, along with bottom-dwelling non-schooling fish. In fresh water they fish in lakes, ponds, rivers, swamps, and commercial aquaculture facilities and catch suckers, shad, catfish, gar, gizzard shad, perch, sunfish, and chubs. They also eat crayfish, shrimp, crabs, frogs, snakes, and eels. About 90% of the prey is under 200 g (7 oz), but fish up to 40 cm (16 in) in length have been recovered from the birds' stomachs. After catching spiny fish such as catfish, they may take them ashore and batter them against rocks or logs until they relax or break the spines to allow easier swallowing. They may eat more than 20% of their weight in fish per day. Indigestible bones and scales are regurgitated as pellets.

REPRODUCTION

Cormorants have been shown to have reproductive potentials considerably exceeding those of most other water birds.

Seasonality Laying has been recorded from December to October, but most breeding is from April to July.

Courtship Males frequently initiate courtship on open water with swimming displays, flapping and splashing the wings, and presentation of water weed. They later display with wing waving and calling *ok-ok-ok* from the nest site. As both members of the potential pair become more selective of their associates, a pair bond is formed and calling ceases. When the male returns to the nest and mate after a pair bond is formed, he will often stretch the neck upward and forward with the bill held wide open to display the blue lining. Copulation is always on the nest. Both members of the pair are physically demonstrative with neck weaving, rubbing of beak and breast, and exchanging of nesting material, along with various grunts, croaks, and gurgles throughout the pre-egg period.

Territoriality They may form nesting colonies of several thousand pairs and may nest with pelicans, gulls, anhingas, and herons. The individual territory is chosen by the male and extends about as far as an incubating bird can reach. Younger adult birds nest at the fringe of the colony and have lower nest success.

Nest and Nest Site Double-crested Cormorants nest in a multitude of elevated situations near fresh or salt water: trees such as mature mangroves and Australian pine; cliff faces; isolated emergent rocks; and many man-made structures such as abandoned wharves, booms of heavy construction equipment, duck blinds and the superstructure of derelict vessels. The birds may nest on the ground when not disturbed by humans or predators. The stick-nest foundation is built by both members of the pair. The male then brings additional nesting material, which is worked into place by the female. Nests must be closely guarded because cormorants are prone to steal material from untended nests. The nest takes about 4 days to build and is often interwoven with seaweed and lined with finer vegetation. Nests from prior years are refurbished, becoming stronger and bulkier over time.

Eggs The greenish-blue eggs are covered with a white, chalky surface layer and measure about 60 by 38 mm (2.4 by 1.5 in) with a weight of about 48 g (1.7 oz). The clutch size is variable and ranges from 2 to 9 with an average of 3 or 4 eggs being laid at 1- or 2-day intervals between eggs. Replacement of lost clutches is common, but individual egg loss is not replaced. Rarely, a 2nd brood is produced in a single breeding season.

Incubation Both parents share in the 28-day incubation period, which begins sporadically after the 1st egg is laid but becomes more consistent as the laying proceeds. The heat for incubation is supplied by the webs of the feet rather than brood-patches on the breast. Incubation at 37.2°C (99°F) and 62% humidity in experimental studies showed a hatching success of over 70%. Eggs left at room temperature for 2 or 3 days before incubation did not show a reduced viability, but eggs left for 5 days showed an 80% loss of viability. The chicks hatch over a 3- or 4-day period.

Fledging At hatching, the dark, naked chicks can only wave their heads. The eyes open at about 3 days, and down becomes evident at 6 days. Complete coverage with a short, thick black down and cessation of brooding, except during bad weather, occurs at 2 weeks of age. The chicks call with a continuous sibilant *seet-seet-eet*. Brood reduction by starvation of the younger and smaller chicks is common. Imported red fire ant predation on hatchlings has resulted in up to 92% reduction of cormorant nest success on ant-infested islands in Texas. At 3 or 4 weeks the young leave the nest and gather in small groups; 1st flight is at 6 weeks. The juveniles are capable of flight from water and of diving by 7 weeks but are provided with supplemental food by the parents until about 10 weeks of age. Nest success averages about 2 chicks per nest, but when food is abundant, many nests will produce 4 chicks for a 95% fledging success. Annual mortality is about 25% per year after 1 year of age and probably lower with full maturity.

Age at First Breeding Double-crested Cormorants usually begin breeding at the age of 3 years, but 17% have been found to breed at age 2. Prebreeding juveniles often attend nesting colonies without breeding.

BEHAVIOR When the bird is landing on water, the tail is flared to contact the water first, then the feet are stretched forward to slow the momentum as the bird coasts to a stop. Takeoff from the water must be into the wind while frantically flapping the wings and paddling the feet. They become airborne with much less fuss when launching from an elevated perch. Although they may preen on the water after feeding, they always rest out of the water. Because cormorants need a long takeoff run and are not very maneuverable in flight, small water bodies enclosed with high vegetation are seldom used. They are quite sociable and often feed and roost in close groups that may number several thousand birds. Flight speed has been recorded as 77 kph (48 mph) with a wingbeat rate of 2.6 per second. Flocks traveling distances of 3 km (2 mi) or more travel in V's or in staggered lines with synchronous short periods of gliding. They often fly very close to the water to take advantage of ground effect, but over land they fly quite high.

MIGRATION Northern and inland birds move south and toward the coast for the winter. Migratory flights travel by day and by night. Florida breeding birds seem to be sedentary.

PREDATORS Gulls, crows, and ravens take the eggs and hatchlings. Human disturbance can have a major negative impact on nesting colonies.

LONGEVITY The oldest substantiated banded bird was 23 years of age.

CONSERVATION ISSUES For 25 years following World War II, the use of DDT and other chlorinated hydrocarbon pesticides in the environment were major factors in the decline of cormorant populations. With the banning of DDT use in the U.S., cormorant populations have increased dramatically. Local populations have shown as much as 26% annual increase when not molested. More recently PCBs and related chemicals are suspected of causing deformities of the beak and head in developing embryos and hatchlings. The depletion of stocks of pilchards, anchovies and sardines by man's overharvest has had detrimental effects on cormorant populations. Fishermen in general and fish farmers in particular consider cormorants to be major competitors and kill large numbers of them. Cormorants have been at the forefront of a long-term controversy due to their feeding on salmon in the Great Lakes and on perch in Minnesota. The great increase in catfish farming in the south-central U.S. in the past 50 years has provided an abundant food supply and contributed to cormorant population growth, much to the chagrin of the fish farmers. Aquaculturists in Florida raising ornamental fish for the aquarium trade have complained of severe economic impact by cormorants feeding in rearing ponds. The increasing development of coastlines has eliminated many colony nesting areas. Because of their habits, cormorants are particularly susceptible to the adverse impacts of oil spills, and they are poisoned by the sick fish they eat during red tide outbreaks. In spite of their strong taste they are sometimes part of the diet of indigenous people, who also use the feathered skins to make clothing.

NOTES The genus name is from the Greek *phalakros* (bald) and *korax* (raven). The species name is from the Latin *auritus* (ear), referring to the tufts of feathers resembling ears on the head. The Latin *corvus marinas* (sea crow) is still a common name in other languages and has been altered from the French *cormoran* into the English "cormorant." In English, other common names are crow-duck and shag; in Spanish *corúa de mar, cormoril, cuevo marino, cormorán orejudo* and *cormorán crestado*; and in French *cormoran à aigrettes*.

SUGGESTED ADDITIONAL READING

Casler, C.L. 1973. The air-sac systems and the buoyancy of the Anhinga and Double-crested Cormorant. *Auk*, 90:324–340.

Hennemann, W.W. III. 1985. Energetics, behavior and the zoogeography of Anhingas and Double-crested Cormorants. *Ornis Scandinavica*, 16:319–323.

Sivak, J.G., J.L. Lincer, and W. Bobier. 1977. Amphibious visual optics of the Double-crested Cormorant (*Phalacrocorax auritus*) and the Brown Pelican (*Pelecanus occidentalis*). *Canadian Journal of Zoology*, 55:782–788.

American Anhinga
Anhinga anhinga | **Anhingidae Pelicaniformes** | **p. 13**

DISTRIBUTION This genus with 2 species is found worldwide in shallow tropical and subtropical waters. The lack of insulating waterproof plumage limits them to warm waters. The member of the family called the Darter (*A. melanogaster*) is found from Africa to Australia. The American Anhinga breeds near fresh or brackish water from North Carolina to Texas, Central America, the Caribbean and South America east of the Andes, south to Argentina. It has been divided into 2 subspecies with *A. a. anhinga* on Trinidad and South America and *A. a. leucogaster* in the U.S., Cuba and Mexico, and as an incidental in the Bahamas and the Antilles. A 3rd subspecies has been suggested for the Pacific coast of Central America. Anhingas lose body heat while swimming and use the sun to regain body temperature while basking after feeding. The northward limit of the winter range of American Anhingas is limited by warmth, with average air temperatures of at least 10°C (50°F) and 160 hours of sunshine per month. Sunny weather allows them to extend somewhat farther north, while cloudy conditions force them to move farther south to maintain body temperature.

FOOD AND FEEDING HABITS

Anhingas fish by swimming underwater and stalking slow-moving prey. The anatomy of the musculature and the hingelike connection between the 8th and 9th cervical vertebrae allows the crook in the neck to be rapidly straightened in a heronlike darting strike. They impale large and small prey with the partly open bill, but may grasp small prey. Large or difficult prey may be pounded on a wooden perch, scraped from the bill on wood or other substrate, or shaken from the bill then manipulated in the air to be grasped for head-first swallowing. They can control buoyancy by controlling the amount of air in the lungs. They are able to float with most of the back exposed but more usually expel air and sink leaving only the head and neck exposed. Anhingas usually surface for only a few seconds between 40- to 60-second dives or to swallow prey. Feeding is in cypress swamps, sawgrass sloughs, marshes, tidal lagoons, bays, and estuaries, which offer open clear water for foraging by sight. They are solitary in foraging, but herons may follow them to take advantage of escaping prey. Anhingas may pause with the wings open to allow fish to seek seeming shelter in the shade. They often maneuver through thick submerged vegetation with surprising agility. There is a general preference for freshwater habitats in which mosquitofish, mollies, pickerel, sunfish, shad, catfish, and warmouth perch are caught and eaten. In salt water they take mullet, killifish, mojarra, pinfish, and silversides. They also eat crayfish, shrimp, leeches, tadpoles, frogs, small snakes, turtles, and alligators. When swimming, the neck is folded back and prepared for a forward strike. Prey items usually have 2 perforations as a result of being stabbed by the slightly open beak. Double-crested Cormorants feed with a similar technique but are not significant competitors because they feed preferentially in open marine ecosystems and catch larger and thicker-bodied fish by grasping. In cold weather anhingas forage more when the sun is bright and often take breaks in feeding to sit in the sun and warm up before continuing to feed.

REPRODUCTION Anhingas form loose nesting associations with other waterbirds.

Seasonality Nesting is usually from March to June, but active nests have been found in every month in southern Florida. They may raise 3 broods in favorable years.

Courtship Breeding readiness is signaled by the development of the blue eye ring. Preliminary flights with swoops and glides near the nesting colony are followed by preening and rubbing bills together. The male displays by raising his tail at a 45-degree angle while waving the wings. The male follows the female and offers her a twig before copulating. Copulation is frequent for about 3 days until the nest site is selected, then diminishes as the nest is constructed. Anhingas are monogamous, with a pair bond that may last several years.

Territoriality The male advertises his territory by peering around and will wave alternate wings, snap-bow, and shake twigs when another bird is seen. The rate of displays is greatly increased when a female is present. As courtship proceeds, the female steps onto the nest and also begins to display. After a nest is constructed, the territory shrinks considerably, with adjoining nests allowed as close as 1 m (1 yd).

Nest and Nest Site The nest platform is built on a fork (or preferably a double fork) in an opening near the tops of trees with a nearby perch site. Nest building or refurbishment is initiated by the male and completed by the female, who uses twigs supplied by the male. A nest may be constructed in as little as 1 day. They may take over heron nests in the owners' absence, while herons and egrets will steal sticks from an unoccupied anhinga nest. Nests range from 1.5 to 6 m (5 to 20 ft) above water with an average of 2.5 m (8.2 ft) elevation. They are most often in colonies with other anhingas, herons, and ibises. The same nest or a new nest on the same site is often used in succeeding years.

Eggs The clutch size averages 3.8 eggs per nest with a range of 2 to 5 white to light-bluish eggs weighing about 35 g (1.2 oz) and measuring 53 by 35 mm (2 by 1.4 in). Usually eggs are laid daily, but a skipped day between eggs is common.

Incubation Parents begin incubation with the feet after the 1st egg is laid. The non-incubating parent often roosts near the nest. Males returning for nest relief often bring small amounts of additional nest material. Eggs hatch after 25 to 28 days of incubation.

Fledging The hatchling is naked at hatching with a yellow skin which is covered in a few days with a tan down except on the grayish neck. Hatchlings produce a continuous and monotonous clicking sound. New hatchlings are fed semidigested fish, but as they grow older they reach down the parent's throat to retrieve solid food. Parents brood chicks for about the 1st week. Hatchlings in a nest are staggered in age with the earlier-hatched larger birds able to get more food per feeding; brood reduction is a common event. By 10 days the tan down on the sides, rump, and belly has been replaced with white down. At 3 weeks the back is still covered with a mixture of white and buff down with some juvenile feathers evident. The chicks will jump out of the nest into the water when they feel threatened and are usually able to climb back up to the nest. They fledge at about 6 weeks of age and are provided with food for about another 2 weeks.

Age at First Breeding The adult plumage is attained in the 2nd or 3rd winter, and 1st breeding is probably the following spring.

BEHAVIOR When swimming, the feathers become fully saturated with water resulting in neutral buoyancy, which allows travel underwater with little effort. They often swim with only the head and neck emerging from the water between dives. When underwater they row with both feet simultaneously, but when swimming on the surface the feet alternate strokes. When chilled or satiated, they emerge from the water and stand on a sunny perch to allow their plumage to dry. They preen extensively while drying. In flight they flap at the rate of 44 wingbeats per second

MIGRATION The populations in the most northerly and southerly part of the range, poleward of the 10˚C (50˚F) isotherm, move toward the equator for the winter. The actual border of winter range is determined by the amount of sunshine available to warm the chilled birds.

PREDATORS Raccoons take the eggs and young chicks when they can get to the nest. Alligators catch inattentive adult birds and young birds that fall out of the nest.

LONGEVITY Adults have been recovered 12 years after banding, and individual birds have lived as long as 16 years in captivity.

CONSERVATION ISSUES Destruction of shallow-water wetlands eliminates feeding habitat, and deforestation may eliminate sites for nesting colonies. DDT and its breakdown products are still present in the eggs of anhingas in the U.S. many years after the use of the pesticide was banned. DDT is still manufactured in the U.S. and exported to many tropical nations for unregulated use.

NOTES The name "Anhinga," meaning devil bird or snake bird, is from the native Brazilian Tupi language. Many of the original native Brazilian names for birds date back to the landmark publication *Historiae rerum naturalum Brasiliae* published in 1648 by G. Marcgrave. Other common names in English are American darter, snake bird and water turkey; in Spanish, *corúa real, anhinga Americano, huizote* or *acoyotl;* and in French, *anhinga noir* or *anhinga d'Amérique.* The flight feathers are molted simultaneously, resulting in a flightless period every year in which the birds elude predation by quietly slipping into the water at any disturbance.

SUGGESTED ADDITIONAL READING

Hennemann, W.W. III. 1982. Energetics and spread-winged behavior of Anhingas in Florida. *Condor,* 84:91–96.

Owre, O.T. 1967. Adaptations for locomotion and feeding in the Anhinga and Double-crested Cormorant. *Ornith Monographs #6.* Lawrence, KS: AOU.

Magnificent Frigatebird
Fregata magnificens | **Fregatidae Pelicaniformes | p. 14**

DISTRIBUTION This genus with 5 species is found worldwide in the trade wind belts of tropical seas. This species is found in the tropical Atlantic from Cape Verde Islands off the west coast of Africa, west through the Caribbean and Florida, and along both coasts of Central and South America through Ecuador on the west and Brazil on the east.

FOOD AND FEEDING HABITS
Frigatebirds feed primarily on flying fish and squid, which they catch in the air or snatch from the surface of the sea without landing. Hatchling sea turtles are taken from the beach and as they swim near the surface. Frigatebirds can take off with considerable difficulty after landing in the sea, but only if they do so promptly before their feathers become saturated with water. A wet frigatebird is doomed unless it can swim to a nearby shore or a piece of flotsam that will allow it to climb out of the water and dry out before attempting to fly. Frigatebirds seem to ignore the smaller herring and fry so avidly pursued by gulls and terns. A significant but highly variable amount of their food is obtained by forcing boobies, gulls, tropicbirds, and other seabirds to regurgitate or drop their prey while in flight. The frigate may also snatch a fish from the bill of its victim. The frigate maneuvers to catch dropped prey before it reaches the sea. Frigatebirds follow fishing boats and scavenge discarded fish entrails or incidental catch of fish too small to market. Frigatebirds also take the eggs and young of their own and other species of birds.

REPRODUCTION After courtship both parents cooperate in nest building, incubation, and feeding of the chick until it is about 3 months of age. At this stage the male often departs from the colony for the summer, then courts another female and begins a new nest the following fall. Due to extended parental duties, the females breed only every other year.

Seasonality Eggs are deposited primarily from October to January, resulting in hatching at the beginning of the dry season in the Caribbean.

Courtship Groups of males assemble on the tops of trees in the breeding colony and display to females flying overhead by inflating the gular sacs, throwing the head and neck back, and vibrating the fully extended wings. Females may land nearby and indulge in mutual head waving with the selected male suitor.

Territoriality The male defends the area around his display site by lunging at any nearby males with ferocious bill snapping. A nest is built on the display territory within 2 or 3 days of establishment of a pair bond. The territory size is the distance the individual adult can reach while it is incubating. Generally frigatebirds seem to be socially tolerant, with nests in clumps corresponding to the original groups of displaying males.

Nest and Nest Site Frigatebirds nest in colonies of up to 2,500 pairs. The rudimentary stick nest is built in the tops of trees or bushes, sometimes over water in red mangroves or black mangroves but often near the beach on the windward side of small islands. Trees utilized include seagrape and almond. Frigatebirds nest on the ground, but this is rare. The site is selected to allow the bird to soar in and land delicately on the nest or nearby branch. While the bird is in flight, twigs are collected from the ground or the sea or are pulled from standing trees. Frigates habitually steal nest material from each other's nests.

Eggs The clutch is a single white egg that is 5% or 6% of the female's weight.

Incubation The incubation period of about 45 days is often disturbed by social turmoil resulting in the egg's being lost from the nest. When an egg is lost, a replacement is usually laid in 12 to 14 days. Other birds often use a nest that is not continuously occupied after an egg is destroyed.

Fledging The very sparse food supply results in an extremely long fledging period. The naked hatchling with a dark-bluish skin is brooded by the parents until it is covered by a smoky-gray down. The brooding begins to diminish within 2 weeks, and by 6 weeks of age the young are seldom visited except to be fed. Most feeding of young takes place in the late afternoon. By 2 months of age, the juvenile flight and scapular feathers have grown to provide a black cape in contrast with the down. The young have a grating screech, which they use to beg for food and at a higher intensity use as a defensive call. They bob up and down with spread wings while calling for food. First flight is at about 5 to 6 months of age. Post-fledging feeding by the female may continue for 6 months to a year while the young bird learns how to capture enough food to survive in an impoverished environment. The young bird and its mother recognize each other at a distance of over 100 m (328 ft), and supplemental feeding may take place when the young bird flies to the mother if she lands at some distance from the nest site. Young frigatebirds attempt piracy less often than adults and suffer a lower success rate. Overall reproductive success is about 20% or 11 fledged young per 55 eggs laid.

Age at First Breeding The data are very sparse, but it seems almost certain that frigatebirds do not breed before their 5th year of life, and probably most are 7 years of age or more when they first breed. This delayed breeding allows for the practice and perfection of the complex fishing skills that will be required to feed the young.

BEHAVIOR Frigatebirds are normally seen perched in or near the nesting colony but may also be seen resting in groups in the tops of trees (sometimes with pouches inflated) on islands many miles from the home colony. The individual distance between perched birds may be as little as 1 m (3 ft). Frigatebirds in flight watch each other at great distances and rapidly join another bird that seems to be feeding.

MIGRATION Frigatebirds do not migrate, but the young birds may disperse several thousand kilometers from the nesting colony.

PREDATORS Untended eggs may be

taken by other frigatebirds. Feral cats may eat chicks and adversely influence reproductive success for an entire colony.

LONGEVITY Frigatebirds are long lived and have a low mortality once adulthood is attained. Individual banded birds have been recovered after 34 years, and it is likely that some individuals live over 40 years in the wild.

CONSERVATION ISSUES The frigatebird world population has been estimated at 500,000. The remoteness of the nesting areas probably protects most of the population from interference, resulting in stable numbers within the normal range of variation. Disturbance and nesting habitat destruction are problems for a few local populations. Harvest of trees for construction material or as a source of charcoal may eliminate entire colonies. Long-term concerns relate to pollution and overfishing of the world's oceans, which will further restrict the already limited food supply for this oceanic forager.

NOTES The genus is named for the light, swift-sailing warships of the same name. The species name is from the Latin word meaning "magnifi-cently." This bird is also known locally in English as man o' war bird, scissors tail, hurricane bird and cobbler; in Spanish as *rabihorcado, rabijunco, tijereta*; and in French as *frégate superbe* and *queue en ciseaux*.

Frigatebirds have evolved several energy conservation strategies for living in areas of low food density. Stealing prey saves energy by taking advantage of the hunting by other birds. The slow growth rate and lengthy fledging period allow the parents to provision the nest at a lower rate per day. By breeding only every 2nd year, females have a greater time to recover and to store new energy reserves for future egg production. Finally, the high-efficiency flight allows lengthy patrols with little energy expenditure.

SUGGESTED ADDITIONAL READING

Carmona, R., J. Guzman, and J.F. Elorduy. 1995. Hatching growth and mortality of Magnificent Frigatebird chicks in southern Baja California. *Wilson Bulletin*,. 107:328–337.

Diamond, A.W. 1973. Notes on the breeding biology and behavior of the Magnificent Frigatebird. *Condor*, 75:200–209.

Great Blue Heron
Ardea herodias | Ardeidae Ciconiiformes | p. 15

DISTRIBUTION This genus with 10 species is found in North and South America, sub-Saharan Africa, India, Southeast Asia, and Australia. The similar Grey Heron of Europe and the Cocoi Heron of South America may be part of the same species. The Great Blue Heron breeds from the Atlantic to the Pacific from northern Canada through Central America and northern South America. It is most commonly called *A. herodias*, but sometimes is variously subdivided into subspecies. The Great White Heron, generally called *A. h. occidentalis,* breeds in southern Florida through the Caribbean to northern South America.

FOOD AND FEEDING HABITS
The diet is composed of about 70% fish up to 30 cm (12 in) and 17% invertebrates (grasshoppers, dragonflies, crawfish, and crabs) with lesser numbers of reptiles, amphibians and more rarely birds (particularly nestlings such as those of Coots and Common Moorehens) or mammals. This heron may depart from tradition and hunt far from water, walking about in cultivated fields or open pastures catching small rodents and grasshoppers. Foraging at night is common, and the retinas of the eyes are composed of about 30% cones and 70% rods, which provide enhanced night vision. Spiny fish such as catfish may be speared, shaken, and pounded against a log until the spines are broken or relaxed. The herons do sometimes choke to death on particularly large or spiny prey. Great Blue Herons defend feeding territories of as much as 400 m (1,320 ft) of shoreline against other fish-eating birds and have been observed to peck at and repel small alligators and curious house cats. A Great Blue Heron was seen to lethally peck the skull of a pelican that failed to retreat from a threat display. Territoriality is abandoned in feeding areas of high prey density such as drying ponds, or when prey is highly dispersed by floods.

The Great Blue Heron prefers to feed along the shallow edges of fresh- and saltwater bodies but may also be found strolling about and feeding in open fields miles from the nearest water. The typical feeding behavior is a very slow walk with long strides on land or in water up to the abdomen. The bird may remain immobile for long periods while awaiting prey to come within range of a sudden stab of its beak. In the Caribbean they are frequently seen perched on emergent rocks seemingly totally ignoring breaking waves while waiting to nab the many small fish that feed on the vegetation in the wave break zone. The Great White Heron feeds primarily on fish, crabs, and shrimp in shallow marine habitats such as mud-flats and seagrass beds, but sometimes strays into nearby freshwater marshes and swamps.

REPRODUCTION Great Blue Herons are usually monogamous within a breeding season but court new mates in each succeeding year.
Seasonality In Florida, nesting may begin in the early fall and be as late as midsummer, but most eggs are laid in

March, April, or May. In the northern part of the range, nesting is climatically limited, being later the further north the nest is located.

Courtship The courtship display is quite variable and may include vertical neck stretches, decisive bill snaps, and erections of head, neck and breast plumes. Bill chattering seems to be part of maintaining a pair bond.

Territoriality The nesting territory has a radius of about 2 m (6 ft) beyond the boundaries of the nest. Feeding territory is not fixed because it moves with the bird.

Nest and Nest Site Nesting is usually in colonies and may be shared with other herons and egrets. The nest is usually placed in a tall tree in an established colony, but on predator-free islands the nest may be built on top of small shrubs or even on the ground. The male gathers twigs and sticks, which are used to form a platform by the female. After the platform is complete, a depression in the center is lined with dry grass, leaves or other fine material. New material continues to be added throughout the nesting cycle. Nests are often reused in subsequent years with no particular fidelity and may become quite massive due to annual additions of material. Colonies may occupy the same site for many years if the trees survive and nesting is not excessively disturbed by predators.

Eggs The pale-blue egg is a long oval about 6.3 cm long (2.5 in) with a width of 4.6 cm (1.8 in) and a weight of about 70 g (2.5 oz). Clutch size varies from 2 to 6 with a distinct trend to larger clutches in the north. The Great White Heron in Florida averages fewer than 3 eggs per clutch, while the Great Blue Heron in central Canada averages 5. The eggs are laid at about 2-day intervals.

Incubation Both parents share incubation duties, the male primarily during the day and the female at night. Incubation begins after the 1st egg is laid. The 1st egg hatches about 27 days later. The entire clutch will hatch over a period of 2 to 8 days.

Fledging The new chicks are covered with a pale-gray down with a particularly bushy crown at hatching (Great White Heron chicks have white down). Chicks begin to vocalize shortly with a repetitive *tick-tick* call. They are able to stand at 2 weeks of age and walk steadily by 3 weeks. Although both parents deliver food to the nest, the largest young usually manage to get the most food. Brood reduction is more frequent when small prey items are delivered to the nestlings and monopolized by the larger individuals. Flapping in the 4th week leads to short hops to nearby branches by the 7th week and sustained flight by 8.5 weeks. Chicks leave the nest area at 9 to 13 weeks of age but return to be fed for another 2 or 3 weeks. For the first 2 months after leaving the nest their prey capture success rate is only about half that of adults.

Age at First Breeding Great Blue Herons usually start breeding when 2 years old.

BEHAVIOR The flight speed has been measured at 37 kph (23 mph) with a wing flap rate of 2.1 per second. Feeding territories are defended by several stereotyped threat behaviors. In a forward display the defending heron erects the body plumage, retracts the neck, and walks, runs or flies toward the trespasser. This usually results in the transgressor's departing but may result in a bill duel. A circle flight with the neck fully extended may be made toward the intruder with the usual result being that the intruder departs the territory. The head and neck are held vertically, and the wings may be drooped to show the black shoulder patch in the upright display. This display may escalate to a stance with broadly spread wings.

MIGRATION The most northern breeders must migrate south to find ice-free water for feeding. Many of the young birds east of the Rocky Mountains spend their winters in the southeastern United States and Caribbean. Single birds may make the journey or they may join in flocks of up to 30.

PREDATORS Raccoons may eat the unguarded eggs or newly hatched chicks. Great Horned Owls take the chicks and, less frequently, the adults. Alligators regularly attempt but seldom succeed in sneaking up on an immobile lurking adult.

LONGEVITY One heron has been reported as surviving 23 years after banding.

CONSERVATION ISSUES The reestablishment of beaver populations in North America and the ponds they construct have significantly increased foraging and nesting opportunities for Great Blue Herons in the last half of this century. Great Blue Herons rapidly become habituated to carbide

canons, broadcast alarm calls, and other fright displays at fish-rearing facilities. Habitual trespassers continue to be shot. With the increase in outdoor recreation activities in recent years, it has been found that increased disturbance reduces the number of chicks fledged per nest. Disturbance includes foot traffic, horses, and all forms of boat traffic near nests. Noisy and fast-moving vehicles such as ATVs, water skiers, and personal watercraft are the most disruptive. Slow-moving, quiet observers, such as bird watchers or kayakers, are less disturbing.

NOTES The genus name is from Latin *ardea* (heron). The species name is from the Greek *erodios* (heron). In West Indian English it is called blue gaulin or grey gaulin. It is also (erroneously) called crane or blue crane. In Spanish it is *garza morena, garza azulada, garzón cenizo* or *garzón ceniciento*, and in French *grand héron*.

SUGGESTED ADDITIONAL READING

Andelt, W.F. and S.N. Hopper. 1996. Effectiveness of alarm-distress calls for frightening herons from a fish rearing facility. *Progressive Fish Culturist*, 58:258–252.

Butler, R.W. 1992. Great Blue Heron (*Ardea herodias*). In A. Poole and F. Gill (eds.), *The Birds of North America. No. 25*. Philadelphia: The Birds of North America Inc.

Great Egret

Casmerodius albus | **Ardeidae Ciconiiformes** | **p. 16**

DISTRIBUTION The single species in the genus is found in the southern U.S., South America, Africa, India, Southeast Asia, and Australia. The Great Egret is divided into 4 subspecies. *C. a. egretta* is found in the summer from Oregon and Ontario south through the West Indies and Central America to southern South America east of the Andes. *C. a. melanorhynchos* is found in sub-Saharan Africa, *C. a. albus* is found in Europe, and *C. a. modesta* is found in India, Southeast Asia from Japan south through coastal Australia, and New Zealand.

FOOD AND FEEDING HABITS

This egret wades in water up to its belly using the walking-slowly feeding technique. It also feeds by standing and waiting, crouched with head and neck retracted, peering over, and head or neck swaying. It will also fly from a perch and stab prey near the surface of water too deep to wade. The Great Egret feeds in a broad variety of habitats, including freshwater marshes, swamps, rivers, lakes, damp meadows, and various agricultural lands. The bird may hunt grasshoppers and other insects in grassy uplands and use the services of cattle to flush insects from the grass. It uses most shallow marine habitats, including marshes, sea-grass beds, and sandy, muddy, and rocky shorelines. Feeding territories are strongly defended with various postures which may escalate into attacks and chasing flights. The bird defends its territory against other wading birds and even small alligators. In times of great abundance—when fish are concentrated in the bottom of a drying pond, for instance—territoriality may diminish to undetectable levels. The Great Egret will attempt to steal prey from other birds. Fish is the primary prey, although the diet is extremely varied and includes frogs, crayfish, salamanders, snakes, lizards, insects, small birds, and rodents.

REPRODUCTION

Great Egrets usually nest in colonies, sometimes with other waders. They sometimes nest as solitary pairs.

Seasonality In Florida, territories are selected in March, and nesting starts in April. Because of the benign climate, early and late nesting are not uncommon.

Courtship The early stages of courtship involve circle flights over the nest site. Males build a rudimentary nest platform from which they solicit females. From the host site, males perform a vertical stretch display to announce the claimed territory and reproductive readiness. A display with horizontally extended neck and bill clacking accompanied by erection of the plumes is given regularly until copulation with a mate begins. The magnificent plumes are used prominently in pair formation and maintenance displays such as the greeting ceremony, in which the plumes are erected. This action is often accompanied by the raising of the wings. Aggressive territorial posturing with erected plumes is frequent from the nest site along with stereotyped bows involving lowering the head to grasp a stick while bouncing the erect plumes.

Territoriality Advertisement of the territory is by circle flights and distinctive calls of *frawnk*. After a female has joined a male and copulated on a nest platform, she becomes aggressive to other females in the vicinity. A member of a pair usually utters several low croaks when returning to the nest.

Nest and Nest Site The coarsely constructed nest of twigs and branches is built over or near water, most commonly in mangrove, willow, or cypress trees on islands isolated from terrestrial predators. Nests are often located over alligator-infested water. Old nests are re-used. The 15 to 100 pairs in a colony are often part of a larger group of cormorants, Brown Pelicans and other waders. In mixed colonies, Great Egrets nest in the highest sites.

Eggs The 2 to 5 light-blue eggs per clutch are laid on alternate days and measure about 58 by 42 mm (2.3 by 1.6 in).

Incubation Both parents share incubation duties for the 25-day incubation period. Hatching success is usually better than 80% and may exceed 96%.

Fledging The earliest hatched chicks show the greatest weight gain per day at first because of lack of competition and later because their size provides a competitive advantage over siblings. The last sibling to hatch in a nest seldom survives for more than a week because of food competition from its older and larger nest mates. The chicks leave the nest to climb on nearby branches at about 3 weeks of age and fledge at 6 weeks. Imported red fire ant predation on hatchlings has resulted in up to 92% reduction of heron nest success on infested islands. After fledging, the mortality rate in 1st-year birds may be as high as 76%, but drops to about 26% in older, experienced birds.

Age at First Breeding Great Egrets may attempt to breed as early as 1 year of age, but most begin successful breeding at age 3.

BEHAVIOR The Great Egret has an unusual bathing behavior—it may bend its legs to squat and submerge most of its body for several minutes before embarking on a thorough preening. The birds remain 15 to 30 m (50 to 100 ft) apart on feeding territories, but territorial inclinations seem to subside after sundown when they roost communally. The flight speed has been recorded at 27 kph (17 mph). Courtship and pair formation behavior is similar to that of Great Blue Herons.

MIGRATION The birds in the northern part of the range (north of the mid-Atlantic states) move south in October to the Gulf of Mexico, Caribbean, Central America, and South America to escape freezing temperatures. The spring migration northward begins in February and March.

PREDATORS Great Egrets generally avoid terrestrial predators by selecting nesting sites inaccessible to them. Avian predators, such as crows and Boat-tailed Grackles, will take momentarily unattended eggs or hatchlings.

LONGEVITY A Great Egret was recovered 24 years after banding.

CONSERVATION ISSUES This species was one of those most highly affected by the millinery trade in the late 1800s. At the fad's peak, plumes sold for more than twice their weight in gold. Plumes from 10 birds sold for more than a factory laborer would make in a year. Feathers from as many as 200,000 birds were sold at a single auction. The National Audubon Society was formed to halt the destruction of egrets, and the whims of fashion moved on to different excesses before the birds could become extinct. Populations have recovered dramatically from near elimination early in the century, due in part to federal protection provided by the Migratory Bird Treaty Act and the Lacey Act. The North American population now exceeds 100,000 breeding individuals. Present-day threats are primarily related to the continuing loss of wetland feeding and nesting areas and to human disturbance of reproductive activities.

NOTES The genus name is from the Greek word *herodios,* meaning "brother or sister," and is the origin of the word "heron." The species name is Latin *albus,* meaning "white." This bird has also been called *Egretta garzetta, Ardea garzetta,* and *Ardea alba.* The common name "egret" is from the French *aigrette* (a tuft of plumes). The meaning of the word has evolved to include the bird wearing the plumes. English common names include American Egret (recently the "proper" common name), great white heron, long white, white crane, white heron, and white gaulin. In Spanish it is *garceta grande, garza real* and *garzón blanco,* and in French it is *grande aigrette.*

SUGGESTED ADDITIONAL READING

Custer, T.W. and D.W. Peterson Jr. 1991. Growth rates of Great Egret, Snowy Egret and Black-crowned Night Heron chicks. *Colonial Waterbirds,* 14:46–50.

Pratt, H.M. and D.W. Winkler. 1985. Clutch size, timing of laying, and reproductive success in a colony of Great Blue Herons and Great Egrets. *Auk,* 102:49–63.

Little Blue Heron

Egretta caerulea | **Ardeidae Ciconiiformes | p. 17**

DISTRIBUTION This genus with 8 species is found worldwide in temperate and tropical climates. The Little Blue Heron breeds on the shores of the Gulf of California and on the U.S. east coast from Massachusetts south to the coast of the Gulf of Mexico and in the Caribbean, Central America, and in South America south to Lima, Peru, and Uruguay. Breeding birds from the northeast U.S. move south to Florida and the Caribbean for the winter as the weather in their areas becomes cold.

FOOD AND FEEDING HABITS

The Little Blue Heron feeds solitarily or in small, dispersed mixed-species groups, preferring water 5 to 15 cm (2 to 6 in) deep. The preferred feeding habitats include shallow marshes, lagoons and other shallow, sheltered fresh or salt water, often at sites with aquatic or riparian vegetation. The primary feeding behavior is walking slowly, but the birds may also peer over, walk quickly, run, stir the feet, hop, and open the wings and flick. Striking efficiency is higher in open water or on shore than in pools. They also use other animals as "beaters" to scare up prey. This heron's feeding with other birds, livestock, alligators, and manatees has been recorded. The main foods are crabs, crawfish, prawns, and fish such as anchovies, killifish, and gobies in salt water. In fresh water they eat sunfish, mosquitofish, shad, perch, mollies, and many introduced species. Pond-dwelling frogs, tree frogs, crayfish, and grasshoppers may make up a signifi-

cant part of the diet when available in numbers. The herons also regularly eat crabs, shrimp, isopods, beetles, bugs, and dragonflies. Foraging territories may be maintained except in the presence of abundant prey. They avoid competition with Snowy Egrets and Tricolored Herons by resource partitioning. Little Blue Herons eat many crustaceans, while Tricolored Herons almost exclusively eat fish. Over 80% of the fish caught by Little Blue Herons are over 31 mm (1.2 in) while 79% of the fish caught by Snowy Egrets are under 31 mm. Little Blue Herons have a higher striking efficiency than competitors but are intermediate in calories of prey gathered per minute.

REPRODUCTION Little Blue Herons nest in mixed-species groups with other waders, pelicans, cormorants and anhingas.

Seasonality In Florida most birds are in the breeding colony by late March or early April. Further north, nesting may be delayed until mid-May. In tropical areas with no climate-limiting factors, the nesting period may be spread over a much longer period.

Courtship Males claim breeding territories 3 to 5 m (10 to 16 ft) in diameter by patrolling, displaying, and defending at the boundary. The primary male territorial display is a vertical stretch with erection of the feathers on the crest, neck, and upper back. The full forward threat display toward trespassers is similar to that of the other herons. The pair bond is formed and maintained by bill nibbling and other appeasement displays, copulation, and nest fidelity. The defended territory contracts as courtship proceeds. The pair are seasonally monogamous with some promiscuity between neighbors, and may copulate as many as 16 times per 7 hours.

Territoriality After pair formation and nest construction, the nesting territory extends about 1 m (40 in) from the nest site and is defended by both members of the pair. Typically Little Blue Herons travel 3 to 10 km (1.8 to 6.2 mi) from the breeding colony to foraging sites. Feeding territories may be claimed and defended.

Nest and Nest Site The nest construction is completed 3 to 5 days after the pair bond is established. The nest may be placed in cypress, buttonbush, willow, or mangroves from less than a meter (yard) to more than 7 m (23 ft) above ground or water level. The nest site is typically near or over water. Upland vegetation on predator-free dredge spoil islands is readily used. The birds' dark plumage absorbs heat to the extent that they exhibit gular fluttering on hot, still days and generally place the nest in a shady spot. The male seems to go without feeding and seldom leaves the nest site until the eggs have been laid. His only absence is when he departs to gather twigs and deliver them to the female, who constructs the nest with a leaf-lined central depression. Late-nesting birds may occupy a previously used nest. The effects of removing twigs for nest material and the deposit of abundant guano commonly results in the stunting or death of the trees in a nesting colony.

Eggs The pale bluish-green eggs average 44 by 33 mm (1.7 by 1.3 in). The average clutch is 3 or 4 eggs (with a range of 2 to 6) laid every other day, beginning when the nest is completed. Clutch size may vary within a single site due to variation in seasonal and annual environmental factors. Replacement clutches are laid to replace clutches lost early in the season, but multiple broods in a single season have not been recorded.

Incubation The incubation period begins after the 2nd egg is laid and lasts 22 to 23 days. Both parents incubate. A Little Blue Heron repeatedly disturbed by an observer was seen to sequentially move its clutch of 4 eggs away from the disturbed nest, presumably to an available abandoned nest. Hatching success may exceed 92%.

Fledging Asynchronous hatching produces a range of age and size of chicks. Brood reduction is common due to starvation of the youngest chicks, which seldom survive to fledge. Young chicks grow and thrive at a normal rate if accidents remove older siblings from the nest. Hatchlings develop a coat of gray down with a few filaments standing erect above the crown. Thermoregulation is developed enough to maintain body temperature in mild weather at 11 days and for colder weather at 16 days. The amount of time adults spend brooding the chicks decreases rapidly when they obtain thermal independence. About 50% of nestlings survive to 2 weeks of age. At this age, the feet and legs develop rapidly and allow the chicks to leave the nest at 2 weeks of age to climb laboriously about on nearby vegetation, grasping with the bill or waving the wings to maintain balance. By 3 weeks they do not need parental care except for feeding. They may roost and be fed by the parents as far as 3 m (10 ft) away from the nest. The diet fed to nestlings includes about 35% fish and 20% crayfish. By day 35, the young show sustained flight and the parents provide less food. A week later the juveniles regularly forage for themselves and soon begin to spend the night at other roosts away from the colony. After fledging, the juveniles are significantly less effective than adults at feeding.

Age at First Breeding One-year-old Little Blue Herons make up a significant number of the courting individuals at breeding colonies, but they seldom pair with other young birds and have lower reproductive success when paired with older birds.

BEHAVIOR Little Blue Herons show a greater response to mosquitoes and biting sandflies than most other herons do. The wingbeat is a continuous solid stroke at 2.7 beats per second with glides only when losing altitude or landing. The flight speed over distances averages about 40 kph (25 mph).

MIGRATION The populations in the U.S. east of the Mississippi migrate south through Florida. The western U.S. populations move south along the coast of Mexico. Post-breeding dispersal is in all directions from the colony.

PREDATORS Eggs and chicks are subject to predation by raccoons, opossums, mink, weasels, night herons, crows, owls, and rat snakes. Hawks, owls, and alligators take the adults. An alarm call is given in response to predators, but mobbing and other defensive measures are lacking.

LONGEVITY The greatest recorded longevity of a banded Little Blue Heron is 13 years 11 months.

CONSERVATION ISSUES Because of the dark color and lack of plumes, Little Blue Herons escaped the population devastation associated with the plume trade. A general, slow population decline is due primarily to loss of foraging habitat in wetlands and alteration of natural ecosystems by developers. Little Blue Herons are still shot at some fish hatcheries. Careful studies have shown that disturbance of nesting colonies by man can lead to nest abandonment or decline in reproductive success. Actual flushing distances vary considerably, but it seems that a 100 m (328 ft) radius no-entry buffer zone will prevent most of the man-induced disturbance.

NOTES The genus name is from the French *aigretta*. The name was also used for the bird that produced the plumes. The species name is from the Latin, meaning "dark blue." This heron was originally named *Ardea caerulea*. It was subsequently placed in its own genus, *Florida*, and later in *Hydranassa*. Most of the small and intermediate herons have now been grouped in *Egretta*. Other English common names are calico bird, blue gauling, and pied or spotted heron (for the transition plumage of the white young molting to blue adults). In Spanish it is *garza azul* or *garceta azul*, and in French *petit héron bleu*, *aigrette bleue* or *crabier bleu*.

SUGGESTED ADDITIONAL READING

Frederick, P. C. and M. W. Collopy. 1989. Nesting success of five ciconiiform species in relation to water conditions in the Florida Everglades. *Auk,* 106:625–635.

Rogers, J. A. Jr. and H. T. Smith.1995. Little Blue Heron (*Egretta caerulea*). In A. Poole and F. Gill (eds.), *The Birds of North America. No. 145.* Philadelphia: The Birds of North America, Inc.

Werkschkul, D. F. 1981. Nesting ecology of the Little Blue Heron: Promiscuous behavior. *Condor,* 84:381–384.

Tricolored Heron

Egretta tricolor | **Ardeidae Ciconiiformes** | **p. 18**

DISTRIBUTION This genus with 8 species is found worldwide in temperate and tropical climates. Three subspecies have been proposed; of these, *E. t. ruficollis* is found in North America and the Caribbean. Tricolored herons breed from Maine south through southern Florida, from the Gulf coast of Mississippi through the Gulf and Caribbean coasts of Mexico and Central and South America, and along the Atlantic coast of South America south to Brazil. They nest on many of the Caribbean and Bahamas islands. They are found on the Pacific coast from Baja California, to northern Peru.

FOOD AND FEEDING HABITS

Topminnows captured in shallow water make up over 90% of the diet. Small fish such as killifish, mollies, mosquitofish, and flagfish in the range of 20 mm to 35 mm (0.4 to 1.4 in) are also a regular part of the diet. They also take snails, shrimp, frogs, tadpoles, and aquatic insects. On land they take lizards and grasshoppers. The primary feeding habitat is marine mudflats, mangrove swamps, tidal creeks, and estuaries. They feed by day using the modes of walking quickly, hopping, running and open-wing feeding. When chasing prey they often crouch and stab horizontally into the water. Their strike efficiency is highest when they stand and wait and walk slowly, but they may see more prey by disturbing and chasing. Fishing is likely to be along protected shorelines, canals, and pools and seldom on the edges of open water. The chicks are mainly fed small fish such as killifish for the 1st few weeks of life. Feeding territories are sometimes vigorously defended against long-legged waders, and Tricolored Herons are dominant over Snowy Egrets. In times of plenty the herons are sometimes quite tolerant of other birds. When feeding in mixed-species flocks they are often on the periphery. They tend to wade in deeper water than the other small herons do and often wet the belly feathers or even float. Tricolored Herons usually travel 1.6 km to 14.5 km (1 to 9 mi) between nesting colonies and feeding sites but may occasionally travel as far as 25.3 km (16 mi) in times of need. They avoid competition with Snowy Egrets and Little Blue Herons by resource partitioning. Tricolored Herons eat primarily fish while Little Blue Herons eat many crustaceans and Snowy Egrets eat many prawns.

REPRODUCTION Tricolored Herons nest in colonies with their kind or other species of herons. The availability of food seems to influence breeding attempts, and there is little or no nesting when food is scarce. Tricolored Herons often form single-species aggregations within mixed-species nesting colonies.

Seasonality Most nesting is between March and June, with a few pairs earlier and later.

Courtship Circle flights around the territory with deep wingbeats produce a characteristic *whomp, whomp,* which invites females. The male usually selects the nest site and builds the initial foundation of sticks as a display platform. The male performs stretch-and-snap displays, and when a female approaches he performs a twig-shake display. After pairing, the male collects twigs and delivers them to the female, who works them into the nest structure. The pair bond only lasts for 1 season. A Tricolored Heron was recorded mating with a Snowy Egret and producing a brood of 4 offspring.

Territoriality Males often select 4 to 10 m (13 to 33 ft) diameter territories before females arrive at the colony. Males gradually allow females to enter the territory, which decreases to 2 to 3 m (7 to 10 ft) after pair bonding. Nearest nest distance averages 1 to 2 m (3.3 to 6.5 ft). Aggressive displays include an alert posture with feathers sleeked, or a forward display in which the crest, scapular aigrettes, and neck feathers are erected. This display may lead to aerial fighting, with 2 males flying up from the ground, lunging at each other with beaks, and clawing at each other with the feet.

Nest and Nest Site The nest is a platform of sticks with a central depression and is usually 2 to 4 m (6.5 to 13 ft) off the ground below a canopy that provides protection from sun and aerial predators. Nest sites are adjacent to salt water 75% of the time, in bushes or 1 of the 4 species of mangroves. In freshwater habitat they may nest in cypress, pondapple, willow, or other wetland hardwoods with low-hanging tree branches on small islands or in inundated vegetation. The nest is primarily constructed by the female of sticks brought to her by the male and has material added throughout incubation. The inland nest site is often over water containing alligators, which deter terrestrial predators. The nest seldom survives to subsequent seasons, but the same tree crotch may be reused annually.

Eggs The normal clutch is 3 or 4 eggs, but up to 9 have been found in 1 nest. The greenish-blue eggs average 44 by 32 mm (1.7 by 1.3 in) and weigh about 21 g (.75 oz). An interval of 2 days is normal between the first 2 eggs, with subsequent eggs usually being laid more frequently. Replacement clutches are laid an average of 5 days after a 1st clutch is destroyed. Second clutches are rare but have been recorded. Probable egg dumping in another Tricolored Heron's nest has been recorded.

Incubation Incubation starts sporadically and becomes effective after the laying of the 2nd or 3rd egg. Both sexes sit on the eggs for the 23-day incubation period. Relieving parents often perform a greeting ceremony in which the arriving bird, with all feathers erect and wings held out to the side, passes a twig to a mate. Snowy Egrets, Little Blue Herons, and Tricolored Herons have been recorded laying eggs in each other's nests with the adoptive parents rearing the chicks.

Fledging Eggs show pip holes and chicks begin peeping a day before hatching. The chicks hatch with a dark-gray down, white underparts, and hairlike plumes on the crown. Brooding is continuous for about the first 12 days. After about the 1st week the chicks keep up a constant sibilant whining when not sleeping. When the chicks start to climb about the branches near the nest at 11 or 12 days of age they often hook the lower beak over branches while scrabbling for purchase with wings and feet. At first the chicks return to the nest for feeding, but within a few weeks they are fed elsewhere in the colony. Adults are able to recognize their own young in the colony and do not feed other chicks. By 14 days of age, temperature control, preening, begging, threats, and aggressive vocalizations are present. At 24 days of age the young perch above the nest and only return to it to be fed. Juvenile plumage is mostly complete at 30 days, when the 1st flights begin. The young are initially fed in treetops by the parents, but as the chicks mature, the parents lead them on short flights around the colony before feeding. Independence is reached at 7 or 8 weeks. Brood size is significantly reduced by predation, malnutrition, disease, abandonment, and incle-ment weather. Colony nest success rates have been measured from 11% to 100%. Studies of nestling survival using posture-sensing radio transmitters have shown that other standard methods such as color banding tend to greatly underestimate mortality.

Age at First Breeding Based on molts and plumage, Tricolored Herons probably breed when 2 years of age.

BEHAVIOR When traveling across country from nesting colonies to feeding areas, Tricolored Herons average 15.3 kph (9.5 mph), but this average probably includes some feeding stops.

MIGRATION Tricolored Herons from the northern part of their range migrate south to Florida and the Caribbean coast in September and October for the winter and begin the spring migration back to the breeding grounds in February or March. Migration is generally along coastal habitats, but migrating flocks have been seen 160 km (100 miles) offshore.

PREDATORS American Crows, Fish Crows, and Boat-tailed Grackles take the eggs when the nest is unguarded. Black-crowned Night Herons, Bald Eagles, and Turkey Vultures take unguarded newly hatched chicks. Raccoons, opossums, mongooses, and feral cats may prey on the young if water levels fall and allow predators access to the nest site. Alligators take chicks that fall out of the nest and may jump to catch chicks climbing about on lower branches.

LONGEVITY The oldest recovered banded Tricolored Heron was 17 years 8 months of age.

CONSERVATION ISSUES Although Tricolored Herons were seldom harvested for the plume trade, the nesting colonies were disrupted to the point of failure by the plume hunters' depredations in mixed-species colonies. In less-developed countries the eggs, chicks, and adults are still taken for food. The recent, large increase in the aquaculture industry has resulted in increased shooting of Tricolored Herons at fish-rearing ponds. Water management practices in south Florida have reduced the rate of successful reproduction. In the past 50 years the breeding range has extended northward to New York, with some nests reported as far north as Maine.

NOTES The genus name is from the French *aigrette.* The name was also used for the bird that produced the plumes. This heron was originally classified in the genus *Ardea,* then placed in its own genus, *Hydranassa.* After further study of its behavior and skeleton, it was combined with the genus *Egretta.* The Tricolored Heron is also called gaulin or Louisiana Heron in English, *garceta tricolor* or *garza pechiblanca* in Spanish, and *aigrette tricolorée* or *crabier* in French.

SUGGESTED ADDITIONAL READING

Frederick, P.C. 1997. Tricolor Heron (*Egretta tricolor*). In Poole and F. Gill (eds.), *The Birds of North America. No. 306.* Philadelphia: The Birds of North America, Inc.

Kent, D.M. 1986. Foraging behavior, habitat use and food of three egrets in a marine habitat. *Colonial Waterbirds,* 9:25–30.

Reddish Egret
Egretta rufescens | Ardeidae Ciconiiformes | p. 19

DISTRIBUTION This genus with 8 species is found worldwide in temperate and tropical climates. The Reddish Egret breeds on both coasts of the southern half of Florida, the Bahamas, Cuba, Hispaniola, and the coast of Venezuela and Colombia. It breeds on the Gulf Coast from Alabama through the Yucatan peninsula to Belize and on the west coast of Mexico in Baja California. The literature is inconsistent on the number of races present but seems to agree that the form in Florida is *E. r. rufescens*. The population breeding on the Baja peninsula and the Pacific coast of Mexico has been named *E. r. dickeyi*.

FOOD AND FEEDING HABITS
Reddish Egrets feed near low tide on shallow (less than 15 cm or 6 in), tidally influenced flats, shoals, grassbeds, and on the lagoon side of undeveloped coastal barrier islands. They are found more rarely in shallow freshwater habitats. This egret is active strictly during the day and feeds more actively than any of the long-legged waders in our area. They may stand and wait or walk slowly but more frequently walk quickly with a distinct stride. They are typically more active than other herons and typically disturb and chase when foraging. They run, prance, and dart as they chase schools of small fish in a zigzag path, often with the head tilted to one side. They use the wings to assist in abrupt changes of direction, to take flight for short distances when running after prey, and to use open-wing feeding and canopy feeding, in which a pause with wings spread is used to lure disturbed fish into the seeming safety of the shade. Alternatively, a quick flick of 1 or both wings is used to flush prey from hiding. When open-water prey is not in evidence, Reddish Egrets may use the feet to stir mud or sea grass to scare prey into the open. They eat fish, small crabs, shrimp, and snails. When feeding in freshwater wetlands they may include frogs, lizards, and small snakes in the diet. The feeding territory is often vigorously defended.

REPRODUCTION
Reddish Egrets nest on predator-free islands on the ground or in low shrubs but seem to prefer to place nests just below the canopy of clumps of red or black mangrove trees. On dredge spoil islands they may nest in Brazilian pepper or other introduced trees.

Seasonality Nesting season is variable, and active nests may be found in any month of the year, although there is usually a distinct peak for a specific year or location.

Courtship Males often perform circle flights and spiral-descending flights to the territory. Rival males chase one another, with the pursued making rapid turns and zigzags while close to the water and between trees and bushes. The male in pursuit maintains an erect crest and returns to the female and nest site with full erection of the bristlelike plumes on the back, neck and shoulders. In the early stages of courtship the male may pursue the female for several hundred yards in a graceful aerial duet. At the nest the male bows to the female, his head and neck feathers erect, and performs head tossing in which the head is rapidly raised and lowered vertically. The advertising call of a male in peak breeding condition is an *arg* given from an elevated perch or in flight. After further display the pair rub necks together, then copulate. No discrimination is evident in pair formations—the 2 color phases seem to mate at random. Reddish Egrets sometimes have extra-pair copulations, and new mates are commonly selected in succeeding years.

Territoriality The nesting or feeding territories are defended with a series of display postures showing increasing erection of crest and other plumage with increasing forward inclination of the head and neck.

Nest and Nest Site Reddish Egrets nest in colonies of their own species or more commonly with groups of anhingas, cormorants, herons, ibises, pelicans, and spoonbills on small islands or in coastal mangroves. They build a sturdy stick nest at least 5 m (16.4 ft) from the ground and 1 m (3 ft) or more under the canopy on the outer end of a springy branch. The nest is about 60 cm (2 ft) in diameter with an inner depression about 30 cm (12 in) wide by 9 cm (4 in) deep, lined with soft grasses, leaves, and vines.

Eggs The light-bluish-green eggs average 52 by 38 mm (2 by 1.5 in). An average clutch is 3 or 4 eggs, but a range of 2 to 7 has been observed.

Incubation Both parents share the 26-day incubation period. Hatching rate has been observed to be in the range of 65% to 85%.

Fledging The red-phase young have a gray down with cinnamon-colored tints on the head and neck. Young that are destined to be white at maturity have a pure-white down. The chicks make their 1st flights at about 45 days of age but are fed near the nest for 2 or 3 more weeks. Most juveniles are fully independent by 65 days of age. Full adult foraging efficiency is not attained until the 3rd year of age. Depending on predators, weather, and food supply, the fledging rate may vary from 4% to 75%, with a normal productivity of about 1.3 fledglings per breeding pair.

Age at First Breeding Adult plumage is attained by the 2nd year, and breeding commences in the 2nd, or more usually, the 3rd year.

BEHAVIOR A flight speed of 32 kph (20 mph) has been recorded.

MIGRATION Populations are mostly sedentary, but dispersal after breeding is common.

PREDATORS Raccoons and crows are major potential predators of eggs and chicks. Dogs can have a huge negative impact by disturbing a colony and allowing aerial predators access to unguarded nests. Reproductive success of colonies may be eliminated by individual Bald Eagles, that develop a prey preference for young Reddish Egrets.

LONGEVITY One Reddish Egret was recovered 12 years 3 months after banding.

CONSERVATION ISSUES Plume hunting virtually exterminated Reddish Egrets in Florida by early in this century, but dispersals seeded a new population that has slowly continued to increase in numbers and expand in range. The loss of natural shorelines due to dredging and filling of wetlands and associated development has eliminated huge amounts of feeding habitat. Human use or habitation of coastal barrier islands constantly disturbs feeding or nesting birds, and introduced predators have rendered many of the islands unfit for nesting. The largest part of the population lives in Florida Bay and is likely to be adversely affected by the recent change in ecology from a seagrass bottom with clear water to a mud bottom with turbulent water. The Reddish Egret continues to be the rarest heron in the United States.

NOTES The genus name is from the French *aigrette,* for the breeding plumes previously used as millinery decoration. The species name is from the Latin *rufous* (reddish). This bird has also been placed in the genera *Ardea* and *Dichromanassa.* At one time the white phase was considered a separate species, *A. pealii.* The Reddish Egret is also called gaulin in the English Caribbean. It is called *garza rojiza* in Spanish and *crabier* or *aigrette roussâtre* in French.

SUGGESTED ADDITIONAL READING

Meyerriecks, A.J. 1960. Comparative breeding behavior of four species of North American Herons. *Nuttall Ornithology Club,* 2.

Paul, R.T., H.W. Kale II, and D.A. Nelson. 1979. Reddish Egrets nesting on Florida's east coast. *Florida Field Nat,* 7:24–25.

Rodgers, J.A. Jr. and H.T. Smith. 1995. Set-back distances to protect nesting bird colonies from human disturbance in Florida. *Conservation Biology,* 9:89–99.

Snowy Egret

Egretta thula | **Ardeidae Ciconiiformes** | **p. 20**

DISTRIBUTION This genus with 8 species is found worldwide in temperate and tropical climates. A very similar species, *E. garzetta,* is found in Europe, Africa, Asia, and Australia. Two races of Snowy Egrets have been described: *E. t. brewsteri,* which is somewhat larger and is found on the Pacific coast of the U.S. south to the shores of the Gulf of California in Mexico; and *E. t. thula,* which breeds on the Atlantic and Gulf coasts through the Caribbean and Central America to southern Argentina and Chile.

FOOD AND FEEDING HABITS

Most feeding habitats are bordered by salt water or fresh water although the birds may seek insects in dry brush or grasslands. They may join Cattle Egrets utilizing the insects disturbed by grazing livestock or agricultural machinery. In freshwater habitats they are most often associated with willows, reeds, and other emergent plants. In saltwater habitats they favor shorelines, shallow seagrass beds, and mudflats. They may forage in excess of 20 km (12 miles) from the colony. Actively feeding Snowy Egrets are often joined by others on the feeding grounds. The bright-yellow feet are often used to stir, rake, probe, and paddle; feet are also used to drag and stir while the egret is in flight. When seeking active prey they employ a series of rapid moves including walking quickly, flicking wings, using open wings, hopping and running, as well as hovering and dipping while in flight. When feeding on abundant, tiny minnows they may make a series of dips while flying slowly forward dragging the feet. More typical heron feeding behavior, such as standing and waiting, walking slowly and peering over, is also regularly used. Competition among Snowy Egrets, Little Blue Herons, and Tricolored Herons feeding in the same area is reduced by partitioning of the resource. Snowy Egrets eat fewer and smaller fish than Tricolored Herons do, and many more prawns than Little Blue Herons do. Snowy Egrets may use Red-breasted Mergansers as beaters in shallow water and livestock as beaters when foraging in open pastures. The diet is diverse and utilizes locally abundant prey, including fish 20 to 50 mm (0.8 to 2 in) in length, shrimp, crayfish, crabs, snails, clams, aquatic and terrestrial insects, frogs, lizards, and small snakes.

REPRODUCTION Snowy Egrets like to nest in waterfront trees with Great Egrets, Little Blue Herons, and Tricolored Herons.

Seasonality Nest construction may begin as early as March in the U.S., with April and May the peak months of laying. Historically, nesting was 2 or more months earlier in Florida. In Trinidad and Panama, breeding is in the summer, while south of the equator the nesting season is in the austral summer, November through January.

Courtship The extravagant, lacy nuptial plumes are an essential part of courtship displays in flight and while perched. Courting males arrive 1st at the breeding colony to perform circle flights and tumble flights near the territory. When perched they perform stretch and head-pumping displays while erecting the plumes and giving the *wah-wah-wah* call. The female performs reciprocal displays and is soon accepted on the territory by the courting male. Joint nest building helps to cement the pair bond and copulation occurs on the nest. The pair bond is usually only maintained through a single nesting cycle, and promiscuity has been recorded.

Territoriality Males select a territory for nesting and sexual display. The territory is ferociously defended with crest raising, forward display, and face-to-face fighting. The initial territory shrinks when pair bonds have formed and nest building is under way. Both sexes defend a small area around the nest against other Snowy Egrets and other heron species.

Nest and Nest Site Nesting colonies may form in dense stands of mangroves, cypress or cedar swamps, willows, reeds, rushes or on the ground on small predator-free islands. When in trees the nest is usually 2 to 5 m (6 to 16 ft) above the ground or water. The male brings sticks, then twigs and reeds for the female, who builds the platform nest near or over water. The nest is a flat ellipse with a modest central depression and continues to have material added even after the chicks have hatched. The same nest site may be used in subsequent years, but a new nest is constructed each year, sometimes including the sticks from old nests.

Eggs The pale blue-green eggs average 43 by 32 mm (1.7 by 1.3 in) and weigh 17 g (.6 oz). Clutch size ranges from 2 to 6 with an average of 4 in northern nests and fewer in tropical nests. Eggs are laid every other day until the clutch is complete. Renesting after a lost clutch is common, but there is no record of a 2nd brood being raised.

Incubation Both sexes participate in incubation, which begins as soon as the 1st egg is laid. The incubation period has been reported as 24 days. A new nest is built before a replacement clutch of eggs is laid.

Fledging Hatchlings have sparse, hair-like down, with the longest forming a topknot on the crown. The characteristic yellow feet of the adult are present even in young hatchlings. Both parents bring food to the nest. Hatching of young sequentially over a period of a week or more often results in brood reduction due to starvation of the youngest chicks. Imported red fire ant predation on hatchlings has resulted in up to 92% reduction of heron nest success on infested islands. At 3 weeks of age the chicks leave the nest and begin to walk around on nearby branches. At 5 weeks of age they begin to take short flights, and a week later they are able to fly to the feeding grounds and forage for themselves.

Age at First Breeding The minimum age of reproduction has not been recorded, but it is likely that some juveniles breed at the age of 1 year, although most breed in their 2nd spring.

BEHAVIOR This egret often travels in bunched flocks between roosts, feeding sites, and breeding colonies. Outside the breeding season they gather for the night in communal roosts, commonly in mixed-species groups with White Ibis. Flight speed between colonies and feeding grounds has been recorded as 35 to 39 kph (21 to 24 mph) with a flap rate of 3.2 per second. They may increase the speed to 48 kph (30 mph) when pressed.

MIGRATION The southerly migration begins with frost, inspiring birds from Virginia north to travel south through Florida and the Caribbean. Florida Snowy Egrets are not believed to migrate.

PREDATORS Crows and raccoons take the eggs. Raccoons and alligators take the young, and the adults are eaten by hawks and owls.

LONGEVITY The oldest recovered banded Snowy Egret was 11 years of age.

CONSERVATION ISSUES This egret was one of the most sought after in the plume trade, and populations did not recover from the hunting devastation until the 1950s. Since then an overall decline of Snowy Egret populations in Florida has been correlated with a loss of wetland feeding habitat. While outright drainage eliminates feeding habitat, water management in the south Florida ecosystem has altered natural cycles of water depth and prey availability over thousands of square miles. Reproductive success of Snowy Egrets in the central U.S. has declined due to the influence of the DDT breakdown product DDE, which

they might have accumulated while wintering in Mexico. (Sale of DDT in the U.S. is prohibited, but it is still manufactured in the U.S. and sold to other countries.) PCBs and other pesticides have also been found in Snowy Egret eggs.

NOTES The genus name is from the French *aigrette* for the breeding plumes previously used as millinery decoration. The name was also used for the bird that produced the plumes. The species name is a Chilean Indian name for the Snowy Egret. This bird has also been known as *Ardea thula* and has been placed in the genus *Leucophoyx* by itself. In English it is also called white gaulin, little white heron, common egret, and bonnet martyr; in Spanish *garza blanca, garza rizos* or *garza real;* and in French *crabier blanc, aigrette neigeuse* or *aigrette blanche.*

SUGGESTED ADDITIONAL READING

Findholt, S.L. 1984. Organochlorine residues, eggshell thickness, and reproductive success of Snowy Egrets nesting in Idaho. *Condor,* 86:163–169.

Jenni. D.A. 1969. A study of the ecology of four species of herons during the breeding season at Lake Alice, Alachua County, Florida. *Ecological Monographs,* 39:245–270.

Cattle Egret
Bubulcus ibis | **Ardeidae Ciconiiformes** | **p. 21**

DISTRIBUTION The single species in the genus is found worldwide. The activities of man in converting forest to pasture on a worldwide scale have greatly facilitated the colonization and expansion of the range of Cattle Egrets in the past 100 years. This heron was first seen in the New World at the end of the 19th century and was widely established and breeding in South America, Central America, and the Caribbean in the 1950s. Since then it has expanded its range to breed in all of the contiguous 48 states and two Canadian provinces. Between 1948 and 1963 it spread from Asia through the Malay Archipelago to New Guinea and Australia. Three subspecies are generally accepted. *B. i. coromanda* is found in Asia, Australia, and Japan. *B. i. seychellarum* is found in the Seychelles, and *B. i. ibis* is native to Africa but more recently has colonized the New World.

FOOD AND FEEDING HABITS

This egret specializes in accompanying large, hooved mammals (ungulates), which it uses as beaters to flush insect prey for capture. Cattle Egrets have been seen to follow almost every type of large animal moving on a grassland and often perch on the backs of hosts. Efficiency in feeding is increased by feeding near active hosts, where the birds expend less time and fewer steps per prey item captured. Cattle make ideal hosts as they occur in adequate numbers in predictable areas foraging at consistent rates. Cattle Egrets follow and use mowing and harvesting machinery as beaters, and in tilling operations they follow the tractor to catch exposed soil invertebrates. Leapfrog feeding is common when birds at the rear of the flock fly forward to become leaders of the flock and are themselves supplanted in turn. Prey capture behavior on grasslands includes walking quickly, running, swaying the neck and head, hopping and pecking. They are regularly found foraging without hosts on grasslands such as pastures, parks, road verges, and lawns. They are attracted to grass fires and feed heavily on toasted insects and those seeking to escape the fire front. They are often abundant at city dumps, where they feed on flies by standing, waiting or flying. They feed along aquatic habitats using techniques similar to those of other herons. Foraging is usually in small flocks, but individuals feeding singly are not uncommon and seem to gain a feeding advantage when they are the solitary consort of a grazing animal. Cattle Egrets select ungulates that are moving at a rate that allows the egret to forage at its optimum speed of 10 to 30 steps per minute. The antagonistic forward display with plumes raised or a stiff-legged supplanting run is sometimes used to defend a feeding territory around a host. Cattle Egrets are attracted to actively feeding flocks of other Cattle Egrets. Diet and foraging behavior are very flexible and adapt readily to transient or unusual food sources. Foods include grasshoppers, crickets, flies, spiders, beetles, wasps, lizards, frogs, snakes, butterflies, and moths. They take the eggs and hatchlings of other birds. Unlike the African Red-billed Oxpecker (*Buphagus erythorynchus*), which regularly removes ticks from its hosts, Cattle Egrets eat only unattached crawling ticks. The daily feeding cycle involves morning flights from the colony to feeding sites as far as 60 km (37 miles) distant. In late afternoons individuals assemble and return to the roost in close V-shaped flocks.

REPRODUCTION Cattle Egrets nest on a great variety of sites, often in mixed-species colonies with other herons, ibises, spoonbills, anhingas, and cormorants.

Seasonality Eggs may be laid from March to September, but local laying is often influenced by rainfall, which increases insect populations. Nesting may be inhibited by high winds, dry weather, or disturbance.

Courtship Males establish breeding territories with a series of intense, complex, aggressive displays. Forward displays may lead to bill fighting or aerial fighting of such ferociousness that injuries result. Initially, females are repulsed from the territory, but several gather within an 8 m (26 ft) radius and approach the male by landing next to him or sometimes on his back. With female persistence over 3 or 4 days, the male eventually allows 1 female to remain on the territory. Seasonal monogamy is usual but 2 females with 1 male is not uncommon early in the season. Extra-pair copulations are regularly observed, but they usually take place outside the fertile period of the female.

Territoriality Pairs on adjacent nests may alternately stab back and forth at each other. The defended nest territo-ry is originally 2 to 3 m (7 to 10 ft) in radius but shrinks to 80 cm (32 in) when incubation begins. Cattle Egrets are very aggressive and generally out-compete native North American herons, egrets, and ibises for nest material and nest sites in mixed-species colonies.

Nest and Nest Site The mated male leads the female to a nest site separate from the display territory to begin construction. The nest is constructed on almost any surface that will sup-port the nest platform or even on the ground where no nest sites are avail-able in the trees of a colony. Nests are always clumped in colonies and may be as dense as one nest per 0.8 sq m (9 sq ft). Trees at roost and nest sites are often destroyed over time by pruning and excessive deposits of guano. The male brings the nesting materials, including twigs with green leaves, which the female uses to construct the nest, sometimes with the assistance of the male. The 1st egg is laid about 6 days later, but nest construction con-tinues through incubation and after hatching. Nest platforms of previous years' nests may be refurbished in sub-sequent years. In North America, roosting sites are also used as breeding territories and nest sites.

Eggs The sky-blue eggs vary consider-ably in shape and average 45 by 33 mm (1.8 by 1.3 in) with an average clutch size of 3 or 4. Individual eggs make up 4% to 11 % of the female's weight and are usually laid every 2nd day. Females will renest, often in a new nest, if a clutch is lost before comple-tion, but 2nd broods have not been recorded in North America.

Incubation Incubation usually begins after the 1st egg is laid but may be delayed until the 2nd or even 3rd egg. Both parents participate in incubation duties. Hatching success varies from 14% to 97%.

Fledging The hatchling produces an almost continuous, sibilant *zi-zi-zi* call when not sleeping or eating. The 1st pinfeathers begin to emerge, and leg development allows them to leave the nest at 6 days. Chicks are constantly brooded or guarded by a parent until the 10th or 11th day of age when the chick is able to control its own body temperature. By the end of the 2nd week the chicks leave the nest and climb on nearby branches. Competition for food delivered to the nests by the parents is fierce, with the loser growing more slowly and sometimes starving to death. Nests with hatchlings may be defended by parents using pecking attacks against intruders. First tentative flights are at 25 days with more sustained flight to nearby feeding areas at 30 days. Parents continue to provide supplemental food near the nest site until 7 or 8 weeks, when most of the chicks' feathers are fully grown. Nestling survivorship is influenced by many environmental factors and varies from 15% to 94%. An adult feeding 4 chicks captures about half its body weight per day in prey. If the prey is entirely grasshoppers, more than 1,700 grasshoppers per day are required to feed an adult and nestlings. Young birds disperse widely to considerable distances from the colony with very few returning to the natal colony or its vicinity.

Age at First Breeding Cattle Egrets do not usually breed before their 2nd year of age.

BEHAVIOR Cattle Egrets usually gather in flocks near feeding sites and return to night roosts as flocks. Flocks have been recorded traveling at an average of 43 kph (28 mph) with wingbeats of 4 or 5 per second while migrating. They make dramatic, evasive flight maneuvers when pursued by hawks.

MIGRATION Cattle Egrets migrate seasonally toward the equator to avoid freezing weather. Migration travel takes place in daylight hours with clear skies and light or tail-winds. They disperse widely when not breeding and have been observed from ships in the mid-Atlantic.

PREDATORS Grackles, crows, and raccoons take the eggs. Nestlings are sometimes killed by fire ants or eaten by hawks, owls, night herons, or raccoons. Adults are taken by hawks and owls.

LONGEVITY The oldest recorded banded Cattle Egret was 23 years of age.

CONSERVATION ISSUES The diet of the Cattle Egret is considered to be beneficial to man in general and to agriculture in particular. Nesting colonies are sometimes considered to be nuisances due to excrement that falls on the works of man, or to the birds' flightlines between breeding and feeding areas, which cross airport operational areas. Analysis of tissues has shown the presence of chlorinated hydrocarbons such as DDT, DDE, and dieldrin as well as PCBs. The wide, annual dispersal has been the main contributing factor to rapid range expansion.

NOTES The genus name is from the Latin *bubul* (of or concerning cattle). The Swedish explorer Fredrik Hasselqvist was erroneously informed that the Cattle Egret was the sacred ibis. His papers were used as a resource by Linnaeus, who perpetuated the error in the species name of the Cattle Egret. The Cattle Egret has also been placed in the genera *Ardea* and *Egretta*. In English it is also called cow heron, cattle gaulin or tick bird. In Africa it is variously called by the names of the ungulates it follows, such as rhinoceros egret or buffalo egret. In Europe it is called a buff-backed heron in reference to the color of its breeding plumes. In Spanish it is called *garza de vaguera* or *garza del ganado,* and in French *héron garde-boeuf.*

SUGGESTED ADDITIONAL READING

Burger, J. 1978. Competition between Cattle Egrets and native North American herons, egrets, and ibises. *Condor,* 80:15–23.

Telfair R.C. II. 1994. Cattle Egret (*Bubulcus ibis*). In A. Poole and F. Gill (eds.), *The Birds of North America. No. 113.* Philadelphia: The Birds of North America, Inc.

Green Heron

Butorides striatus | **Ardeidae Ciconiiformes** | **p. 22**

DISTRIBUTION This genus with 4 species is found worldwide in the warm parts of the world. The Green Heron population that lives in North America is called *B. s. virescens* by many authors, or *B. virescens* by the American Ornithologists Union checklist. The species has more than 30 named subspecies in tropical America, Africa, Asia, Australia, and the Pacific Islands. The arrangement of species and subspecies in the genus is presently still being debated.

FOOD AND FEEDING HABITS

The Green Heron's primary feeding habitat is thick swamps and marshes in both fresh and salt water. The Green Heron is a remarkably consistent resident of red mangrove stands. It will feed in the open when food is available. It hunts by wading in water less than 5 cm (2 in) deep but also fishes in deeper water from perches on overhanging branches, floating logs, or emergent rocks. The birds typically lurk in a crouched posture, then lunge forward with a darting stroke of the head and neck. The prey is usually grasped but may be speared. When prey is out of reach, the birds may dive after it from a perch. They also lunge with the entire body while grasping a branch with strong feet, then regain an upright stance without releasing the perch. The primary food of this heron is fish. Opportunistically, they will eat crustaceans, mollusks, insects, spiders, reptiles, amphibians, and rodents. The Green Heron actively lures fish to a feeding site using a variety of baits and even artificial lures including bread, worms, insects, feathers, and sticks. Feeding territories are defended by erecting the crest, extending the head and neck, uttering loud calls or supplanting other birds in flight.

REPRODUCTION The Green Heron may nest solitarily or form a loose aggregation with other Green Herons slightly apart from other colonial birds. The birds are probably seasonally monogamous, but data from marked birds is lacking.

Seasonality The wide climatic range of nesting controls the timing of egg laying. Eggs are laid in Florida as early as March and in northern New England as late as June. In all areas the birds are likely to renest following nest failure, and in the more southern latitudes a 2nd nesting is common after the 1st brood has reached independence.

Courtship Territory is first declared when a male initiates circling, crooked-necked flights and calls from lookout posts. He begins the new nest or takes possession of an old nest before pairing. The male then displays at the nest site by extending the head and neck outward and downward, then snapping the bill. Before the female enters the nest, the male performs a stretch display by stretching the head and neck upward then backward to almost touch the back while the plumes on the back are erect. After the female enters the nest, the circling flights, calling, and snap displays cease.

Territoriality The initial territory is quite large and is often centered around an old nest. The defended area around the nest shrinks as work on the nest proceeds and incubation begins.

Nest and Nest Site The nest is usually well hidden over or near water, often in mangroves, but may be as far as 0.8 km (0.5 mi) from water if no satisfactory sites are closer. The flimsy nest is typically situated in a fork 1 to 2 m (3 to 7 ft) high with overhanging branches. The male selects the nest site, which may be the old nest of a Green Heron, Night Heron, or Snowy Egret. After pairing, the female does most of the nest construction with material provided by the male, which may be freshly broken twigs or material pirated from other old or active nests. The nest is 20 to 30 cm (8 to 12 in) in diameter composed of 200 to 300 twigs 5 to 8 mm (0.2 to 0.3 in) in diameter. The nest cup is shallow and has no lining. The incubating bird continues to build and repair throughout the nesting period. The nest may be reused after a successful brood is reared, but relocation is likely if the 1st nesting effort fails. They may nest solitarily or in loose aggregations in which nests may be less than 0.5 m (20 in) apart, but the nearest neighbor is typically 7 to 15 m (23 to 50 ft) away.

Eggs The light-green eggs measure about 38 by 29 mm (1.4 by 1.1 in), and the clutch size ranges from 2 to 5 with an average of 3. Eggs are laid an average of every other day. The eggs often become stained by mud from the adults' feet. Crows and grackles are vigorously driven from the vicinity of a nest containing eggs.

Incubation Intermittent incubation begins with the 2nd egg but becomes more regular after the 3rd egg is laid. The male tends to incubate during midday and at night, while the female incubates early in the morning and late in the evening. Each bird is consistent in the route used to approach the nest. The incubation period varies from 19 to 21 days. When not in contact with the eggs, the parents will stand and provide shade to prevent lethal overheating. Windstorms often destroy significant numbers of the nests.

Fledging The newly hatched chick has a grayish-brown down with a distinctive crest on the head. Shortly after hatching, the chicks vocalize monotonously with a *tik-tik-tik* call. The parents brood the chicks continuously for the 1st week, then with decreasing regularity until they leave the young unattended after 3 weeks. The chicks can climb at about 1 week, jump between branches at 2 weeks and leave the nest at 16 or 17 days of age. First flight takes place at about 3 weeks, but the parents continue to feed the chicks, at first in the nest tree, then in other nearby trees. At 25 days, the juvenile plumage is complete with only traces of down on the head, and the chicks begin to accompany the adults to the feeding grounds. The juveniles are essentially independent after 7 weeks, although parental feeding may continue for several more weeks.

Age at First Breeding Some records indicate that breeding may take place rarely in the 1st year, but most birds do not breed until their 2nd year. The juveniles have a heavily streaked neck and buff spots on the wings.

BEHAVIOR The Green Heron is solitary except in the breeding territory (in which only the mate is allowed) or night roosts. They are very adept at walking through jumbles of branches and roots. When walking, excited in feeding, or in antagonistic encounters, they erect and depress the crest and flip the tail up and down. When flying, they hold their necks in an S curve with the head retracted and the legs extended. For short flights and when landing, the head and neck are fully extended. The flight speed has been recorded at 35 kph (22 mph) with a flap rate of 2.8 per second. When recently flushed and hurried, the rate increases to 3.8 per second. They swim well but seldom do. They are astonishingly tolerant of mosquitoes and make only mild head shaking motions when enveloped in a fog of thousands of the hungry bloodsuckers.

MIGRATION Birds nesting in northern latitudes disperse widely before wandering south in the early fall to spend the winter in Florida and on Caribbean coasts. The northern migration in the early spring is usually more organized into flocks, and travel is primarily at night to allow resting and foraging by day.

PREDATORS Snakes have been blamed for high predation rates on eggs and chicks. Grackles and crows eat untended Green Heron eggs, and raccoons take eggs and chicks.

LONGEVITY For a bird that is difficult to band even as a chick and very difficult to catch as an adult, it is not surprising that not many band return records exist. One bird was recovered almost 8 years after banding.

CONSERVATION ISSUES The solitary, secretive nature of the Green Heron in its soggy habitat makes any estimates of population numbers or trends suspect. The birds have been shot for food and continue to be eliminated as part of predator control efforts at fish hatcheries. The draining and clearing of wetlands along with increasingly vigorous human recreational use of areas adjoining suitable habitat have had an adverse influence on both feeding and nesting activity.

NOTES The genus name is from the Latin *butio* (bittern or heron) and the Greek *ides* (resembling). The species name is from the Latin *striatus* (streaked). The subspecies name is from the Latin *virescens* (greenish). This heron is sometimes grouped with the other very similar birds of South America, Africa, India, China, Southeast Asia, Australia, and the Pacific Islands into 1 species called *Butorides striatus*. It is called little gaulin or pond gaulin in the West Indies. Other English common names include green-backed heron, little green heron, mangrove heron, and striated heron (referring to its appearance and habitat). The more rustic names shite-poke (a bag of excrement) and chalk-line refer to the bird's habit of releasing a white stream of defecation when taking flight as a result of human disturbance. In Spanish it is *gaulching, garcita verdosa* or *martinete*, and in French *héron vert* or *valet de caïman*.

SUGGESTED ADDITIONAL READING

Davis, W.E. and J.A. Kushlan. 1994. Green Heron (*Butoroides virescens*). In A. Poole and F. Gill (eds.), *The Birds of North America. No. 129.* Philadelphia: The Birds of North America, Inc.

Gavino, G. and R.W. Dickerman. 1972. Nestling development of Green Herons at San Blas, Nayarit, Mexico. *Condor,* 74:72–79.

Black-crowned Night Heron
Nycticorax nycticorax | **Ardeidae Ciconiiformes** | **p. 23**

DISTRIBUTION This genus with 3 species is found worldwide foraging along shorelines and wetlands. The White-backed Night Heron is irregularly distributed in sub-Saharan Africa. Black-crowned Night Herons are found worldwide except in Australasia, where the very similar Nankeen or Rufous Night Heron *(N. caledonicus)* occupies the same ecological niche. The distribution of the Black-crowned Night Heron extends 53 degrees north and south of the equator and to an elevation of 4,816 m (15,800 ft), but it is absent in arid areas with no surface water. Habitat utilized is very broad but includes trees such as oak, cypress, mangrove, or bamboo for roosting and nesting near fresh, brackish, or salt water. Four subspecies are generally recognized: *N. n. falklandicus,* resident in the Falkland Islands; *N. n. obscurus* from northern Chile and Argentina to Tierra del Fuego; *N. n. nycticorax* from Europe, Africa and India to Japan; and *N. n. hoactli* from southern Canada through Central America to northern Argentina and Chile.

FOOD AND FEEDING HABITS

The highly variable diet is usually composed of about 50% fish and 40% invertebrates. Raiding of nests of gulls, terns, White Ibis, Cattle Egrets, Great Egrets, and coots for eggs or chicks is common. Blackbird and Common Moorhen nest contents may make up a seasonal preponderance of the diet. Reptiles, amphibians, and rodents have all been reported as prey. Hunting is primarily by standing and waiting, particularly when the bird is perched on protuberances such as rocks, logs or pilings projecting from the water. They also walk slowly and, with surprising agility, among mangrove roots. Almost all heron feeding techniques are used at times including hovering, bill vibrating, underwing feeding, swimming feeding, and, rarely, plunging into the water from flight in pursuit of fish. Prey is grasped but not stabbed, and it may be vigorously shaken or thumped against a hard object before manipulation and swallowing. Each bird typically defends a feeding territory except when flocks are feeding on a temporarily abundant resource. Feeding is primarily nocturnal and crepuscular, with roost departures after sunset and returns before sunrise. Diurnal feeding is seen when nestling food demand is high. Night feeding results in capture of fewer but larger fish for a greater food intake per hour. Day feeding results in the capture of more small fish suitable for feeding to nestlings. Attempts to scare Black-crowned Night Herons from commercial fish ponds with recorded distress calls are initially effective but the birds soon acclimate to the recordings and return to the abundant food resource in numbers.

REPRODUCTION The stick nest may be built in small, monospecific colonies or large, mixed colonies of wading birds near salt water or fresh water.

Seasonality Nesting may begin as early as December in south Florida but is usually considerably later, with birds beginning to arrive in the northern part of the range in late March. Breeding dates are probably subject to local weather conditions.

Courtship The male selects the site and begins to build a nest, which he uses as a display platform. On the platform the male may sway from one foot to the other in a lively dance display. The male displays to an attracted female by raising the crest and the feathers on the back and neck, then terminates the display by assuming a hunched posture while giving a hissing vocalization. The attracted female responds in kind by fanning her head and neck feathers and erecting her plumes. The male solidifies the relationship with the presentation of twigs, which the female weaves into the nest.

Territoriality Black-crowned Night Herons often nest in colonies, with less than a meter (40 in) separating some of the nests of conspecifics or other herons. The horizontal distance to the territory boundary is about twice the vertical distance defended.

Nest and Nest Site Males choose the nest site and begin the nest as a display platform. When a pair bond is formed, the male brings construction material while the female forms it into a nest. New nests are often small and flimsy, but in subsequent years of reuse they become more bulky. The nest is almost always in thick cover and may be on the ground, in bushes or reeds in areas free of terrestrial predators or in tall trees, often on islands or in the interior of swamps. Nesting colonies may stay in the same general area for 30 to 50 years. They are surprisingly tolerant of urban conditions when not overtly harassed and have established colonies in Boston, New York, Baltimore, and Washington, D.C. Windstorms may eliminate all the nests in a colony.

Eggs Beginning about 3 days after the 1st copulation, the pale blue-green eggs, about 53 by 37 mm (2 by 1.5 in), are laid every other day until the clutch of 2 to 5 is complete. Renesting occurs when eggs or young chicks are lost.

Incubation Both parents share the 25-day incubation period, starting with the 1st egg. Hatching success of up to 96.3% has been recorded.

Fledging The hatchlings, which have dark-buff down with a lighter crest on the crown and cream underparts, are brooded continuously by the parents until about 10 days of age. Chicks hatch several days apart, and in times of insufficient food the younger nestlings often die of starvation. Imported red fire ant predation on hatchlings has resulted in up to 92% reduction of heron nest success on infested islands. Both parents work at provisioning the young. By about 3 weeks of age the chicks are able to leave the nest and walk about on nearby branches until an average of 2.3 birds per nest fledge at 6 to 7 weeks. The juvenile, with buff spots on an olive-brown back with brown-streaked underparts, has a 1st-year mortality rate of 60%.

Age at First Breeding Sexual maturity with 1st breeding is reached at 2 or 3 years and is followed closely by full adult plumage.

BEHAVIOR The flap rate when traveling is reported at 2.6 to 2.8 flaps per second, producing a flight speed of about 32 kph (20 mph), which can be accelerated to 56 kph (35 mph) when the bird is stressed.

MIGRATION Postbreeding dispersal and inaccurate spring migration lead to their arrival on isolated oceanic islands and places outside their normal breeding range.

PREDATORS Ring-billed Gulls and vultures eat the eggs. Raccoons, opossums, Boat-tailed Grackles, and Fish Crows eat the eggs and young chicks. Great-horned Owls take the larger chicks from branches, and more rarely the adults. Storms may destroy nests, and human disturbance may cause abandonment.

LONGEVITY Black-crowned Night Herons have been recovered 21 years after banding, and captive birds have lived to 30 years of age.

CONSERVATION ISSUES Human disturbance of Black-crowned Night Heron colonies during or just prior to laying may result in nest abandonment, increased predation on the uncovered eggs, or even abandonment of eggs. Disturbance can also discourage nest building by late-breeding pairs and cause increased chick mortality. Black-crowned Night Herons are shot while feeding at commercial fish ponds and are still hunted as food

in certain areas. Habitat loss and disturbance of nesting colonies continue as a corollary of coastal development. Some data indicate that the population may be declining in the mid- and north Atlantic states.

NOTES The genus and species names are from the Greek *nyctos* (night) and *corax* (raven). They are also called black-capped night heron in English, *martinete común, yaboa real, guanaba* or *guaco* in Spanish and *bihoreau gris* or *bihoreau couronne noire* in French.

SUGGESTED ADDITIONAL READING

Davis, W.E. Jr. 1993. Black-crowned Night Heron (*Nycticorax nycticorax*). In A. Poole and F. Gill (eds.), *The Birds of North America. No. 74.* Philadelphia: The Birds of North America, Inc.

Erwin, R.M., J.G. Haig, D.B. Stotts and J.S. Hatfield. 1996. Reproductive success, growth and survival of Black-crowned Night Heron (*Nycticorax nycticorax*) and Snowy Egret (*Egretta thula*) chicks in coastal Virginia. *Auk,* 113:119–130.

Wolford, J.W. and D.A. Boag. 1971. Food habits of the Black-crowned Night Heron. *Auk,* 88:435–437.

Yellow-crowned Night Heron

Nyctanassa violacea | **Ardeidae Ciconiiformes** | **p. 24**

DISTRIBUTION The single species in the genus is found from the southern U.S. along both coasts of Mexico south through Central America and the Caribbean to Brazil and Peru. Six geographic subspecies have been described based on bill size and color of underparts.

FOOD AND FEEDING HABITS

Crustaceans are the main food item of most Yellow-crowned Night Herons. Foraging is in salt marshes, mud-flats, sandy beaches, rocky shorelines, and among mangrove roots. Favored foraging areas are usually on the edge of habitat types and are often synchronized with tidal cycles. Man-disturbed areas including golf courses, agricultural land, and household lawns also serve as hunting grounds. Foraging methods include standing and waiting, peering and walking slowly. They catch small 5-cm (2-in) black land crabs, but have not been recorded tackling the large, strong and heavily armored land crabs that live near mangroves. On mud-flats they swallow fiddler crabs, on sandy beaches they capture swift-running ghost crabs, and on rocky shorelines they take sally lightfoot crabs from above the surf zone. In shallow water they catch a broad diversity of crabs, including the active and aggressive blue crab. In fresh water they feed almost exclusively on crayfish. When feeding on a large crab, the legs and claws are removed and the body is broken into pieces small enough to swallow. The body parts are eaten first, followed by legs and claws. Yellow-crowned Night Herons are opportunistic feeders and will also eat snails, clams, worms, terrestrial insects, scorpions, centipedes, fish, frogs, tadpoles, snakes, hatchling turtles, eggs, young birds, and mice. Night heron predation may be a major source of mortality in nesting colonies of gulls, terns, and other birds. Groups of night herons may congregate to prey on hatchling sea turtles as they emerge from a sandy beach at night and crawl to the sea. Indigestible hard parts such as crab shells and beetle wing covers are regurgitated as pellets.

REPRODUCTION Yellow-crowned Night Herons often breed in small loosely organized colonies with others of their kind, but single nesting is not uncommon.

Seasonality The onset of breeding in cooler climates is controlled by the emergence of hibernating crabs and general weather conditions. Breeding in Florida may be as early as March, but further north it may be delayed until May. In the tropics they may nest in any month.

Courtship The early part of courtship involves male flight displays around the selected nest site. The *huh* call is important in pair formation and is often given when several birds are perched in the same tree or just prior to a stretch display. In a stretch display a bird extends the head and neck vertically, then retracts the neck fully until part of it is resting on the back. The plumes on the back are raised, the wings are slightly opened, and the bird bows with the head lower than the tail. The *whoop* call is given by the male to the female at the completion of the stretch display. Mutual preening is part of courtship and increases in frequency prior to copulation. Bill clattering is often associated with courtship and copulation. The pair bond is usually maintained in subsequent seasons. The *up* call is a greeting during courtship and is used just prior to nest relief. If habitat allows, each pair will select a separate tree. The *ahhh-ahhh* call is given when an intruder approaches the nesting territory and it may escalate to a *squawk* call, which is a warning of imminent attack.

Nest and Nest Site Yellow-crowned Night Herons nest on man-made dredge spoil islands, small predator-free natural and man-made islands, swamps and forested uplands near bodies of water. They may form mixed-species colonies with other waders, particularly Black-crowned Night Herons. The nest may be placed in shrubs, thorny thickets, mangroves, or forests with an open understory. Nesting is not uncommon in wooded residential neighborhoods with an open understory. The nest site is of-ten selected to overhang creeks or swamps. Nesting areas are usually less than 2 km (1.2 mi) from feeding areas. The male delivers twigs to the female, who constructs the nest in a shady spot. The lining may include many forms of fine vegetation. When a clutch or brood is lost, the nest is extensively refurbished before a new clutch is laid. The nest may be added to and reoccupied in subsequent years and become more than 1 m (40 in) across. Twig stealing from unoccupied nests is common.

Eggs The pale blue-green or olive-col-ored eggs measure 51 by 37 mm (2 by 1.5 in) and weigh about 40 g (1.4 oz). Clutch size varies from 2 to 6 but is usually 3 or 4 eggs. The clutch and egg size decrease with proximity to the equator. With the loss of all eggs or brood, renesting is usual, but only 1 brood is raised to independence per year.

Incubation The 25-day incubation period begins when the 1st egg is laid. If disturbed by predators while incubating, the parents slink quietly away from the nest before quietly taking flight. The eggs hatch asynchronously.

Fledging One day after hatching, the chick is covered with a pale-gray down and has its eyes open, although it is unable to lift its head or sit upright. Parents feed the young by regurgitating food into the nest. Dominance behavior between the chicks begins within 2 weeks of hatching, and brood reduction is common. The young show preening and stretching movements at 3 weeks of age and often sunbathe facing the sun with an erect posture and wings partly spread. Full juvenile plumage is attained by 5 weeks of age, and fledging with short flights occurs a few days later. Young return to the nest to be fed for 2 weeks after fledging and sleep on the nest for 3 weeks after fledging. They have not usually attained adult size when they leave the nest. Reproductive success is highly variable and depends in part on seasonality of nest loss with no replacement clutches for late season nest losses.

Age at First Breeding Most of the adult plumage is acquired in the 2nd year, prior to the 1st breeding at the age of 2 years. The full adult plumage is acquired at the age of 30 months, after the 1st breeding season. Exceptional individuals may breed at 1 year of age.

BEHAVIOR Various reports show considerable variation in the amount of feeding by day at dusk or at night. Individual distance of at least 5 m (16 ft) is maintained on feeding grounds. The flight speed is about 40 kph (25 mph).

MIGRATION The northern populations in the U.S migrate south for the winter, but the populations in warm climates are sedentary.

PREDATORS Red-tailed Hawks and several species of owls take adults and juveniles. The eggs and small young are taken by Fish Crows, opossums, raccoons, and domestic dogs and cats. Juvenile Yellow-crowned Night Herons continue to be hunted by humans as a succulent delicacy in some areas in spite of legal protection.

LONGEVITY Maximum longevity has not been determined.

CONSERVATION ISSUES The major threat to this species' well-being is loss of breeding and feeding habitat due to shoreline development. Pesticides containing dieldrin and mercury are accumulated from the environment in the adults and eggs. The population trend is not recorded due to their secretive habits of nesting in small colonies under vegetative cover. Significant illegal kills of adults feeding at commercial crawfish ponds continue.

NOTES The genus name is from the Greek *nykteros* (nocturnal) and *anassa* (queen or ruler). The species name is from the Latin *viola* (violet). This species has also been placed in the genus *Nycticorax,* but recent genetic studies indicate that the 2 night herons are as distinct from each other as either is from the day heron group. Other common names in English are crabcatcher, crabeater, crabcracker, and night gaulin; in Spanish it is called *guanabá real, yaboa común* or *rey congo;* and in French it is *grosbec, crabier gris* or *crabier de bois.*

SUGGESTED ADDITIONAL READING

Watts, B.D. 1995. Yellow-crowned NightHeron (*Nyctanassa violoacea*). In A. Poole and F. Gill (eds.), *The Birds of North America. No. 161.* Philadelphia: The Birds of North America, Inc.

Wingate, D.B. 1982. Successful reintroduction of the Yellow-crowned Night Heron as a nesting resident in Bermuda. *Colonial Waterbirds,* 5:104–115.

Wood Stork

Mycteria americana | Ciconiidae Ciconiiformes | **p. 25**

DISTRIBUTION This genus with 4 species is found in North and South America, Africa, and from India through the Southeast Asian islands. The Milky Stork *(M. cinerea)* is found in Malaysia and Indonesia, the Yellow-billed Stork (*M. ibis*) is found in sub-Saharan Africa, and the Painted Stork (*M. leucocephala)* is found from India to South China. The Wood Storks are the only true storks in North America. They breed in the U.S. in Florida, Georgia, and South Carolina. They breed in Cuba, Mexico, and south along the coasts of Central America and in South America east of the Andes south to northern Argentina. West of the Andes they breed in Ecuador.

FOOD AND FEEDING HABITS

Wood Storks feed in shallow water along estuaries, mangrove-fringed creeks, rivers, marshes, swamps, wetlands, and canals. They usually fish in calm, uncluttered water 5 to 40 cm (2 to 16 in) deep. Extensive movements are sometimes undertaken to find productive feeding habitat where low and declining water levels have concentrated prey species. Alternatively they may depart an area when heavy rainfall raises water levels, as commonly happens with summer rains in south Florida. Wood Storks are tactile feeders and catch most of their prey by feel. The time between 1st contact with the very sensitive touch receptors on the beak and the capture of prey has been found to be less than 25 milliseconds, which is one of the fastest reflex reactions known in vertebrates. Small fish less than 2.5 cm do not seem to stimulate the bill-closing reflex. The storks feed by swinging the partially open bill through the water and between vegetation while either walking slowly or standing. Wood Storks also use foot stirring and wing flicking to flush prey into the open. When both techniques are used, the limbs on the same side are used simultaneously. Experiments have demonstrated that individuals with occluded vision continue to catch fish at a normal rate. Thus they should be able to forage as efficiently in muddy water or at night as by day. In clear water and adjacent uplands they hunt by sight. The absence of feathers on the head (as in vultures) makes for easier cleanup after feeding in messy circumstances. The primary prey is shallow-water fish. They generally select the larger fish in the population. Prey also includes reptiles, amphibians, crustaceans, and rodents. Small nestling birds are also eaten when they can be found. They often feed in small flocks that move through the habitat together and frequently soar upward on a thermal then glide to the next thermal when traveling to feeding sites more than 10 km (3.7 miles) away. Travel distance to feeding sites is usually less than 70 km (43 miles) but has been recorded to be as much as 140 km (87 miles). An adult Wood Stork requires about 520 g (18 oz) of prey per day for self-maintenance and up to an additional 250 g (9 oz) per day per chick in the nest.

REPRODUCTION Wood storks are gregarious and nest in compact colonies.

Seasonality Wood Stork breeding seasons are dependent on continuously falling water levels that concentrate aquatic prey in small areas. The storks may omit nesting entirely when water levels are not conducive to generation of high prey densities.

Courtship Groups of males begin courtship by displaying with wing flapping and bill-clattering fights in "bachelor groupings." When a display site is claimed, it is defended against males and females by a beak-clattering threat display until a female approaches with wings spread open and the beak gaping. Males often reject the 1st approaches of a female but eventually allow her on the nest site. Posturing and gaping cease after the pair bond has allowed the female on the territory. New mates and nest sites are often selected in succeeding years.

Territoriality The territorial radius is about the 1 m (3 ft) reach of a Wood Stork from a nest site. In compact colonies as many as 50 nests have been recorded in 1 tree. As 1 member of a pair arrives for nest relief it may give a hissing *fizz* call.

Nest and Nest Site The nest site is usually in tall cypress, black gum, willow, buttonbush, or mangrove trees growing from the water or on small islands isolated from terrestrial predators by alligator-inhabited water. The 0.5 to 1.5 m wide (2 to 6 ft) stick nest, lined with softer material, is built in 3 days, with the male providing most of the building material and the female placing it on the nest platform. They may nest in mixed-species colonies with other long-legged waders.

Eggs The white but often brown-stained eggs measure 68 by 46 mm (2.7 by 1.8 in) and average 80 g (3 oz). An average clutch is 3 eggs, with a range of 2 to 5. The eggs are laid at about 2-day intervals. A 2nd clutch can be produced if the eggs are lost early in the nesting season.

Incubation Parents take turns at incubation for the 28- to 30-day period beginning after the 1st egg is laid.

Fledging The hatchlings have a pale-gray down and weigh about 62 g. By 10 days of age the body is covered with a woolly, white down. At least 1 parent remains in attendance at the nest until the chicks are about 3 weeks old. By the 3rd or 4th week the juveniles are able to stand and exercise their wings. Juveniles fledge at 8 or 9 weeks of age and may be provided with supplemental feeding at the nest site for another 3 to 5 weeks. Fledging success is often less than 1 chick fledged per adult pair per year. Mortality is estimated at 40% for 1st-year young and 20% for adults.

Age at First Breeding Sexual maturity seems to be reached in some birds in the 3rd year but most do not breed successfully until 4 or 5 years of age.

BEHAVIOR They often soar as groups in thermals to gain altitude before gliding to distant feeding sites. Flight is with slow powerful wingbeats at the rate of 3 per second. Straight-line flight speed has been measured from 25 to 35 kph (16 to 22 mph). They often sleep standing on 1 leg.

MIGRATION A considerable post-breeding dispersal is normal. In South Carolina, Georgia, and northern Florida, the Wood Stork is more numerous in summer than winter, indicating a migration south to avoid chilly weather.

PREDATORS Crows take unguarded eggs and hatchlings. Occasional persistent raccoons will climb into the nesting colony to eat eggs and hatchlings. Nesting colonies in trees immersed in water are frequently protected from predatory raccoons by alligators. Drying of the swamp and departure of the alligators may lead to massive consumption of eggs and chicks by raccoons. They also eat young that fall to the ground and are unable to return to the nest. Alligators sometimes catch unwary adults. Environmental conditions sometimes wreak havoc on reproduction. Parents may desert the young during cold spells. Storms may destroy most of the nests in a colony, and stable or rising water levels may cause a scarcity of food concentrations leading to nest desertion.

LONGEVITY Wood Storks have lived for over 30 years in captivity, but survival in the wild has only been recorded up to 11 years, 8 months.

CONSERVATION ISSUES Loss of habitat due to urban and agricultural development and alteration of natural drainage regimes are the major threats to long-term population stability. Breeding colonies from Alabama to Texas have disappeared in the past 50 years, and Wood Storks have been given protection under the U.S. Endangered Species Act. Water management that produces continuously wet or dry habitats has significantly interfered with concentrations of prey in residual wetlands, which are needed for feeding offspring. Mercury and other heavy metals in levels sufficient to produce adverse health effects have been found in adult and nestling Wood Storks. The DDT metabolite DDE and PCBs have been have been found in high levels in eggs from Florida, but no direct influence on reproduction has been recorded. Hunting and collection of eggs for human food, more common in Latin America, adversely impacts local populations.

NOTES The genus name is from the Greek *mykter,* meaning "snout" or "nose," and the species name makes reference to the American origin of the bird. The Wood Stork is also called wood ibis, flinthead, stonehead, ironhead, gourdhead, and preacher in English, *tántalo americano, cigüeña cabeza pelada, cabeza de piedra* and *faisán* in Spanish and *tantale d'Amérique* in French.

SUGGESTED ADDITIONAL READING

Bancroft, G.T., W. Hoffman, R.J. Sawicki and J.C. Ogden. 1992. The importance of water conservation areas in the Everglades to the endangered Wood Stork *(Mycteria americana). Conservation Biology,* 6:392–397.

Kahl, M.P. Jr. and L.J. Peacock. 1963. The bill-snap reflex: A feeding mechanism in the American Wood Stork. *Nature,* 199:505–506.

Ogden, J.C., J.A. Kushlan and J.T. Tilmant. 1976. Prey selectivity of the Wood Stork. *Condor,* 78:324–330.

White Ibis

Eudocimus ruber (albus) | **Threskiornithidae Ciconiiformes | p. 26**

DISTRIBUTION This single-species genus breeds from Baja California, to Virginia and south along both coasts of Central America, the Gulf of Mexico, Greater Antilles, and northern South America. The White Ibises in northern South America are smaller, and a dominant percentage of those nesting are the scarlet form. Some authors treat the white form as *E. albus* and the red form as a separate species, *E. ruber*. Both color forms are nomadic and are frequently seen dispersed far beyond their breeding range outside the breeding season. In south Florida, Scarlet Ibises continue to appear among White Ibises as a result of dispersal, expressions of recessive genes, or escapes from captivity.

FOOD AND FEEDING HABITS

This ibis uses freshwater or saltwater wetlands and the nearby open shallow water. Feeding is primarily by rapid, tactile probing in exposed or submerged mud while slowly walking. Ibises may also sweep the partially open bill from side to side in water over 10 cm (4 in) deep, snapping down when they feel a prey item. The sweep feeding may be accompanied by foot stirring to scare fish and crustaceans up into the water column, and/or fully extending a wing to shade the water and provide a perceived refuge for fish. They take advantage of almost any ephemeral source of food and may be seen probing in shallow marshes, willow or sawgrass-lined ponds, the soggy spots of an interstate highway median, or wet agricultural land. This ibis usually feeds in flocks. When feeding on the exposed soil surface, they select their prey items by vision rather than feel. Prey includes small crabs (particularly hermit crabs), aquatic insects and larvae, crayfish, snails, clams, worms, frogs, and small fish. They become particularly adept at catching coquina clams exposed at the surface by strong surf. Small prey is swallowed with a forward thrust of the head, while larger items are dismembered by stabbing and biting. Indigestible hard parts are cast as pellets. Ibises steal large prey from each other and are sometimes the thief and sometimes the victim with other wading birds. Other wading birds as well as kingfishers use feeding ibises as beaters to flush prey, and ibises use livestock as beaters. Nestlings become salt stressed when fed prey from salt water or brackish water; thus, accessible shallow freshwater feeding sites are required for successful reproduction. Recent studies have shown that the White ibis and Glossy Ibis partition food resources by selecting different foods when feeding outside the breeding season. White Ibises feeding in flooded ricefields avoid competition by feeding selectively in muddy fields on 48% crabs, 37% aquatic insects, and 15% fish. The Glossy Ibis feeds in shallowly flooded fields on a diet composed of 58% grains, 26% insects, and 15% crabs.

REPRODUCTION

The White Ibis nests in large, densely packed colonies. It is nomadic in its selection of breeding colony sites. They may use a particular site for as long as a decade, then all or a part of the colony may join another occupied site or found a new breeding colony. Because of frequent changes of nesting colony sites, local changes in abundance do not reliably reflect changes in population size.

Seasonality Timing of breeding in White Ibises is influenced by environmental conditions that provide a source of food for the young. In interior Florida, ibises usually nest in April but may deposit eggs as early as March and as late as September. The renesting as a result of nest loss early in the season may account for the records of late-nesting pairs.

Courtship Behavior such as exaggerated preening, head rubbing, and bill popping and twig grasping are all included in male courtship displays. The female approaches displaying males very cautiously, bowing and showing the brightly colored side of her face. The male often responds with a forward display and may attack the female and shake her head. After the pair bond is formed, the pair performs greeting displays, stick shaking, display preening, and standing with body contact. Birds do not usually touch each other except in courtship and fights. The female may give squealing vocalizations in response to the *hunk* call of the male. Extra-pair copulations are common, with an estimated 6% of eggs fertilized by an outside male. Mated males returning to the nest site and encountering intruding males sometimes pull feathers and inflict head injuries on the interloper. At times the male's ire extends even to his mate.

Territoriality Males strongly defend their display sites by supplanting flights and by making forward lunges at an opponent from a horizontal posture. On the territory, the male display behavior includes exaggerated preening, head rubbing, and bill popping with twig grasping. The nest territory is the reach of the incubating bird, with close spacing of nests common.

Nest and Nest Site The preferred nesting colony site seems to be on a predator-free natural or man-made island along the coast or inland in a lake. It seems to evolve from a roost site. Nearly 30% nest in mangroves. The balance nest in stands of Australian pine, Brazilian pepper, live oak, cypress, or in grasses or sedges when higher nest sites are not available. The female selects the nest site on or near the male display site and constructs the nest of twigs brought by the male. When the territorial male is gone, other males will attempt extra-pair copulation and steal twigs from other nests. Fresh leaves are often incorporated in the nest structure and may be replenished during incubation. The leaves probably help camouflage the exposed nest. The nest is completed enough to receive the 1st egg after 7 days of construction. Maintenance and repairs continue through hatching.

Eggs The cream to blue-green, brown-splotched, dull-surfaced eggs are variable in shape from ovate to elongate. Average egg size is 5.8 cm by 3.9 cm (2.3 in by 1.5 in) with a weight of 50.8 g (1.8 oz). The eggs are laid in the morning every other day beginning 5 or 6 days after copulation. A normal clutch size is 2 to 3 eggs with a range of 1 to 5.

Incubation The 21-day incubation period begins after the last egg is deposited and is shared by both parents. The eggs hatch at 1- or 2-day intervals.

Fledging The newly hatched chick cannot hold its head up for the 1st day. The adult feeds the chick by grasping its beak and regurgitating food into its mouth. The heads and necks of hatchlings are covered with a black down. The beak is straight and flesh-colored. The initially pink skin turns gray within a few days. The primaries begin to emerge on the 5th day and the balance of the juvenile plumage is in place by the end of the 4th week except for patches of down showing on the head and neck. On hot days, adult birds will stand with their backs to the sun with spread wings to provide shade to young birds, which cannot regulate their body temperature. When the young become mobile at 2 weeks of age, they seek shade in vegetation near the nest. The shrill *ziu* begging call of the nestlings is present at 1 week of age. At 2 weeks of age the feet and legs have matured sufficiently for the juveniles to leave the nest, seek shade, and join a crèche. The young play by manipulating twigs, grass, and foreign objects in their environment. They leave the colony at 7 to 8 weeks of age with beaks significantly shorter than those of the adults. After the 1st year, they are still not as successful at foraging as adults; they do not reach adult weight until 2 years of age. Nesting success is only about 50% under most circumstances and declines to near zero in very dry years. The adults undergo a postnuptial molt at the end of the breeding season and replace the feathers, which have become soiled and stained while nesting.

Age at First Breeding Juvenile birds are brown with a white belly and rump. A gradual change to adult plumage takes place over 2 years. Breeding commences in the 3rd summer.

BEHAVIOR An individual distance equal to the reach from the nest is maintained on the nesting territory. On the feeding grounds, individual distance is vigorously enforced with jabs and bites. The spacing increases on the feeding grounds when the likelihood of piracy increases due to capture of large or difficult-to-handle prey. The flight speed when traveling between nest and feeding site may exceed 45 kph (28 mph). They bathe by crouching in the water and are not inclined to swim. When overheated, the adults and young gular-flutter with the bill open.

MIGRATION Populations are highly nomadic and often move before breeding and show extensive dispersal outside the normal range of occurrence after breeding. Movements are also influenced by the amount of local rainfall, which affects the amount of suitable habitat.

PREDATORS Egg loss to avian predators in general ranges from 7% to 75%. Fish Crows may steal 44% of the eggs in a colony. Raccoons and opossums may steal the eggs or eat the chicks or adults. Black-crowned Night Heron adults and ambulatory chicks, crows, and other predatory birds eat chicks not attended by adults. Renesting after nest loss has been recorded.

Alligators catch a few inattentive adults.

LONGEVITY Free-ranging banded birds have been recovered after 16 years 4 months, while captive birds may live beyond 20 years.

CONSERVATION ISSUES The eggs, young, and adults are prized for their culinary properties, perhaps due to their diet of crustaceans. In northern South America and parts of Louisiana a large number of waders are taken for food or decorative feathers. In the U.S. "reclamation of wetlands" and "water management" for various corporate gains are the largest threats to local populations. Due in part to the flexibility of feeding conditions, the species in the U.S. seems to be showing a gradual long-term increase.

NOTES The genus name is from the Greek *eudokimos* (famous or well known). Linnaeus originally named the species *ruber*, from the Latin word for "red." When the white form is treated as a distinct species it is *albus*, from the Latin word for "white." Common names in English include Spanish curlew, white curlew, and brown ibis (juvenile). In Spanish they are called *ibis blanco, coco blanco, corocoro blanco* and *coclito blanco*. In French they are *ibis blanc*. The red form has similar names in most languages, with substitution of the appropriate red term for the white.

SUGGESTED ADDITIONAL READING

Bildstein, K.L. 1990. Status, conservation and management of the Scarlet Ibis *Eudocimus ruber* in the Caroni swamp, Trinidad West Indies. *Biological Conservation*, 54:61–78.

Frederick, P.C. 1987. Responses of male White Ibises to their mate's extra-pair copulations. *Behavioral Ecology and Sociobiology*, 21: 223–238.

Kushlan, J. and M. Kahl. 1992. *Storks, Ibises and Spoonbills of the World*. San Diego: Academic Press.

Glossy Ibis

Plegadis falcinellus | **Threskionithidae Ciconiiformes** | **p. 27**

DISTRIBUTION This genus with 3 species is found worldwide in temperate and tropical climates. The similarly colored White-faced Ibis, *P. chihi*, is found from the western U.S. south through Argentina, with vagrants occasionally visiting Florida or the Caribbean. The Puna Ibis, *P. ridgwayi*, is found in the highlands of Peru, Bolivia, and Chile. Glossy Ibises have extended their range extensively in North America over the last century. The Glossy Ibis nests from New Brunswick, Canada, south to Florida and west to Texas. It also nests through the Bahamas and the Greater Antilles; northern South America; the Black, Caspian and Aral Seas; Africa; northern India; Southeast Asia and Australia. Glossy and White-faced Ibises have interbred in captivity but do not seem to do so when nesting in a mixed colony in the wild. Some authors consider all members of the genus to be members of the same species.

FOOD AND FEEDING HABITS

The preferred feeding areas are marshes, swamps, shallow lakes, river floodplains and the adjacent muddy soils, including river deltas, rice paddies, and other irrigated land. They also feed in shallow marine habitats and wetlands that are sheltered from large waves. They feed in mixed groups with American White Ibises and Snowy Egrets. They also feed in monospecific flocks and as solitary individuals walking slowly along while rapidly probing into a soft muddy substrate. Other waders often follow them to catch the prey that the ibises have spooked from hiding places. The Glossy Ibis feeds on crustaceans, worms, mollusks, reptiles, amphibians, and insects. They take advantage of transient local prey abundance such as locust swarms and tadpoles in ephemeral ponds. Recent studies have shown that the Glossy Ibis and White Ibis partition food resources by selecting different foods. The Glossy Ibis diet is composed of 58% grains, 26% insects, and 15% crabs when feeding in flooded ricefields outside the breeding season. White Ibises feeding in the same areas reduce competition by feeding selectively in muddy fields on 48% crabs, 37% aquatic insects, and 15% fish.

REPRODUCTION

Glossy Ibises nest clustered in small clumps with others of their own kind but sometimes nest in mixed-species colonies with Cattle Egrets and American White Ibises.

Seasonality In Florida, birds may start breeding as early as March. Re-nesting or late-breeding birds may have eggs as late as August.

Courtship The pair bond is generated and maintained by the rubbing of bills, with mutual bowing and cooing vocalizations. The birds often indulge in aerobatic maneuvers, of which the most common is falling from a great height with wings partly folded and legs fully extended downward.

Territoriality They do not tolerate other species nesting within 4 m (12 ft) of their nest.

Nest and Nest Site The female selects the specific nest site within the territory. Nesting colonies are highly mobile and often move considerable distances after using the same nesting area for several years. The colony is usually in reeds but may be on the ground or in trees or bushes. In Florida they build their platform nest of sticks in the lower parts of trees as solitary pairs or with large colonies of other wading birds. The nests are typically 3 to 6 m (10 to 20 ft) high in willow, elderberry, wax-myrtle, salt bush, and mangroves that form dense thickets or overhang water. Males collect most of the nest material and assist the female in building the nest. Additional green leaves and grass are added to the nest throughout the incubation. Renesting with a new nest and eggs is common when a nest is destroyed by weather or predators.

Eggs The clutch varies from 2 to 6 but the average is 3 dark-blue eggs measuring 53 mm by 36 mm (2 in by 1.4 in) with a weight of 35 g (1.3 oz). The eggs are laid at intervals of 24 hours, and incubation begins the day after the last egg is laid. Laying dates within the colony are not synchronous and may spread over more than a month.

Incubation Both parents participate in the 21-day incubation, with the male taking the day shift. Both sexes croon softly when approaching the nest.

Fledging The chicks are black with a red patch of skin on the crown and a white patch of feathers on the head. The chick is attended constantly by at least 1 parent for the 1st week. By the end of the 2nd week, they leave the nest and join nearby crèches. They fledge by the end of the 4th week and may join their parents on the feeding grounds or remain in the colony for as many as 3 more weeks. Substantial brood reduction is common, with an average of less than 1 chick fledging per nest. The nesting effort and nest success are highly variable from year to year. Full adult size is not reached until the bird is 6 months old.

Age at First Breeding The full sheen of the adult plumage is attained at the age of 2 years, when first breeding usually begins.

MIGRATION In the fall, birds from the U.S. move south to Florida and the Caribbean. Eurasian birds move south and winter from Africa through India. Australian birds move north to New Guinea and winter there. Individuals and flocks are highly nomadic and disperse to wander far outside the normal range of regular occurrence.

PREDATORS Fish crows, owls, Herring Gulls, night herons, and raccoons that gain access to colonies eat untended eggs. Cold or rainy weather can lead to substantial loss of eggs and chicks.

LONGEVITY Glossy Ibises have been known to live more than 21 years.

CONSERVATION ISSUES The population numbers recorded in one geographic area may increase, although the numbers elsewhere are declining, probably due to changing distributions and breeding conditions. Dramatic local population declines have followed drainage of wetlands.

NOTES The genus name is from the Greek *plegas* (sickle). The species name is from the Latin *falcis* (sickle). Linnaeus originally named this bird *Tantalus falcinellus*. It seems that the sickle-shaped bill is the outstanding feature of the bird. It is also called green ibis, black curlew, and Spanish curlew. In Spanish, it is called *coco, coco oscuro, coco prieto, morito* and *cigüeña;* in French it is *pêcheur, ibis falcinelle* or *ibis noir.*

SUGGESTED ADDITIONAL READING

Burger, J. and L.M. Miller. 1977. Colony and nest site selection in White-faced and Glossy Ibises. *Auk,* 94:664–676.

Miller, L.M. and J. Burger. 1978. Factors affecting nest success of the Glossy Ibis. *Auk,* 95:353–361.

Ogden, J.C. 1981. Nesting distribution and migration of Glossy Ibis in Florida. *Florida Field Naturalist,* 9:1–6.

Roseate Spoonbill
Ajaia ajaja | Threskiornithidae Ciconiiformes | p. 28

DISTRIBUTION The single species genus is the only spoonbill native to the western hemisphere. The other spoonbills of the world are classified as 5 species in the genus *Platelea* found in Europe, Africa, Asia, and Australia within 40 degrees of the equator. Some authors place all spoonbills in the genus *Platelea*. It breeds from the northern coast of the Gulf of Mexico through Florida, the Bahamas, the Greater Antilles, and in South America primarily east of the Andes south to Buenos Aires. They disperse widely after breeding and are seen as accidentals in suitable habitat beyond their breeding range.

FOOD AND FEEDING HABITS Spoonbills feed in hypersaline, tidal, brackish, and fresh water including ephemeral pools. The main qualifying criterion seems to be prey density. Spoonbills are gregarious and readily join flocks of their kind or other actively feeding long-legged waders. When feeding, they stalk about in a grave and dignified manner, periodically scything the partially opened bill side to side in the water or soft mud. When small organisms are detected, the bill snaps closed rapidly and the morsel is swallowed with a backward toss of the head. Small shallow-water fish are preponderant in the diet, followed by aquatic insects, shrimp, and accidentally swallowed plant material. They have been seen to swallow fish as large as a 15 cm (6 in) mullet. Feeding sites may be as far as 35 km (22 mi) from the nest and typically are less than 20 cm (8 in) deep. They may feed in chest-deep water and scythe with the entire head and neck submerged.

REPRODUCTION Roseate spoonbills often nest in association with other long-legged waders.

Seasonality The nesting season in Florida varies with the location in the state (see Migration). Because of the spoonbills' distribution south of the equator and variation in breeding seasonality within geographic areas, active nests can be found in every month.

Courtship The birds begin courtship upon their arrival at the breeding grounds. The courting flocks take to the air as a group and circle the colony site. Groups of standing birds point their bills at the sky when another bird flies over. Paired birds display by preening in a stereotypic manner in which they shake the head and preen the upper wing coverts, primaries, or neck ruff. Copulation may be more frequent than once per hour 2 weeks after pair formation. There is no evidence of pair bonding beyond a single breeding season.

Territoriality The breeding territory is often in a mixed colony which includes ibises and herons.

Nest and Nest Site Spoonbills prefer tall mangroves but will nest in other trees such as cypress or even on the ground in the absence of trees on predator-free islands. Isolation from raccoon accessibility may influence choice of colony nesting sites. The male gathers most of the nest material and delivers it to the female, who does most of the arranging. The nest is a sturdy foundation of twigs and sticks lined with finer and softer vegetation. Nest enhancement continues through incubation and reaches a crescendo just before the eggs hatch.

Eggs The white eggs are 64 mm by 44 mm (2.6 in by 1.8 in) and are marked with variously hued brown spots and blotches; the eggs vary considerably in shape. The average clutch size is 2.7, but varies from 1 to 5 eggs per nest. Beginning about 6 days after copulation, eggs are deposited every other day.

Incubation Both the male and female begin to incubate when the clutch is complete, and hatching is complete at about 22 days. Hatching success of 76% has been recorded.

Fledging The hatchling is covered with sparse down and weighs about 50 g (1.8 oz). The feet, skin, and cylindrical bill are a rich pink at hatching. The bill and legs begin to darken at 2 days. At 7 days spoonbills are covered with a thick coat of short, white woolly down. Their begging call has been aptly described as "a chorus of tremulous trilling whistles." The distinctive spoon on the bill begins to form at day 9. Chicks leave the nest at about 30 days and are fed nearby by the parents until they are 8 weeks old. About half of the eggs laid result in a fledged young. At independence they have white juvenile plumage tinged with light pink and feathers on much of the head, which will be bare as an adult. The legs and feet are gray-brown. The bill is dull yellow to green with a distinct spoon that is less than full adult length.

Age at First Breeding The full pink and carmine of the adult plumage is not reached until at least the 3rd year when breeding commences.

BEHAVIOR As with many of the long-legged waders, they seem to be quite comfortable standing on 1 leg for periods exceeding 1 hour.

MIGRATION Adults migrate north from Cuba to Florida Bay in September and October, then nest from November to January. A 2nd group migrates north from the Caribbean in March and occupies southwest Florida north through Tampa Bay. The 2nd group nests April to June.

PREDATORS Raccoons, grackles, and crows eat the eggs. The young are taken by birds of prey such as Peregrine Falcons, Bald Eagles, and Great Horned Owls.

LONGEVITY Banded birds have been recovered after 8 years of living in the wild.

CONSERVATION ISSUES The species was brought close to extirpation at the turn of the century in the U.S. by plume hunters' disturbance of nesting colonies. Although they were still exploited for food in the 1930s, the populations are recovering. Breeding colonies have increased in Texas and been re-established as far north as Tampa Bay and Merritt Island in Florida. In recent times the greatest threats have been from wetland drainage projects for agriculture, real estate development, and mosquito control. Nestings in south Florida have had mercury concentrations that produce emaciation, weakness, and disease.

NOTES The genus and species names are from the native Brazilian Tupi name for this bird. The Roseate Spoonbill has also been called pink curlew, paddlebeak and banjo-bill flamingo for the similarity in color and feeding habits. In Spanish, it is called *espátula rosada, flamenco espátula, cucharón*; and in French it is *spatule rouge or spatule rosé*.

SUGGESTED ADDITIONAL READING

Robertson, W.B. Jr., L.L. Breen and B.W. Patty. 1983. Movement of marked Roseate Spoonbills in Florida with a review of present distribution. *Journal of Field Ornithology*, 54:225–226.

White, D.H., C.A. Michell and A.J. Krynitsky. 1982. Nesting ecology of Roseate Spoonbills at Nueces Bay, Texas. *Auk*, 99:275–284.

Greater Flamingo
Phoenicopterus ruber | **Phoenicopteridae Phoenicopteriformes | p. 29**

DISTRIBUTION This genus with 3 species is found in a patchy distribution worldwide in warm climates except for Southeast Asia and Australia. The recently published material on flamingos is not taxonomically consistent. *P. r. ruber* breeds in the Bahamas, the Caribbean, and the Galapagos. They are regularly seen in south Florida along the southern border of the Everglades, but those birds are probably vagrants from the Bahamas or escapees from a captive breeding flock maintained at Hialeah Racecourse.

FOOD AND FEEDING HABITS

Flamingos may feed in hypersaline or alkaline lakes with salinity twice that of seawater, alkalinity above a pH of 10 and temperatures to 68°C (155° F). They are able to fulfill their drinking needs with water as salty as seawater. Due to harsh environmental conditions, fish are often absent in feeding areas, thus allowing the small prey of flamingos to reach high densities. Flamingos also feed on marine sandbanks, mudflats, or in lagoons. When the flamingo is feeding, its head and neck are usually submerged while the feeding bird walks slowly forward. The pistonlike action of the tongue sucks water and mud into the partially open beak where lamellae on the bill and spines on the tongue and palate retain small items and direct them down the throat while the water is expelled. Tongue pumping progresses at the rate of about 5 cycles per second. The opening of the beak on the intake stroke is about 5 mm, and the spacing of the lamellae result in the retention of prey between 0.5 and 5 mm (0.02 to 0.2 in). They sometimes use a foot to stir the bottom and bring prey into the water column. Animal foods include brine shrimp, gammarus, copepods, various tiny mollusks, aquatic insect adults and larvae. In the West Indies the diet is primarily composed of brine fly larvae and tiny snails. They occasionally take small crabs and fish. Plant foods include the seeds or stolons of ditch grass, rushes, reeds, and sedges as well as incidental algae, diatoms, and particles of dead leaves. It has been calculated that a Greater Flamingo needs to eat 50,000 larvae of brine flies per day to satisfy its caloric requirements. They can feed effectively in water as much as 130 cm (51 in) deep by swimming, then upending like dabbling ducks to reach the bottom. They are highly gregarious and never feed alone unless injured or infirm. Feeding at night is common.

REPRODUCTION Flamingos nest in colonies of up to 200,000 pairs or as few as 50 pairs except in the Galápagos, where groups of 3 pairs have bred. **Seasonality** Nesting is from March through June in the Bahamas and Caribbean but varies considerably through the tropics. Flooding in wet years can inundate nests, and dry years may expose nests to easy access by predators. **Courtship** Before pairing, flocks of flamingos often perform movements and displays which stimulate hormones and synchronize nesting efforts. The pink coloration is essential in stimulating reproduction. When females gather in groups in shallow water, the males display by head wagging, wing salute, and inverted wing salute with a bow, false preening, false bathing and feeding, and a forward dash with the neck crooked forward. The females disperse into deeper water and the bickering males threaten each other with erected feathers; then the males, with the beak angled upward, individually approach the female of their choice. Copulation is in the water with the female sometimes almost submerged. The pair bond is formed after multiple copulations. Flamingos in captivity are often monogamous, with pair bonds which last through several years. Wild flocks have been observed to switch mates 98.3% of the time between seasons and for 2nd nesting attempts in the same season.

Territoriality The territory is limited to areas immediately around the nest. Birds may be so close that neighbors' beaks can touch while each bird is sitting on its own nest. Most chicks and adults return to their native colony to breed.

Nest and Nest Site Flamingos nest in shallow water or on isolated islands with no vegetative cover near the nest. The nest is a cone of mud, usually about 40 cm (15 in) tall with a small cup at the peak for the egg. Nest mounds built in areas of suitable substrate have been measured at 122 cm (48 in) tall and a basal diameter of 80 cm (31 in). The nest mounds may be built on land near the water on predator-free islands. The mound protects the egg from rising water and is often cooler than the ground in the area. Nesting colonies are often in shallow

water, with each nest being a small sun-baked mud island. When flamingos nest on rocky islands, they build a small pile of stones with a central depression. Nests may be used in subsequent years after they are repaired and enhanced.

Egg The normal clutch is 1 chalky-white egg 5.5 by 9.1 cm (2.0 by 3.6 in) long that weighs about 140 g (5 oz). Replacement eggs are laid only if the 1st egg is lost early in incubation.

Incubation The incubation, shared by both parents, is 27 to 31 days. The very long legs are folded under the bird with considerable finesse as it settles to incubate or brood. Nest relief varies from 1 hour to several days, depending on food availability. Nest desertion is not uncommon when heavy rains inundate nests or drought results in falling water levels that expose the colony to terrestrial predators.

Fledging The chick hatches with a straight bill and a pale-gray, velvety down that is replaced with a darker down at 4 weeks. Within 4 hours of hatching the chick can swim and run to escape predators. The chick usually remains perched on the nest and is regularly brooded until it leaves the nest within a few days. When chicks leave the nest they are able to swim and walk effectively, and soon form large crèches. Flamingos, like pigeons, feed their young with a milk produced in the upper digestive tract, having a fat and protein content similar to mammal milk. Prolactin secretion, which controls the production of the milk in both parents, is induced by the constant begging calls of chicks. The begging calls can even induce prolactin and subsequent milk production in nonbreeding birds. The chicks and adults recognize each other by voice and approach each other at feeding time. Although the beak has developed so chicks can feed themselves to some extent by 35 days of age, parents continue to provide supplemental food until fledging at 75 to 77 days. The fledging period is dependent on abundance of food. About 40% of nests produce a fledgling in years when climatic conditions do not produce a complete nesting failure.

Age at First Breeding Flamingos have been recorded breeding as early as 3 years of age but normally do not nest successfully until 5 or 6 years old.

BEHAVIOR Takeoff requires a short run into the wind, and landing birds run a few paces to disperse the forward momentum after landing. Flamingos may sustain speeds as high as 60 kph (37 mph) when traveling as a flock. Individual distance when feeding or resting may be less than a wingspread apart and require sequential rather than simultaneous takeoff when disturbed. They often rest and even sleep while standing on only 1 leg.

MIGRATION Flamingos in the Caribbean do not migrate in the classic sense, but they may travel as a flock to new feeding or breeding areas. The Flamingos from Great Inagua are known to travel to Hispaniola, Cuba, and south Florida. Seasonal migrations are annual events in many populations. When traveling as a flock they usually fly in V or diagonal formations, and sustained flights are usually at night with a cloudless sky and a favorable wind.

PREDATORS Mammal and bird

predators take the eggs and very young chicks, but the rate of predation declines when the chicks become mobile.

LONGEVITY The oldest recovered banded Greater Flamingo was 33 years old and still nesting. Flamingos have lived over 44 years in captivity. An annual survival rate of 94% has been calculated for a population in southern France.

CONSERVATION ISSUES The conversion of natural saltpans into commercial salt production facilities has eliminated much nesting and feeding habitat. Flamingos and their eggs are still sold for food in some subsistence-level societies outside the U.S. Low-flying aircraft can devastatingly disturb nesting colonies. Flamingos did not suffer from the plume trade in the late 19th century because they did not have plumes and their feathers faded when removed from the bird.

NOTES The genus name is from the Greek *phoenix* (crimson) and *pteron* (wing). The species name is Latin *ruber* (red). In English it is also known as West Indian flamingo, rosy flamingo, American flamingo, and scarlet flamingo; in Spanish it is *flamenco común*, and in French, *flamant rose*. The pink coloration is from canthaxanthin produced by the liver from carotenoid pigments synthesized by prey. Captive animals fed a nutritionally sound diet missing the essential pigments lose most of their pink coloration. Pink feathers are restored after the addition of carrot juice to the captive diet. Phalaropes sometimes use feeding flamingos as beaters to stir up sedentary inverte-brate prey, making it easier to detect.

SUGGESTED ADDITIONAL READING

Allen, R.P. 1956. *The Flamingos: Their life history and survival. Research Report 5.* New York: National Audubon Society.

Arengo, F. and G.A. Baldassarre. 1995. Effects of food density on the behavior and distribution of non-breeding American Flamingos in Yucatan, Mexico. *Condor,* 97: 325–334.

Lesser Scaup
Aythya affinis | **Anatidae Anseriformes** | **p. 30**

DISTRIBUTION This genus with 11 species is found worldwide. The Lesser Scaup breeds in the spring from Montana and North Dakota north through Canada and Alaska. They winter from California to Pennsylvania and south through Central America and the Caribbean to northern South America. They are often found in large rafts in inland lakes and protected waters of the Gulf of Mexico. Large rafts of Lesser Scaup have been seen out of sight of land in the Gulf of Mexico.

FOOD AND FEEDING HABITS

When feeding they may upend in shallow water or dive in water to a maximum of 8 m (26 ft) deep, with dives lasting about 30 seconds interspersed with surface intervals of 10 to 12 seconds. They execute a small leap forward and upward, then allow gravity to help develop downward momentum for the dive. In the winter they feed and rest in protected bays, marshes and estuaries. Feeding activity is greatly influenced by the tide, and they feed at night when suitable conditions exist. Tactile feeding is assumed when they insert the beak into the substrate and chatter the bill while sweeping the head from side to side. They also feed at night. One radio-tracking study showed Lesser Scaup spent more than twice as much time feeding at night as during the day. Diet is determined opportunistically and may vary from 10% to 90% vegetable matter, with the balance animal matter. Animal matter includes mollusks, worms, insects, small fish, and various crustaceans. The vegetable component of the diet includes water lettuce, pond weeds, muskgrass, waterlilies, arrowheads, smartweed, grasses, and sedges. Lesser Scaup often make daily movements if freshwater ponds are available near wintering ground estuaries. They feed primarily in marine ecosystems but drink and preen in fresh water.

REPRODUCTION After moving north in the spring, Lesser Scaup nest in groups on the shores of open water. **Seasonality** The northward migration begins in early March, with stopovers in suitable habitat while waiting for the northward-moving thaw. Large groups may still be along the shores of the Gulf of Mexico until mid-April. Most eggs are deposited from late May to the end of June. The southward movement begins in September, with most birds on the wintering grounds by November. Stragglers continue to arrive in Florida through December.

Courtship Most courtship takes place before or during stopovers in migration. Male display behavior includes a coughlike movement with a whistled *whew*, head throw, head shakes, sneaking behavior, turning the back of the head, and mutual preening behind the wing. Females often respond by nipping at the male, diving with him and uttering a rattling purr, *kwuh-h-h*, which is answered by a low whistle from the male. Copulation is on the water. They are generally monogamous within a breeding season, but the females usually select a new mate in subsequent years.

Territoriality Adult females often return to the same pond and nesting area in subsequent years. The home range of 1 to 2 ha (2 to 5 acres) is shared with other Lesser Scaup with no obvious defense of territory other than opposing other drakes that approach the hen.

Nest and Nest Site The nest is located on grassy freshwater shorelines, wetlands, islands, or on river deltas adjacent to water at least 3 m (10 ft) deep. The nest is usually placed under heavy vegetative cover on dry ground, close to the edge of the water, which allows the female to move to and from the nest inconspicuously. Nests may be placed in uplands several hundred meters (yards) from a suitable body of water for chick rearing or among emergent vegetation over water. The highest nesting density is in bulrush marshes bordering lakes with high amphipod populations. The nest is a depression in the ground with some added dry vegetation. Dark down from the hen's breast falls out or is plucked out and added to the nest gradually as the eggs are laid and incubation proceeds. Pairs nesting on peninsulas have a nest success of only 17%, but when predator barriers are installed the nest success increases to 54%. Many birds do not nest in dry years that leave mud banks between open water and shoreline vegetation. Those scaup that do nest are often preyed upon by skunks and other predators.

Eggs The olive-buff eggs measure 57 by 40 mm (2.2 by 1.6 in), have a weight of 48 g (1.7 oz) and are laid daily until the clutch of 10 to 12 is completed. The clutch may weigh up to 70% of the female's body weight. Renesting after nest failure is uncommon, with subsequent clutches smaller than the original.

Incubation Females do all the incubation while the drakes leave their mates and travel to other lakes for the flightless molting period. Incubation begins after the full clutch is deposited. Eggs hatch after 22 days of incubation but may take as long as 27 days if the female is disturbed or otherwise less attentive while incubating. The female voids a smelly fluid on the eggs when she is flushed from incubation by a potential predator. The entire clutch generally hatches within a day, with a usual hatching success of 80% to 90%.

Fledging The newly hatched downy ducklings have brown upperparts and yellow underparts with stripes on the head. The hen leads the brood to water soon after all the eggs have hatched. Ducklings feed themselves in a habitat with emergent and submerged vegetation that supports a large invertebrate fauna. Broods from 2 or more hens often combine and are cared for by all the involved adult females. The ducklings are able to dive at the age of 2 days. As the ducklings mature, the females are more inclined to take flight when disturbed. The ducklings then run and flap across the water and dive. Food of the ducklings in the preflight stage is almost entirely animal matter taken while diving. Juvenile feathers entirely replace the down, and 1st flight is about 50 days of age. Hens stay with the brood until almost ready for flight, then fly to other lakes for molting. Nesting success is variable and determined in large part by water levels. With high water levels nesting success may be as high as 90%. With low water levels, predation increases significantly and food supplies may be limited, leading to nesting success of less than 10%.

Age at First Breeding Most females are physiologically capable of breeding at 1 year of age but seldom reproduce successfully until 2 years of age. With abundant rich habitat in wet years, most individuals breed. An excess of males in the population usually prevents young males from breeding until the age of 2 years.

BEHAVIOR Scaup arrive on the wintering grounds late in the fall and often form large flocks on lakes, rivers, estuaries, and protected marine waters. When the scaup are swimming on the surface, the feet are stroked alternately, but when diving they are stroked together. When disturbed, Lesser Scaup may mingle with other species of ducks, but flocks and rafts seldom have other species present.

MIGRATION Scaup tend to gather in large flocks for the fall migration. Males molt and migrate south early in mostly male flocks. Females and juveniles may delay departures until forced south by freeze-ups. They are often the last ducks to leave the breeding grounds in the fall and among the last to arrive in the spring.

PREDATORS Crows, foxes, coyotes, raccoons, skunks, weasels, and mink take the eggs. Pike and mink take the ducklings. Hawks, owls, and mammalian predators take the adults and chicks when they can catch them. Alligators and snapping turtles catch a few unlucky individuals. Ring-billed Gulls have been seen pirating food from Lesser Scaup.

LONGEVITY Lesser Scaup banded as hatchlings have been recovered as much as 18 years 4 months later.

CONSERVATION ISSUES With annual mortality from 40% to 80%, population stability depends very much on successful nesting. Lesser Scaup have a high reproductive potential and rapidly rebuild populations when climatic conditions are favorable. They are the most abundant species of diving duck in North America. Lesser Scaup have consistently shown residues of DDT and its metabolites, but the levels have significantly declined in recent years. Scaup often pick up residual lead shot from the bottom of marshes. The shot lodges in the gizzard and is slowly corroded, abraded, and released into the digestive tract, producing lead poisoning. The present prohibition of lead shot for waterfowl hunting will further reduce the prevalence of this problem in years to come.

NOTES The genus name is from the Greek *aithya*, a seabird mentioned by Aristotle. The species name is the Latin *affinis* (related), probably referring to the similar Greater Scaup. This duck has also been placed in the genus *Marila*. Other common names in English are black jack, bluebill, and creek broadbill. In Spanish they are *costero chico, pato del medio, pato turco* and *pato morisco;* in French *petit milouinan* or *canard tête-noir.* Most consumers rate the flavor of Lesser Scaup as less than satisfactory, often commenting on a rank taste that is particularly evident in Florida birds. Others have found them desirable table fare. The difference seems to be related to the diet of the duck in the previous month.

SUGGESTED ADDITIONAL READING

Austin, J.E., C.M. Custer and A.D. Afton.1998. Lesser Scaup (*Aythya affinis*). In A. Poole and F. Gill (eds.), *The Birds of North America. No. 338*. Philadelphia: The Birds of North America, Inc.

Custer, C.M., T.W. Custer and D.W. Sparks. 1996. Radio telemetry documents 24-hour feeding activity of wintering Lesser Scaup. *Wilson Bulletin,* 108:556–566.

Rogers, J.P. and L.J. Korschgen. 1966. Foods of Lesser Scaups in breeding, migration and wintering areas. *Journal of Wildlife Management,* 30:258–264.

Blue-winged Teal

Anas discors | **Anatidae Anseriformes** | **p. 31**

DISTRIBUTION This genus with 46 species is found worldwide with several endemic species on island groups. The Atlantic flyway population has been proposed as a different race, *A. d. orphna,* from the central and western population, *A. d. discors.* The majority of Blue-winged Teal nest in the prairie potholes of central Canada and the U.S., with fewer numbers breeding along the coasts east of the Appalachian Mountains and west of the Rocky Mountains. A small part of the population of Blue-winged Teal winter in the southern U.S., but most move further south through Central America and the Caribbean to northern South America, extending sometimes to Argentina and Chile. Large numbers may breed considerably farther south than normal when heavy rains produce an abundance of wetland habitat. A few Blue-winged Teal regularly remain and breed in Florida in the spring and summer.

FOOD AND FEEDING HABITS

About 75% of the Blue-winged Teal's diet is vegetable matter represented by many types of filamentous algae, sedges, grasses, duckweeds, pondweeds, and smartweeds. Seeds are particularly favored. The balance of the diet is a variety of insects, snails, clams, crustaceans, and other invertebrates. Foraging in the winter is in shallow freshwater or saltwater marshes, mangroves, and estuaries, which allow teal to feed on the bottom by extending the neck underwater or tipping up. They often feed in association with Green-winged Teal.

REPRODUCTION Courtship proceeds during the migration north to the prairie pothole nesting areas.

Seasonality The northward migration in the spring begins as early as February in the most southern part of the winter range and reaches its peak in the northern states in April. Nesting is in May, June, and July.

Courtship Males begin to molt into breeding plumage in December when courtship begins on the wintering grounds. Males display by jump flights toward the female, ritual foraging, stereotyped comfort movements, and turning the back of the head in response to female incitement. Pair bonds are established as both sexes become more ardent on beaches and on the water in the wintering grounds. Courtship behavior continues through migration to the breeding grounds. Copulation takes place on the water after mutual head pumping. Wild populations of Blue-winged Teal have a male preponderance of up to 60% of the population.

Territoriality Males defend the female against the close approach of other males by chin lifting and other aggressive postures. Both members of the pair participate in selecting the nest territory, but the female selects the actual nest site. Territorial disputes in nesting and feeding areas have not been recorded, but nests are dispersed. Blue-wing Teal do not routinely return to the same nest in subsequent years and are thus able to take advantage of changing water and habitat conditions.

Nest and Nest Site The nest is a scraped depression in the soil; it is lined with grasses and sedges and is built in vegetation that is 30 to 60 cm (12 to 24 in) tall. Down is added to the nest daily after about 4 eggs are laid, and the female continues to pluck down from her breast to add to the nest throughout incubation. Some preferred vegetation types for the nest site are bluegrass, marshgrass, and alfalfa. The distance from nest to water averages 38 m (125 ft); some nests may be on vegetation over water and others may be built more than 1,600 m (1 mi) from water. Nest density averages from about 20 nests per 100 acres in typical habitat, to 60 per 100 acres in ideal habitat such as islands in marshes. Renesting females select a new nest site an average of 183 m (600 ft) from a plundered nest.

Eggs Average clutch size is 9 eggs (range 6 to 15) laid 1 per day just after sunrise. Renesting clutches contain about half as many eggs. The olive to creamy-white eggs measure 46 by 33 mm (1.8 by 1.3 in) and weigh about 29 g (1 oz). Prior to nest construction, eggs are commonly dropped at random or in nests of other birds. With a nest loss of up to 6 eggs, the female continues to lay until she produces a full clutch. With 8 or more eggs lost, there is a time-lag before renesting. The interval before renesting increases with the duration of the incubation of the lost clutch. Females with clutches lost in the last week of incubation generally do not renest.

Incubation Within 24 hours after the last egg is laid, the female begins incubation and continues till hatching at about 22 to 24 days. The female loses about 1% of her body weight per day while laying and incubating. She usually defecates on the eggs if she is flushed from the nest. Males become less attentive and desert the females about 2 weeks after incubation begins.

Fledging The hatchlings, covered with a brown down with large yellow patches, follow the female to water within 12 hours of hatching. The rearing habitat is typically shallow water with various species of bulrushes and cattails. Initially the ducklings are brooded by the female but soon become independent. After about 2 weeks the brown juvenile feathers become evident. The females then leave the brood, which aggregates with other flightless juveniles. Full feather growth with coloration similar to that of the female is attained by fledging at about 42 days of age. By mid-August most young can fly but do not develop full adult plumage until their 2nd summer. Due to the number of predators and environmental conditions, nest success rates vary from 13% to 72%. About 40% of nests do not produce any viable offspring. An average of 3 ducklings per brood are raised to fledging.

Age at First Breeding Most Blue-winged Teal begin to breed at the age of 1 year.

BEHAVIOR Blue-winged Teal are very sociable ducks and aggregate in flocks after nesting and remain in flocks for the fall migration, on the winter feeding grounds and for the spring migration. Early in the season on the breeding grounds, individual pairs separate and select home ranges of about 40 ha (100 acres). They often rest perched on boulders, logs or branches and roots overhanging water. They usually travel at 50 to 65 kph (30 to 40 mph) and have been recorded flying considerably in excess of that. When traveling locally, small flocks often wheel and change direction abruptly in unison. Blue-winged Teal almost never dive for food and only rarely to escape predators.

MIGRATION Blue-winged Teal usually migrate 130 to 160 k (80 to 100 mi) per day during the morning and evening hours and may travel more than 11,300 k (7,000 mi) from breeding to wintering grounds. They travel at an elevation of 150 to 900 m (500 to 3,000 ft) above ground level in single-species flocks, but a few may intermingle with other species of waterfowl or have a few individuals join their flocks. The males begin their postnuptial molt and flightless period shortly after deserting the females and lead the fall migration in August. Females begin their postnuptial molt shortly before the juveniles fledge. Females and juveniles often migrate in separate flocks in late August and September. Most Blue-winged Teal winter south of the U.S.

PREDATORS Eggs are eaten by foxes, skunks, weasels, mink, magpies, and crows. Hawks, owls, pike, and mink take the juveniles, while hawks and owls eat the adults. Blue-winged Teal are heavily hunted, with total annual mortality from all causes estimated at 50% of the population.

LONGEVITY The oldest recorded individual lived to be 17 years of age.

CONSERVATION ISSUES The North American annual breeding population averages about 5,000,000. An early fall migration allows a large percentage of the population to pass unscathed before duck-hunting seasons open. But when the season opens they are heavily hunted as a challenging target. Audubon commented on their tender and savory flesh. Drought and agricultural activities such as overgrazing, tilling and mowing of nesting habitats are the most significant factors controlling populations. Drainage of wetlands continues to reduce the amount of nesting and rearing habitat available.

NOTES The genus name is from the Latin *anas* (duck). The species name is from the Latin *discors* (discordant or different). In English they are also called blue-wing, white-faced teal, Mexican duck, or teal. In Spanish they are *cerceta de alas azules, zarceta de estoño, pato zarcel* or *pato de la Florida,* and in French they are called *sarcelle soucrourou* or *sarcelle à ailes bleues.*

SUGGESTED ADDITIONAL READING

Bennett, L.J. 1938. *The blue-winged Teal, its ecology and management.* Collegiate Press. Ames Iowa.

Glover, F.A. 1956. Nesting and production of the Blue-winged Teal (*Anas discors*) in Northwest Iowa. *J Wildl Mgmt,* 20:28–46.

Dane, C.W. 1968. Age determination of Blue-winged Teal. *J Wildl Mgmt,* 32:267–274.

White-cheeked Pintail
Anas bahamensis | Anatidae Anseriformes | p. 32

DISTRIBUTION This genus with 46 species is found worldwide. Three subspecies of the White-cheeked Pintail have been named: *A. b. galapagensis* is found in the Galápagos Islands, and *A. b. rubirostris* occurs from southern Brazil south to Argentina and Uruguay and on the west coast of South America in Ecuador, Bolivia and Chile. *A. b. bahamensis* is found from Florida and the Bahamas through the Caribbean to northern Venezuela, the Guianas, and northern Brazil. The White-cheeked Pintail is probably under-reported from Florida because its ideal coastal habitat from Naples to Homestead is difficult to access and rarely subject to the scrutiny of bird watchers. Florida records probably include escapees from captivity.

FOOD AND FEEDING HABITS
Feeding is by head dipping, upending and diving in saltwater lagoons and hypersaline saltponds, and less frequently in small freshwater lakes and ponds. Flocks of these ducks congregate on ponds that have good growths of widgeon grass. The algae also seem to be a particularly favored food. Animal matter is at least a seasonal component of the diet. Pintails are seen actively feeding in areas with no apparent vegetation and have been reported feeding behind foraging yellowlegs and feeding flamingos. Ducklings' diets include aquatic invertebrates and several species of grass seeds.

REPRODUCTION White-cheeked Pintails nest singly on the ground in areas not prone to disturbance or predation.

Seasonality The breeding season is extensively varied; in Trinidad nesting is reported from August to November, while in Surinam it is from May to October. In the Virgin Islands the peak of egg laying is from April through June, but fluffy ducklings have been found in December.

Courtship Females incite the interest of males with a stiff-necked display and vocalizations. Males follow and show the back of the head to the females. Copulation is preceded by head pumping by both birds, and is followed by male displays while the female bathes. Forced extra-pair copulations with fertile females are often attempted by mated territorial males.

Territoriality Although nesting is solitary, groups of ducklings may combine in good habitat to form larger flotillas. Territorial behavior in the wild has not been recorded, but only single nests have been found on islands up to 4 ha (10 acres).

Nest and Nest Site The nest is built on the ground in a dense thicket of sedge, grass, weeds, or vines. The site may be on a dry island at some distance from suitable chick-rearing habitat, requiring the female, accompanied by chicks, to walk up to 100 m and swim up to 3 km (2 miles) in the open sea to reach a secure environment.

Eggs The creamy-white to buff eggs measure 57 by 38 mm (2.2 by 1.5 in) and weigh about 34 g (1.2 oz). The complete clutch is 5 to 12 eggs.

Incubation When disturbed on the nest, the incubating adult slinks silently through the grass for 20 ft or more before explosively taking flight.

Fledging At hatching, the chicks are rich yellow with brown markings. When all the eggs hatch, the flock of ducklings is led to protected water by the mother. When threatened by predators they are capable of escape by diving. Fledging is at 45 to 60 days.

Age at First Breeding White-cheeked Pintails have been recorded as breeding at the age of 1 year.

BEHAVIOR White-cheeked Pintails may form mixed flocks with Blue-winged Teals, but usually form small, single-species flocks. They become very tame, and free-living individuals have adapted to begging at seashore restaurants. Flight speed has been recorded at 56 kph (35 mph).

MIGRATION Individuals of the South American race *A. b. rubirostris* move outside their breeding range when not nesting. The balance are sedentary with only small local movements related to changing food supplies.

PREDATORS The eggs are taken by Laughing Gulls and mongooses. The ducklings are taken by snook and barracuda when swimming in open water, and Peregrine Falcons take the adults.

LONGEVITY The maximum longevity recorded is 14 years 2 months.

CONSERVATION ISSUES Hunting and wetlands loss are the major threats to continued population stability. Successful nesting has never been recorded in the presence of mongooses, thus successful nesting on the larger Caribbean islands is limited to small, mongoose-free satellite islands.

NOTES The genus name is from Latin *anas* (duck). The species name refers to the Bahama Islands as the source of the original specimen described by Linnaeus. Other names in English are Bahama duck, Bahama pintail, brasswing, and whitehead; in Spanish it is called *pato gargantillo, pato quijada colorada, pato de la orilla* and *anade gargantillo;* in French *canard des Bahamas, canard tête blanche.* They are noted to be particularly good eating.

SUGGESTED ADDITIONAL READING

Raffaele, H. 1975. Bahama Duck exploiting feeding habits of yellowlegs. *Wilson Bulletin,* 87:276–277.

Sorenson, L.G. 1994. Forced extra-pair copulation in the white-cheeked pintail: Male tactics and female responses. *Condor,* 96:400–410.

Red-breasted Merganser
Mergus serrator | **Anatidae Anseriformes | p. 33**

DISTRIBUTION This genus with 4 species is found worldwide. The Chinese Merganser (*M. squamatus*) is found from Siberia south through Manchuria and China. The Common Merganser (*M. merganser*), sometimes called goosander, is found worldwide in the Arctic and adjacent temperate zones. The Brazilian Merganser (*M. octosetaceus*) is found in the Amazon basin. The Red-breasted Merganser breeds worldwide in the Arctic and subarctic from Alaska to Canada, Greenland, Iceland, Scotland, Scandinavia, Siberia, northern Japan, and the Islands of the Bering Straits. In the winter, they may go to the Atlantic, Pacific, and Gulf coasts of the U.S., with stragglers in Bermuda and the Caribbean, and to Europe, the Black and Caspian Seas, Korea, China, and Japan.

FOOD AND FEEDING HABITS
The primary feeding habit is to pursue fish at high speed, but mergansers are also inclined to poke into holes and crevices to flush prey into the open. They have been reported as using the wings to aid the feet in propulsion, but if they do, it is a rare event. Synchronous diving is common when feeding in small cooperative groups. In shallow water they swim at the surface with the head submerged while searching for prey. Feeding is usually in clear water that is protected from waves and seldom more than 4 m (13 ft) deep. The feet are stroked together when moving underwater, but at the surface they are stroked alternately. Underwater feeding dives usually last less than 30 seconds, but dives to escape predators frequently exceed 1 minute. Small food items are swallowed underwater, with larger prey brought to the surface for manipulation. Fish-stealing attempts by other mergansers are common on the surface. In the winter mergansers are primarily marine, but some winter in open water in the Great Lakes. Mergansers are responsive to prey abundance and eat a broad variety of fish and invertebrates. Aquatic invertebrates and small fish are the most important food source of developing young. Red-breasted Mergansers raise the ire of recreational fisherman when they regularly consume trout and salmon fingerlings in freshwater streams. Mergansers also help fishermen by consuming lampreys, which parasitize sport fish. After feeding they often preen extensively, tipping sideways to gain access to the breast and belly feathers. Herons and gulls sometimes follow feeding mergansers to catch small fish disturbed by the mergansers.

REPRODUCTION The Red-breasted Merganser builds a simple nest near water.
Seasonality Peak egg laying is variable with latitude but is usually in June.
Courtship Red-breasted Mergansers usually form pair bonds as a result of extensive displays in the winter and early spring before migration. The female displays include inciting behavior—she makes a forward dash with her head held high and the beak pointed downward. She may also per-

form a ritualized upward stretch, wing flapping, and bathing. The male displays include a sprint in which he rushes through the water near females leaving a bow wave and wake, a salute in which the head and neck are extended, uttering of yeow call, a curtsy in which the body is tilted forward, and head turning with fully erect crest. A ritualized upward stretch, wing flapping, and bathing are also part of the male courtship repertoire. Polyandry and polygeny have been recorded.

Territoriality The female selects the nest site, usually within 10 m (33 ft) of water. The territory around the nest site only extends about 1 m (40 in) from the nest.

Nest and Nest Site Nests lined with grass and down are built in crevices or holes or among thick vegetation or exposed tree roots near the water. In thickets of reeds and other nonwoody vegetation the female may develop a tunnel-like path from the nest to the water. Nests may be found in dispersed groups near estuaries and lakes or along swiftly flowing rivers with gravel bottoms. The same nest site may be used again in subsequent years.

Eggs The average clutch size is 9 eggs laid over about a 15-day period. The creamy-white or buff-colored eggs measure 65 mm by 45 mm (2.6 by 1.8 in) and weigh about 72 g (2.6 oz). Replacement clutches average about 1/3 fewer eggs than 1st clutches.

Incubation The female begins to pluck a gray-brown down from her breast and add it to the nest surface after a few eggs have been laid; she continues to add down during incubation. She covers and surrounds the eggs with down when she leaves the nest. Males may share incubation duties early in the cycle, but most terminate the pair bond and depart early in incubation. Incubation begins after the clutch is complete. The entire clutch hatches within a few hours after a variable incubation time of 29 to 35 (usually 32) days. Mergansers often gather in small flocks when not incubating.

Fledging The female leads the young to water soon after they hatch but continues to brood them at night for a week or so. Ducklings initially skitter along the surface in response to danger but later dive when threatened. The young feed themselves from the beginning and soon make shallow feeding dives. Several broods may combine to form groups of ducklings that are accompanied by a single female. They are independent at 7 weeks of age and are capable of long-distance flight by about 9 weeks. The productivity averages less then 2 viable young per year per pair due to high loss rate of both eggs and chicks.

Age at First Breeding Most Red-breasted Mergansers breed in their 2nd spring, but in captivity, some may reproduce at 1 year of age.

BEHAVIOR The Red-breasted Merganser is generally shy, skeptical, and vigilant. The flight speed has been measured at 72 kph (45 mph) when traveling peaceably and 114 kph (71 mph) near an aircraft. When in flight the wings whistle.

MIGRATION The northward migration begins in late March and reaches its peak in April. The southward migration in the fall seems to be driven by freeze-ups in late October, with many birds remaining at the northern edge of ice-free waters until November when they move south along the Atlantic and Pacific coasts. When migrating in groups, they fly in Vs or diagonal lines.

PREDATORS Weasels, foxes, ravens, and gulls take the eggs. Pike, gulls, and otters take the ducklings, and hawks capture the adults.

LONGEVITY The longest reported lifespan is 9 years 8 months.

CONSERVATION ISSUES Mergansers are often shot when feeding in commercial aquaculture facilities and by fishermen who consider them to be competitors. They are seldom hunted, as the meat of Red-breasted Mergansers is generally considered unpalatable by humans. Red-breasted Merganser populations have been affected by environmental DDT and DDE, which has caused eggshell thinning and reduced nest success. Mercury concentrations potentially harmful to ducklings have been found in Red-breasted Merganser eggs. With the decline in environmental concentrations of chlorinated hydrocarbon pesticides, nest success has returned to normal levels.

NOTES The genus name is from the Latin *merges* (diver) and the Latin *anas* (duck). The species name is Latin *serrator* (one who saws), in reference to the saw-edged bill. It is also called saw-bill or fish duck in English; *pato serrucho, mergo cristado, serrata mediana* and *mergansa pechirroja* in Spanish; and *harle huppé* or *sechotier* in French.

SUGGESTED ADDITIONAL READING

Des Lauriers, J.R. and B.H. Brattstrom. 1965. Cooperative feeding behavior in Red-breasted Mergansers. *Auk,* 82:639.

Munro, J.A. and W.A. Clemens. 1939. The food and feeding habits of the Red-breasted Merganser in British Columbia. *Journal of Wildlife Management,* 3:46–50.

Osprey
Pandion haliaetus | **Pandionidae Falconiformes** | **p. 34**

DISTRIBUTION This unique bird is placed in its own family, *Pandionidae*, and its own genus, *Pandion*. The single species in the genus is found worldwide. Four or more geographic subspecies are generally recognized: *P. h. haliaetus* from Scandinavia and the Mediterranean to Japan; *P. h. cristatus* from Australia to the Philippines; *P. h. ridgwayi* in the Bahamas and Caribbean; and *P. h. carolinensis* from Alaska and Canada south to Florida and Arizona, wintering in northern South America.

FOOD AND FEEDING HABITS
Hunting is generally solitary, but Ospreys may gather in small groups to exploit local concentrations of fish. The diet is almost exclusively live fish weighing up to 1.2 kg (2.6 lbs) but usually 150 to 300 g (5 to 10 oz) and 20 cm to 40 cm (8 to 16 in). Ospreys often plunge dramatically from 10 to 30 m (33 to 100 ft) to catch a fish. They fly 5 to 40 m (16 to 130 ft) above the water when actively fishing, and often circle or hover when a suitable prey is spotted. The dive may be in a series of steps with pauses at intermediate altitudes. The legs swing forward at the last second and enter the water, with the full momentum of the body pushing the talons into contact with the fish. Fish are carried headfirst in both talons and aligned with the body while en route to the nest or feeding perch. Ospreys often seem to submerge but seldom go far beneath the surface to catch fish with their talons. They feed in shallow fresh, brackish, and salt water but are most abundant in protected marine waters. This raptor has several adaptations that assist in its life as a fisherman. The outer toe can be reversed to allow 2 toes to grasp each side of a fish. The talons are long, sharp, and strongly curved, with spiny foot pads to enhance the grip. The compact plumage resists wetting, and its smaller volume allows easier penetration of the water upon impact from the plunge. Ospreys hunt by sight and do not forage at night or in windy or rainy weather. Forty to 70% of the dives successfully capture a fish. The dense, compact, oily plumage and nasal valves allow Ospreys to dive and return to the air with little inconvenience. Prey items in northern marine waters include winter flounder, herring, menhaden, and pollock, with carp, pike, and trout in fresh water. Mullet and sea catfish are the primary prey in warmer marine waters further south, while shad, sunfish, crappie, and bass are taken from fresh water. Shad seem to be particularly susceptible to Osprey capture.

REPRODUCTION Ospreys nest as single pairs or small groups in the tops of tall trees near water.
Seasonality Ospreys in Florida may have eggs from December to March, but migrants to northern areas may lay as much as 3 months later.
Courtship The pair display by circling high over the nest and uttering a *cree-cree-cree* call. The male performs a spectacular dive and upward swoop series of flights often while carrying a stick or fish. Most courtship revolves about the nest site and courtship feed-

ing of the female by the male. A female copulates often with a mate who feeds her and seldom with one that does not. Poorly fed females are more likely to copulate with males that are not their mate. Most pairs are monogamous, but some males form trios with 2 females on nearby nests. Males copulate frequently and closely guard their mates in periods of high fertility to maximize probability of paternity.

Territoriality Ospreys returning to a breeding colony establish a nesting territory. The territory is defended with guard calls as an intruder approaches. Territorial defense a-gainst other Ospreys is usually only by the resident of the same sex as the intruder. The resident assumes a stereotyped erect posture with wings partly open and back feathers erect. Intruders may be chased on close approach, and in extreme cases the birds strike each other and tumble to the ground as they grapple. Ospreys do not defend a home range or feeding territory. Nest site defense against predators is vigorous and involves calling, high-speed dives, and hitting the intruder with the talons.

Nest and Nest Site They easily become accustomed to human activity and will build nests in suitable trees near roads and houses. They nest along the shores of lakes, bays, marshes, and estuaries and have a great preference for islands free of terrestrial predators. Nest sites are generally chosen to be in the top of tall trees such as cypress, pine, and red mangrove. Standing dead snags are often preferred. On predator-free islands with no disturbance they sometimes nest on the ground or on rocky promontories. The nest platform is a bulky collection of sticks and other flotsam

and is lined with grass, seaweed and leaves; it takes about 3 weeks to construct. In subsequent years of use much additional material is added until nests may reach almost 2 m (7 ft) in depth. Nest material continues to be added throughout the fledgling development. The nest is usually on the very top of a tree, exposed to the sky and easily approached by food-carrying adults. Natural nest sites seem to be a limiting factor. Ospreys nest on the crossbucks of electric power poles and on navigation markers when natural nest sites are not available. This willingness to use artificial structures has led to the erecting of artificial nest platforms on poles as a very successful conservation program.

Eggs The eggs are buff with chestnut-colored swirls and blotches, measure 61 by 46 mm (2.4 oz) and weigh about 70 g (2.5 g). The normal clutch is 3 eggs with a range of 1 to 4. Eggs are laid at 2- or 3-day intervals. Replacement clutches are laid after nest loss, but only 1 brood is raised per year.

Incubation The incubation period is about 33 days and begins after the 1st egg is laid. The female provides most of the incubation, but males regularly provide nest relief, particularly when the female leaves the nest to consume prey that the male has provided. Chicks in a 3-egg clutch hatch over an average period of 4 days and may hatch at 1- to 7-day intervals.

Fledging Females usually stay on the nest to tend the chicks while males capture and deliver fish. The chicks continue to be brooded in cold weather and shaded in hot weather until about 14 days of age, when their original white down is replaced by a sooty-colored down. The male often feeds from a fish before he delivers it to the female, who tears off small bits for the chicks. As the chicks grow larger they are provided with entire fish; they are able to dismantle prey and feed themselves after 6 weeks of age. For a nest with large chicks, the male needs to deliver 100 g of fish per hour in daylight hours. Larger, earlier-hatched chicks dominate others at feeding, and in times of food scarcity the smaller chicks starve. After about 10 days of wing-flapping exercise, chicks are urged by the parents to fledge at about 53 days of age. Supplemental feeding by the parents may continue until 100 days of age. Nest success has been found to decrease with increasing human disturbance, but pairs acclimated to human proximity are not adversely affected. Mortality is about 50% in the 1st year and less than 20% per year thereafter.

Age at First Breeding Ospreys breed at 3 or 4 years of age if nest sites are plentiful but may delay to 5 or 6 years old if nest sites are scarce. It has been estimated that only 30% of fledged young survive long enough to reproduce.

BEHAVIOR The flight speed is 2.6 wingbeats per second, which is considerably increased when hovering. Level flight has been recorded in excess of 65 kph (40 mph). A vigorous doglike shake rids the oily feathers of much of the water after a plunge. Ospreys habituate to human presence, and with regular exposure tolerate humans' close approach to nesting trees.

MIGRATION Most Ospreys north of Florida and the Gulf Coast states migrate south for the winter as far as the Amazon River in South America. Banded birds data from eastern and midwestern populations show that 24% were south of the equator, 26% in South America north of the equator, and 40% in Central America, the Caribbean and the U.S. They are known to be capable of migrations of 2,000 km (1,250 mi) over water, taking as long as 60 hours.

PREDATORS Crows take untended eggs, and raccoons take eggs and chicks when accessible. Bald Eagles steal prey from adult Ospreys and sometimes eat the chicks.

LONGEVITY A banded Osprey was retrapped and released 22 years after the original banding. Unsubstantiated reports claim the same pair has been using the same nest for over 30 years.

CONSERVATION ISSUES Osprey populations in the U.S. declined drastically after World War II because of DDT and other pesticide-induced thinning of egg shells. The population stabilized in the early 1970s after DDT and dieldren were banned for use in the U.S. Reproductive success has increased to levels characteristic of pre-DDT populations. Continued public support in the form of artificial nest platforms should allow us to enjoy this magnificent bird for many generations to come.

NOTES The genus name is that of a mythological Greek king whose daughters metamorphosed into birds. The species name is from the Greek *hals* (sea) and *aetos* (eagle). They are also called fish hawk and fish eagle in English, *águila pescadora* or *gavilán pescador* in Spanish, and *balbuzard pêcheur* in French.

SUGGESTED ADDITIONAL READING

Berry, J.D. and C.J. Henny. 1995. Osprey polygyny in Wyoming. *Journal of Raptor Research,* 29:279–281.

Bowman R., G.V.N. Powell, J.A. Hovis, N.C. Kline and T. Wilmers. 1989. Variation in reproductive success between subpopulations of the Osprey (*Pandion haliatus*) in south Florida. *Bulletin of Marine Science,* 44:245–250.

Szaro, R.C. 1978. Reproductive success and foraging behaviour of the Osprey at Seahorse Key, Florida. *Wilson Bulletin,* 90:112–118.

Swallow-tailed Kite

Elanoides forficatus | **Accipitridae Falconiformes** | **p. 35**

DISTRIBUTION The single species in the genus is found from the U.S. south to Argentina. Two subspecies have been described, with *E. f. yetapa* from southern Mexico through tropical South America, and *E. f. forficatus* breeding in the southeastern U.S.

FOOD AND FEEDING HABITS Swallow-tailed Kites soar low over saltwater and freshwater swamps and marshes as well as bottomland hardwood forests while gleaning prey from vegetation or catching flying insects. They catch prey in trees and grasses. Primary prey items are beetles, grasshoppers, dragonflies, and butterflies. Bees, ants, and wasps often constitute an important part of the diet. Wasp nests may be torn from their moorings and carried away before being dismantled to allow consumption of the larvae. When feeding young, the adults also take frogs, lizards, and small snakes by swooping down and plucking them from the vegetation. Small birds with exposed nests such as Mocking Birds are robbed of their nestlings. After plucking the entire nest from a tree with its talons, the kite reaches with its beak as it swings the nest forward to extract and consume the nestlings. In return kites are often mobbed by songbirds such as kingbirds. Gleaning insects from foliage is most common in morning and evening, although more flying insects are captured during midday. Kites pick bats from the air, fish from calm water, and ripe fruit directly from trees. They are attracted to wildland fires and feast on flustered, fleeing small animals. Prey is captured, carried in the talons, and usually consumed in flight. When delivering prey to mate or offspring, the item is transferred to the beak just before landing. Forays with continuous hunting have been radiotracked as far as 24 km (15 mi) from the nest or roost.

REPRODUCTION Swallow-tailed Kites nest in open groups in the top of the tallest trees in the area.

Seasonality Swallow-tailed Kites return to Florida in late February or early March. Nesting is from late March to early June.

Courtship Both members of the pair chase, swoop, and dive in courtship. Females solicit and males provide courtship feeding as a prelude to copulation. Copulation is initiated by the female facing into the wind while perched on an exposed limb. The male flies in and lands on the female's back. After adjusting his balance he brings his tail under hers as he rests his bill on her back. Total time from landing to takeoff is about 30 seconds and may be repeated several times per hour. Unmated males may attempt to interfere with copulation. Pairs seem to be monogamous within a season, but no data have been collected on long-term pair bonds. Nonbreeding 1-year-olds and unmated adults are often present in nesting colonies and offer food and nesting material to mated females, who usually decline.

Territoriality The area around the nest site for a radius of 50 to 100 m (164 to 328 ft) is defended by both sexes and is advertised by the owners' circling above the nest. Particular animosity is shown to Red-tailed Hawks and vultures, which are chased from the vicinity of the nest. Home range, determined by radiotracking, varies from 10 to 360 sq km (4 to 139 sq mi) with smaller core areas being occupied most of the time.

Nest and Nest Site Nests are often placed in the top of large pine, cypress, Australian pine, or other trees extending above the canopy. Nesting trees are often in clumps of trees in standing water or in riparian zones. Nest sites are often in open groups 75 to 700 m (246 to 2,297 ft)—less than .5 mi apart—near the top of an open irregular canopy. Both sexes collect nesting material by breaking off twigs with the talons in flight. Although they carry nesting material for long distances in the talons, they transfer building material to the beak before landing. The nest is usually composed of pine and cypress twigs in a matrix of epiphytes such as Spanish moss and lichens and commonly includes wasp nests. The nest is constantly supplemented during incubation and chick rearing. Most nesting is with newly constructed nests, but reuse of old nests does occur.

Eggs The creamy-white eggs, blotched and streaked with reddish-brown, measure 47 by 37 mm (1.9 by 1.5 in) and weigh about 35 g (1.2 oz). Swallow-tailed Kites lay 1 clutch with an average of 2 eggs per season.

Incubation The 28- to 31- day incubation period begins after the 1st egg is laid. Both parents share incubation and seldom leave the eggs untended. The female occupies the nest about 30% of the time by day and all night.

While the female is incubating, the male provides food twice a day. The sitting bird often seems to be bothered by mosquitoes in still weather.

Fledging Hatchlings have a continuous short cheeping call that evolves to an adultlike *klee* when begging. Nestlings are brooded continuously by one or the other of the parents for the 1st week. The male ceases to brood after a week and then hunts continuously. The male provides 96% of the prey. It is dismembered by the female, who feeds the chicks. Juvenile plumage is visible at 14 days and complete by 40 days. The nestlings continue to be brooded at night until they are about 3 weeks old. They begin to exercise wings at 33 days and by 35 days take flight if startled. First flights beyond the nesting tree are usually at about 5.5 weeks of age. Siblicide or brood reduction is common, with few nests fledging more than 1 juvenile.

Age at First Breeding Most Swallow-tailed Kites begin breeding in their 2nd spring.

BEHAVIOR A continuous *klee-klee-klee* call attracts other kites, which join in mobbing a potential predator. When taking flight they dive off the perch with partially closed wings until flight speed is attained, then fully extend the wings to swoop back to elevation. In roosting and foraging flocks the distance between individuals may be as little as 1 m (3 ft). Flight speed has been recorded as 40 kph (25 mph). Skimming low and touching water is usually done for drinking, moistening the belly feathers, cooling, and washing prey remains from the belly feathers. Fish are caught at the surface without dunking the body.

MIGRATION The winter migration begins in July with aggregation into premigration roosting colonies composed of hundreds of birds. The departure to South America is complete in September, with most birds returning to the U.S. in February.

PREDATORS Red-shouldered Hawks, Boat-tailed Grackles, and vultures have been recorded taking eggs. Raccoons may take the eggs, young, or nestlings if they can gain access to the nest, and monkeys are thought to be nest predators in Latin America. Hawks, eagles, owls, crows, and vultures near the nest site are attacked and driven away. Groups of kites may collaborate in mobbing Bald Eagles or Great-horned Owls.

LONGEVITY There is no data on longevity of Swallow-tailed Kites.

CONSERVATION ISSUES The historic breeding range of the Swallow-tailed Kite included more than 16 states but is now reduced to small populations in 7 states. Clearing of bottomland hardwoods for development and conversion to pine plantations continues to reduce available feeding and nesting areas. The association of patches of tall, open trees interspersed with suitable rich hunting areas is becoming scarce.

NOTES The genus name is from the Greek *elanus* (kite) and *oides* (resembling). The species name is from the Latin *forficus* (scissors) and *atus* (possessing), in reference to the tail shape. It is also known as scissor tail kite, forked tail kite, and snake hawk in English; *Milano tijereta, elanio tijereta* or *gavilán tijerita* in Spanish; and *milan à queue fourchue* or *le milan de la Caroline* in French.

SUGGESTED ADDITIONAL READING

Meyer, K.D. 1995. Swallow-tailed Kite (*Elanoides forficatus*). In A. Poole and F. Gill (eds.), *The Birds of North America. No. 138*. Philadelphia: The Birds of North America, Inc.

Millsap. B.A. 1987. Summer concentrations of American Swallow-tailed Kites at Lake Okeechobee, Florida, with comments on post breeding movements. *Florida Field Nat,* 15:85–92.

Snyder, N.F.R. 1974. Breeding biology of Swallow-tailed Kites in Florida. *Living Bird,* 13:73–97.

Red-tailed Hawk

Buteo jamaicensis | Accipitridae Falconiformes | p. 36

DISTRIBUTION This genus with 27 species is found primarily in the New World, with several members in Europe, Africa, and Asia. The Red-tailed Hawk is found from Alaska and the provinces of Canada south through Panama and the Antilles. It has been divided into 12 or more subspecies, with *B. j. umbrinus* in Florida and the Bahamas, *B. j. solitudinous* in Cuba, and *B. j. jamaicensis* from Jamaica through the Greater Antilles to St. Kitts.

FOOD AND FEEDING HABITS

The characteristic hunting method is to rest on an elevated perch, then launch on a downward glide when prey is sighted. Preferred feeding habitat is open woodland to savanna. They are generally absent from treeless grasslands or closed-canopy old- growth forests. Glides may be extended with a few wing flaps, and they may weave among terrain obstacles to conceal their approach. The talons are swung forward about 3 m (10 ft) before impact with the prey. A similar technique is used in flight at elevations of less than 60 m (200 ft). They may run and hop about when catching terrestrial prey such as grasshoppers and frogs. They pirate from each other and other raptors, and eat fresh carrion such as recent road kills. Individuals or pairs may specialize in certain prey species, depending on availability and dietary preference. Small mammals make up the majority of the prey. Also regularly present in the diet are reptiles, fish, amphibians, and large insects. Birds up to the size of Ring-necked Pheasants are taken when available. Red-tailed Hawks regularly take bats at cave entrances on the evening emergence of large roosts, and in the Caribbean they take immature mongooses up to a weight of about 200 grams. They do occasionally take young chickens and domestic pigeons. They regurgitate pellets composed of the indigestible remains of prey.

REPRODUCTION

Red-tailed Hawks nest on the canopy of the highest tree around that gives them easy nest access and a good view.

Seasonality Nesting may begin as early as February in the south and may be delayed until June in the northern part of the range. In the northern part of the breeding range, the 1st egg is laid within 2 to 3 weeks of arrival.

Courtship Pair bonds are formed and maintained by flying acrobatic maneuvers, often accompanied by calls. The pair bond is monogamous for life, but lost partners are rapidly replaced. New females may assist in the rearing of the prior female's brood.

Territoriality The territory is first claimed by soaring in circles high above it. A sky dance to show territorial boundaries is performed by diving at high speed, then using the momentum to regain altitude for another dive. Males often occupy a sequence of conspicuous perches along the boundary of the defended territory. The home range of 260 to 520 ha (1 to 2 sq mi) includes hunting areas and is defended as the territory. Territories have a height limit, which allows other hawks to pass over without harassment. Territorial boundaries are often delineated by terrain features such as roads, habitat edges, and streams. Boundaries commonly remain consistent even with turnover of claimants.

Nest and Nest Site Red-tailed Hawks prefer a tall tree with open canopy, which allows them easy access to the nest in the crown. The nest site is located toward the center of the defended territory within the canopy of a tree taller than surrounding forest. The nest may be used seasonally by other species, then refurbished for use by Red-tailed Hawks again in subsequent seasons. Great Horned Owls, which nest earlier in the spring, never build a nest of their own and often usurp Red-tailed Hawk nests. The nest is constructed primarily by the female using sticks broken off the tree by the male's beak or talons and carried to the nest in the beak. The nest platform is 76 cm (30 in) wide and 38 cm (15 in) deep with a central bowl about 10 cm (4 in) deep lined with fine vegetation. Material continues to be added to the nest throughout the incubation period.

Eggs The pale-bluish to white eggs with dark-brown spots and blotches measure 60 by 47 mm (2.4 by 1.9 in). Clutch size is an average of 3 and is variable with latitude and food supply. Eggs are ordinarily laid every other day. Replacement clutches are laid 3 to 4 weeks after nest loss.

Incubation Both parents share nest duties during the 34-day incubation period, with the male sometimes bringing food to the female on the nest. Hatching takes place over a shorter period than laying, indicating the incubation does not occur until the clutch is started.

Fledging Males provide food for the female and brood at the nest, allowing the female to be on guard almost continuously. The last-hatched chick may be less able to compete for food and die of starvation in times of food scarcity. At hatching, the chicks have a short white down that is replaced within a week with a longer, gray-brown down. Females guard and brood the chicks until 4 or 5 weeks of age. Juvenile plumage is evident by the 4th week, with the upper parts mostly covered by feathers by the 5th week. First flight is at 6 or 7 weeks, and sustained flight is 2.5 weeks later. First capture of vertebrate prey occurs about 6 weeks after fledging. Parents provide training and supplemental food for another 30 to 70 days. In flying juveniles, the tail is gray-brown above. The juvenile plumage is retained for the 1st year of flight, then gradually replaced over 4 months with an adult color and pattern. An average of 1.4 young fledge per nest. The mortality rate for birds in their 1st year of flight is 54%, as compared with 20% mortality per year for the adult population.

Age at First Breeding Capable of breeding at age 2, Red-tailed Hawks in crowded habitat often do not breed until several years later.

BEHAVIOR The flap rate is 2.6 per second when traveling in steady flapping flight. Maximum-level flight speed is about 65 kph (40 mph). Density of Red-tailed Hawks in the winter is about 1 pair per 520 ha (2 sq mi) of open country with high perches or edge habitat. Play has been recorded as a small object repeatedly dropped and recovered in flight.

MIGRATION Northern Red-tailed Hawks generally migrate south beginning with the most northern birds, which are urged forward by freezing temperatures. The migration passes through Pennsylvania in October and November with the peak traffic the 1st week in November. The northern migration is diffuse in time and location and is controlled in part by the snow melt, which exposes their rodent prey. Peaks of migration are associated with favorable winds and thermals, while rain and headwinds inhibit travel. Air speed of Red-tailed Hawks in level flight soaring in updrafts along ridge lines has been measured at about 60 kph (37 mph) with a ground speed of 47 kph (29 mph). Individuals migrate alone or in small loose flocks, with waves of adults often occurring separately from juveniles. The migration path is greatly influenced by topographic features such as ridge lines that provide updrafts to assist soaring.

PREDATORS Jays, crows, and ravens take unguarded eggs and hatchlings. Raccoons take the eggs and hatchlings. Owls take the chicks and more rarely adults.

LONGEVITY Several banded Red-tailed Hawks have been recovered more than 20 years after banding, and a captive female was still living at age 29.5.

CONSERVATION ISSUES Because of habitat and dietary preferences, Red-tailed Hawks often supplant Red-shouldered Hawks as an area is deforested. Shooting and direct human interference with nesting activities continue to be significant causes of population limitation.

NOTES The genus name is from the Latin *Butte* (a type of hawk). The species name refers to the origin of the early specimens collected and described. They are also called chicken hawks in English; *aquiline, busardo colirrojo, gavilán del monte* or *guaragao* in Spanish; and *buse à queue rousse* in French.

SUGGESTED ADDITIONAL READING

Janes, S.W. 1984. Influences of territory composition and interspecific competition on Red-tailed Hawk reproductive success. *Ecology*, 65: 862–868.

Preston, C.R. and R.D. Bean 1993. Red-tailed Hawk (*Buteo jamaicensis*). In A. Poole and F. Gill (eds.), *The Birds of North America. No. 52.* Philadelphia: The Birds of North America, Inc.

Snyder, R.L. 1975. Some prey preference factors for a Red-tailed Hawk. *Auk*, 92:547–552.

Red-shouldered Hawk
Buteo lineatus | **Accipitridae Falconiformes** | **p. 37**

DISTRIBUTION This genus with 27 species is found primarily in the New World but has several members in Europe, Africa, and Asia. The Red-shouldered Hawk is found from the Atlantic coast of the U.S. west to Lake Superior and south to eastern Texas. A disjunct population exists on the Pacific coast. The species has been divided into 5 subspecies, with *B. l. lineata* in northeast North America, *B. l. elegans* from southern Oregon to Baja California, *B. l. texanus* from south Texas to Mexico City, *B. l. alleni* in the southeastern U.S. to northern Florida, and *B. l. extima* from Lake Okeechobee through the Florida Keys.

FOOD AND FEEDING HABITS
Red-shouldered Hawks prefer to hunt under the canopy of old-growth forest with an open understory. Hunting territories may be in cypress swamps, bottomland hardwoods, oak/hickory forests, or mixed deciduous/conifers. In every case the feeding territory includes open water and/or seasonal wetlands. They typically launch predatory flights from a perch in the canopy. In more open terrain they use a fence post while watching for prey or fly slowly over short vegetation and wetlands at elevations of 30 m (100 ft) or less. They seem to use sound to help locate small terrestrial prey. The primary prey items are insects, amphibians, rodents and small mammals, and birds. They pluck frogs, snakes, crayfish, and small turtles from the water and steal prey from crows when possible. Specific prey selection is opportunistic, with mammals making up as much as 92% of the diet in some years, while amphibians and arthropods may be 85% of the diet of the same birds in a succeeding year with different ecological conditions. They have been seen to fly for short distances with a Tricolored Heron, a gray squirrel, or a small opossum, each of which equaled or exceeded the weight of the hawk. They have been found on the ground eating prey too large to transport such as mallards, teal, skunks, and muskrats. Chickens are not usually taken even when easily available.

REPRODUCTION Red-shouldered Hawks place their nests close to the trunks of large trees in lowland hardwood forests.
Seasonality Eggs may be laid from January to June in Florida, with a peak in March and April. Migration of northern nesting birds to the breeding grounds is somewhat weather dependent in March and April.
Courtship Courtship activities involve aerial displays with much swooping, diving, and calling. The pair bond seems to last for life, with replacement mates rapidly acquired after the loss of a partner.
Territoriality Nests are separated from each other at distances of 700 to 2,100 m (0.4 to 1.3 mi). Individual pairs defend 100 to 350 ha (250 to 860 acres) nonoverlapping territories. Specific territories are held by their owners and successors for as long as 50 years. American Kestrels and Barred Owls may share the territory, but Red-shouldered and Red-tailed Hawks

have mutually exclusive territories.

Nest and Nest Site Nests are most frequently built below the crown and near the trunk of large trees in bottomland hardwood forests. The nest height averages 14 m (47 ft), with a recorded range from 0 (on the ground) to 36 m (118 ft). A nest is constructed of interwoven sticks, leaves, strips of bark, vines, Spanish moss, and often a few conifer sprigs. The central cavity is lined with fine soft moss, lichens, and shredded bark. A finished nest is about 60 cm (2 ft) in diameter and 30 cm (12 in) thick with a central cavity 20 cm (8 in) in diameter by 5 to 7 cm (2 to 3 in) deep. In reuse of a prior year's nest, only the lining material is refurbished. Intent to repossess a prior nest is announced by leaving sprigs of greenery in the nest.

Eggs The dull-white eggs with brown and lavender blotches measure 55 by 44 mm (2.1 by 1.7 in) and weigh about 58 g (2 oz). Clutch size is geographically variable from a preponderance of 2-egg nests in the southern part of the range to 4 or more in northern nests. Eggs are laid at 2- or 3-day intervals. If the first clutch is lost, a replacement clutch will usually be laid in a different nest within 3 or 4 weeks.

Incubation Males provide food for incubating females and provide short periods of incubation that begin after the 1st egg is laid, and each egg hatches after about 33 days of incubation. Eggs hatch asynchronously, resulting in a range of chick sizes. Brood reduction is common when food is limited.

Fledging At hatching, the chicks have a long, buff-colored down, which is soon replaced with a thick, grayish woolly down on the back, with white below. Brooding by the female is almost continuous for the 1st week, with the male delivering food to the nest or a nearby perch. Chicks are able to feed themselves from delivered food by 18 days. Brooding at night and in cold, rainy weather continues until the chicks are at least 3 weeks old. The chicks leave the nest at 4 or 5 weeks and climb about on nearby branches but return to the nest to be fed and to roost at night. Fledging is at 6 to 7 weeks, with parents providing supplemental feeding for an additional 8 to 10 weeks. On average, less than 2 young fledge per nest.

Age at First Breeding First breeding is usually at age 2, but 1-year-old females may breed successfully with adult males. They often return to claim a territory in the vicinity of their natal site.

BEHAVIOR Red-shouldered Hawks generally do not cross bodies of water greater than 25 km (18 miles) across. Speed has been recorded at 30 to 55 kph (18 to 34 mph) in flap and glide migration flight and at 77 kph (48 mph) when the hawk is gliding between thermals. The wings are held flat when soaring, but when gliding, the wings are bowed with the wrists turned up and the wing tips bent down. The result is a greater amount of lift at the expense of some forward speed. The rate of climb in thermals has been recorded at 1.3 to 4.1 m/s (250 to 800 ft/min).

MIGRATION Northern-breeding birds migrate south alone or in small groups from September through November, depending on weather. Some maintain northern residency in mild winters. The northern migration is in March. California and southern birds are permanent residents and do not migrate. They often use ridge-induced updrafts and thermals as aids in soaring, particularly during migration.

PREDATORS Raccoons, martens, and fishers eat the eggs and young. Great-horned Owls take the chicks and more rarely the adults. Both members of the pair mob Great-horned Owls and Barred Owls when they are discovered on the territory. Red-shouldered Hawks have been recorded taking the chicks of a Great-horned Owl. Red-tailed Hawks are not compatible with Red-shouldered Hawks and have been known to kill them.

LONGEVITY Red-shouldered Hawks have been known to live for more than 20 years.

CONSERVATION ISSUES Eggshell thinning caused by chlorinated hydrocarbon pesticides has been recorded. Direct mortality of adults from pesticide toxicity has also been recorded. Disturbance by human activity, including removal of young from nests by falconers, is a significant source of mortality in some areas.

NOTES The genus name is derived from the Latin *buteo* (hawk), and the species name is from the Latin *lineatus* (striped). This hawk has also been placed in the genera *Falco* and *Asturina*. It is also called winter hawk, red-bellied hawk, and hen hawk in English; *gavilán ranero* or *busardo hombrorrojo* in Spanish; and *buse à épaulettes* in French.

SUGGESTED ADDITIONAL READING

Crocoll, S.T. 1994. Red-shouldered Hawk (*Buteo lineatus*). In A. Poole and F. Gill (eds.), *The Birds of North America. No. 107.* Philadelphia: The Birds of North America, Inc.

Ogden, J.C. 1974. Aspects of Red-shouldered Hawk nesting in southern Florida. *Florida Field Nat,* 2:25–27.

Portnoy, J.W. and W.E. Dodge. 1979. Red-shouldered Hawk nesting ecology and behavior. *Wilson Bulletin,* 91:104–117.

American Kestrel
Falco sparverius | **Falconidae Falconiformes** | **p. 38**

DISTRIBUTION This genus with 38 species is found worldwide. American Kestrels are found throughout southern Canada, Alaska, the U.S., Greater and Lesser Antilles, Central America, and South America south to Tierra del Fuego except for the Amazon basin. They have been divided into 14 subspecies. *F. s. sparverius* is found over most of North America. *F. s. sparveroides* is on Cuba and the southern Bahamas. *F. s. dominicensis* is on Jamaica and Hispaniola. *F. s. caribbearum* occurs from Puerto Rico to Grenada. *F. s. peninsularis* is on Baja California and adjacent Mexican lowlands in Sonora and Sinaloa. *F. s. paulus,* the smallest of the subspecies, is resident in the coastal southeast U.S. from Texas to South Carolina. The other subspecies are found in Southern Central America and South America.

FOOD AND FEEDING HABITS
The primary prey is small vertebrates such as starlings, sparrows, shorebirds, Least Terns, deer mice, voles, shrews, lizards, frogs, and small snakes. Surplus vertebrate prey may be cached in a tree or a spot on the ground. Feeding may be almost exclusively on grasshoppers, dragonflies, beetles, cicadas, or other invertebrates when they are abundant. They may walk about on the ground eating earthworms after heavy rainfall. Unaware bats are taken from behind in pursuit flight, and kestrels may reach into swallow nests with a foot to extract chicks. They are attracted to and feed along the windward edge of grassfires. They are able to transport prey up to 50% of their body weight. They feed in deserts, grasslands, forest openings, marshes, barrier islands, agricultural land, and many urban settings. By using water from the prey and metabolically produced water, they can live and breed without drinking. They are generally absent in mature, closed-canopy forests. Hunting is from perches on snags or other vantage points, or on the wing with frequent hovering pauses while watching prey. Prey is generally captured with the talons and killed by a bite from the bill. Successful ground hunting usually requires a vegetation height of less than 25 cm (10 in). Most prey is captured on the ground, but large insects and small birds may be captured in the air. The great diversity of acceptable prey allows kestrels to maintain population densities of more than a pair per square kilometer in suitable habitat.

REPRODUCTION American Kestrels require holes in trees, cliff faces or buildings for nesting.

Seasonality Seasonal movements north and south are protracted because the individuals of the most northward origin migrate the farthest south, with many intermediate populations remaining as residents or only moving short distances. Laying dates in the U.S. have been recorded from early April to July, and in the Caribbean the kestrels may nest in any month.

Courtship Migratory males usually arrive on the breeding grounds and establish a territory before the females arrive. The reproductive sequence continues in the presence of freezing temperatures but is delayed in late springs when snow cover remains. Courtship, similar to that of other hawks, is a series of *klee* calls at the apex of display dives and climbs near the female. A female then begins to associate with a male in aerial displays and hunting. The female displays by flight with shallow rapid wingbeats interspersed by glides with the fully extended wings arched below the body. As the pair bond develops, the male carries food to the female while chittering. Copulation is frequent with as many as 14 copulations in 36 minutes recorded and an estimated 690 performed for a 5-egg brood. Both members of the pair begin to inspect cavities and search for a nest site. Before eggs are laid, the female frequently visits the nest site and roosts in it at night. Sexes are segregated on the wintering grounds, but pair bonds are renewed each year until 1 member of the pair is lost. Divorces, early season promiscuity with neighbors, and other philandering are recorded for both sexes.

Territoriality Territories may be as small as 22 ha (54 acres), and nearest neighbor distance may be as little as 42 m (138 ft) in productive habitat. Territories and nest dispersion may be 10 times as large in areas with reduced habitat quality. Male kestrels chase other male kestrels from the territory, drive off other raptors, and harass and sometimes strike mammalian intruders near the nest site. Home range and territory seem to be synonymous in American Kestrels. Territories are commonly reused in subsequent years.

Nest and Nest Site A favorite nest site is an old woodpecker hole in a standing dead tree, but they also use nooks in buildings and ledges on cliff faces. The nest is always situated in a cavity. Nest sites are usually in short supply, and American Kestrels are able to evict starlings, woodpeckers, chipmunks, and squirrels from desirable cavities. Selected cavities are more than 5 m (16.4 ft) above ground with openings of 5 to 20 cm (2 to 8 in) that face away from prevailing storms. They are quite willing to use artificial nest boxes. One easily constructed roofed design measures 25 by 25 by 30 cm (10 by 10 by 12 in) tall with a 7 cm (3 in) hole 2/3 of the way up the front. The box should be mounted more than 3 m (10 ft) above ground in an open area with no obstructing branches. Kestrels do not add material to the nesting cavity, so a bit of dry grass, sawdust, wood chips, or pine needles approximate the debris in the bottom of a natural cavity and keep the eggs from rolling around.

Eggs The 35 by 29 mm (1.4 by 1.1 in) egg weighs 15 g (0.5 oz) and is white to light reddish brown with violet, gray, and brown spots and mottling. Eggs are laid at 1- to 3-day intervals. Clutch size ranges from 2 to 6 eggs but is usually 4 eggs. The average number of eggs per clutch decreases from northern to southern latitudes. Replacement laying after loss of a clutch is common, and multiple broods per season are normal in the southern part of the range. Kestrels do not recognize their own eggs and have been recorded incubating Wood Duck eggs. They have also been recorded incubating and raising a screech owl to fledging.

Incubation Incubation begins when about half the clutch is complete and lasts about 29 days; hatching occurs over a 3- or 4-day period. Hatching success has been recorded between 67% and 89%. Both sexes incubate, with the male covering the eggs while the female is hunting. The male reinforces the pair bond by providing food while whine-chittering to the incubating female. The female also hunts on her own and immediately consumes captured prey. It is hypothesized that it is more efficient for the female to catch and consume her own food, leaving the male to provide for himself and the chicks.

Fledging At hatching, the chicks have a sparse, short white down. The male is the sole provider of food for the 1st week or so while the female guards and broods the chicks. Chicks grow rapidly and reach adult weight by 17 days. The chicks show a voluntary decrease in food intake and weight loss just prior to fledging at about 30 days. Fledging success has been recorded from 72% to 98%. Fledglings remain close together and are fed by the parents for up to 2 weeks before they disperse. An adultlike, sexually dimorphic plumage is attained before fledging, but full adult plumage is not present until the summer after their 1st breeding season.

Age at First Breeding American Kestrels usually breed at 1 year of age.

BEHAVIOR The flap rate is 2.8 per second in normal flight but increases up to 4.6 when the kestrel is in a hurry or flying into the wind. A flight speed of 32 kph (20 mph) is easily maintained and may increase to 58 kph (36 mph) when the bird is migrating or facing a headwind.

MIGRATION The most northern populations move south as far as Panama for the winter. Individuals seem to return to the same wintering territory in subsequent years.

PREDATORS Raccoons eat the eggs and chicks when they can gain access to the nest. Red-tailed Hawks, Peregrine Falcons and Barn Owls eat the adults.

LONGEVITY Both sexes are capable of breeding to 10 years of age; the oldest recovered banded bird was age 12. American Kestrels have lived over 17 years in captivity.

CONSERVATION ISSUES Nesting habitat loss has had adverse effects on American Kestrel populations in Florida and the Caribbean. In Florida the conversion of pinelands to orange groves, cleared pastures, agriculture, and commercial development have reduced kestrel populations as nest sites have been eliminated.

NOTES The genus name is from the Latin *falx* (sickle), in reference to the sickle-shaped talons. The species name is Latin *sparvarius* (pertaining to a sparrow). They are also called sparrow hawk, killi killi hawk, and bastard hawk in English; *cernicala chitero, gavilán chitero* or *falcón común* in Spanish; and *crecerelle d'Amérique in* French. *Falco tinnunculus* of the Old World and *Falco bicolor* of South and Central America are also commonly called sparrow hawks.

SUGGESTED ADDITIONAL READING

Miller, K.E. and J.A. Smallwood. 1997. Natal dispersal and philopatry of southeastern American Kestrels in Florida. *Wilson Bulletin,* 109:226–232.

Smallwood, J.A. 1987. Sexual segregation by habitat in American Kestrels wintering in south-central Florida: Vegetative structure and responses to differential prey availability. *Condor*, 89:842–849.

Willoughby, E.J. and T.J. Cade. 1964. Breeding behavior of the American Kestrel. *Living Bird*

Peregrine Falcon
Falco peregrinus | Falconidae Falconiformes | p. 39

DISTRIBUTION The genus with 38 species is found worldwide. Peregrine Falcons are found worldwide from the Arctic to Tierra del Fuego. They thrive in cold, wet maritime climates; in hot, wet tropical rain forests; in cold and hot deserts; and in mountains to 4,000 m (13,000 ft). The species has been divided into 19 geographic subspecies on the basis of size and coloration. The Peregrine Falcon was extirpated in the eastern U.S. and Canada by 1965 due to chlorinated hydrocarbon pesticides such as DDT and dieldrin. With the banning of most of the more pernicious chemicals and the reintroduction of birds reared in captivity, the original population numbers are being restored.

FOOD AND FEEDING HABITS
Birds make up 95% of the diet and are usually disabled or killed in midair with a high-speed dive (stoop) and impact. The speed of the peregrine's stoop has been discussed for centuries and continues to be debated. A 30° dive was recorded at 270 kph (170 mph), and a 350 kph (220 mph) dive at a 45° angle of descent. A vertical stoop has been calculated to reach a maximum of 386 kph (240 mph). While there may be debate on the specific speeds, there is complete agreement that the dive speed far exceeds that of any of the prey species and is a marvel to behold. Straight and level flight has been variously recorded at 50, 64, and 100 kph (30, 40, and 62 mph) with a flap rate of 4.3 flaps per second. Waterfowl and shorebirds are important prey, and feeding habitat typically includes shorelines and wetlands. Males catch birds in the range of 20 to 500 g (0.7 to 17.5 oz), while larger females catch prey 100 to 1,000 g (3.5 to 35 oz), with a record of 2,000 g (4.4 lbs). The peregrine can carry prey heavier than itself only a short distance before landing to dismember and feed on it. Individual peregrines often specialize in 1 taxonomic group of birds such as Rock Doves, shorebirds, or ducks. In the Caribbean they may specialize in fruit pigeons or boobies, or even enter tropicbird nesting crevices to eat the adults and chicks. Rodents, bats, rabbits and other small mammals as well as lizards, grasshoppers, and dragonflies have also been recorded as prey. In strictly concrete urban settings, Peregrine Falcons adapt very well to a diet of starlings and semi-domestic Rock Doves. Prey is usually plucked and dismantled and seldom swallowed whole. Pellets containing feathers, fur, and claws are regularly regurgitated.

REPRODUCTION Peregrine Falcons form long-term pair bonds with attachment to a specific nest site on a ledge near a source of prey.
Seasonality Nesting is in late winter or early spring both north and south of the equator. Due to the broad worldwide distribution it is possible to find a Peregrine Falcon nest with eggs in every month.
Courtship Unmated males roost on a conspicuous spot near the nest site and sail back and forth uttering a *wichew* (rusty hinge) call when a

female approaches. The potential pair begins to develop a pair bond by roosting together at the proposed nest site. Later, extremely acrobatic display flights occur near the nesting cliffs. When pair bonds are established, courtship feeding often precedes copulation. Feeding of the female by the male continues through egg laying, incubation, and the first half of the fledging period. The pair bond usually extends until 1 of the pair dies, with pairs remaining together even in non-breeding season. Bigamy by males has been recorded. In mild climates the pair may occupy the breeding territory throughout the year. Males stay on the territory after losing a mate and most of them choose a 1- or 2-year-old as a replacement mate.

Territoriality The defended nesting territory usually results in nests being spaced at least 5 km (3 mi) apart, but in areas of abundant food supply the nests may be as close as 1 km (0.6 mi). The feeding territory can exceed 10,000 ha (40 sq mi).

Nest and Nest Site The nest is often a ledge on a cliff face and is used annually by a succession of generations. Offspring commonly inherit the nest site of parents. The ledge must be wide and deep enough to allow the young to fully stretch their wings while exercising, and typically has a thin layer of vegetated soil in which a shallow nest scrape is formed. Small, shallow caves in cliff faces inaccessible to mammalian predators are highly favored. Nests are usually located near water. Peregrine Falcons may also use an isolated stick nest of other species. In recent years Peregrine Falcons have successfully nested on ledges of skyscrapers and bridges.

Eggs The glossy eggs are cream colored to reddish brown with spots and blotches of darker red-brown, and measure about 52 by 41 mm (2 by 1.6 in) with a weight of about 45 g (1.6 oz). The clutch is geographically variable and averages about 3 eggs laid at 2- or 3-day intervals. If the nest is lost early in incubation, replacement eggs are laid about 2 weeks later.

Incubation Continuous incubation does not begin until the clutch is nearly complete. Both parents share the incubation period of about 30 days. The eggs all hatch within a 48-hour period, leaving approximately equal-sized chicks in the nest.

Fledging Hatchlings have a white down that is soon replaced with a gray down and are brooded by the female for 2 or 3 weeks while the male provides food. As the chicks mature they are less in need of brooding and the female assists in foraging for the larger appetites, which demand as much as 300 g of food per day per chick. Unlike many other raptors, intense aggression between chicks and siblicide is rare. Some peregrines develop distinct prey preferences for shorebirds, such as Greater and Lesser Yellowlegs, when feeding chicks. Feeding flights average over 5 km (3 mi) from the nest and have been recorded as far as 24 km (15 mi). Fledging is at about 42 days of age, with the juveniles remaining dependent on adult supplemental feeding for another 2 months. Productivity averages 1.7 fledged young per nest, with a 1st-year mortality of 50% to 70%.

Age at First Breeding Peregrine Falcons usually begin breeding in their 2nd year, but females may mate with an older male in their 1st year. Successful breeding of a yearling pair has been recorded.

BEHAVIOR Peregrine Falcons seem to enjoy bathing and do so frequently by wading into shallow water or splashing into deep water at a shallow angle.

MIGRATION Many populations migrate away from the boreal winter across the equator to the austral summer. Wintering birds often establish territories that are reclaimed in subsequent years. Temperate-zone populations may be sedentary and resident throughout the year. Florida and the Caribbean are host only to wintering birds that migrate north to breed.

PREDATORS Great Horned Owls by night and Golden Eagles by day take unguarded young. Adults are sometimes shot by uninformed humans. Raccoons and ringtails are sometimes able to climb to the nest and eat the eggs. Foxes may eat the eggs and chicks from nests built on the ground in the tundra.

LONGEVITY The maximum recorded age for a wild Peregrine Falcon was that of a 20-year-old individual that was still breeding. Annual adult mortality has been estimated at 25% per year, and few members of the population live more than 5 years after attaining breeding age.

CONSERVATION ISSUES World populations of Peregrine Falcons declined drastically in the '60s and '70s due to the adverse impact of chlorinated hydrocarbon pesticides on eggshell thickness and chick mortality. DDT was banned in 1972 in the U.S. and subsequently in many other countries. Falcon populations have shown significant recovery since these chemicals have been banned. Blood samples from Peregrine Falcons during spring and fall migrations indicated that most of their pesticide burden, primarily DDE, was accumulated on wintering grounds in Latin America. Habitat loss due to development of coastal wetlands is now an increasing threat to this species.

NOTES The genus name is from the Latin *falx* (sickle) in reference to the shape of the talons. The species name is from the Latin *peregrinus* (wanderer or foreign). Peregrine Falcons were formerly placed in the genus *Rhynchodon*. They are also known as Barbary falcon, duck hawk, big-footed falcon, and rock peregrine in English; *halcón peregrino*, *halcón pollero* or *halcón de patos* in Spanish; and *faucon pèlerin* or *malfini* in French. This is one of the most sought-after raptors for use in the sport of falconry due to their ability to subdue a variety of fast, powerful game birds. While falconry enthusiasts have been able to induce breeding in captivity and to release these birds into the wild, other groups have been highly critical of the use of peregrines in falconry.

SUGGESTED ADDITIONAL READING

Beyer, W.N, and C.D. Gish. 1980. Persistence in earthworms and potential hazards to birds of soil applied DDT, dieldrin, and heptachlor. *Journal of Applied Ecology,* 17:295.

Cade and Bird. 1990. Peregrine Falcons nesting in an urban environment. *Canadian Field Naturalist,* 104:209–218.

American Coot

Fulica americana | Rallidae Gruiformes | p. 40

DISTRIBUTION The genus with 10 species is found worldwide. The Caribbean Coot is found from south Florida through the West Indies to Venezuela and is sometimes considered to be a subspecies of the American Coot. The American Coot breeds from southern Canada, through the U.S., Caribbean, and Central America, to the central Andes of South America. They also have an established population in the Hawaiian Islands.

FOOD AND FEEDING HABITS

Coots are often found in fresh water but are also regularly found in shallow marine swamps and marshes. Feeding methods are dipping and diving to obtain the primarily vegetarian diet. They can dive to a depth of 8 m (26 ft) but seldom extend themselves to forage that deep. They seem to have a preference for filamentous green algae along with the leaves, seeds, and tubers of water milfoil, pondweed, duckweed, and other aquatic plants. They may graze on newly sprouted grass and readily consume grain to the extent that they may be major pests in freshly seeded or sprouted rice fields. Animal matter is eaten in the form of grasshoppers and aquatic insects, tadpoles, snails, and small fish. They have been seen to pirate vegetable food from ducks. They easily become accustomed to the presence of humans and readily use suitable man-made wetlands and impoundments.

REPRODUCTION Coots nest in marshy areas in all of the 48 contiguous states and in the Canadian provinces.

Seasonality Coots generally nest from May through July, but in Florida young chicks observed in early February indicate nesting in January.

Courtship The males display to the female by swimming toward her with the head and neck extended along the water, wingtips raised above the tail, and the tail spread and elevated to show the white markings. If the female is positively disposed, she will assume a similar posture and follow him as he turns away. Paired coots will often splash water on each other, then preen the mate on neck and back.

Territoriality Male coots are pugnacious in the breeding season. They display extensively and may fight over territories or the attentions of females. A directed run across the surface of the water will generally displace intruders. Fights include grasping the intruder with a foot while slapping with the other foot and pecking. Coots may make aggressive displays and rush at Double-crested Cormorants in the territory, but the cormorants generally seem to ignore them.

Nest and Nest Site Coots may build up to 9 nests to various stages of completion before selecting 1 for egg deposition. The female builds the nest platform by bending over and intertwining living reeds, bulrushes, or cattails. Additional vegetation is added until a nest platform 38 cm (15 in) wide is completed and lined with softer vegetation. The finished nest rim is usually 5 to 20 cm (2 to 8 in) above the water and 1 to 5 m (3 to 16 ft) from open water. Males often build platforms as resting places for the chicks.

Eggs The slightly glossy eggs are buff with dark blotches and average 49 by 34 mm (1.9 by 1.3 in). The usual clutch varies from 8 to 16 eggs laid 1 per day. Early in the breeding cycle the female coot may lay her eggs in another coot's nest. Up to 4 replacement clutches have been recorded. Coots have been observed laying a 2nd clutch of eggs in the same nest before the 1st clutch of eggs has hatched. Two separate broods may be raised per year in the southern part of the range.

Incubation Incubation begins when the 1st egg is laid. Both parents share in the 22-day incubation period. The asynchronous hatching may lead to a total of 5 weeks of incubation before the last laid egg hatches. The male often rests near the female while she is incubating.

Fledging At hatching, coots have seemingly oversize feet, and a black down with an exposed orange to red skin on the top of the head. The red bill shades distally to pink and has a black tip. There is a scatter of orange and yellow bristles on the neck. The dispersed hatching sequence allows the parents to produce a larger number of offspring while decreasing the intensity of parental feeding duties by distributing them over a longer time period. Hatchlings leave the nest within an hour of hatching and are soon able to dive and stay submerged for over 3 minutes. The chicks frequently return to the nest or nearby platforms for brooding and are fed for the first 2 weeks. They gradually learn to feed themselves and become independent, then fledge at about 10 weeks of age.

The legs are green at 1 year, yellow-green at 2, yellow at 3, and orange-red for birds 4 years or older. Chicks sometimes ride on adults' backs and remain in place even when the adults dive. Nesting success of coots 3 years or older may exceed 80% and is considerably higher than that of younger birds.

Age at First Breeding Coots are able to breed at the age of 1 year, with 58% of the yearlings nesting. Second-year coots nest 96% of the time, and all older coots nest annually unless injured or infirm. Young birds nest later in the season, lay fewer and smaller eggs, and fledge fewer young, which are smaller than average.

BEHAVIOR Social groups often congregate in large compact rafts in open water, but strident vocalizations and a large suite of aggressive displays are used to defend nearshore territories. Distress displays include inflation of the shield and erection of the plumage.

MIGRATION The fall migration is from late September to November. Adult males in the northern part of the range move south in the fall with the nonbreeding adults and are followed several weeks later by the females and juveniles. In the spring the northward migration begins in March, and most birds have reached their breeding grounds by the end of April.

PREDATORS Snakes, grackles, crows, mink, and raccoons take the eggs. Largemouth bass and snapping turtles take the chicks and rarely the adults. Bald Eagles, Great Horned Owls, Peregrine Falcons, and alligators take the adults.

LONGEVITY Banded birds have been recovered after 20 years.

CONSERVATION ISSUES Tens of thousands of coots are killed by Florida hunters every year, and the national harvest is almost a million, but a high reproductive rate seems to allow relative population stability.

NOTES The genus name has been explained as the Latin *fulica* (coot). The species name refers to the American origin of this species. The American Coot is also called mud hen, waterfowl, water hen, and splatterer in English; *focha americana* or *gallinazo americano* in Spanish; and *foulque américaine* in French.

SUGGESTED ADDITIONAL READING

Gullion, G.W. 1952. The displays and calls of the American Coot. *Wilson Bulletin,* 61:83–97.

Gullion, G.W. 1953. Territorial behavior in the American Coot. *Condor,* 55:169–186.

Sutter, G.C. and R.A. MacArthur. 1992. Development of thermoregulation in a precocial aquatic bird: The American Coot. *Comparataive Biochemistry Physiology,* 101: 533–543.

Common Moorhen
Gallinula chlorops | **Rallidae Gruiformes** | **p. 41**

DISTRIBUTION The genus is divided into 3 to 8 species by various authors and is found worldwide. The Common Moorhen has a patchy worldwide distribution except for Australia and has been divided into 11 geographic subspecies. The subspecies *G. c. cachinnans* breeds in the U.S. from the Great Lakes south through the Mississippi and Atlantic drainage, and in wetlands across the southern borders of Texas, New Mexico, Arizona, California, Central America, and the Caribbean.

FOOD AND FEEDING HABITS

Diet of the Common Moorhen is primarily shoots, rootlets, seeds, and leaves of various wetland plants such as duckweed, pondweed, rush, sedge, waterlilies, and many other incidental terrestrial and aquatic seeds and sprouts. Filamentous algae is grazed from the prop roots of red mangroves. A small percentage of the diet is animal matter made up of aquatic insects, fish, tadpoles, clams, and snails. Moorhens usually feed on the surface or by submerging the head, but they may dive when feeding if delectable morsels are otherwise out of reach. Terrestrial prey includes insects, spiders, and earthworms. They prefer waters protected from wind and wave action and especially that with emergent vegetation. Open grasslands, parks, and farmland may be grazed if wetland cover is nearby. They often flick the tail while feeding on land and bob the head in unison with swimming strokes.

REPRODUCTION Common Moorhens nest in vegetation near the shores of calm, protected water.

Seasonality Nesting is usually from April to July but may occur in any month that has salubrious weather. In Florida, eggs have been found as late as September, and young have been found as early as January. In cooler climates, nesting is often timed so that new growth of cattails is 0.5 to 1 m (20 to 40 in) tall.

Courtship The male Common Moorhen courts the female by swimming around her, giving his *tikka-tikka-tikka* mating call while arching the neck, opening the wings, and displaying the white feathers under the tail. He may face her while they bill-dip synchronously. Single females may approach a courting pair and attempt to displace the resident female by intimidation and/or overt fighting. The heavier female usually prevails and seeks to pair with a fat male who has enough energy reserves to perform primary incubation duties on multiple nesting attempts. The pair bond is signaled by preening each other and by reduction in courtship displays. After she accepts his advances they move off together to copulate in thick cover. Nest building begins after 3 or 4 days of this behavior. The pair bond is usually monogamous, but late in the season polyandrous trios may develop in which a female forms pair bonds with 2 males. Some pairs maintain relationships for several years, bowing and nibbling each other's plumage to maintain the pair bond throughout the year.

Territoriality After the pair bond is formed in courting flocks, pairs establish individual territories. In the breeding season they call from territories in mornings and evenings and in response to distant sounds such as gunshots or thunder. Charging attacks with or without beating wings are used to defend nesting and feeding territories of 200 or more sq m (240 sq yds). Feeding territories may be vigorously defended against other birds such as American Coots or Black-necked Stilts. A typical territory includes water and a strip of adjacent shoreline. Social rank order seems to be determined by the size of the frontal shield. Maintenance of year-round territory is common in warm climates, and migratory individuals often return to the same territory in subsequent years.

Nest and Nest Site The nest is initiated by the male and is usually constructed of interwoven stems near open water in a dense stand of reeds or rushes. The nest may be floating, suspended in emergent vegetation, on a platform of branches near the water, or in trees or bushes up to 8 m (26 ft) above water level. The nest is a platform of coarse vegetation about 27 cm (11 in) in diameter with a cup that is 5 cm (2 in) deep and lined with fine materials. Separate nests or platforms are sometimes constructed as locations to brood the young.

Eggs The slightly glossy eggs are olive buff irregularly marked with spots and blotches of olive drab and dark brown concentrated at the broad end. The eggs average 43 by 31 mm (1.7 by 1.2 in) with a weight of 25 g (0.9 oz). The average clutch size is 7 eggs and varies from 3 to 12 eggs laid at the rate of 1 per day. Experienced breeders begin nesting earlier than others and have larger clutches. Two broods per season are common, and 3 broods have been recorded. The 2nd clutch usually has fewer eggs and is laid about 4 weeks after the 1st clutch. Up to 4 replacement clutches may be laid after nest loss. Laying for replacement clutches begins about 9 days after nest loss.

Incubation Males incubate for 72% of the 21-day incubation period, which begins when the last egg is laid. Hatching is synchronous. Incubation begins about halfway through the laying period for 2nd and replacement clutches, but later eggs seem to develop faster, resulting in less of a spread of hatching time than the laying interval would suggest. Nest loss due to predators and flooding is quite high, but hatchlings usually have about a 90% survival rate.

Fledging The newly hatched chicks have a glossy black down on the upperparts except the beak, crown and wingtips, which are rose red and bare. Underparts are dull black. In begging, the red wingtips and crown are displayed to the parent before the parent feeds them; food is larvae of aquatic insects. Chicks are capable of leaving the nest and swimming shortly after hatching but usually remain in the nest for 1 or 2 days. They swim well by day 3 and are able to dive by day 8. The parents brood the chicks on old nests or specially built platforms for about 2 weeks in cold or wet weather. The chicks are able to feed themselves at 3 or 4 weeks, but the parents continue to provide supplemental food until the young fledge at about 7 weeks and become independent several weeks later. In surviving broods with more than 4 chicks, each parent may lead a part of the brood to different parts of the territory for feeding. Juveniles of the 1st brood will sometimes assist parents with nest maintenance, incubation, and feeding of subsequent broods. Most juveniles disperse from the territory by 10 weeks of age. The juvenile plumage is similar to that of the adult but has a lighter gray with white on the throat and underparts. Full adult plumage is attained at the first postnuptial molt at the age of 14 months.

Age at First Breeding Common Moorhens form pair bonds and breed at 1 year of age, but nest success of 1st-time breeders is quite low.

BEHAVIOR Common Moorhens often become very habituated to man in parks and other situations when not molested. When alarmed they often flick the expanded tail to show a flash of white. Outside the breeding season they often form amicable, loose feeding aggregations. Night roosts, often in trees overhanging water, are entered before full dark. They are often active and call on moonlit nights.

MIGRATION Northern populations move south to escape snow and ice, but more tropical populations are stable residents.

PREDATORS Eggs of Common Moorhens are taken by grackles, crows, raccoons, and night herons. Chicks are taken by raccoons, mink, hawks, alligators, snapping turtles, and largemouth bass.

LONGEVITY Common Moorhens have been recovered up to 11 years after banding.

CONSERVATION ISSUES Waterfront development continues to shrink available feeding and nesting habitat.

NOTES The genus name is Latin (little hen). The species name is from the Greek *khloros* (greenish) and *pous* (foot). This bird has also been placed in the genus *Fulica*. The common name "mud hen" is used for Common Moorhens as well as American Coots, both being dark birds of similar shape found in similar habitat. The Common Moorhen is also called chicken-foot coot, American gallinule, common gallinule, red-billed mud hen and water hen in English; *gallina de agua, gallineta común* or *gallareta pico rojo* in Spanish; and *poule d'eau* or *poule d'eau à cachet rouge* in French.

SUGGESTED ADDITIONAL READING

Bryan, D.C. 1981. Winter breeding of the Common Gallinule in the Florida Panhandle. *Florida Field Nat,* 9:8–9.

Petrie, M. 1983. Female moorhens compete for small fat males. *Science,* 220:413–415.

Siegfried, W.R. and P.G.H. Frost 1975. Continuous breeding and associated behavior in the moorhen *Gallinula chlorops. Ibis,* 117:102–109.

Black-bellied Plover
Pluvialis squatarola | **Charadriidae Charadriiformes** | **p. 42**

DISTRIBUTION This genus with 3 species is found worldwide along shorelines. The Black-bellied Plover breeds in the high arctic on the west and north coasts of Alaska, on many of the Canadian arctic islands and in the Old World Arctic from Finland to Siberia.

FOOD AND FEEDING HABITS

Typical feeding behavior is for a single bird to stand motionless on a beach, then run forward a short distance to pick a prey item or stand still for a few seconds before another short dash. Capture attempts vary from 3 to 15 per minute, with a success rate of about 2 prey per minute, depending on prey density and substrate. Feeding is primarily by sight of the prey or surface indications such as water flowing from worm holes or sand movements. They are active primarily by day but may feed on moonlit nights at the same rate as by day. Nocturnal feeding may allow exploitation of nocturnally active invertebrates such as polychaete worms. Feeding rate is reduced on nights with no moon. Feeding habitat is coastal beaches, estuaries, tidal flats, and salt marshes, but it may also be found on cultivated agricultural land and wet pastures. On the breeding grounds they prey primarily on insects and terrestrial invertebrates. On their winter range they eat worms, clams, mussels, crabs, shrimp, and amphi-pods. Sand and mud are often removed from prey by a shake in shallow water.

REPRODUCTION Black-bellied Plovers migrate to the high Arctic and tundra to breed in the very brief annual summer.

Seasonality The dates of nesting are quite variable depending both on latitude and the rate of snow melt. On the tundra, laying is usually complete in May. Most birds reach the high Arctic breeding grounds by early June and have nests with eggs by the middle of June.

Courtship The males arrive first on the breeding grounds to select territories. Over the territories they perform courtship flights composed of shallow wing strokes above the body leading to a jerky flight similar to that of a butterfly. The display call during flight is a *whee-li-ee*. After gliding to the ground with slightly upraised wings, the male approaches a female at a run with the body tilted forward and the head and neck extended. He then poses in a stance with head down and tail up. If the female finds him enticing, copulation often follows. The pair bond is seasonally monogamous and often continues in succeeding years.

Territoriality On both feeding and nesting territories, threats are often made by the resident bird, which assumes a forward-hunched posture with feathers ruffled, then runs at the intruder. Territorial displays disperse nesting pairs to 2 per square mile on territories that usually do not contact a neighbor's territory. Some individuals hold territories in the range of 0.4 ha (1 acre) on the wintering grounds and return to them in consecutive years.

Nest and Nest Site The nest is a 12 cm (5 in) scrape started by the male and deepened by the female. It is lined sparsely with lichens, pebbles, leaves, and twigs. It is placed on a dry site in exposed patches of gravel on ridges and hills within a few miles of rivers, deltas, or the sea. Territories are often reclaimed in subsequent years, with the new nest site within 50 m (164 ft) of the previous site.

Eggs The gray to buff eggs with darker spots and blotches measure 52 by 36 mm (2 by 1.4 in) and weigh about 35 g (1.2 oz). The typical clutch is 4 eggs laid at intervals of about 36 hours. Each egg represents about 16% of the weight of the female. Replacement clutches are laid when the eggs are lost in early incubation.

Incubation The male often begins incubation after the 1st egg is laid and is the sole incubator until the clutch is complete. The female is presumably absent while feeding to produce the clutch, which may exceed half of her body weight. Both sexes share the balance of the 27-day incubation period. Several distraction displays are used to lure predators away from the nest. A 65% nest success has been recorded.

Fledging The parents lead the newly hatched, yellow, pebble-patterned downy chicks away from the nest to feeding areas within 20 to 30 hours after hatching. The parents do not provide food for the chicks, which begin to feed on their own within 12 hours of hatching. Within a day the chicks may be more than 50 m (164 ft) from the nest but are still regularly brooded by the parents for 2 or 3 days. Both parents attend the newly hatched chicks for the first 2 weeks, then the females leave the brood and soon migrate south. The juveniles accompanied by the male parent seldom venture more than 1.5 km (0.9 mile) away from the nest site before fledging at about 23 days of age. Some males continue to lead the brood for several days after fledging. Juveniles fledge in middle August, and most adults have started south by the end of August with the juveniles following as much as a month later.

Age at First Breeding Black-bellied Plovers are capable of breeding in their 2nd year, but some do not nest until their 3rd year.

BEHAVIOR The individual distance for foraging is about 100 m (328 ft) and is attained by mutual avoidance rather than aggression. They gather in flocks of up to 400 when traveling, roosting, and migrating and may join mixed-species flocks of other shorebirds. Flight speed has been recorded at 38 to 80 kph (23.6 to 50 mph) with a flap rate of 3.5 to 4 flaps per second. They usually roost and sleep standing on 1 leg facing the wind. Dunlins, Red Knots and other shorebirds often feed near Black-bellied Plovers and use them as alert sentinels.

MIGRATION North American Black-bellied Plovers winter on the coasts of the southern U.S., the Caribbean, and Central and South America. European and Asian birds migrate south to Africa, southern coastal Asia, and northern Australia. The northward migration begins in the tropics in March and April, while only 20% of the birds have attained full breeding plumage. One-year-old birds often remain on the wintering grounds.

PREDATORS Skuas, jaegers, gulls, foxes, and weasels eat the eggs and small chicks. Peregrine Falcons and Snowy Owls take the adults.

LONGEVITY A Black-bellied Plover was recovered 20 years after banding.

CONSERVATION ISSUES Market hunters found them to be in high demand and severely reduced the population in the 19th century. The species has recovered with protection but shows a lack of genetic heterozygosity, which may be the result of the low surviving numbers.

NOTES The genus and common names are from the Latin *pluvia* (rain). The origin of the species name may be an ancient Venetian name for a plover. In the Old World this bird is known as the gray plover. In Caribbean English it is called lapwing (erroneously) and soldier bird, in Spanish *playero cabezón* and *chorlito gris,* and in French *pluvier argente* or *pluvier gris.*

SUGGESTED ADDITIONAL READING

Baker, M.C. 1974. Foraging behavior of Black-bellied Plovers (*Pluvialis squatarola*). *Ecology,* 55:162–167.

Paulson, D.R. 1995. Black-bellied Plover (*Pluvialis squatarola*) In A. Poole and F. Gill (eds.), *The Birds of North America. No. 186.* Philadelphia: The Birds of North America, Inc.

Townshend, D.J. 1985. Decisions for a lifetime: establishment of spatial defense and movement patterns by juvenile Grey Plovers (*Pluvialis squatarola*). *Journal of Animal Ecology,* 54:267–274.

Wilson's Plover
Charadrius wilsoni | **Charadriidae Charadriiformes** | **p. 43**

DISTRIBUTION This genus with 31 species is found worldwide along shorelines and on open lands. Wilson's Plover breeds from Baja, California, to Peru on the Pacific coast, and from Maryland through the Caribbean south to Guyana. Four subspecies have been described: *C. w. beldingi* is on the Pacific coast, and *C. w. cinnamominus* is resident along the north coast of South America. *C. w. wilsonius* on the Atlantic and Gulf coasts through Mexico is not rufous on the crown, but *C. w. rufinucha*, resident in the West Indies, is strongly rufous on the crown.

FOOD AND FEEDING HABITS

Feeding is along sandy beaches and mudflats, often near the mouths of streams. Hunting is mainly standing still until prey is sighted, then running quickly to catch it. They generally stay on the dry part of the beach and seldom wade in the surf or walk in soft mud. They feed at low tides at night. Fiddler crabs are a significant component of the diet, along with marine worms and other invertebrates as available.

REPRODUCTION Wilson's Plovers nest in loose colonies on soft, sandy beaches and islands.

Seasonality Most Wilson's Plovers are on their nesting grounds by April, with peak nesting in May and renesting in June.

Courtship Males initiate courtship by chasing other males away from the female and making preliminary nest scrapes in front of the females. The male displays by stamping his feet with lowered head, drooped wings, and spread depressed tail while he circles the female on the territory. After the pair bond is formed, the male mounts the female and grasps the nape of her neck. Mounting may last more than a minute, with the pair toppling on culmination.

Territoriality After the pair bond is formed, the male makes several nest scrapes on the breeding territory, from which the female chooses 1 in which to lay her eggs. Territories are usually less than 30 m (100 ft) in radius but may be as large as 91 m (300 ft). Agonistic displays directed at other males and females include fluffing and expanding the neck band and chasing the other bird on the ground at a running crouch.

Nest and Nest Site The nest site is in sand or gravel well above the high-tide line near a clump of vegetation of a windbreak such as a log or other lump of flotsam. Nests are often among or sometimes under overhanging, scattered vegetation. Plovers generally do not nest near thick vegetation. The nest may be lined with broken shells or other bits of locally collected debris.

Eggs The creamy buff-colored eggs, streaked and spotted with dark brown, measure 36 by 26 mm (1.4 by 1 in) and weigh about 12.4 g (0.4 oz). The normal clutch size is 3 with a range of 2 to 4.

Incubation Incubation begins after the clutch is complete. The female usually incubates by day and the male at night until the young hatch at about 24 days. Adults' departure from the nest when disturbed is by running rather than flying.

Fledging The buff-colored chicks with dark mottling above and white below are able to run and feed themselves when led away from the nest at a few hours to 1 day of age. Parents lead them to nearby feeding areas and accompany them for at least 3 weeks, when they are capable of flight.

Age at First Breeding This has not been determined.

BEHAVIOR Wilson's Plovers are often solitary when feeding. Injured-bird distraction displays, which include distress calls and flopping an extended wing, are given when a predator approaches the nest or the young brood.

MIGRATION Northern birds withdraw to warmer climates for the winter. Wilson's Plovers in warm climates do not seem to migrate.

PREDATORS Gulls, crows, grackles, foxes, coyotes, and raccoons sometimes take the eggs and small chicks.

LONGEVITY Maximum life span has not been determined.

CONSERVATION ISSUES Nesting habitat loss due to increasing public use of beaches is an increasing problem. The populations on the mid-Atlantic coast may benefit from the protection enjoyed by the federally threatened Piping Plover, which also nests on open beaches.

NOTES The genus name is from the Greek *kharadrios* (a ravine-dwelling bird). The species name honors Alexander Wilson, who collected the 1st described specimens. Wilson (1766–1813), a Scottish immigrant, became one of the fathers of American ornithology. His natural history observations and taxonomic work have survived the test of time much better than those of his rival, Audubon. He is also honored in the name of the *Wilson Bulletin,* one of the major American ornithological journals. Wilson's Plover has also been called thick-billed plover in English, *chorlitejo picogrueso* or *playero maratimo* in Spanish, and *pluvier de Wilson* in French. Compared with other plovers, the large, sturdy bill is probably a result of selection for a diet of fiddler crabs and not of great taxonomic significance.

SUGGESTED ADDITIONAL READING

Bergstrom, P.W. 1988. Breeding displays and vocalizations of Wilson's Plover. *Wilson Bulletin,* 100:36–49.

Morrier, A. and R. McNeil. 1991. Time activity budget of Wilson's and Semipalmated Plovers in a tropical environment. *Wilson Bulletin,* 103:598–620.

Thibault, M. and R. McNeil. 1994. Day/night variation in Habitat use by Wilson's Plovers in Northeastern Venezuela. *Wilson Bulletin,* 106:299–310.

Semipalmated Plover

Charadrius semipalmatus | Charadriidae Charadriiformes | p. 44

DISTRIBUTION This genus with 31 species is found worldwide along shorelines and on open lands. The very similar sister species, the Ringed Plover (*Charadrius hiaticula*), breeds in the Arctic of eastern Canada, Greenland, Europe, and Asia and winters in Africa. The Semipalmated Plover breeds in the tundra from Alaska along the north coast of North America east to Hudson Bay, Newfoundland, and Nova Scotia. The wintering grounds are on the coast from the southeast Atlantic coast of the U.S., the Gulf of Mexico through the West Indies, and Central America to Southern Chile and Argentina. Ringed Plovers are reported to interbreed with Semipalmated Plovers on Baffin Island where their breeding ranges overlap.

FOOD AND FEEDING HABITS

The Semipalmated Plover runs about the sand or mudflat with its head held high until it pecks at prey of small marine worms, crustaceans, and mollusks. They sometimes feed on worms and insects such as flies, mosquitoes, and grasshoppers in grasslands or recently cultivated fields.

REPRODUCTION
The Semipalmated Plover chooses dry sand or gravel substrate for a simple scrape nest in the New World Arctic.

Seasonality Nesting is limited by the spring thaw but is usually under way by late April or early May.

Courtship On the ground the male spreads and depresses the tail feathers, slightly opens the wings, and puffs the feathers while continuously calling. When the female first enters the territory, she is met with aggression, which declines as courtship proceeds. Pairs tend to stay together in subsequent seasons while both are alive.

Territoriality The male advertises the nesting territory by flying over it with a distinctive, slow-flap, butterfly-like flight.

Nest and Nest Site The nest site is a scrape located in full sun but often out of the wind on sand or gravel bars in rivers, pebbly coastal beaches, or gravely ridges with sparse vegetation overlooking water on the tundra. Land cleared by heavy equipment is often found acceptable. The nest is a scrape in the ground that may be enhanced by the addition of a few pebbles or other objects that enhance camouflage.

Eggs The olive or brown-buff eggs marked with dark-brown or black splotches are about 33 by 24 mm (1.3 by 0.94 in) with an individual weight of 9.6 g (0.3 oz) and a clutch size of 3 or 4.

Incubation The clutch is laid over a period of about a week, followed by an incubation period of 23 or 24 days. Incubation may begin before the clutch is complete, leading to the last egg's hatching as much as 30 hours after the balance of the clutch.

Fledging The chicks fledge at 3 to 4 weeks of age depending on food availability.

Age at First Breeding Most young breed at 1 year of age, but some remain on the wintering ground until their 2nd year.

BEHAVIOR They are often found in mixed flocks with other shorebirds, and at high tide often roost and sleep in dense flocks. They are normally alert and wary, but the flushing distance is surprisingly close. The flap rate on a flushed bird departing was recorded as 5.6 flaps per second.

MIGRATION The southward migration of adults begins as early as July, with the young traveling in August and September. Some (presumed young) individuals remain on the wintering grounds while the balance of the population travels north.

PREDATORS Foxes and weasels take the eggs and chicks.

LONGEVITY The oldest banded bird recovered was banded 8 years previously.

CONSERVATION ISSUES The population is recovering from the devastation caused by hunting in the late 19th century.

NOTES The genus is from the Greek *kharadrios*, a name for a nocturnal waterbird nesting in ravines. The species name is from Latin, referring to the semiwebbed toes. In English it is also called semipalmated ringed plover, in Spanish *chorlitejo semipalmado* or *playero acollarado,* and in French *pluvier semipalmé.* The ringed plover (*C. hiaticula),* which is very similar in appearance and habits, interbreeds with the Semipalmated Plover on Baffin Island. It also breeds on Greenland and from Scandinavia to Siberia but winters from the British Isles south to central and southern Africa.

SUGGESTED ADDITIONAL READING

Burton, J. and R. McNeil. 1976. Age determination of six species of North American Shorebirds. *Bird Banding,* 47:201–209.

Sutton, G.M. and D.F. Parmelee. 1955. The breeding of the Semipalmated Plover on Baffin Island. *Bird Banding,* 26:137–147.

Killdeer

Charadrius vociferus | **Charadriidae Charadriiformes** | **p. 45**

DISTRIBUTION This genus with 31 species is found worldwide along shorelines and open lands. The Killdeer breeds across North America, Central America, and the West Indies. Three races have been described: the largest, *C. v. vociferus,* breeds in every state of the U.S. and in Canada from British Columbia to James Bay and Nova Scotia. The smaller and grayer *C. v. ternominatus* is permanently resident in the West Indies, and *C. v. peruvianus,* with more distinctive rufous edges on the feathers, is found in coastal Peru and Chile.

FOOD AND FEEDING HABITS

Feeding areas are open wetlands or grassy habitat including gravel or sandy beaches, golf courses, cemeteries, pastures, tilled fields, and airport median strips. The usual feeding pattern is a search, run and peck, but foot pattering and chasing are also common. Killdeers are primarily insectivorous, with beetles making up the preponderance of the diet, but they are opportunistic and may prey almost exclusively on outbreaks of grasshoppers, weevils, small crabs, or swarms of postlarval frogs. The chicks are led to moist areas to feed for themselves.

REPRODUCTION Killdeers nest on open land, frequently near shallow water, and commonly produce 2 broods per season.

Seasonality The return to the northern breeding grounds begins in February and is complete by April. Chicks are all flying by July.

Courtship The aerial courtship includes hovering high in the air and a lower bouncy flight on stiff, slowly beating wings, which resembles the flight of a butterfly. The *vociferus* of the species name is well earned with the repeated calling of *killdeer* while in flight or on the nesting territory. It is not uncommon for pairs to reunite in subsequent breeding seasons.

Territoriality Shortly after arrival on the breeding grounds, the males disperse and announce their territories by standing on a prominence and repeatedly calling *di-yeet.* The male often circles the area, calling in flight. Creating nest scrapes and pseudoincubating begin as a part of pair bonding and are followed by copulation and use of 1 of the nest scrapes. The area near the nest is vigorously defended by both sexes, with the female expending more effort against other Killdeers, and the male expending more energy attacking or distracting predators. When chasing other Killdeers on the ground, Killdeers hold the body horizontal and fluff the back feathers. Nest densities may be as high as 3 pairs per ha (7.4 acres). The same nest territory is often used by males in succeeding years. Females changing mates usually join the new mate on his territory.

Nest and Nest Site The nest site is on soil soft enough for digging, free of vegetation, but with a reference object nearby. Small, flat, white stones are often used to line the nest. It is not unusual for a Killdeer to use the flat roofs of buildings as a predator-free nest site.

Eggs The buff eggs splotched with black and brown measure 3.8 by 2.7 cm (1.5 by 1.1 in). The 4-egg clutch is laid within an average of 3.7 days, with the laying interval usually increasing in length as the clutch is filled. It takes about a week to begin laying to replace a lost clutch. Killdeers commonly raise 2 broods in a single season.

Incubation The incubation period begins after the last egg is laid and is about 25 days, with both parents participating. Hatching of an individual egg is prolonged over a period of about 20 hours. When predators approach to within 15 to 30 m (50 to 100 ft) of a nest, the incubating adult surreptitiously leaves the nest, using a hunched-over run, and at some distance performs an extensive broken-wing distraction display by dragging a wing and appearing to struggle while calling continuously. The broken wing display may continue while the Killdeer lures a predator as far as 100 m (328 ft) from the nest. An incubating bird may lunge toward an approaching hooved mammal or run toward it with wings raised. In spite of the disproportionate size of the contenders, the intruder usually alters course to avoid the Killdeer and its nest.

Fledging The chicks leave the nest within a day or so to begin foraging. Chicks of roof-nesting adults must jump off the roof at 1 or 2 days of age or face death by starvation or dehydration. Chicks frequently die when jumping off roofs and landing on hard surfaces. Others die because they are unable to surmount parapets. Capture of chicks on flat roofs and release into nearby grassy areas greatly increases survival. On 2nd broods, the female often deserts the broods shortly after hatching, leaving the male to protect and brood the chicks. The 1st flight is at about 30 days of age, but they often remain with parents another 10 days.

Age at First Breeding Killdeers 1st breed at the age of 1 year.

BEHAVIOR Outside the breeding season, Killdeers are found solitarily or in loose aggregations from a few individuals to groups of 25. Flight speeds have been recorded up to 88 kph (55 mph).

MIGRATION Some birds lag behind in the southern migration until forced to move by freezing temperatures. The migrating North American race and the resident West Indian race mingle in the Caribbean in the winter.

PREDATORS Foxes, mink, weasels, mongooses, house cats, gulls, and grackles take the eggs. Predatory mammals take the chicks, and raptors catch the adults.

LONGEVITY The maximum age of a recovered banded bird was 11 years.

CONSERVATION ISSUES In the late 19th and early 20th centuries, Killdeer populations were reduced by market hunting. They are now probably the most abundant shorebird in North America.

NOTES The genus name is from the Greek *kharadrios*, a name used by Aristotle for a nocturnal waterbird nesting in ravines. The species name is from the Latin *vociferus* (vocal) in reference to its energetic and frequent calling. The most frequently used English common name is an onomatopoetic representation of its call. It is also called pasture bird and field plover in English. In Spanish it is called *playero gritón, chorilejo culirrojo* and *chorlitejo gritón,* and in French it is *pluvier kilder.*

SUGGESTED ADDITIONAL READING

Mundahl. J.T. 1982. Role specialization in the parental care and territorial behaviour of the Killdeer. *Wilson Bulletin,* 94:515–530.

Phillips, A.R. 1972. Sexual and agonistic behavior in the Killdeer. *Animal Behavior,* 20:1–9.

American Oystercatcher
Haematopus palliatus | Haematopodidae Charadriiformes | p. 46

DISTRIBUTION The published taxonomy of oystercatchers is inconsistent. This genus with 4 to 11 species is found worldwide. The American Oystercatcher has been divided into several races. The western race breeds from Baja, California, south through Central America. The eastern race *(H. p. palliatus)* breeds from Massachusetts south to Florida, along the coast of the Gulf of Mexico, and in the Caribbean. Seasonally they are found as far south as Chile and Argentina.

FOOD AND FEEDING HABITS

The American Oystercatcher specializes in feeding on marine bivalves and other mollusks found in the intertidal zone. Oysters, clams, and mussels are opened with a quick stab that severs the muscles between the partially open shells. Prey may be removed to a spot away from the water while a hole is hammered into the shell. In the Caribbean, large sturdy snails, locally called whelks, are hammered open and consumed. Limpets are pried from rocky surfaces. Many species of snails, sea urchins, starfish, and crabs are also regularly eaten. Feeding is commonly in the lower part of the tidal cycle, and the bird roosts nearby at high tide. Clams and worms may be located visually or by probing into mudflats. When marine worms are abundant they may make up a significant part of the diet. Marine worms grasped while probing may be extracted from the mud with a twisting motion generated by the bird's walking in a circle around the burrow. Oystercatchers are rarely seen away from the coast.

REPRODUCTION American Oystercatchers breed only on marine coasts. **Seasonality** The females arrive on the breeding grounds and may take up territories as much as 3 weeks before the males arrive. Eggs are laid over a 1-day period that may begin from early April to the end of June. In the Caribbean, nesting is in May or June.

Courtship Two birds walk in parallel giving single pipe calls, then stretch forward and down. As courtship proceeds, the birds run together calling more loudly, then fly in parallel with more vocalizations. American Oystercatchers usually form long-term pair bonds that last as long as both birds live, but divorce and bonding with a new mate along with polygamy have been observed. One male and 2 females may nest communally.

Territoriality The territory is formed soon after the birds arrive on the breeding grounds. Pairs that stay together usually nest in the same territory in subsequent years. On small islands in the Caribbean it appears that territories are maintained all year. On islands less than 2 ha (5 acres) in size with rocky shorelines, pairs seem to claim the entire island as feeding and nesting territory. Nest density has been observed from 0.7 to 13 pairs per ha (0.3 to 5 pairs per acre). Feeding territories at some distance from the breeding territory may be defended. Oystercatchers nest in mixed-species colonies with Least Terns, Common Terns, and Black Skimmers, but not gulls.

Nest and Nest Site The nest is a simple scrape in the sand or gravel, sometimes lined or edged with shells, pebbles, or seaweed. Multiple scrapes in a sand, shell, or gravel substrate are completed before 1 is chosen to receive the eggs. In the northern part of the range the birds often nest on islands surrounded by mudflats or marsh grass. They may also nest on beaches or well above water level on dunes. Dredge spoil islands with open sand or gravel substrates are particularly favored.

Eggs The buff-gray, brown-speckled eggs measure 57 by 39.5 mm (2.2 by 1.6 in). Eggs vary considerably in color and pattern, but those of individual females are quite consistent. The clutch size averages slightly less than 3 eggs per nest. Replacement eggs for lost clutches are generally laid within 2 weeks of the loss.

Incubation The incubation period is about 27 days and begins after the 2nd egg is laid, with the first 2 eggs hatching almost synchronously and the 3rd about a day later. Replacement clutches may be repeated several times if nests are destroyed or the chicks eaten by predators.

Fledging The drab gray-brown chicks with black stripes and speckles are precocious and leave the nest within a few hours of hatching. The downy chicks threatened by predators may swim on the surface by paddling the feet, or dive for short distances using the wings as propulsion. At 4 weeks of age the weight and body measurements equal those of adults. At 5 weeks the typical bill begins to be evident. The parents spend 24% of the time during the 35-day chick-rearing period searching for food. After fledging, the parents provide supplemental food to the flying juveniles for a month or more while they learn to feed themselves. Young birds often accompany parents on the wintering ground and regularly steal food from foraging adults.

Age at First Breeding Two-year-old American Oystercatchers court, pair, show territoriality, and dig nest scrapes but do not breed. It is assumed that first breeding occurs at 3 or 4 years of age. They usually do not return to their natal location to breed.

BEHAVIOR Oystercatchers prefer to walk or run and seldom take flight unless disturbed by an intruder. They sleep with the bill tucked into the feathers of the back and may stand on 1 or both legs or sit.

MIGRATION Oystercatchers in the northern part of their range migrate south in the winter to avoid freezing conditions. In the winter, the American Oystercatchers from Virginia to Florida are a mixed population of residents and migrants that form compact roosting flocks at high tide before dispersing to feed as the tide drops.

PREDATORS The adults are preyed upon by owls, Peregrine Falcons, dogs, cats, foxes, mink, skunks, and weasels. The eggs are eaten by gulls, crows, night herons, rats, skunks, raccoons, and mink. A variety of distraction displays such as crippled bird and mock brooding are used to lure predators away from eggs or chicks. Nest loss due to the flooding of storms is common.

LONGEVITY An American Oystercatcher banded as an adult was still alive at a minimum age of 17 years.

CONSERVATION ISSUES The population declined in the 19th century when American Oystercatchers regularly appeared in markets, and the eggs have been regularly collected as human food. Since the Migratory Bird Treaty Act of 1918 the direct consumption has declined, allowing a population recovery. The present threat to the species is loss of feeding habitat due to coastal development and recreational use. Increased use of beaches by humans and dogs continues to adversely affect nesting areas.

NOTES The genus name is from the Greek *haima* (blood) and *pous* (foot). The species name is from Latin *palliatus* (cloaked). Other English common names are whelk-cracker, red-bill, pied oystercatcher, and common oystercatcher. In Spanish they are *ostrero* or *caracolero* and in French *l'huotrier-pie* or *l'huotrier d'Amérique*. Oystercatchers have had their beaks caught by bivalves, which hold them until they drown with a rising tide.

SUGGESTED ADDITIONAL READING

Nol, E., A.J. Baker and M.D. Cadman. 1984. Clutch initiation dates, clutch size and egg size of the American Oystercatcher in Virginia. *Auk,* 101:855–867.

Tuckwell, J. and E. Nol. 1997. Foraging behavior of American Oystercatchers in response to declining prey densities. *Canadian Journal of Zoology,* 75:170–181.

Tuckwell, J. and E. Nol. 1997. Intra- and inter-specific interactions of foraging American Oystercatcher on an oyster bed. *Canadian Journal of Zoology,* 75:182–187.

Black-necked Stilt
Himantopus mexicanus | Recurvirostridae Charadriiformes | p. 47

DISTRIBUTION This genus with as many as 8 geographic species is found worldwide on tropical and subtropical shores. The primary difference in the species is variations in the black-and-white pattern. Some authors have combined all the members of the genus into a single, highly variable species, *H. himantopus,* in which case the birds in Florida and the Caribbean are called *H. h. mexicanus.* The Black-necked Stilt has been recorded in most of Florida, with higher concentrations near Lake Okeechobee and the Everglades. It is found on all the major Caribbean islands.

FOOD AND FEEDING HABITS

Black-necked Stilts are found on tidal flats, pools, grassy marshes, and on shallow fresh, alkaline or saline lakes. They pick food from the surface of the mud or water, probe in mud or chase prey in shallow water. They may scythe the beak from side to side in muddy water or soft mud when feeding. They are carnivorous and eat a broad variety of invertebrates, including predaceous diving beetles, dragonflies, mayflies, earwigs, caddisflies, waterbugs, brine shrimp, brine flies, aquatic worms, clams, snails, crabs, and various aquatic crustaceans. They also eat small vertebrates such as minnows and tadpoles. The muscles of the jaws allow very rapid closing when prey is contacted. Adults aggressively defend feeding territories when accompanied by juveniles.

REPRODUCTION This very cosmopolitan bird breeds in a great variety of habitats adjacent to suitable feeding grounds.

Seasonality The northern breeding populations migrate south to the nesting areas in March and have nests by the end of April. They travel north from August to November. Stilts breeding in Florida and the Caribbean are present in all months of the year.

Courtship No nest preparation ceremonies have been recorded for stilts. Both sexes may show ritualized pecking movements followed by brief preening of the breast feathers before the female assumes a horizontal invitational posture. The very brief copulation is followed by the male standing by the female with fluffed neck feathers and crossing his bill over hers.

Territoriality Stilts usually nest in loose colonies of as many as 50 pairs but may nest as a solitary pair. In one carefully studied colony, the nests were regularly arranged with an average distance of 22 m (72 ft) between nest sites. Mixed colonies may be formed with gulls, terns, and waterfowl.

Nest and Nest Site The nest is usually a depression scraped in the sand or gravel but sometimes is hidden under a clump of vegetation. The nest may be lined with pebbles, shells, or bits of vegetation, supplemented by materials the departing bird tosses over its back as part of the nest-relief behavior. The nesting habitat is along grassy shorelines of fresh or brackish pools, coastal lagoons, flooded agricultural fields, or on the shores of hypersaline ponds and lakes. The nest sites are usually in the open to allow visibility in all directions. Stilts commonly return to the same nest site in subsequent years.

Eggs The eggs are buff to olive brown and spotted or blotched with dark brown. The eggs measure 44 by 31 mm (1.7 by 1.2 in) and weigh about 23 g (0.8 oz). The usual clutch is 4 eggs with 3- or 5-egg clutches occurring in less than 10% of nests. Replacement clutches are laid after nest loss.

Incubation Eggs are deposited on a daily basis with an occasional skipped day. Incubation is by both parents and begins after the full clutch is deposited. Hatching is synchronous after about 24 days of incubation.

Fledging The downy young have a pebblelike pattern of black spots on their back and remain on the nest after hatching for up to 24 hours. Fledging is at about 28 days, and they remain dependent on their parents for a time as they share their parents' feeding territory. Chicks often feed on the young of flies and beetles. Stilts can usually fly by the age of 30 days, but some may require another week to master the art. Juvenile stilts make considerably more intentional movements but have a lower feeding success rate than adults do.

Age at First Breeding Most stilts breed for the first time at age 2, but successful nesting at 1 year of age has been reported. Young birds often return to their hatching site when they are old enough to breed.

BEHAVIOR The long strides suggest total stability when walking or running. The gait is decisive and graceful, with the feet firmly planted, and there is no indication of wobble from the long legs. When approached, they bob their head and call before taking flight. After landing, they stretch their wings above the body before closing them neatly over their back. Displays include a tall, slim posture as a pecking threat. A flight pattern with head and legs held below the level of the body is used as a threat display both to other stilts and to territorial intruders. Stilts acclimate easily to regular nonthreatening human presence. When eggs or young are approached, the adults perform feigned injury distraction displays. Broken-wing and broken-leg acts are followed by crouching and distressed flapping. Stilts also distract predators by feigning incubation at some distance from the nest.

MIGRATION The journey north to the breeding grounds begins in March or April. Banding studies are needed to confirm that the seeming winter-resident stilts on Caribbean islands are the same ones breeding on these islands. For northern breeders, the journey south begins in late July.

PREDATORS Foxes, raccoons, mink, and crows take untended eggs and young. Hawks sometimes take adults.

LONGEVITY One Black-necked Stilt lived more than 19 years in a zoo.

CONSERVATION ISSUES Stilts are susceptible to secondary poisoning when eating prey disabled by pesticides. They may be among the victims of avian botulism outbreaks.

NOTES The genus name is from the Greek *himantos,* meaning "strap" or "thong," and *pous,* meaning "foot," in reference to the legs, which are as long and thin as a leather thong. The species name refers to the Mexican origin of the first individuals of this species described. The common name comes from the Scandinavian *stilta* or *sylta*, describing wooden poles on which to stand. Other common names are longshank, redshank, soldier, yelper, and telltale. In Spanish it is called *cigüeñela, viuda,* and *arcagüete,* and in French *échasse blanche,* and *pigeon d'étang.*

SUGGESTED ADDITIONAL READING

Cullen, S.A. 1994. Black-necked Stilt foraging site selection and behavior in Puerto Rico. *Wilson Bulletin,* 106:508–513.

Hamilton, R.C. 1975. Comparative behavior of the American Avocet and the Black-necked Stilt (*Recurvirostridae*). *AOU Monograph 17,* NY: American Ornithologists Union.

James, R.A. Jr. 1995. Natal philopatry, site tenacity and age of first breeding of the Black-necked Stilt. *J Field Ornithol,* 66:107–111.

American Avocet
Recurvirostra americana | Recurvirostridae Charadriiformes | p. 48

DISTRIBUTION This genus with 4 species is widespread. *R. andina* is found at high elevations in the central Andes from northern Chile and southern Peru to Argentina and Bolivia. *R. novaehollandiae* lives in Australia, while *R. avocetta* has a range extending from Sweden and the coasts of Africa through central Asia to Mongolia and the coast of eastern Asia. The North American *R. americana* breeds in an area ranging from the prairie provinces of Canada south to California and New Mexico, with a few individuals recorded nesting on the Atlantic coast of the U.S. The winter range includes southern California, both coasts of Mexico, the Gulf Coast states, and the Antilles.

FOOD AND FEEDING HABITS
The characteristic feeding habit is a scythelike swinging of the partially open bill from side to side with a rapid closing when food is contacted. Avocets scythe in mud but not in sand. The head and neck may be totally submerged during feeding sweeps in water to about 20 cm (8 in). They may swim in somewhat deeper water while continuing to feed. Avocets sometimes feed in a moving line, with each bird gaining the prey startled into its direction by the birds on the right and left. Individual distance in these feeding lines may be less than 1 body width. Feeding habitat includes almost any shallow muddy area such as salt marshes, mudflats adjacent to mangroves, and various man-made impoundments. They feed in fresh water, inland saline ecosystems, tidal ecosys-

tems, and on land. Prey is a variety of insects, small animals, and seeds of wetland plants. Intestinal worms parasitizing avocets feeding in ephemeral waters are usually avocet specialists, but avocets feeding in permanent water also harbor worms generally found in Lesser Scaup. The duck parasites compete with the avocet parasites for space on the intestinal walls.

REPRODUCTION
Breeding is in open groups that may aggregate to form large colonies on the shores of saline and often alkaline lakes or coastal estuaries.

Seasonality The American Avocets arrive at the northern breeding grounds in April, and they usually lay their eggs by mid-May. With renesting and late nesting, some nests are initiated as late as July.

Courtship Pairing seems to take place on the wintering grounds and during migration as flocks separate into pairs upon reaching the breeding grounds. The courtship includes elegant dances with bowing and side-to-side tipping with wings extended. Studies of banded birds indicate that the pair bond may last for more than 1 season.

Territoriality Early in the breeding season before egg laying, the territory is based on a feeding area. A second territory used for nesting is often established a short distance away from the feeding territory. The individual nests in typical open colonies may be less than a meter (3 ft) to over 100 m (328 ft) apart. The spacing of nests, due to territorial defense, places them far enough apart to enhance concealment but close enough to enjoy the advantages of group predator defense. After the chicks become fully mobile, the defended territory centers on the location of the chicks.

Nest and Nest Site The nest is a simple scrape, typically 20 cm (8 in) in diameter and 2 cm (1 in) deep, made by resting on the breast and kicking out the soil with the feet. The nest may be unlined or lined with vegetation gathered by both members of the pair within a few meters of the nest site. The birds pick up nesting material with their bills and toss it laterally in the direction of the nest. In areas subject to flooding, the nest may be built up to a height of 38 cm (15 in). Avocets prefer to nest in areas with sparse vegetation on islands or dikes. Most nests are within 5 m (16 ft) of water. They avoid islands used for nesting by American White Pelicans or gulls but may form mixed-species colonies with Common and Forster's Terns.

Eggs The olive-buff, pear-shaped eggs, profusely marked with dark-brown or drab spots, measure about 34 by 50 mm (1.3 by 2.0 in) and weigh about 32 g (1.1 oz). The clutch of 4 eggs is laid over 4 or 5 days and fits together in the nest very snugly when the small end of each egg points inward.

Incubation Both sexes incubate, and nest relief takes place about once an hour. Incubation begins after the next-to-last egg is laid, so most of the eggs hatch after 24 days. In cool weather, incubation may begin when the 1st egg is laid, and in hot weather the adults may cool the eggs by shading them. The eggs may be pipped (a small hole is pecked in the egg by the chick) as long as 4 or 5 days before

hatching. Hatching is usually complete within a day or so, but if some eggs are late, 1 parent leads the chicks to feeding areas while the other parent continues to incubate. Incubation for infertile eggs often persists for 40 days after the clutch has been initiated. Avocets will return a displaced egg to the nest by straddling and rolling it. Renesting is prompt after desertion or loss of eggs.

Fledging The downy young are dry and able to leave the nest within an hour or so but usually stay in or near the nest for a day unless disturbed. When first mobile, the hatchlings are light brown with black stripes through the eye and on the body. The parents do not feed the young but are very attentive toward them and aggressive toward the presence of other animals, including avocets. The young preen and bathe after the 1st week. Downy young readily swim from nesting areas to nearby mainland feeding areas. Chicks can dive and swim underwater to escape predators. On land, chicks hide from predators by lying flat in cover, but after 3 weeks they run when disturbed. Young separated from their parents are often attacked by other avocets. The first flight is at 4 or 5 weeks of age, at which time the young birds join large postbreeding flocks.

Age at First Breeding Avocets molt into breeding plumage in their 1st winter but do not usually nest until the age of 2.

BEHAVIOR The American Avocet is gregarious and is often seen feeding and resting in flocks of up to several hundred individuals. They often rest standing on 1 leg with the bill tucked under the feathers of the back. Partially webbed feet allow them to swim across stretches of deep waters encountered while foraging. The response to hawks, gulls, and other avian predators flying over group nesting areas is loud calling followed by mobbing (a group attack). In response to terrestrial predators, the nesting group moves away from the nests and gives extensive distraction displays on the ground.

MIGRATION The spring and fall migrations are gradual and dispersed over several months, with stopovers at intermediate feeding sites. Most of the northbound birds migrate from March to May, with the southbound journey in the fall from July to October. Some nonbreeding 1-year-old birds do not migrate to the breeding grounds.

PREDATORS The adults are taken by falcons, owls, and foxes. The eggs are taken by gulls, raccoons, foxes, and snakes.

LONGEVITY Banded American Avocets have been recovered 9 years after banding, but the potential longevity probably approaches that of the Pied Avocet, which can live to 24 years.

CONSERVATION ISSUES Hunting and trapping in the 19th century resulted in the extirpation of the East Coast breeding population and severe reduction of the Western population. Loss of wetland habitat in the western U.S. due to human uses for land and

water is the greatest present threat to populations. Irrigation drainwater contaminated with selenium compounds seems to produce embryo deformities and reduce hatchability of eggs. Avocets are sometimes the victims of outbreaks of botulism.

NOTES The genus name is from the Latin *recurvus,* meaning "turned up" or "bent," and *rostrum,* meaning "beak" or "bill." The species name refers to the American origin. The common name "avocet" is derived from the Italian *avocetta.* Other English common names are blue stocking, blue shanks, and Irish snipe. It is known in Spanish as *avoceta Americana,* and in French as *avocette Américaine.*

SUGGESTED ADDITIONAL READING

Burger, J. and M. Gochfeld. 1986. Age differences in foraging efficiency of American Avocets, *Recurvirostra americana. Bird Behavior,* 6:66–71.

Hamilton, R.C. 1975. Comparative behavior of the American Avocet and the Black-necked Stilt *(Recurvirostridae). AOU Monograph 17.* NY: American Ornithologist's Union.

Robinson, J.A., L.W. Oring, J.P. Skorupa and R. Boettcher. 1997. American Avocet *(Recurvirostra americana).* In A. Poole and F. Gill (eds.), *The Birds of North America. No. 275.* Philadelphia: The Birds of North America, Inc.

Greater Yellowlegs

Tringa melanoleuca | Scolopacidae Charadriiformes | p.49

DISTRIBUTION This genus with about a dozen species is found virtually worldwide. Breeding is in or near the Arctic, and migrations may extend across the equator, sometimes to temperate regions of the southern hemisphere. This species breeds from British Columbia and Lake Iliamna in Alaska across Canada to Newfoundland. It winters on both coasts of the U.S. and south through the Caribbean and Central and South America to Tierra del Fuego.

FOOD AND FEEDING HABITS

They may rush about in chest-deep water chasing fish and small invertebrates. They may form groups feeding in a line and chasing small fish into a declivity in the shoreline for easy capture. They skim the surface with side-to-side sweeps of the bill for minnows, water boatman, and surface-dwelling water beetles. They feed by scything in open water on moonlit nights. They probe in the mud for worms and crustaceans and run about on land catching ants, flies, and grasshoppers. On the wintering grounds they use a variety of wetlands including tidal flats, littoral zones of estuaries, and ponds with emergent vegetation.

REPRODUCTION These birds nest in muskeg country far from human disturbance.

Seasonality Nesting begins in early May.

Courtship The courtship display is an undulating flight with a yodeling *toowhee* call. The flight path is a continuous back-and-forth over the territory for periods of as long as 15 minutes.

Territoriality Pairs disperse widely on the breeding grounds, with a density of only a half dozen pairs per square mile. Feeding territories are sometimes defended.

Nest and Nest Site The muskeg nesting habitat is wet with many ponds and swamps, but the nest is a very well hidden, unlined depression on the ground. Usually it is beside a log or branch with overhanging vegetation. The nests are on dry soil, often in open woodlands with sparse undergrowth around marshy ponds but may be as far as a mile from open water.

Eggs The egg is deep buff and spotted with dark brown and lavender. The markings are thicker at the large end of the egg. Eggs measure about 33 by 49 mm (1.3 by 2 in) and weigh about 28 g (1 oz).

Incubation The clutch of 4 eggs is incubated for 23 days. If the 1st clutch is lost, a 2nd or even 3rd nesting attempt will be made nearby.

Fledging The downy young are variably striped with dark-brown markings along the back and sides. They are led to the nearest water soon after hatching and are tended by both parents.

Age at First Breeding The minimum breeding age has not been determined but is estimated to be 1 year.

BEHAVIOR This species is very wary and is often the 1st of a group of shorebirds to flush. They may form loose flocks of up to a dozen individuals but more commonly forage alone

and may defend feeding territories. In areas of concentrated prey, large groups may join egrets and ibises in a feeding frenzy. They take flight over small areas of deeper water rather than swim to reach foraging areas on the other side.

MIGRATION Departure from the wintering grounds is in March, and most of the breeding range is occupied by April. The population begins to leave the breeding grounds in mid-July. Some birds may linger in the northern part of their range until forced south by freezing temperatures.

PREDATORS Foxes, mink, and weasels take a heavy toll on both eggs and chicks. Hawks are the primary predators of adults.

CONSERVATION ISSUES Many Greater Yellowlegs were shot by hunters at the turn of the century because they were easily lured within range by decoys and imitations of their calls. They were not hunted with such persistence as certain other shorebirds because their flesh did not rank as high for the table. Populations have recovered significantly with protection by the Migratory Bird Treaty Act. Today the yellowlegs is one of the most commonly seen shorebirds on North American coasts.

NOTES The genus name is from the Greek *tryngas* applied by Aristotle to a waterbird with a white rump. The species name is from the Greek *melanos* (black) and *leukos* (white), referring to the black and white spots on the bird. This bird has also been placed in the genera *Totanus* and *Scolopax*. The British common name "tattler" refers to the frequent loud calls given when an intruder is approaching. Other common names include greater yellowshank, big yellow-legged plover, and big cucu in English; *tigüi-tigüi grande*, *archibebe patigualdo grande* or *archibebe patiamarillo* in Spanish; and *chevalier criard á pattes jaunes* and *grand chevalier* in French.

SUGGESTED ADDITIONAL READING

Elphick, C.S. and T.L. Tibbitts. 1998. Greater Yellowlegs *(Tringa melanoleuca)*. In A. Poole and F. Gill (eds.), *The Birds of North America. No. 355.* Philadelphia: The Birds of North America, Inc.

Wilds, C. 1982. Separating the Yellowlegs. *Birding,* 14:172–178.

Zusi, R.L. 1968. "Ploughing" for fish by the Greater Yellowlegs. Wilson Bulletin. 80:491–492.

Lesser Yellowlegs
Tringa flavipes | Scolopacidae Charadriiformes | p. 50

DISTRIBUTION This genus with about a dozen species is found virtually worldwide. Breeding is in or near the Arctic, and migrations may extend across the equator, sometimes to temperate regions of the southern hemisphere. The Lesser Yellowlegs breeds from western Alaska across Canada to the Hudson Bay. It winters on both coasts of the U.S. from California and South Carolina south through the Caribbean, and in Central and South America to Tierra del Fuego. They are found as vagrants from Scandinavia to Africa and east to Japan, and more rarely on Pacific Islands.

FOOD AND FEEDING HABITS
Lesser Yellowlegs forage at exposed mudflats of coastal estuaries and lagoons behind barrier islands, freshwater marshes and salt marshes with emergent vegetation, temporarily flooded grassland, inundated farmland, hypersaline ponds and lakes, mangrove fringes, or on almost any other muddy area. They often feed in flocks, moving about with an elegant, high-stepping gait, usually delicately picking visible prey from the surface rather than probing. They may probe or swing the bill laterally in soft mud or pick insects off vegetation. Pecks are directed forward at about a 25° angle above the substrate. They typically move with a rapid but decisive pace and rarely dash about except when chasing insects on land. They may feed at night using a tactile sweeping technique. Lesser Yellowlegs usually feed in water less than 3 cm (1.3 in) deep, but they may wade in water up to their breast feathers and may feed while swimming. They swim across small areas of deeper water to reach nearby foraging areas. The diet includes the larvae and adults of terrestrial and aquatic insects, spiders, snails, worms, fish, and crustaceans. Feeding territories are sometimes defended on the winter range.

REPRODUCTION Lesser Yellowlegs prefer to nest on hills and ridges of burned-over woodlands (often with early 2nd-growth trees) of the Canadian muskeg country.
Seasonality Most breeding birds arrive on the nesting areas by late April and have nests by May or June and independent chicks by August.
Courtship The undulating aerial courtship display is a prolonged series of flapping and gliding flights over the nesting territory. The flights are usually accompanied by an almost continuous, yodeling *pell-e-wee*. The call may also be given from an exposed perch on a stump, rock, or treetop. When landing after a display they often stretch the wings upward. Copulation follows a chase by the male and often takes place on the stump of a dead tree. This species is believed to be monogamous within a single breeding season, but the males reinforce this with diligent mate guarding during courtship and egg laying.
Territoriality They tend to nest in loose colonies with a density of 1 pair per 10 ha (25 acres) or fewer. During migration and wintering, many individuals defend feeding territories of 0.1 to 0.5 ha (0.25 to 1.25 acres) or

areas along a shoreline of up to 100 m (328 ft).

Nest and Nest Site The nest is a scraped depression in the soil on a ridge in an area of charred stumps and trunks, or in clearings in open woodland with open undergrowth. It is often placed near a stump, under a tuft of overhanging grass, or under an overhanging shrub. The bird on the nest blends remarkably with the dead wood and is almost impossible to see.

Eggs The eggs are buff and usually boldly splashed with dark brown or lavender. The average egg measures 49 by 29 mm (1.9 by 1.1 in) and weighs about 18 g (0.6 oz). The usual clutch is 4 with a range of 3 to 5. A clutch of eggs approximates the weight of the laying female. Renesting after loss of eggs is implied by late season nests but has not been documented.

Incubation One egg per day is laid, and both parents begin incubation after the last egg in the clutch is deposited. The young hatch synchronously after 22 or 23 days of incubation. They sit tight when incubating and usually do not flush until a predator is closer than a meter (3 ft).

Fledging The downy young are light gray below and variably striped with dark-brown markings along the back and sides. They are able to leave the nest within a few hours of nesting. Both parents initially participate in caring for the chicks and leading them to feeding sites, but females generally depart the breeding grounds before the chicks fledge. Chicks have been reported as fledging at 20 to 25 days after hatching.

Age at First Breeding Some yearlings return to the breeding grounds and have been reported to be breeding. A greater proportion are 2 years old or older when returning to breed.

BEHAVIOR The Lesser Yellowlegs is often more tame and approachable than the Greater Yellowlegs. They are readily attracted to a whistled imitation of their call. Flight speed has been recorded at 64 kph (40 mph) to 75 kph (47 mph). They often sleep while standing on 1 leg.

MIGRATION The migration north begins in March, with most of the population arriving on the breeding grounds by May. Nonbreeders often stay on the wintering grounds over the summer. Southbound, they begin to leave the breeding grounds by early July, and some arrive in South America by late August. Some adults and most immatures tarry and move south a month later, while some do not migrate until freeze-up forces them to move in October.

PREDATORS Foxes, coyotes, mink, weasels, ravens, gulls, and magpies eat the eggs and chicks. Hawks and owls take the adults.

LONGEVITY Recoveries of banded birds indicate a minimum longevity in the wild of 5 years 11 months.

CONSERVATION ISSUES These birds were heavily hunted for food and sport around 1900 and paid heavily for their habit of flying back and forth and hovering near a downed individual. With protection, populations are now recovering, and the world population is estimated to be about 500,000.

NOTES The genus name is from the Greek *tryngas,* applied by Aristotle to a thrush-sized waterbird with a white rump. The species name is from the Latin *flavus* (yellow) and *pes* (foot). This bird has also been placed in the genera *Scolopax* and *Totanus.* In Europe, the common name "tattler" refers to the frequent loud calls given by this genus when an intruder is approaching. Other English common names include common yellowlegs, little tell-tale, lesser yellowshanks, yellow-legged plover, and little stonebird. They are called *archibebe patigualdo chico, archibebe patiamarillo menor* or *playero guineilla pequeña* in Spanish, and *petit chevalier à pattes jaunes* in French.

SUGGESTED ADDITIONAL READING

Skagen, S.K. and F.L. Knopf. 1994. Migrating shorebirds and habitat dynamics at a prairie wetland complex. *Wilson Bulletin,* 106:91–95.

Tibbitts, T.L and W. Moskoff. 1999. Lesser Yellowlegs *(Tringa flavipes).* In A. Poole and F. Gill (eds.), *The Birds of North America. No. 427.* Philadelphia: The Birds of North America, Inc.

Wilds, C. 1982. Separating the Yellowlegs. *Birding,* 14:72–178.

Willet

Catoptrophorous semipalmatus | Scolopacidae Charadriiformes | p. 51

DISTRIBUTION This genus with a single species has a western race, *C. s. inornatus*, that breeds in the central prairies from Manitoba and the Dakotas west to the Rocky Mountains and winters on the Pacific coast from California to Peru, with a few individuals regularly moving to the Gulf and Atlantic coasts. An eastern race, *C. s. semipalmatus*, inhabits the Atlantic and Gulf of Mexico coasts of the U.S. and the Caribbean year-round. The birds breeding in the northernmost part of that range drift south to escape frozen coastlines.

FOOD AND FEEDING HABITS

They are found feeding on salt marsh mudflats, sandbars, oysterbeds, sandy beaches, and rocky shores. Feeding and resting is solitary, in small groups, or in flocks in excess of 25. They also feed in freshwater habitats, in marshes, and along the shores of lakes and reservoirs. They walk steadily along, pecking individual items and probing when the substrate allows. The typical prey is small clams and snails, marine worms, amphipods, aquatic insects, crabs, and tiny fish, which the Willets locate visually and by probing. They take larger prey such as fiddler crabs, which are often dismembered before consumption. They may wade belly deep in the water when stalking small fish. Beetles, flies, and other terrestrial arthropods may be taken from temporarily flooded pastures. They may actively feed at night when food resources are limited and they can escape piracy from gulls.

REPRODUCTION The eastern race breeds along the coast on sandy islands with thick grass, on the upper levels of beaches and dunes, and under shrubs behind salt marshes. They show a preference for spoil piles left from mosquito ditching in meadows of salt marsh grass. The western race nests near ponds and lakes and shows a distinct preference for those with brackish or alkaline water.

Seasonality The breeding territories are occupied by late April, and eggs are deposited in May or early June.

Courtship Early courtship takes place in flocks on communal grounds. In subsequent courtship flights, males fly in circles around the territory, holding the wings arched downward and making short, rapid wingbeats. These flights often induce similar behavior in males on nearby territories. On the ground the male walks slowly and deliberately toward the female while calling *dik-dik-dik* and waving the wings above the back, emphasizing the white markings. Females make a soft grunting call during copulation, while males make clicking sounds.

Territoriality They are generally territorial but may form loosely clumped breeding aggregations with nests 60 m (200 ft) apart. In some instances, feeding territories are separate from nesting territories.

Nest and Nest Site The nest is a scrape located near water and carelessly lined with small reeds and grass. The nest may be placed in open sand or gravel but more commonly is carefully concealed in thick grass. The nest site is chosen by the female.

Eggs The pointed egg is greenish white to dark olive-brown strongly marked with spots of dark brown and lavender. The eggs average 5.4 cm (2.1 in) by 3.8 cm (1.5 in) and weigh about 40 g (1.4 oz).

Incubation The typical clutch of 4 eggs is laid with intervals of 1 to 4 days between eggs. The female incubates by day, and the male takes over the duties at night. Incubation may begin before the clutch is complete, leading to a variable incubation period from 21 to 29 days. The resultant staggered hatching and departure of the brood may result in the abandonment of some unhatched eggs.

Fledging The downy young are grayish, with dark dorsal markings that include a central stripe and symmetrical lateral bars. The parents are attentive to the newly hatched chicks but do not normally brood or feed them. An adult has been reported carrying each member of a new brood individually across creeks and marshes between its thighs. When the adults leave the breeding area before the young fledge, the young birds become very secretive in their habits and exist on their own until they learn to fly.

Age at First Breeding Most Willets breed in the spring of their 2nd year, but some may delay until their 3rd year if they are in a poor nutritional state.

BEHAVIOR The Willet is of an alert and nervous disposition and is often the 1st shorebird to give alarm calls at the approach of a threat. They are generally territorial year-round but may form loose feeding groups in the win-

ter. Flight speed has been measured at a range of 43 kph (27 mph) to 75 kph (47 mph).

MIGRATION The adults of the eastern race move south as early as June or July before the young birds fledge. Some travel as far as the Caribbean and northern South America. The western race moves west and south along the Pacific coast from California to Peru, with some birds moving onto the Caribbean coast of northern South America. The northern migration begins as early as March and proceeds as weather permits. Both migrants and residents lay most of their eggs in May. It is reported that Willets from Nova Scotia migrate over water directly to the West Indies. Migrating flocks often travel at night.

PREDATORS Foxes, mink, weasels, raccoons, house cats, and snakes prey on the eggs and chicks. Hawks prey on adult Willets.

LONGEVITY The maximum longevity of Willets has not been reported.

CONSERVATION ISSUES In the days when shorebirds were hunted, the assertive Willet was looked upon with disfavor as often warning other birds of the approach of gunners. Willets began to repopulate shorelines after receiving protection by the Migratory Bird Treaty Act. Loss of estuarine feeding and nesting habitat has resulted in a negative population influence in the later 20th century.

NOTES The genus name is a Latinized form of the Greek *katoptron* (mirror) and *phoros* (bearing), in reference to the white wing patches visible in flight. The species name is from the

Latin, referring to the partially webbed feet. Willet, the common name, is onomatopoetic. This bird is also called Spanish plover, duck snipe, will willet, pill-will-willet, and pied-winged curlew. In Spanish it is called *playero aliblanco* or *archibebe aliblanco*, and in French *chevalier semipalmé*.

SUGGESTED ADDITIONAL READING

Burger, J. and J. Shisler. 1978. Nest site selection of Willets in a New Jersey salt marsh. *Wilson Bulletin*, 90:599–607.

Howe, M.A. 1982. Social organization in a nesting population of Eastern Willets *Auk*, 99:88–102.

Sordahl, T.A.. 1979. Vocalizations and behavior of the Willet. *Wilson Bulletin*, 91:551–574.

Spotted Sandpiper

Actitus macularia | Scolopacidae Charadriiformes | p. 52

DISTRIBUTION This genus with 2 species is found almost worldwide. The Common Sandpiper, *A. hypoleucos,* nests from Scandinavia to Siberia and winters in subequatorial Africa, southern Asia, and Australia. The Spotted Sandpiper has the widest breeding range of any sandpiper in North America, where it nests across the U.S. from Virginia to California and north to the tree line from Labrador to Alaska. In the winter it is found from the southern U.S. south to Chile and Argentina.

FOOD AND FEEDING HABITS

The Spotted Sandpiper may be found feeding in ponds and streams, on a soggy spot in a field, on mudflats, or at the edge of booming surf. Foraging is primarily at dawn and dusk with continuation into midday hours or even moonlit nights, if necessary. They work the edges of open water but seldom wade. A great variety of prey is consumed, including terrestrial insects and their larvae, aquatic crabs, gastropods, small fish, and carrion. Local populations depend heavily on mayflies, midges, and brine flies. Feeding selectivity increases with food abundance. They prefer a firm substrate for feeding. Feeding Spotted Sandpipers often make short rushes at prey followed by a forward thrust of the bill for capture. They may stalk insects by extending the body parallel to the ground and sneaking, or they may catch flying insects with remarkable skill.

REPRODUCTION The Spotted Sandpiper practices sequential polyandry in which a female mates with several males and lays several clutches of eggs over a short period of time.

Seasonality The breeding season is quite extended. Birds in the more southern part of the range nest as early as April, but those in the north are delayed until the thaw in May or early June.

Courtship Females arrive 1st on the breeding grounds and select territories. The female is the dominant sex and displays to males by flying up and landing near another bird with the tail up and spread and the wings drooped. Female competition for males may become intense with much chasing and fighting. Pair bonds seem to be formed within minutes. Paired females may show sequential polyandry with subsequent males. The female resumes singing and aerial displays to attract a new male after depositing 3 eggs in her current nest. Copulation usually is not preceded by specific displays, but a wing-fluttering courtship has been described. Cases of a single female simultaneously forming pair bonds with 2 males have been recorded.

Territoriality The territory includes shoreline for feeding, open habitat for nesting, and dense patches of vegetation available as cover for chicks. Nesting is often in colonies with densities of 3 nests per acre. The males defend specific nest sites. Females defend areas that include several male territories or move between several nesting territories. Nest density may be as much as 20 females and 32 males on a 1.6 ha (4 acre) island but is typically about half that density.

Nest and Nest Site The nest is a depression scraped in the ground, sometimes on the same day that a pair bond is formed. It is well lined with grass, leaves, and stems. Nests are usually located within 100 m (328 ft) of the shore of stony, fast-flowing rivers, ponds, lakes, and sheltered seacoasts. Habitats include shorelines, sagebrush scrub, grassland, and forest at elevations from sea level to 4,700 m (15,420 ft). The nests may be well hidden near trees and shrubs or relatively exposed under sparse weeds along a gravelly shore.

Eggs The eggs are creamy buff to grayish and are blotched with blackish or purplish gray. The eggs are about 32 by 23 mm (1.28 by 0.92 in) and weigh about 9.6 g (0.34 oz) or about 20% of the female's body weight. The clutch size is usually 4 eggs, and as many as 5 complete clutches may be produced with different males in 1 season.

Incubation The 1st egg of the 4-egg clutch is laid as soon as 3 days after the male arrives on the female's territory. Subsequent eggs are laid daily. Incubation becomes decidedly more constant after the 3rd egg is laid. In areas with a high incidence of disturbance, incomplete clutches of 2 or 3 eggs are common. Replacement clutches are initiated 5 to 6 days after nest failure. The male does most of the brooding and does not leave the nest unless closely approached. The female may share incubation duties with the male at her last nest of the season. The incubation period is 20 to 24 days.

Fledging The chicks are able to leave the nest a few hours after hatching. The male broods the chicks for the 1st few days and leads them to foraging spots where they eat small, soft-bodied terrestrial arthropods. The chicks are dark brown on the back, nape, and crown with a lighter stripe on the back. The lighter-colored sides of the head contrast with a dark stripe that runs through the eye. The chicks fledge at 17 or 18 days and are attended by the male, who is sometimes assisted by the female, until the chicks are 4 weeks of age.

Age at First Breeding Spotted Sandpipers breed at the age of 1 year.

BEHAVIOR The Spotted Sandpiper tends to avoid groups of the more gregarious shorebirds and perches easily on trees, posts, and moored boats. It frequently rocks its body in a teetering motion that increases in frequency with anxiety. Teetering ceases with courtship activity, alarm, or aggression. Flight speed has been recorded at 40 kph (25 mph).

MIGRATION The spring migration begins in South America in March and progresses north until the northern breeding territories are occupied by the end of May. The fall migration starts with favorable winds with the females leaving 1st in early July, followed by the males and eventually the juveniles. The spring migration is of single individuals, while the fall migration may have single individuals or flocks of up to 200. When flying in flocks at an elevation or on migration, all members of the flock alter direction simultaneously.

PREDATORS Deer mice, weasels, foxes, mink, and birds take the adults. Chicks are taken by Common Grackles, American Crows, gulls, weasels, and many raptors including Peregrine Falcons. House cats are a threat to the chicks in some areas.

LONGEVITY A Spotted Sandpiper was recovered 12 years after banding.

CONSERVATION ISSUES Due to its great variety of acceptable nesting habitat and the high reproductive potential, this is probably the most abundant shorebird in North America.

NOTES The genus name is from the Greek word meaning "coast dweller." The species name is from the Latin *macula* (spot) and *arius* (possessing), in reference to the spotted breast. It has also been known as *Tringa macularia*. English names include teeter-peep, teeter-tail, tip-up, see-saw, peet-weet, and sand snipe. In Spanish it is called *andarríos masculado* and *arríos manchado*, and in French *chevalier grivelé*.

SUGGESTED ADDITIONAL READING

Lank, D.B., L.W. Oring and J.S. Maxson. 1985. Mate and nutrient limitation of egg laying in a polyandrous shorebird. *Ecology,* 66:1513–1524.

Oring, L.W., and M.L. Knudson. 1972. Monogamy and polyandry in the Spotted Sandpiper. *Living Bird,* 11:59–73.

Oring, L.W., J.M. Reed and S.J. Maxson. 1994. Copulation patterns and mate guarding in the sex role reversed, polyandrous Spotted Sandpiper, *Actitis macularia. Animal Behaviour,* 47:1065–1072.

Ruddy Turnstone
Arenaria interpres | Scolopacidae Charadriiformes | p. 53

DISTRIBUTION This genus with 2 species occupies the seacoasts of the world. The Black Turnstone (*A. melanocephala*) nests on southwest coastal Alaska from Norton Sound and Bristol Bay south to Canada, and it winters on the Pacific coast from Alaska to Baja, California. The Ruddy Turnstone breeds on Arctic coasts and islands. It winters on the Atlantic and Pacific coasts of North America from Oregon and Connecticut south to Chile and Argentina. The birds breeding on Ellesmere Island and in Greenland winter on the coast from Scotland through northwest Africa. The birds nesting from Scandinavia to Siberia winter in Africa, southern Asia, Australia, and New Zealand. Nonbreeding birds often spend the summer on the winter range.

FOOD AND FEEDING HABITS
Six different feeding techniques have been recorded: flicking and plowing seaweed, probing, turning stones, hammering, digging, and surface pecking. Status in a dominance hierarchy determines in part which techniques are used. The bird earned its name by its habit of industriously turning over small stones to catch concealed invertebrates on almost any bare, stony, or rocky seacoast that is free of ice. They are capable of over-turning flat rocks equal to their own weight. They may feed on sandy beaches by flipping seaweed to expose arthropods such as crabs, isopods, and amphipods, or they may dig substantial holes in pursuit of crabs. They readily scavenge bits of prey over-looked by oystercatchers and will take a broad variety of carrion, including such unlikely items as soap, suet, and sheep and human corpses. When they arrive early on the breeding grounds, they sometimes eat plant material until other food becomes available. They enthusiastically scavenge both raw and cooked fish parts, bread, potato peels, and oatmeal from camp-sites and picnic areas near the sea. For-aging away from the water's edge, they eat caterpillars, grasshoppers, and spi-ders. Ruddy Turnstones eat the eggs of terns and other birds. If an egg is undefended the turnstone may peck it open and consume its entire contents. When feeding on the ineffectually defended eggs of Royal Terns, the turnstone may only peck the egg open and gain a mouthful of contents before being chased away, then peck another egg open. Egg predation by turnstones has caused Royal Terns to abandon nesting colonies and has adversely influenced reproductive success of many other terns. On the breeding grounds the adults and lar-vae of midges are the primary food source.

REPRODUCTION
The Ruddy Turnstone makes long annual migra-tions to the open tundra of the high Arctic.
Seasonality The adult birds arrive in the nesting areas above the Arctic Cir-cle in late May or early June as the last of the snow melts.
Courtship Males advertise territories from the ground by perching on rocks or other elevated sites while crouching

and calling with a metallic clicking note. Aerial displays are 10 to 50 m above the ground; the turnstone uses deep, slow wingbeats while giving the *tchee-tchee-tchee* calls at the rate of 3 per 2 seconds. The male may call when pursuing the female in the air. Displays and territorial disputes are greatly reduced at the onset of incubation.

Territoriality The territory is variable within the range of 15 to 30 ha (40 to 80 acres) per pair but may show a clumped distribution with several nests close together.

Nest and Nest Site The nest sites chosen are often on small islands but may be more than a mile from the coast and typical of the tundra, being wet and hummocky with dwarf willow and heather vegetation. Nests are always near marshes, ponds, or streams. The nest is a bare scrape in the open with only a few vegetation fragments, or if it is located in cover, it may be a hollow lined with grass or seaweed.

Eggs The greenish-gray egg, spotted and blotched with various tones of brown, measures about 40 by 30 mm and weighs about 17 g. The normal clutch is 4 eggs.

Incubation Both sexes share in incubation, with the incubating bird leaving the nest when it sees an approaching predator or is warned of one by the mate. Injured-wing displays are common as a distraction to lure predators away from the nest. Average incubation is 22 days, and all eggs hatch within a 1- or 2-day period. Both parents initially tend the young as they leave the nest a day or so after the last egg hatches. Hatching seems to be timed to occur near the peak annual population of midges. Loss of eggs is often followed by renesting in the southern part of the breeding range.

Fledging One study reported that 74% of chicks that hatched fledged. The chicks are gray with a complex darker pattern on the back and a white-tipped powder-puff down forming a concealing pattern well adapted to lichen-covered tundra nesting areas. The young leave the nest the day after hatching and are led to feeding grounds by the parents to feed themselves. The female leaves the breeding grounds long before the chicks fledge at about 19 days of age. The males depart when the chicks fledge, leaving them to gather in small flocks on beaches and to fatten on midges until they migrate south in late August. On the wintering grounds after migration, older birds show greater efficiency in finding and handling prey than do the recent fledglings.

Age at First Breeding One-year-old birds usually remain on the wintering grounds. Even though they often molt into breeding plumage, the gonads do not develop. Two-year-old birds migrate and breed.

BEHAVIOR They prefer to feed and travel in flocks of about a dozen. The flight is very fast in diagonal lines or closely bunched, with the flocks often performing aerobatic maneuvers in unison. Flight speed has been recorded at 55 kph (34 mph). When migrating, they fly high and fast in flocks of thousands. When feeding, solitary birds are not uncommon but closely gathered groups are more frequent. They swim well and readily land on water.

MIGRATION The migration south begins in mid-July and reaches its maximum a month later. A seasonal increase in basal metabolic rate seems to assist the birds in preparing for their migration flights.

PREDATORS Foxes and weasels are the major threats to the eggs and chicks. Kestrels may take the adults, and skuas take fledged young.

LONGEVITY About 1/2 of the juveniles survive the 1st year and about 2/3 of the adults survive each succeeding year. A banded bird was recovered 19 years 8 months after banding.

CONSERVATION ISSUES Habitat loss due to coastal development on the wintering grounds is the primary concern for Ruddy Turnstones.

NOTES The genus name is from the Latin *arenarius* (sand). The species name is from the Latin *interpres*, meaning "messenger" or "go between." This name was mistakenly given to this bird after it was coined for another shorebird that gives warning calls. Other common English names are sea dotterel, stone-pecker, bead bird, chicken plover, calico-bird, streaked-back, and bishop plover. In French it is called *tournepierre à collier* and in Spanish *playero turco* or *vuelve piedras*.

SUGGESTED ADDITIONAL READING

Groves, S. 1978. Age related differences in Ruddy Turnstone foraging and aggressive behavior. *Auk,* 95:95–103.

Loftin, R.W. 1979. Ruddy Turnstones destroy Royal Tern colony. *Wilson Bulletin,* 91:133–135.

Nettleship, D.N. 1973. Breeding ecology of Turnstones *Arenaria interpres* at Hazen Camp, Ellesmere Island, N.W.T. *Ibis,* 115:202–217.

Sanderling

Calidris alba | **Scolopacidae Charadriiformes | p. 54**

DISTRIBUTION This genus with 20 species is found worldwide. The Sanderling breeds in the high Arctic, north of the 5°C (40°F) July isotherm, which has an annual precipitation of less than 25 cm (10 in). This circum-Arctic distribution is on land closest to the north pole from Alaska east to Baffin Island, Greenland, and northern Eurasia. The American population winters from British Columbia and Massachusetts south along the coasts to the Caribbean and southern South America. The Eurasian population winters south to South Africa, India, and New Zealand.

FOOD AND FEEDING HABITS

The primary feeding behavior is rapidly chasing waves back and forth on slightly sloping sandy shorelines capturing exposed prey items with darting dexterity. Tide level is a critical factor, but Sanderlings seem to prefer to feed on mudflats by day and beaches at night. Sensors in the beak allow them to detect worms moving in the mud as far as 2 cm (1 in) from the inserted beak. Feeding may also be by rapid, shallow probes in the wet sand to capture worms, small mollusks, sand flies, and ostracods. Mole crabs may make up over 70% of the diet in some places. On the breeding grounds they eat the adults and larvae of the multitude of midges, mosquitoes, and other diptera present on the tundra. On the wintering grounds they eat insects, small shrimp, horseshoe crab eggs, mollusks, worms, jellyfish, and small fish. Wintering birds show a high degree of site fidelity in successive years.

REPRODUCTION Sanderlings breed as dispersed pairs in the high Arctic.

Seasonality Sanderlings arrive on the high Arctic breeding grounds in late May or June, but environmental conditions do not usually allow laying until mid-June or later.

Courtship The male advertises the breeding territory by flying with rapidly vibrating wings punctuated with short glides while holding the head and body in a hunched position. The loud song is given while in flight over the territory. Display flights cease after a pair bond is formed, and the 2 birds become inseparable. Copulation is initiated by the female by posing on a nest scrape (usually of another species and not used subsequently as a nest) with head down and tail up. The male runs to her and eases her out of the scrape to copulate 3 m (10 ft) away. Pairing is variable and may be monogamous or include 2 simultaneous clutches with each bird incubating a separate nest, or there may be successive bigamy.

Territoriality Breeding territories about 400 m (1,300 ft) in diameter are selected by males and show a density of 1.5 to 3 pairs per sq km (4 to 8 pairs per sq mi) but may reach 6.5 pairs per sq km (17 pairs per sq mi) under ideal circumstances. The territory is sometimes inland but is always near a body of water to provide feeding habitat for prefledge young.

Nest and Nest Site The nest is a leaf-lined scrape selected by the female and open to the sky but near a clump of willows, saxifrage, or other vegetation. It is located on stony, well-drained ridges, slopes or alluvial plains.

Eggs The buff to greenish-olive eggs are marked with darker spots, measure 35 by 25 mm (1.4 by 1 in) and weigh about 11.2 g (0.4 oz). The eggs are laid at slightly greater than 1-day intervals, and incubation does not begin until the 4-egg clutch is complete.

Incubation Eggs are incubated by both parents when they have 1 clutch. When the female lays clutches in 2 separate nests, the male incubates the 2nd nest and the female returns to incubate the 1st nest. The 24- to 27-day incubation period may be extended due to the delayed start of incubation while the 2nd clutch is completed.

Fledging Chicks remain on the nest for about 12 hours after hatching, then follow a parent that leads them to foraging habitat. The brood may move as far as 65 m (213 ft) within 2 hours of leaving the nest and may be 2 to 3 km (1.2 to 1.87 mi) away after 2 weeks. The chicks fledge at about 17 days of age. A parent may leave the chicks untended while it flies to other nearby, more-productive foraging areas, but 1 or both parents usually attend the brood until they fledge. A skulking run is used when departing the nest due to the presence of a predator. Injury feigning, with tail fanned and 1 wing beating the ground while calling pitifully, is particularly well developed as a distraction for predators.

Age at First Breeding Sanderlings breed in their 2nd year, but some yearlings migrate north and may attempt to breed in the 1st year.

BEHAVIOR They often feed in single-species flocks of up to 20 birds and may roost in groups with other species of shorebirds. The flight speed has been recorded at 66 kph (41 mph), and the flap rate has been recorded as 6.3 flaps per second for a bird traveling across the wind. A variety of calls have been recorded on the breeding grounds.

MIGRATION A part of the adult population migrates from the high Arctic to southern South America every year for an annual round trip of 32,000 km (20,000 miles). A seasonal increase in basal metabolic rate seems to assist the birds in preparing for their marathon flights. Adults usually leave the breeding grounds in late July and early August, with young of the year moving south in late August or early November.

PREDATORS Skuas and foxes take the eggs and young when they find them.

LONGEVITY The oldest banded Sanderling recovered was 11 years old.

CONSERVATION ISSUES As with many shorebirds, coastal development has consistently reduced available habitat. The annual population mortality in a small study showed 44% of the individuals died every year, but 62% of the 1st-year birds died.

NOTES The genus name is from the Greek *skaladris* used by Aristotle for a gray, speckled shorebird. The species name is from the Latin *alba* (white).

Sanderlings have also been placed in the genus *Crocethia* by themselves due to the lack of a hind toe. "Sanderling" is derived from the Icelandic *sand* and *erla* meaning "sand-wagtail." The common name "stint" used for these birds and several similar birds in the genus refers to their small size. The American common name for this group is "peep," in reference to their diminutive calls. The Sanderling has been called beach plover and bull peep in English. In Spanish it is called *correlimos blanco* or *correlimos tridáctilo*, and in French *bécasseau sanderling*.

SUGGESTED ADDITIONAL READING

Burger, J. and M. Gochfeld. 1991. Human activity influence and diurnal and nocturnal foraging of Sanderlings (*Calidris alba*). *Condor*, 93:259–265.

Myers, J.P. 1983. Space, time and the pattern of individual associations in a group-living species: Sanderlings have no friends. *Behavioral Ecology and Sociobiology*, 12:129–134.

Parmalee, D.F. and R.B. Payne. 1973. On multiple broods and the breeding strategy of Arctic Sanderlings. *Ibis*, 115:218–226.

Semipalmated Sandpiper
Calidris pusilla | Scolopacidae Charadriiformes | p. 55

DISTRIBUTION This genus with 12 species is found worldwide. Many of the members of this genus migrate from breeding grounds in the Arctic or sub-Arctic across the equator to winter in temperate zones in the southern hemisphere. The Semipalmated Sandpiper breeds in the tundra of Canada, Alaska and northeastern Siberia. They winter on the northern coasts of South America with fewer numbers in Florida and the Caribbean.

FOOD AND FEEDING HABITS
The winter feeding sites are preferably mudflats. Feeding areas before the migrations are shallow fresh- and saltwater wetlands with a soft clay or silt bottom. Feeding is by pecking at visible prey and probing for prey in the mud. They are opportunistic feeders, taking insects, crustaceans, small snails, clams, and worms. They walk at 3 to 13 cm/s (1 to 5 in/s) or run between feeding attempts. They may claim feeding territories of various sizes depending on prey density. In areas of abundant food and high bird density, territories are not defended. Females selectively include lemming bones in their diet as a calcium source before and during egg laying.

REPRODUCTION The Semipalmated Sandpiper breeds near water but often travels 2 or 3 km (1.3 to 1.8 mi) to a feeding area.

Seasonality Males claim territories with display flights and vocalizations that decrease greatly after they are paired. The 1st egg is laid in mid-June at the peak of the insect hatch.

Courtship Males arrive on the breeding grounds and set up territories of about 1 ha (2.5 acres) before the females arrive. They display over the territory with hovering flight and vocalizations such as a pulsating buzz. Courting males may utter a trilled *yu-yu* while chasing a female. After the pair bond is established the male follows the female almost continuously until incubation begins. Semipalmated Sandpipers are monogamous within a breeding season even when renesting. Pairs often reunite in succeeding years.

Territoriality The males often claim the same territory used the previous year. Threat displays given on the ground include erecting neck feathers while rushing at another bird, chasing, and fighting. The nest site is defended with scolding calls by both sexes. Breeding territory distribution is patchy with a density as low as 0.11 pairs/ha (0.28 pairs per acre).

Nest and Nest Site The nest site is located near water and often on islands in ponds, streams, or river deltas in clumps of willow or birch with an understory of grass or sedge. The female selects 1 of the several nest scrapes created by the male. The nest cup selected may be lined with bits of leaves or moss and have nearby vegetation bent over the nest as camouflage. The same nest cup may be used in succeeding years, or it may be 1 of the alternates offered to the female.

Eggs The smooth, glossy, white to olive-buff eggs with light- and dark-brown markings are 3 by 2.1 cm (1.2 by 0.8 in) and weigh 7.3 g (0.26 oz). Egg laying may be as soon as 4 days after pairing but may be delayed up to 2 weeks if abundant food supply is not available. The eggs are laid daily until the clutch of 4 is complete. The females only produce 4 eggs per clutch and do not replace an egg lost during the laying period. Renesting occurs as soon as 5 days after a clutch is lost early in the season. Replacement eggs laid after the 4th of July do not succeed in producing young.

Incubation Incubation is sporadic until the laying of the last egg in the clutch; then it becomes continuous. Both sexes participate in the 20-day incubation of the egg. The adults sit tight on the nest, but if flushed they use distraction displays such as a rodent run or a scolding call.

Fledging The newly hatched downy chicks have stripes on the head and a buff back with dark, speckled blackish-brown markings. The chicks leave the nest and begin to peck for flies within hours of hatching. The female deserts the brood shortly after hatching and soon migrates south. The young are brooded for the 1st week and guarded closely for the 2nd week. The chicks fledge at 16 to 19 days of age. The male parent often emits a scolding alarm call from the ground while the chicks are mobile but still flightless.

Age at First Breeding Up to 10% of yearling birds migrate north and breed, but most young birds stay on the winter feeding grounds and migrate north to breed in their 2nd year.

BEHAVIOR The Spotted Sandpiper feeds, roosts, and migrates in groups that may be as large as several hundred thousand with a very small individual distance between them when flying, feeding, or loafing. They often stand on 1 foot while resting or sleeping with the head under the wing. They may even hop on 1 foot when feeding.

MIGRATION The spring migration to the breeding grounds passes through the U.S. from April to June with a peak in late May. The males arrive on the breeding grounds several days before the females. Female adult Semipalmated Sandpipers start south in mid-July followed about 5 days later by adult males; there is a lull in the migration until the juveniles migrate 2 to 4 weeks later. The summer migration to the wintering grounds may involve nonstop transoceanic flights of 3,000 to 4,300 km (1,860 to 2,666 mi) from the Bay of Fundy and the northeast United States and Canada to South America. The birds feed heavily before they depart and accumulate significant fat reserves to fuel the long overwater flight. Migrating flocks usually travel at night except for long overwater passages that require constant flight. Experiments indicate that Semipalmated Sandpipers probably use both celestial clues and the Earth's magnetic field to navigate while migrating. Fat reserves totaling about 40% of the bird's dry weight must be accumulated to fuel the 90 km/hr (56 m/hr) flight, which lasts for 40 to 60 hours.

PREDATORS Jaegers, gulls, owls, weasels, and foxes take the eggs or chicks. Jaegers, hawks, and owls take the adult birds. Predation on shorebirds increases significantly when Arctic rodents are in low abundance.

LONGEVITY The oldest banded bird recorded was 12 years of age.

CONSERVATION ISSUES The world population of Semipalmated Sandpipers is presently estimated at 2 million, with the population regulated by natural predation and climatic factors.

NOTES The genus name is from the Greek *skaladris* used by Aristotle for a gray, speckled shorebird. The species name is from the Latin *pusillus,* meaning "tiny" or "petty," referring to the small size of the bird. It has also been placed in the genus *Tringa.* The common European name "stint" used for this bird and several similar birds in the genus refers to their small size. The American common name for this group is "peep" in reference to their diminutive calls. The Semipalmated Sandpiper is also called sand peep, black-legged peep, and sand ox-eye. In Spanish it is *correlimos semipalmeado* or *playerito gracioso,* and in French it is *bécasseau semipalmé.*

SUGGESTED ADDITIONAL READING

Dunn, P.O., T.A. May, M.A. McCollough and M.A. Howe. 1988. Length of stay and fat content of migrant Semipalmated Sandpipers in eastern Maine. *Condor,* 90: 824–835.

Gratto-Trevor, C.L. 1992. Semipalmated Sandpiper *(Calidris pusilla).* In A. Pool and F. Gill (eds.), *The Birds of North America. No. 6.* Philadelphia: The Birds of North America, Inc.

MacLean, S.F. Jr. 1974 Lemming bones as a source of calcium for Arctic Sandpipers *(Calidris spp).* *Ibis,* 116:552–557.

Western Sandpiper
Calidris mauri | Scolopacidae Charadriiformes | p. 56

DISTRIBUTION This genus with 12 species is found worldwide. Many of the members of this genus migrate from breeding grounds in the Arctic or sub-Arctic across the equator in order to winter in temperate zones in the southern hemisphere. The Western Sandpiper nests in extreme northwest Alaska and northeastern Siberia. They winter on the Pacific coast from California to Peru and on the mid-Atlantic coast south to the Gulf of Mexico and Caribbean.

FOOD AND FEEDING HABITS
On the breeding grounds, freshwater bottom-dwelling invertebrates, along with adult and larval flies and beetles and spiders, make up the primary diet. When the bird is migrating and on the wintering grounds, the diet is composed of amphipods, copepods, worms, and small clams. Some studies have shown large numbers of beetles in the stomach contents. Foraging habitat varies from slightly submerged to exposed mud and sand near the waterline. The birds gather in flocks to follow the tides in and out while feeding at the edge of the waterline in areas of high prey density. They forage by pecking at exposed food items above the waterline and probing in the mud when it is covered with water. They tend to feed in deeper water than do Semipalmated Sandpipers. Western Sandpipers may drive away Least Sandpipers from a feeding site and be driven away in turn by Dunlins.

REPRODUCTION Western Sand-

pipers are synchronous in their arrival at the northern breeding grounds before the snow is melted.

Seasonality Males generally depart on the spring migration in mid-April and reach the breeding grounds in mid-May as the snow begins to melt. Females arrive a week or so later, form pair bonds, and usually have a full clutch of eggs by late May or early June.

Courtship Males arrive on the breeding grounds in flocks but soon show aggression by chasing and supplanting other males. As aggressive encounters increase in duration and intensity, males disperse to individual territories. Males sing with a series of slightly ascending notes followed by a buzzy trill to attract mates and inform other males of territorial claims on the breeding grounds. The call has been represented as an ascending *t-e-e-e* or *ti-ti-ti*. Monogamy is normal, and the pair bond may extend into subsequent seasons.

Territoriality Males make frequent display flights to announce the territory until incubation begins, in which case the frequency of flights is much reduced. Display flights are rare after the clutch hatches. Males and females often return to the same territory in subsequent years and have been known to reuse the preceding year's nest cup. Nesting territories have been recorded as small as 0.2 to 0.3 ha (0.5 to 0.75 acres), leading to nest densities of 3.4 to 4.9 pairs per ha (2.47 acres). They communally use adjacent, freshwater wetland feeding habitat.

Nest and Nest Site Males may make

up to 6 nest scrapes over 2 or 3 days until 1 is chosen by the female. The chosen nest site is usually on slightly higher ground, often under a small shrub such as dwarf birch or between clumps of overhanging grasses. The lining may be of willow or birch leaves, grasses, sedges, or lichens. The finished nest cup is about 6.5 cm (2.6 in) wide by about 5.5 cm (2.2 in) deep.

Eggs The typical clutch is 4 cream to brown sturdy eggs measuring 31 by 22 mm (1.2 by 0.86 in). Ground color and the elongate brown markings are quite variable among nests but are consistent within nests. Eggs are laid at daily intervals within a few days of establishment of the pair bond. As with other shorebird eggs they are distinctly tapered so that 4 eggs with pointed ends inward fit nicely together in the nest cup, providing easy coverage by the parent and minimizing heat loss. Renesting may replace nest loss early in the breeding season, but 2nd nesting does not take place after a brood has been reared.

Incubation Both parents share in the 21-day incubation duties beginning when the next-to-last egg in the clutch is laid. The female usually incubates morning, evening, and night, with the male covering the eggs in midday and taking on longer periods as incubation proceeds. Females may abandon the nest and mate before hatching.

Fledging At hatching, the downy, precocial chicks have stripes and spots on the head and dense white spots on the black down of the body. Hatchlings remain in the nest until the last chick has hatched and dried. Both parents or the adult male leads the chicks to suitable feeding habitat. An adult will brood the young chicks at night in cold or rainy weather. Females commonly abandon the young and join other females in flocks in preparation for migration. First flight is at 17 to 21 days, at which time the male deserts the brood and migrates. The fledglings remain feeding vigorously in the breeding area until about the 1st week in August.

Age at First Breeding Some yearlings return to the breeding grounds at the age of 1 year, but others remain on the wintering grounds and migrate north to breed in their 2nd year.

BEHAVIOR When roosting at high tide, Dowitchers and Red Knots settle near the water with Dunlins above them and Western Sandpipers still higher on the beach. When traveling in flocks they move with synchronous grace. Flight speed has been recorded at 70 to 84 kph (44 to 52 mph).

MIGRATION Western Sandpipers often gather in huge flocks numbering over 10,000 birds for migration. Females depart the breeding grounds 1st, followed by adult males in mid-July. Then the juveniles leisurely travel south several weeks later. The early southern migration seems to be in response to a declining food supply on the breeding grounds. Some evidence indicates that the sandpipers show considerable flock and location fidelity on the wintering range. Studies of fat stores and behavior indicate that migrations are a series of flights with intervening feeding stops, rather than the long, nonstop flights of some other shorebirds.

PREDATORS Red foxes and jaegers are the primary predators on the breeding grounds, while falcons may take significant numbers on the wintering grounds.

LONGEVITY The maximum longevity of a recovered banded bird was 9 years 2 months. The annual survival rate of adults has been estimated at 70%.

CONSERVATION ISSUES Winter and migratory stopover and feeding areas are of critical importance in maintaining population numbers. World population is estimated to exceed 2 million.

NOTES The genus name is from the Greek *skaladris* used by Aristotle for a gray, speckled shorebird. The species name honors Ernesto Mauri. They have also been placed in the genus *Ereunetes*. The common name "stint" used for this bird and several similar birds in the genus refers to their small size. The American common name for this group is "peep," in reference to their diminutive calls. They are also called pond bird in English; *playerito occidental, correlimos occidental* or *correlimos de Alaska* in Spanish; and *bécasseau d' Alaska* in French.

SUGGESTED ADDITIONAL READING

Senner, S.E. and E.F. Martinez. 1982. A review of Western Sandpiper migration in interior North America. *Southwest Nat,* 27:149–159.

Stevenson, H.M. 1975. Identification of difficult Birds: III Semipalmated and Western Sandpipers. *Florida Field Nat,* 3:39.

Wilson, W.H. 1994. Western Sandpiper (*Calidris mauri*). In A. Poole and F. Gill (eds.), *The Birds of North America. No. 90.* Philadelphia: The Birds of North America, Inc.

Least Sandpiper

Calidris minutilla | Scolopacidae Charadriiformes | p. 57

DISTRIBUTION This genus with 12 species is found worldwide. The Least Sandpiper breeds from the Queen Charlotte Islands of British Columbia across Alaska and northern Canada to Nova Scotia. The birds winter from California and Florida south through the Caribbean and Central America to the Amazon basin and northern Chile. They are often common throughout their wide range.

FOOD AND FEEDING HABITS

Least Sandpipers feed on bay flats, river beaches, mudbars, tidal pools on rocky shorelines, and particularly the muddy or short-grass margins of brackish creeks. They also feed along the shores of freshwater lakes and ponds, on marsh edges, and in rain pools. They seldom wade in water over 4 cm (1.6 in) deep or at a distance of more than 1 m (3 ft) from the water's edge. They probe into the mud and peck (at a very high rate) at exposed small organisms on the surface. The food is almost entirely bottom-dwelling invertebrates smaller than 6 mm (.24 in) captured by day and night. Food items include small snails, beach hoppers, horseshoe crab eggs, isopods, and seed shrimp, as well as larval, pupal, and adult flies. They feed on inland fields when worms are forced to the surface by saturated soil.

REPRODUCTION The nesting grounds are just to the south of tree-less tundra. There the sandpipers build a grass- and leaf-lined nest on a slight rise close to a pond, river estuary, or seashore.

Seasonality Males arrive on the breeding grounds in early May, and the females arrive about a week later.

Courtship Males perform aerial displays with rapid ascents and a hovering flight with alternating gliding and bursts of rapid wingbeats. The display flight area is vigorously defended against other males until a pair bond is formed. Then the males allow other males to use much of the previously defended territory. Males use a variety of calls on the breeding grounds, including a complex song, a repeated 3-part chatter, and variations of rhythmically repeated calls associated with aerial displays. Pairs are monogamous, and the pair bond often continues in subsequent years.

Territoriality The nesting territory is vigorously defended. Nesting has been recorded as being as dense as 90 pairs per ha (36 pairs per acre). Males usually return to the same nesting territory in succeeding years.

Nest and Nest Site Males establish a territory and start several nest scrapes about 6 cm (2.4 in) in diameter by 4 cm (1.6 in) deep, one of which is selected by the female. The female may add a sparse lining of dead leaves during egg laying and incubation. Pairs show considerable fidelity to a nesting site in subsequent years.

Eggs The buff-colored, conical eggs, blotched or spotted with dark brown, measure 21 by 29 mm (0.8 by 1.1 in). The 4 eggs in the normal clutch are usually laid at intervals of about 30 hours. Replacement clutches are laid to replace nests lost early in the breeding season.

Incubation The male does most of the incubation for the 20-day period beginning after the 4th egg is laid. Predation rates of clutches have been recorded as being from 11% to 40%. Of the clutches not eaten by predators, the hatch rate is 86% to 93%.

Fledging The hatchling is black with yellow to brown markings on the back with light underparts. Both parents tend the young as they leave the nest less than 24 hours after hatching, but the female deserts the brood a week or so later. Parents do not feed the chicks but lead them to habitat that allows them to feed on small insects. Chicks fledge at 14 to 20 days, and the male deserts the brood soon thereafter. Hatchling mortality until fledging has been reported as 38% to 67%.

Age at First Breeding Most chicks return to their hatching area at the age of 1 year for breeding.

BEHAVIOR Flight speed has been recorded at 80 kph (45 to 55 mph).

MIGRATION Males arrive on the breeding grounds a week or so before the females. At the end of the breeding season the migration proceeds in 3 waves. The females are the first to depart, followed by the adult males a week or 2 later, then the juveniles within the following month. The western populations move south along the Pacific coast of North and Central America, but the eastern populations migrate over water from the vicinity of the Gulf of St. Lawrence and the Bay of Fundy to the Lesser Antilles and northeastern South America. Studies of energy consumption and fat reserves show that fat individuals are able to make overwater journeys in excess of 3,000 km (1,863 mi).

PREDATORS Ravens, crows, gulls, owls, weasels and Arctic and red foxes all take eggs or chicks when they can. Domestic livestock sometimes trample significant numbers of nests. Falcons often target Least Sandpipers on the wintering grounds. Solitary individuals are 3 times more likely to be killed by predators than are individuals in a flock.

LONGEVITY The maximum recorded longevity was 16 years; this individual was still breeding.

CONSERVATION ISSUES The wetlands used as staging areas and wintering grounds are threatened with modification and development by drainage and construction and modification to agricultural land.

NOTES The genus name is from the Greek *skaladris* used by Aristotle for a gray, speckled shorebird. The species name is from the Latin *pusillus,* meaning "very small." The Least Sandpiper has also been placed in the genus *Erolia.* The common name refers to its small size, as it is the smallest of the American sandpipers. Other English common names are least stint, mud peep, sand peep, and ox-eye. It is known as *correlimos menudillo* or *minutilla blanca* in Spanish, and as *bécasseau minuscule* in French.

SUGGESTED ADDITIONAL READING

Burton, J. and R. McNeil. 1976. Age determination of six species of North American Shorebirds. *Bird Banding,* 47:201–209.

Butler, R.W. and G.W. Kaiser. 1994. Migration chronology, length of stay, sex ratio and body mass of Least Sandpipers (*Calidris minutilla*).

Butler, R.W., G.W. Kaiser and G.E.J. Smith. 1987. Migration chronology, length of stay, sex ratio, and weight of Western Sandpipers (*Calidris mauri*) on the south coast of British Columbia. *J. Field Ornith.*, 58:103–111.

Cooper, J. 1994. Least Sandpiper (*Calidris minutilla*). In *The Birds of North America*. No. 115 (A. Poole and F. Gill eds.). Philadelphia, PA: The Birds of North America, Inc.

Cooper, J.M. and E.H. Miller. 1992. Brood amalgamation and alloparental care in Least Sandpipers (*Calidris minutilla*). *Can J. Zool.*, 70:403–405.

MacLean, S.F. Jr. 1974. Lemming bones as a source of calcium for arctic sandpipers (*Calidris* spp.). *Ibis*, 116:552–557.

Miller, E.H. 1979. Egg size in the Least Sandpiper (*Calidris minutilla*) on Sable Island., Nova Scotia, Canada. *Ornis Scand.*, 10:10–16.

Miller, E.H. 1979. Functions of display flights by males of the Least Sandpiper (*Calidris minutilla*) on Sable Island Nova Scotia. *Can. J. Zool.*, 57:876–893.

Miller, E.H. 1983. Habitat and breeding cycle of the Least Sandpiper on Sable Island Nova Scotia. *Can. J. Zool.*, 61:2880–2898.

Miller, E.H. 1983. Structure of display flights in the Least Sandpiper. *Condor*, 85:220–242.

Miller, E.H. 1983. The structure of aerial displays in three species of *Caladridinae*. *Auk.*, 100:440–451.

Miller, E.H. 1985. Parental Behavior in the Least Sandpiper (*Calidris minutilla*). *Can. J. Zool.*, 63:1593–1601.

Miller, E.H. 1986. Components of variation in nuptial calls of the Least Sandpiper (*Calidris minutilla*; *Aves, Scolopacidae*). *Syst. Zool.*, 35:400–413.

Miller, E.H. and R. McNeil. 1988. Longevity record for a Least Sandpiper: a revision. *J. Field Ornithol.*, 59:403–404.

Spaans, A.L. 1976. Molt of flight and tail feathers of the Least Sandpiper in Surinam, South America. *Bird Banding*, 47:359–364.

Stilt Sandpiper

Calidris himantopus | Scolopacidae Charadriiformes | p. 58

DISTRIBUTION This genus with 20 species is found worldwide. The Stilt Sandpiper breeds north of the tree line along the west coast of the Hudson Bay, the Canadian Arctic coast, and along the north coast of Alaska to Barrow. The birds winter in southern California, the northern Gulf of California, the Gulf of Mexico near the mouth of the Rio Grande, and in Florida and the Caribbean. Wintering populations are present in southern Florida and the Caribbean. The majority of the population winters in central South America from Peru and Chile to Argentina and southern Brazil.

FOOD AND FEEDING HABITS

On the wintering grounds they prefer protected waters, shallow pools, and marshes and are seldom seen on unprotected coasts or sandy beaches. They frequently feed belly deep in ponds and shallow lagoons and use rapid, irregular vertical probes that submerge the head. They feed on vegetated edges of exposed mudflats by pecking and probing. In the summer they forage by wading in water and pecking at individual prey located by sight and by using feel and smell as they probe in soft bottoms. Foods include larvae and adult diving beetles, snails, adult flies, larval insects, and small seeds. Larval midges are a significant food for young birds. Adults swim well but have not been seen to forage while swimming. While nesting they may feed on the breeding territory or travel as much as 8 km (5 mi) to suitable foraging habitat. They often feed and associate with yellowlegs and dowitchers.

REPRODUCTION

The Stilt Sandpiper nests north of the tree line in dry, open tundra.

Seasonality Stilt Sandpipers can be found on Floridian and Caribbean coasts most abundantly during seasonal migrations and are usually present in modest numbers in the winter months.

Courtship Males advertise breeding territories with display flights at a height of 20 to 60 m (65 to 200 ft) lasting several minutes. In display flights the bird uses shallow wingbeats, with the tail often spread, and often accompanies this by gliding and singing with *eree* calls. Males often sing while chasing females. They also fly ahead of females, raise their wings almost vertically, and sing as they tilt side to side while falling almost to the earth in front of the female. After landing, the males often stretch their wings upward and give an *errit* call. First-time breeders and unmated males vocalize and perform flight displays much more frequently than reuniting pairs do.

Territoriality The usual breeding territory is about 8 ha (20 acres) with nests more than 100 m (330 ft) apart, but in favorable circumstances they may have territories as small as 1 ha (2.5 acres). Territorial defense is maintained until incubation duties supersede. Fidelity to mate and territory is high, with about 50% of the pairs remaining together in succeeding years.

Nest and Nest Site The male initiates

the nest scrape and may initiate 5 or more before the female selects 1 as satisfactory. The nest, a depression in the ground, is about 10 cm (4 in) across by 3 cm (1 in) deep and is lined with grass and leaves. It is usually placed over 152 m (500 ft) from the tree line, often in wet tundra with dwarf willows, dwarf birch, and other tundra, shrubs, and lichens. The nest may also be placed on adjacent drier slopes or in dry sedge meadows. The nest may be well hidden in dry vegetation or exposed on gravel ridges or sedge hummocks. Pairs often reuse the same nest in subsequent years.

Eggs The eggs are grayish white, 36 by 25 mm (1.4 by 1 in), marked more boldly on the large end with chestnut, brown, and lavender. The eggs weigh about 11 g (0.4 oz) each and are deposited at intervals of about 36 hours. The average clutch size is 3.9 eggs with a range of 2 to 5 per nest. In 1 measured instance, the weight of the clutch of 4 eggs was 75% of the weight of the female. Late-hatching clutches are thought to be the result of renesting. Rapid gonadal regression would indicate that renesting is unlikely more than a week after incubation begins.

Incubation Continuous incubation begins after the last egg is deposited and lasts 19 to 21 days. Nesting in local populations is highly synchronous, with 80% of the eggs hatching within a 7-day period. The nest is continuously attended by the male during the day and by the female at night, except in some periods of severe inclement weather. Unincubated eggs exposed to below-freezing temperatures for several days can still hatch, as can incubated eggs that are aban-

doned for several days. Adult birds flushed from the nest by potential predators show injured-bird and rodent-run distraction displays.

Fledging The entire clutch hatches within a period of 10 to 14 hours, and the parents lead the chicks away from the nest as soon as all the chicks are dry. At hatching, the dusky white down is marked with black stripes on the head and is marbled with black and brown on the back, wings, and thighs. The weight doubles in the 1st 10 days of life. Young chicks crouch when parents give an alarm call, but older chicks run to cover before crouching and becoming immobile. The young are led to wet marshy areas to feed and may be as far as 2 miles from the nest site within 2 weeks. Males have been reported tending chicks other than their own offspring. Females leave the young after 2 to 7 days, and the males depart when the chicks are about 2 weeks of age. The young fledge when about 17 or 18 days old and begin to move from the nesting areas before they are a month old.

Age at First Breeding Most individuals remain on the wintering grounds in their 2nd summer and begin breeding at 2 years of age. A small percentage breed at 1 year of age.

BEHAVIOR In the winter they are quite gregarious and form groups of 10 to 100 birds. They often form mixed-species flocks with Semipalmated Sandpipers.

MIGRATION Stilt Sandpipers often gather in flocks for migration. The main route south is through the center of the North American continent, but significant numbers move along the east coast of the U.S. Failed breeders migrate south first in late June. Postbreeding females depart in early July, and postbreeding males travel several weeks later. Juveniles move south from late July until September with peak numbers in the U.S. in mid-August. The migration north begins in March and April in South America, with peak numbers arriving in the southern U.S. in mid May and at the breeding grounds in early June. Non-breeders often remain on the wintering grounds.

PREDATORS Weasels and Arctic and red foxes seek the eggs in the nests and sometimes catch unwary chicks. Migrating birds are taken by owls, hawks, and jaegers. In years with low lemming populations, hungry predators destroy more nests.

LONGEVITY Wild birds have been recaptured as long as 9 years after banding.

CONSERVATION ISSUES Overgrazing by geese is degrading summer habitat in Canada. Development on coastal lagoons in South America is reducing winter habitat.

NOTES The genus name is from the Greek *skaladris* used by Aristotle for a gray, speckled shorebird. The species name is from the Greek *Himanto*

(strap or thong) and *pous* (foot), in reference to the legs, which are as long and thin as a leather thong. This bird, originally described as a member of the genus *Tringa*, has also has been placed in the monospecific genus *Micropalama*. The American common name for this group of sandpipers is "peep," in reference to their diminutive calls. The common name "stint" used for this bird and several similar birds in the genus refers to their small size. Other common names are bastard yellowlegs, frost snipe. and long-legged sandpiper. In Spanish it is called *correlimos patilargo* or *correlimos zancolín*, and in French *bécasseau échasse*.

SUGGESTED ADDITIONAL READING

Burton, P.J.K. 1972. The feeding techniques of Stilt Sandpipers and dowitchers. *San Diego Soc Nat Hist Transactions,* 17:63–68.

Jehl, J.R. Jr. 1970. Sexual selection for size difference in two species of sandpipers. *Evolution,* 24:311–319.

Klima, J. and J.R. Jehl Jr. 1998. Stilt Sandpiper (*Calidris himantopus*). In A. Poole and F. Gill (eds.), *Birds of North America. No. 341.* Philadelphia: The Birds of North America, Inc.

Short-billed Dowitcher

Limnodromus griseus | Scolopacidae Charadriiformes | p. 59

DISTRIBUTION This genus with 3 species is found in the temperate and tropical New World and in Asia. The Asian Dowitcher (*L. semipalmatus*) breeds in Siberia and winters in Southeast Asia and northern Australia. The Long-billed Dowitcher (*L. scolopaceus*) breeds in Siberia and Alaska and winters from Oregon south through Central America. The Short-billed Dowitcher breeds only in the New World. Three subspecies are recognized, with *L. g. caurinus* breeding in Alaska and the Yukon and wintering from California to Peru. *L. g. hendersoni* breeds in British Columbia and Manitoba, wintering from the southeastern U.S. to Panama. *L. g. griseus* breeds in northern Quebec and Labrador and winters on the south Atlantic through the Caribbean to Brazil. The aerial songs of the 3 subspecies on the nesting grounds are quantitatively different.

FOOD AND FEEDING HABITS

On the wintering grounds they feed on worms, snails, clams, and crustaceans. They usually feed in flocks that gradually work their way across the flats, but when a local resource is discovered, they may become very territorial and aggressive about a small resource area. Feeding is primarily by vertical thrusts of the long beak into soft tidal mudflats or shallow pools in marshes. Pits near the end of the beak probably protect sensors that help identify prey when the beak is deeply inserted into the bottom mud. When probing in shallow water the birds commonly submerse the entire head to allow full penetration of the beak into the substrate. On the breeding grounds the primary prey are adults, pupae and larvae of various flies as well as beetles, snails, and seeds gathered from muskeg, bogs, wet sedge meadows, and coastal tundra. When available at feeding stops during the birds' migration, the eggs of horseshoe crabs may make up most of their diet. Feeding is by day and night, often in large flocks.

REPRODUCTION Dowitchers nest on seasonally soggy ground in the brief Arctic summer.

Seasonality Eggs are laid in late May or early June, with replacement clutches laid sometimes as late as July.

Courtship A call described as a liquid, musical contralto gurgle has accompanied the hovering display flight over the territory.

Territoriality Males declare territories before the females arrive on the breeding grounds.

Nest and Nest Site The nest is located on a small hummock near or surrounded by water in bogs or muskegs.

Eggs The usual clutch is 4 dark-flecked, buff-green to brown eggs measuring 41 by 29 mm (1.6 by 1.1 in) and weighing about 17.5 g (0.6 g). The clutch averages about 60% of the body weight of the female.

Incubation Both sexes share in the typical incubation period of 20 days.

Fledging At hatching, the chicks have a pattern of paired dark lines on the back and sides. The young are led to feeding areas shortly after hatching and are tended primarily by the male, as the female deserts the brood and migrates south.

Age at First Breeding Most individuals breed in their 1st year, but some juveniles spend their 1st summer on the wintering grounds without molting into full breeding plumage.

BEHAVIOR The Short-billed Dowitcher is more commonly found near salt water, while the Long-billed Dowitcher is usually near fresh water. When roosting at high tide, dowitchers and Red Knots settle near the water with Dunlins and Western Sandpipers higher on the beach.

MIGRATION Adults in the tropics begin moving north in March and arrive at the breeding grounds in May, with most laying complete in early June. Females begin assembling in migratory flocks after the clutch hatches and begin departing southward in early July. They are followed in about 2 weeks by the males and eventually by the juveniles. They arrive on the wintering grounds from mid-August to early October.

PREDATORS Foxes and weasels take the eggs and chicks. The adults are sometimes part of the habitual prey of Peregrine Falcons.

LONGEVITY There is no published data on the longevity of dowitchers in the wild.

CONSERVATION ISSUES The world population of Short-billed Dowitchers is now estimated at over 100,000 birds, but at staging areas in the eastern U.S., the population declined 46% between 1972 and 1983.

NOTES The genus name is from the Greek *limno* (lake) and *dromos* (running). The species name is named from the Greek for its grizzled, gray color. This bird has previously been placed into the genus *Scolopax*. When in breeding plumage, they are also called common dowitcher, eastern dowitcher, brown snipe, or red-breasted snipe in English. They are called *agujata gris* in Spanish, and *bécasseau* or *bécasseau roux* in French.

SUGGESTED ADDITIONAL READING

Burton, P.J.K. 1972. The feeding techniques of Stilt Sandpipers and Dowitchers. *San Diego Soc Nat Hist Transactions,* 17:63–68.

Mallory, E.P. and D.C. Schneider. 1979. Agonistic behavior in Short-billed Dowitchers feeding on a patchy resource. *Wilson Bulletin,* 91:272–278.

Miller, E.H., W.W.H. Gunn and R.E. Harris. 1983. Geographic variation in the aerial song of the Short-billed Dowitcher (*Aves, Scolopacidae*). *Canadian Journal of Zoology,* 61:2191–2198.

Laughing Gull

Larus atricilla | **Laridae Charadriiformes** | **p. 60**

DISTRIBUTION This genus with 38 species is found worldwide foraging along marine and freshwater coasts. Two subspecies are recognized, with *L. a. megalopterus* breeding along the coast from Nova Scotia to Florida and both coasts of Mexico. In the winter the northern birds move south and disperse widely in Central America and northern South America. The subspecies *L. a. atricilla* breeds in the West Indies and most of the suitable Caribbean islands adjacent to South America, wintering as far south as Brazil. This is the only gull commonly found on the islands of the Caribbean, and it is rarely seen except in the breeding season from March to November. It is one of the most abundant coastal breeding birds in the southeastern United States.

FOOD AND FEEDING HABITS

The Laughing Gull eats a very broad variety of organic material. Shallow-water marine invertebrates eaten include snails, clams, crabs, shrimp, worms, and horseshoe crab eggs and larvae. They catch fish and squid by hovering at less than 3 m (10 ft), then dropping lightly on the prey, seldom becoming completely submerged. They scavenge dead fish and other offal from fishing boats at sea and after it has washed ashore. When rough seas or high tides make foraging difficult, they go inland to feed on insects, which they catch in the air and pluck from meadow foliage. Flocks may assemble to feed on exposed worms as fields are tilled or to feed on outbreaks of grasshoppers or crickets. They may "plow the water" for small fish by flying close to the surface with the lower mandible submerged. Although primarily diurnal, they do regularly forage at night. They make considerable use of food resources provided by man such as french fries, pizza crust, and chicken bones dropped near fast-food vendors, as well as a cornucopia of scraps from landfills. They steal food from terns, pelicans, and skimmers and have food taken from them by Herring Gulls and Frigatebirds. They are particularly adept at landing on the head of a surfacing Brown Pelican and stealing fish from the side of the pouch. Laughing gulls are reported to eat the eggs of Sooty Terns and Noddy Terns, but both terns may nest in colonies adjacent to gull colonies without any obvious concern for predation. Eggs in untended booby nests are quickly taken by gulls. Although they have salt glands that allow them to drink seawater, they prefer to drink freshwater from shallow bodies of water.

REPRODUCTION Laughing Gulls are the most abundant breeding marine bird in the southeastern United States. They nest in colonies of up to several thousand pairs in a variety of habitats isolated from terrestrial predators.

Seasonality Laughing Gulls return to the breeding colony at least a month before copulation and egg production. First eggs are laid in April or May, depending on geographic location.

Courtship The male advertises with a series of calls and head tosses. When a female lands on the territory the male faces away, hiding his black head. As courtship proceeds, the female solicits food, and the male provides offerings. After mounting the female, the male gives an extended copulation call, which continues through the act. Afterwards the birds bathe, preen, and sleep. The pair bond is monogamous for at least 1 season and often continues for several more.

Territoriality The nest site is claimed soon after the annual return to the breeding colony. The nesting territory extends 0.5 to 3 m (2 to 10 ft) beyond the nest, with smaller territories in dense vegetation and larger territories in sparse vegetation. It is defended against predators by the gulls' swooping close to them while making threat calls, or by making threat calls and displays from the ground. Other Laughing Gulls may intrude on the territory seeking copulations and thieving nesting material; they may be territorial interlopers, or just neighbors that accidentally land. Laughing Gulls are often displaced from breeding colonies by Herring Gulls.

Nest and Nest Site The nest is often on a natural or dredge spoil island and may be placed on a sandy beach or rocky shoreline, but it usually is in marsh vegetation. Both members of the pair usually participate in nest building, but unpaired males may build a nest as an additional enticement to unpaired females. The nest is started before egg laying begins, but additions may continue throughout incubation. Nest density is variable, with demand due to colony density. On small islands with large populations, density may be as high as 1 nest per 3 sq m (33 sq ft) with some as close as 1 m (3 ft).

Eggs The normal clutch is 2 or 3 eggs but may be as many as 5. The eggs are brown or greenish buff with irregular brown and black splotches. The eggs average about 5.2 by 3.7 cm (2 by 1.5 in) and weigh about 40 g (1.4 oz) with each egg in the clutch usually slightly smaller than the prior one. Eggs are laid at 1- to 3-day intervals, usually at night. Replacement eggs may be laid, but 2nd broods are never attempted.

Incubation Incubation begins after the 2nd egg is laid. The eggs hatch at 1- or 2-day intervals after an incubation period of 24 days. Both parents incubate with a nest relief cycle of 20 minutes to 3 hours. The eggs are continuously covered. The first 2 eggs hatch within 6 hours of each other, but the 3rd egg may not hatch until 1 to 5 days later. This late-hatched egg may facilitate brood reduction because it is much smaller than the other residents of the nest. The range in size and needs of chicks also allows the adults to use a wider array of food items. Laughing gulls may be an indicator species demonstrating the detrimental effects of low-level, long-term oil pollution. Experimentally 0.02 ml (0.004 tsp) of oil applied to eggs resulted in 83% mortality, as compared with 2% mortality in untreated eggs. Oil applied to the breast of incubating Laughing Gulls also caused a significant mortality of the eggs. Hatching success in natural colonies may exceed 90% when predators and disturbance are absent.

Fledging The hatchlings are covered

with a light gray-brown down with mottled darker markings. For the 1st week, chicks stay on or very near the nest where they are fed primarily marine prey. At 1 week of age the chicks are mobile, fully recognize the parents' voices, and begin to wander farther from the nest. Parental voice recognition is essential to sort out the melee in colonies with high nesting density in which the chicks wander across other territories to form into flocks. The chicks fledge at about 42 ± 5 days. The parents continue to feed the chicks on or near the nest for 2 or 3 weeks after fledging. Fledging success for 3-egg clutches in one study was about 44%, producing 1.3 young per nesting pair. For 2-egg nests the success rate was only 36%, producing 0.71 young per pair.

Age at First Breeding Laughing gulls begin breeding at age 3.

BEHAVIOR Laughing Gulls usually roost, feed, travel, and nest in flocks. The flap rate of 2.9 flaps per second is considerably accelerated when urgent movement is needed.

MIGRATION Laughing Gulls in the northern part of their range gather into flocks in September and October and move south an average distance of 3,100 miles to Latin America and the coast of the Gulf of Mexico. U.S. Gulf Coast birds tend to overwinter on the Gulf Coast. Laughing Gulls of unknown origin arrive in Puerto Rico and the Virgin Islands in March to nest in May. This is the first of the many summer migrant seabirds to arrive in the Caribbean. Adults and immatures depart in the fall, leaving an absence of gulls in the winter. Birds too young to breed often stay in the wintering areas instead of migrating with the adults.

PREDATORS Egg predators include rats, Fish Crows, Common Crows, American Oystercatchers, and Herring Gulls. Chicks are taken by gulls and owls. Chicks dabbling in shallow tropical marine waters may be grasped by the tentacles of carpet anemones and drowned as waves wash over them. Owls, hawks, and foxes regularly take adults, while house cats and domestic dogs wreak havoc if they gain access to a colony with young chicks.

LONGEVITY The maximum recorded longevity of a banded bird is 19 years.

CONSERVATION ISSUES The habit of roosting and feeding on landfills has probably assisted population expansion, while roosting and feeding at airports has resulted in various population control activities including shooting and poisoning the birds and destroying their eggs. The population seems to be stable at around 500,000 in spite of the many tribulations set upon the species.

NOTES The genus name is from the Latin, meaning "rapacious seabird." The species name is from the Latin *ater* (black) and *cilla* (tail). In Spanish it is called *guanaguanare*, *galleguito*, *gaviota gallega*, *gaviota risueña* and *cabecinegra*. In French it is *mauve à tête noire*, *goéland atricille* and *pigeon de la mer*.

SUGGESTED ADDITIONAL READING

Beer, C.G. 1979. Vocal communication between Laughing Gull parents and chicks. *Behaviour,* 70:118–149.

Burger, J. 1996. Laughing Gull (*Larus atricilla*). In A. Poole and F. Gill (eds.), *The Birds of North America. No. 225.* Philadelphia: The Birds of North America, Inc.

Hahn, D.C. 1981. Asynchronous hatching in the Laughing Gull (*Larus atricilla*): Cutting losses and reducing rivalry. *Animal Behaviour,* 29:421–427.

Ring-billed Gull
Larus delawarensis | **Laridae Charadriiformes** | **p. 61**

DISTRIBUTION This genus with 38 species is found worldwide foraging along marine and freshwater coasts. Ring-billed Gulls nest in the northern U.S. and southern Canada, with the eastern population wintering on the Gulf of Mexico and Atlantic coasts through the Bahamas and Greater Antilles to the Virgin Islands.

FOOD AND FEEDING HABITS

This gull is extremely omnivorous. They catch fish such as killifish and silversides in salt water, and alewives and rainbow smelt in fresh water. Along the coast they catch crabs, shrimp, and worms. Inland, as they feed on pastures or tilled soil, they capture mice, grasshoppers, grubs, and earthworms. The gulls eat grains when available. Many forms of carrion are eaten, from the most minute beach detritus to whales, and the gulls regularly form aggregations that feed at garbage dumps and parking lots of fast food restaurants. Ring-billed Gulls steal food from shorebirds, ducks, Pied-billed Grebes, coots, pelicans, and egrets. They eat the eggs and chicks of terns, ducks, night herons, cormorants, avocets, and many songbirds. Mammalian prey includes mice, moles, shrews, ground squirrels, pocket gophers, and rabbits. They eat orchard fruit, palmetto berries, blueberries, strawberries, and dates both from the ground and plucked off the tree by the gull in flight. Most feeding is within 15 km (9 mi) of the colony, with some birds ranging as far as 32 km (20 mi).

REPRODUCTION Ring-billed Gulls usually nest on the ground in areas remote from predators and human disturbance.

Seasonality Most eggs are laid between early May and mid-June, with most young fledged by mid-August.

Courtship Males advertise from the ground by giving long calls and head tosses to flying females. With extensive calling, displaying, and flying about, the mutual hostility between male and female declines and the pair bond is formed. The male often feeds the female just prior to copulation. Most pairs remain together for at least 2 years, although an annual divorce rate of 14% has been recorded in one colony. Nesting in subsequent years is often within 6 m (20 ft) of the prior year's nest site. Female-female pairs are formed, with each female laying eggs in a mutual nest, resulting in superclutches of 5 to 7 eggs. Males readily fertilize both members of the pair but do not participate in incubation or rearing the young. Polygynous parental groups have been recorded with 1 male and 2 females.

Territoriality Pairs select a territory of 1 to 4 sq m (11 to 44 sq ft) after the pair bond is formed. Territories often expand during incubation due to failure of nearby nests. Nearest neighbor distance is usually less than 1 m (40 in). California Gulls are dominant in selecting nesting areas and may disperse Ring-billed Gulls to less desirable sites. The nest site is defended from conspecifics by ritualized displays on the territory such as head tosses and running charges with the bill open. Physical combat may ensue with pecking, wing pulling, and bill locking. The territory is defended against predators by swooping at a predator with a charge call, defecating, and swooping upward.

Nest and Nest Site Nesting colonies are situated in low vegetation on peninsulas or islands in freshwater lakes, rivers, or the sea. Ring-billed Gulls often nest in mixed-species colonies with other gulls such as Herring Gulls and California Gulls. The typical nest is a scrape enhanced with weeds and grasses on sandbars, beaches, rock, or bare earth. They avoid dense cover but favor a nest site under low plants that provide cover from aerial predators. Both members of the pair participate in bringing twigs, grass, leaves, and moss to build a nest with an outer diameter of 43 cm (17 in). The inner cup is 23 cm (9 in) wide and 5 cm (2 in) deep. They rarely build stick nests in low trees. Nest sites are reused in subsequent years. Nest density may be as high as .54 nests/sq m (.45 nests/sq yd).

Eggs Eggs measure 58 by 42 mm (2.3 by 1.7 in) and weigh 59 g (2 oz), making up 12% of the female's weight. The clutch of 3 light-brown eggs is marked with dark-brown, lavender, and gray splotches. Eggs are laid every other day, with inexperienced birds and individuals on the periphery laying a week or 2 after the experienced birds in the center of the colony. Individuals in immature plumage or breeding for the first time have fewer and smaller eggs. Replacement clutches are rare after nest loss.

Incubation Both parents share the 26-day incubation period, which begins sporadically after the 1st egg is laid and becomes fully effective when the clutch is complete. They retrieve eggs rolled out of the nest or rebuild the nest around the eggs. They may also retrieve and incubate pebbles with markings similar to those of eggs. Most eggs in a nest hatch within a 24-hour period. Ring-billed Gulls' hatching success has been recorded from 15% to more than 90%.

Fledging Hatchlings are covered with a smoke-gray to buff down with darker spots on the head and mottling on the back. Brooding is almost continuous at hatching and declines daily, ending when the chicks are 7 days old. By the 2nd day of age, the chick begins to make short excursions from the nest. Both parents feed the chicks fish and insects via nearby regurgitation. Chicks over 1 day of age approach to be fed when an adult gives a *mew* call. Adults accept any chicks in the nest or territory until the brood is 5 days old. Five-day-old chicks can distinguish the parents individually, and the parents recognize their own chicks after 5 days. Some adoption of chicks among nonrelatives seems to occur. The chicks are able to swim at 2 or 3 days of age. Chicks hide, crouch, and become silent when nearby gulls give an alert call. Some chicks 15 to 20 days old band together in crèches. Fledging is at about 36 days, with considerable improvement in skills evident with 1 week of experience. Hatching success and fledging success are highest in nests centrally located in the colony. Family groups disintegrate and depart the colony about 11 days after fledging when the chicks are about 47 days of age.

Age at First Breeding Full adult plumage is not attained until the 3rd year of age. In one study 33% of the breeding birds captured were 2 years old.

BEHAVIOR
Individual distance is about 1 m (1 yd) when gathered in aggregations outside the breeding season. Flight speed has been recorded up to 70 kph (44 mph) with wingbeats of 3.2 per second. They float buoyantly on the water and may dip the head to catch near-surface prey.

MIGRATION
The southern migration is gradual and dispersed. Early-nesting birds begin to travel south as early as July when their young fledge. Others may remain on the nesting grounds until September. The northward migration may begin in late February and March, but the rate of movement is dependent on prevailing weather and snowmelt in the breeding colonies.

PREDATORS
Raccoons, foxes, coyotes, weasels, mink, skunks, crows, and ravens eat the eggs, chicks, and adults but may create greater havoc by generating a panic in which gulls knock eggs from the nest and temporarily desert the colony, allowing the eggs to die of cold. Repeated visits by predators such as Great-horned Owls may lead to abandonment of the nesting colony.

LONGEVITY
The maximum-recorded age of a Ring-billed Gull was 31 years 9 months, but band wear and loss has probably depressed the maximum-recorded age.

CONSERVATION ISSUES
Populations declined drastically due to harvest of adults for the millinery trade and of the eggs for human consumption and because of disturbance of nesting colonies. Most population indices show an increase in populations over the past 30 years. Abundance at airports has been considered a flight hazard, and colonies in urban areas are sometimes unwelcome due to their droppings. Gull control at nesting colonies in the Great Lakes has been implemented to reduce gull-human conflicts and to reduce gulls' competition with nesting terns.

NOTES
The genus name is from the Latin, meaning "rapacious seabird." The species name refers to the Delaware River, the origin of the first specimen described. They are also called common gull and lake gull in English, *apipizca pinta* or *gaviota piquianillada* in Spanish, and *goéland à bec cerclé* in French.

SUGGESTED ADDITIONAL READING

Haymes, G.T. and H. Blokpoel. 1980. The influence of age on the breeding biology of Ring-billed Gulls. *Wilson Bulletin*, 92:221–228.

Ryder, J.P. 1993. Ring-billed Gull (*Larus delawarensis*). In A. Poole and F. Gill (eds.), *The Birds of North America. No. 33*. Philadelphia: The Birds of North America, Inc.

Southern, W.E. 1974. Florida distribution of Ring-billed Gulls from the Great Lakes region. *Bird Banding*, 45:341–352.

Caspian Tern

Sterna caspia | **Laridae Charadriiformes** | **p. 62**

DISTRIBUTION This genus with 30 species is found worldwide. Caspian Terns breed worldwide in northern temperate regions from the Baltic, Black, Caspian, and Aral Seas, through Africa, Asia, Australia, and New Zealand. They are generally absent from oceanic islands. They breed in America from the northwest coast of Mexico north to Canada and across Canada to the Great Lakes, Quebec, and Newfoundland. Nesting colonies are found inland in North Dakota and Minnesota and on the southeastern Atlantic and Gulf of Mexico coasts. They generally avoid water colder than 13°C.

FOOD AND FEEDING HABITS

The diet of Caspian Terns is almost exclusively fish. The selection seems to be based on availability of a species 8 to 26 cm (3 to 10 in) long. As ecosystems change through the year the most abundant fish in the diet may change substantially. Caspian Terns may fish near shore in clear, calm water or 32 km (20 mi) or more offshore in deeper water. They fish by flying slowly at 5 to 20 m (16 to 60 ft) above the water, hovering briefly, then plunging to grasp a fish with the bill. They may submerge completely for very brief periods. When predatory fish force schools of baitfish to the surface, Caspian Terns may surface dip or rest on the water surface and submerge the head to catch fish. They are willing to travel long distances to use a concentrated food source. In Finland they have been found with fish tags applied 70 to 85 km (43 to 53 mi) from the colony, and in California fish have been found with trout tags applied 60 km (37 mi) away. In fresh water they commonly eat rainbow smelt and alewives, and in marine ecosystems they eat anchovies, shiner perch, herring, sardines, topsmelt, mullet, pinfish, and staghorn skulpin. Pellets cast contain fish bones, scales, remains of crayfish, clams, snails, and insects. They pirate food from other gulls and terns when opportunity presents.

REPRODUCTION

Seasonality Most eggs are laid along the coast of the Gulf of Mexico in April or May, but further north laying may be delayed until late May, June, or early July. Replacement clutches in southern latitudes may be laid as late as August or September. In northern Australia, nesting occurs in every month.

Courtship Unmated males and females may visit several different colonies in the course of a day. Males court females away from the colony by flying over them with a fish and calling. Females take flight and chase the male, who lands and offers the fish with bowing movements of the head. As the female gradually accepts the male she will accept the fish, sometimes with begging in a hunched posture. Copulation often follows courtship feeding. Established pairs perform a display flight, climbing to as much as 200 m (656 ft), then descending with a series of glides, dives, and vocalizations. A soft buzz is often produced by the feathers while the bird is in a display dive. When copulation is initiated by the male he carries a fish as he approaches the female in a forward-erect posture, then bows with the crest raised. If she is receptive he flies onto her back, reaches forward over her head offering the fish while she raises her tail and he lowers his. Females may initiate copulation by begging, and the males respond with a forward erect posture and mild bowing before mounting. Caspian Terns are generally monogamous, but female-female pairs do produce nests with larger-than-normal fertile clutches. About 25% of the pairs in one study remained together in a subsequent year.

Territoriality Caspian Terns may nest as solitary pairs, as small colonies and as densely occupied large colonies. Colonial nest densities have been recorded from .39 to 1.29 nests per sq m (.32 to 1 nest per sq yd), with individual territories .5 to 1.5 m (20 to 60 in) in diameter. Territories are defended with an open beak and wings bent with elbows out. Nesting colony fidelity is about 75%, but pairs with reproductive failures often move to other colonies. Colony sites may be used repeatedly for over 100 years but may be completely and abruptly abandoned if disturbed early in the nesting season. Plant succession on the preferred, bare ephemeral habitat may cause the colony to move away.

Nest and Nest Site Many scrapes are made by both sexes in various parts of the colony until a single location is selected. The nest is a shallow depression frequently situated on a small island less than 2 ha (5 acres) in extent. The substrate is usually sand, shell, or gravel with sparse or no vegetation, but hard soil, dead vegetation, and depressions in bedrock are also used. Dredge spoil islands and shell berms are often favored. It is common for Caspian Terns to form subcolonies (with no mixing of types) within or adjacent to other colonies of nesting seabirds.

Eggs The light-buff to brown eggs with brown or black speckles measure 45 by 64 mm (1.8 by 2.5 in) with an average weight of 64 g (2.2 oz). The normal clutch is 1 to 3 eggs, laid 2 or 3 days apart, with the average number varying from 1.6 to 2.8 in various populations. Renesting birds' clutches average smaller than first-time clutches. Second broods have not been recorded.

Incubation Both parents share in the 27-day incubation period, which begins when the 1st egg is laid. Hatching success is influenced by weather and predators and is usually about 80%. While one bird is incubating, the partner often stands nearby. In hot weather the adults stand near the nest cup to shade the eggs.

Fledging The chicks come in 2 color phases—one is pale cream with faint spots, yellowish skin and orange feet, and the other is grayish brown with distinct dark spots, dark skin, and olive feet. Chicks are capable of leaving the nest by 6 hours of age but usually remain on the nest for several days. By 3 days of age the chicks leave the nest and crouch nearby on the ground upon hearing the adult's alarm call. Adults usually adjust the size of fish captured to the needs of the chicks being fed, but if too large a fish is offered, a chick may accept it and leave the tail hanging out of the mouth until the chick can digest the head. Chicks may be killed by adults if they wander into the wrong territory. By 1 week of age the chicks are highly mobile and may move 200 m (656 ft) to nearby water to escape predators. Fledging is at 5 or 6 weeks, but parental care is prolonged, extending sometimes even onto the wintering grounds. Fledging success has been reported from 1 to 1.5 chicks per nest, with most of the loss due to storms and very high tides. Asynchronous hatching results in a graded series of chick sizes in a nest, leading to brood reduction. First-hatched chicks are fed more frequently and have a higher fledging rate than their siblings do. Juveniles at 2 years of age often have not yet developed adult proficiency at capturing fish.

Age at First Breeding Some Caspian Terns return to the breeding ground and nest at 2 years of age but most do not breed successfully until their 3rd or 4th year.

BEHAVIOR They often roost with other gulls and terns, particularly the very similar Royal Tern, on large lakes and estuaries. The individual distance is about 1 m (3 ft) when roosting in neutral areas. When heat stressed, they tilt the head to avoid direct sun radiation on the black cap.

MIGRATION North American populations migrate south leisurely and winter from California and South Carolina south through the Caribbean and Central America to Colombia. Populations breeding in warm climates do not migrate. The spring migration to the breeding grounds is usually rapid.

PREDATORS Chicks and eggs are taken by gulls, ravens, Great Horned Owls, skunks, mink, weasels, foxes, coyotes, northern pike, and diamond-back rattlesnakes. Nests near the periphery of the colony are considerably more subject to predation. Defensive behavior includes a *gakkering* call while swooping at the intruder's head. They may inflict wounds on the heads of colony intruders. Other Caspian Terns will kill chicks when they wander into territories other than their own.

LONGEVITY A Caspian Tern banded in Michigan was recaptured 26 years 2 months later. Annual mortality for adult individuals has been estimated at 11% to 18% and an average life span at 11.9 years.

CONSERVATION ISSUES Egg harvest has been and continues to be detrimental to populations. Increasing human use of nesting areas has had a significant negative effect on many colonies.

NOTES The genus name is from the old English name *starn* used for this group of birds. The species name and common name derive from the original described specimen in the Caspian Sea. This tern also appears in the literature as *Hydroprogne caspia* or *Hydropogne tschegrava*. It is also known as *gaviota de caspia, charrán caspica* or *pagaza piquirroja* in Spanish, and *sterne caspienne* in French.

SUGGESTED ADDITIONAL READING

Cuthbert, F.J. 1985. Reproductive success and colony-site tenacity in Caspian Terns. *Auk,* 105:339–344.

Cuthbert, F.J. and L.R. Wires. 1999. Caspian Tern (*Sterna caspia*). In A. Poole and F. Gill (eds.), *The Birds of North America. No. 403.* Philadelphia: The Birds of North America, Inc.

Lampman, K.P., M.E. Tayor and H. Blokpoel. 1996. Caspian Terns (*Sterna caspia*) breed successfully on a nesting raft. *Colonial Waterbirds,* 19:135–138.

Royal Tern
Sterna maxima | **Laridae Charadriiformes** | **p. 63**

DISTRIBUTION This genus with 30 species is found worldwide. Royal Terns have been divided into 2 races. The race *S. m. albidorsalis* breeds on small islands off the north coast of Mauritania and winters on the west coast of Africa from the Straits of Gibraltar south to Angola, with the highest concentrations in the Gulf of Guinea. The American race of the Royal Tern, *S. m. maxima,* breeds from Maryland through Florida, Louisiana, and Texas and in Mexico south to the Yucatan, with some terns breeding on the Pacific coast. They also breed in the Bahamas and Caribbean. In the winter they are found from the southern U.S. south to Argentina and Peru.

FOOD AND FEEDING HABITS
This tern is an opportunistic feeder on small fish and invertebrates that approach the surface of the sea. The birds forage singly or in small groups but may gather in large, boisterous flocks when predatory fish chase shoals of baitfish to the surface. Royal Terns dive readily but seldom penetrate more than 60 cm (2 ft) under the sea and usually resume flight promptly after each splash. They feed in lagoons and estuaries, along mangrove coastlines, and in open water within 20 km (12 mi) of land; they may travel as much as 65 km (40 mi) from the nesting colony along the coast to feeding sites. In the winter they may venture as much as 145 km (90 mi) offshore in feeding flocks. The diet includes small blue crabs, shrimp, silversides, menhaden, croaker, drum, thread herring, squid, sardines, anchovies, and whatever suitable prey is abundant. Prey fish are generally less than 10 cm (4 in) in length and are swallowed whole. Royal Terns regularly scavenge jetsam from fishing boats.

REPRODUCTION Royal Terns nest in dense colonies near the water and often on low sandy islands.

Seasonality Most Royal Terns in the U.S. and Caribbean lay eggs in May and June, but eggs have been found from April to July. Some colonies lay eggs over a 2-month period, but others are very synchronous and lay all their eggs within less than a week.

Courtship Much of Royal Tern courtship is complex flight maneuvering and feeding of the female by the male. On the ground the male raises the crest and sleeks the neck feathers as he approaches the female with a small food offering. After much circling and strutting, the female may accept and swallow the food. Both members of the pair select the nest site after making several preliminary scrapes. Pairs are monogamous within a breeding season, but continuation of the pair bond has not been reported.

Territoriality The territory is limited to the nest site and only extends to the reach of an incubating bird. Nest densities may become so high that packing results in hexagon-shaped territories.

Nest and Nest Site The nest is usually placed on a sandy substrate on a small island free of mammalian predators. The terns may also place the nest in small depressions on a steep, rocky slope, or among short grass or on bare rock on an elevated plateau. Fidelity to approximate colony site is continuous over years if the colony is not disturbed. Individual pairs seem to stay with others in the colony if an alternative nesting site is selected. Nests are usually close together and have a density of 7 per sq m (6 per sq yd) in some colonies. They often nest in confluence with Sandwich Tern colonies.

Eggs The eggs are a light olive drab with dark-brown and black blotches and measure 64 by 45 mm (2.5 by 1.8 in) and weigh about 64 g (2.2 oz). The clutch is 1 egg; only a small percentage of nests have 2 eggs. The 2-egg nests may be the result of accidental jostling that rolls an egg into an adjacent nest. Up to 3 renesting attempts are made after nest loss, but only 1 brood per year is raised.

Incubation Both parents share in the 30- to 31-day incubation after the egg is laid.

Fledging Hatchlings have a buff down with irregular dark markings and are able to leave the nest and seek nearby cover within 24 hours. Within a few days the chicks form a crèche. Parents recognize their chicks by voice and appearance and feed only their own chicks in the crèche. Chicks recognize their parents by voice. For about the first 4 days the young freeze or climb under vegetation when hearing the alarm call of the parent. When in an established crèche they often take to water in response to a perceived threat. Fledging is at 4 to 5 weeks of age. Feeding juveniles have a dive success rate that is only 62% of adults' and continue to be provided supplemental food for 5 to 8 months after hatching—throughout the migration and on the wintering grounds.

Age at First Breeding Royal Terns usually first breed successfully at the age of 4 but may nest at age 3. Most juveniles visit the breeding colony at age 2, and rarely precocious individuals may nest.

BEHAVIOR The primary aggressive display is an upright stance with the beak slightly elevated, the crest raised, the neck and back feathers ruffled, and the wings held away from the body. Traveling flight speed has been recorded at up to 65 to 80 kph (40 to 50 mph).

MIGRATION The southern migration of mid-Atlantic coastal birds to the Caribbean and South America is primarily in October. Most breeding birds in the Greater and Lesser Antilles also seem to migrate south for the winter. Adults return to the breeding grounds in March and April.

PREDATORS Gulls and crows take unguarded eggs by day, and rats can be serious predators at night. Ruddy Turnstones feed on ineffectually defended eggs of Royal Terns. The turnstone may only peck the egg open and gain a mouthful of contents before being chased away, then return and peck open another egg. This egg predation by turnstones has caused Royal Terns to abandon nesting colonies. Night Herons, hawks, and owls take chicks. Sharks and other predatory fish take members of the crèche when they are swimming offshore. Adults of the colony vocalize while they dive at intruders but seldom approach within 2 m (6 ft) of them and rarely make contact.

LONGEVITY A young, banded Royal Tern was recaptured after 17 years.

CONSERVATION ISSUES Loss of nesting habitat due to coastal development and disturbance by increased use of coastal beaches and recreational boating are of significant concern for the long-term well-being of Royal Terns.

NOTES The genus name is from the old English name *starn* used for this group of birds. The species name is from the Latin *maximus* (greatest). The Royal, Cayenne, Elegant, and Sandwich Terns have been grouped together into the genus *Thalasseus*. They are also called sprat bird in English, *charrán real* in Spanish, and *sterne royale* in French.

SUGGESTED ADDITIONAL READING

Ashmole, N.V. and H. Tovar. 1968. Prolonged parental care in Royal Terns and other birds. *Auk,* 85:90–100.

Blus, L.J., R.M. Prouty and B.S. Neely Jr. 1979. Relation of environmental factors to breeding status of Royal and Sandwich Terns in South Carolina, USA. *Biological Conservation,* 6:301–320.

Buckley, F.G. and P.A. Buckley. 1972. The breeding ecology of Royal Terns, *Sterna (Thalasseus) maxima maxima. Ibis,* 144:344–359.

Sandwich Tern

Sterna sandvicensis | **Laridae Charadriiformes** | **p. 64**

DISTRIBUTION This genus with 30 species is found worldwide. The Sandwich Tern is dispersed widely around the world and has been divided into 3 species. *S. s. sandvicensis* is found on the coasts of Africa and Eurasia. It is absent from the Indian Ocean east of 80° longitude and from the entire Pacific except for birds wintering on the Pacific coast of Central America. The Cayenne Tern (*S. s. eurygnathus*) in South America has an all-yellow bill and has been treated as a separate species. The northern New World form, *S. s. flavidus,* also called Cabot's Tern, breeds from Virginia along the Atlantic and Gulf Coast, through Central America and the Caribbean, with large colonies on the Chandeleur Islands in Louisiana.

FOOD AND FEEDING HABITS

Sandwich Terns plunge-dive from as high as 10 m (33 ft) to penetrate over a meter (3 ft) below the surface for a submergence time of up to 3 seconds. When predatory fish such as tuna drive baitfish to the surface in feeding frenzies, terns may dive from less than 1 m or pluck them from the water while still in flight. Fish are captured crosswise in the beak and immediately swallowed headfirst unless they are intended for feeding to the female or chicks. The sight of diving birds brings a congregation of birds to use the temporarily abundant food supply. They catch and swallow fish up to about 14 cm (5.5 in) in length. Black-headed Gulls frequently steal the catch of Sandwich Terns. Prey species include shrimp, anchovies, sardines, silversides, menhaden, sand lance, and squid.

REPRODUCTION Sandwich Terns nest in dense colonies on small islands.

Seasonality Eggs are laid in May or June, and members of a colony are quite synchronous.

Courtship Courtship is similar to that of other terns, with aerial displays followed by male offerings of small fish.

Territoriality Nesting territories may be as dense as 10 per sq m (1.2 sq yds) but more usually 6 per sq m or as distant as 2 per sq m on the periphery of the colony. The defended area is sometimes as small as the radius of reach of an incubating bird. In stable colonies the pair may use the same nest site in succeeding years. Nesting colonies are mobile and often move to nearby islands in subsequent years or when renesting after being disturbed.

Nest and Nest Site In the U.S. they always form mixed colonies with Royal Terns and in many instances have gull colonies nearby. The nest is a shallow nest scrape in sand, coral rubble or short grass or on bare rock. They nest on the beaches of barrier islands and regularly use small dredge spoil islands.

Eggs The buff to cinnamon-colored eggs are spotted and scrawled with darker-brown markings. Clutch size is 1 to 2 eggs, with average clutch size about 1.5. Eggs are laid at 2- to 5-day intervals. Renesting occurs after nest loss but it is usually successful only if in a group of other pairs that are also renesting.

Incubation Both parents share the 25-day incubation period, which begins when the 1st egg is laid. Eggs hatch an average of 2.5 days apart in nests with 2 eggs. Hatching success of the eggs in the center of the colony is higher than for those on the edge because the edge nests serve as buffers against predators. In hot weather the incubating adult may leave the nest momentarily to dip the belly in the sea before returning to incubate. Storms and high tides are common sources of extensive nest losses.

Fledging Hatchlings have a buff to gray-brown down with black speckles. Parents may travel as far as 25 km from the colony to catch fish for the young and may be seen returning to the colony with several fish held crosswise in the bill. Fish 5 cm (2 in) or less in length are selected for hatchlings. At about 2 weeks of age the young may form crèches but continue to be fed by their own parents. Fledging is at about 27 days, and within a few days most fledglings depart the breeding area with the parents, who continue to feed them for several months.

Age at First Breeding Juveniles remain on the wintering ground until their 3rd spring when some migrate to the breeding grounds late in the season. Most Sandwich Terns first breed at 4 years of age or older.

BEHAVIOR Flight speed is up to 50 kph (31 mph) when the tern is traveling over water.

MIGRATION Sandwich Terns from northern Europe migrate south to spend the winter off the coast of Africa. Northern populations in the U.S. move south to Florida, Cuba and the Bahamas for the winter. Adults arrive in the Virgin Islands in May to nest, then adults and juveniles depart for an unknown wintering ground by the end of September. Large numbers of birds of unknown origin winter in Panama. Seasonal movements of Sandwich Terns in the Caribbean continue to be an intriguing question.

PREDATORS Gulls take the eggs and chicks. Crows and oystercatchers take the eggs. Hawks and owls take the juveniles and adults. Nesting colonies are generally located on islands that are free of mammalian predators, but rats, weasels, mink, foxes, or dogs can devastate a colony if they gain access.

LONGEVITY Maximum age for recovery of a banded Sandwich Tern is 23 years 7 months.

CONSERVATION ISSUES Development and recreational use of nesting areas will continue to make reproduction more difficult. Human disturbance of colonies results in increased mortality for chicks that move outside their territory and are attacked by adults. Continued disturbance by humans and dogs may lead to complete abandonment of the colony site. Fuel oil has been found to be very toxic to Sandwich Tern eggs.

NOTES The genus name is from the old English name *starn* used for this group of birds. The species is named for the town of this name in England. These terns have also been placed into the genus *Thalasseus*. This tern has also been called Cabot's tern, Kentish tern, or gullie bird in English. In Spanish it is called *charrán de Cabot*, *charrán patinegro* or *gaviota piquiaguda*, and in French *sterne caugek*.

SUGGESTED ADDITIONAL READING

Blus, L.J., R.M. Prouty and B.S. Neely Jr. 1979. Relationship of environmental factors to breeding status of Royal and Sandwich Terns in South Carolina, USA. *Biological Conservation,* 16:301–320.

Hutchison, R.E., R.E. Stevenson and W.H. Thorpe. 1968. The basis for individual recognition by voice in the Sandwich tern (*Sterna sandvicensis*). *Behaviour,* 32:150–157.

Shealer, D. 1999. Sandwich Tern (*Sterna sandvicensis*). In A. Poole and F. Gill (eds.), *The Birds of North America. No. 405.* Philadelphia: The Birds of North America, Inc.

Roseate Tern
Sterna dougallii | **Laridae Charadriiformes** | **p. 65**

DISTRIBUTION This genus with 30 species is found worldwide. The Roseate Tern has been divided into 4 subspecies with *S. d. bangsi* in the western Indian Ocean eastward to China and the Sunda Islands, *S. d. korustes* in the Bay of Bengal, *S. d. gracilis* in Australia and New Caledonia, and *S. d. dougallii* in the temperate Atlantic and Caribbean. Roseate Terns are generally absent from the open waters of the central and eastern Pacific. In America they breed from southeast Canada south along the coast to Central America, the Bahamas, and Antilles.

FOOD AND FEEDING HABITS
Roseate Terns feed primarily on saltwater fish 2 to 8 cm (1 to 3 in) long with a maximum length of 15 cm (6 in) and a weight of 15 g (0.5 oz). They require clear water for foraging and frequently find it in deeper waters offshore. Feeding may be solitary while they watch for shoaling fish, or they may join in boisterous mobs with other terns and gulls when baitfish are chased to the surface by schools of predators. They readily steal fish from other terns when opportunity presents. Typical fishing technique is a rapid but shallow plunge 15 cm (6 in) into the water from about 6 m (20 ft) with a submergence of 1 to 2 seconds. Terns feeding alone may make dives to 75 cm (30 in) deep lasting 2.5 seconds from an altitude of 12 m (40 ft). The duration of the submergence is proportional to the height of the dive. Solitary, diving terns are likely to be joined by others when baitfish are forced to the surface. Fish are seized crosswise in the beak, and up to nine have been reported to be carried simultaneously to be fed to chicks in the colony. Prey includes sand lance, herring, young mackerel, silversides, pilchards, dwarf herring, anchovies, menhaden, and sardines. These terns have also been observed catching airborne insects.

REPRODUCTION
Roseate Terns are quite adaptable and may lay their eggs on any flat, undisturbed area.
Seasonality Spring migration takes place in April, with most birds laying eggs from mid-May to mid-June. The migration south is in August and September and may be hastened by a precipitously dropping barometer such as that which precedes a hurricane.
Courtship Courtship includes aerial and ground displays. An unmated bird may fly in circles over the colony while carrying a small fish and giving the *chiVIK* advertising call. Small groups may spiral to 150 m (500 ft) in a stylized flight then glide back to the ground while passing each other. Much of the ground courtship takes place on roosts outside the colony. An essential part of courtship on the ground is the male's offering small fish to the female.
Territoriality Pair bonds are established before the territory is claimed. Then the pair walks around the proposed territory and makes several experimental scrapes. Nest site density may exceed 4 per sq m (2.7 sq ft) per nest, but more commonly it is around 1 nest per 2 sq m (20 sq ft). Nearest-neighbor distance may be as little as

45 cm (18 in). Entire colonies may abandon a site that is disturbed. They are less inclined to abandon the site as incubation and chick growth proceed.

Nest and Nest Site A scrape in the substrate near a plant, boulder, log, or beach flotsam that provides cover is the full extent of nest preparation. Bits of debris are added to the nest during incubation. The eggs may be laid in a depression on open, exposed rock. In cooler climates the nest is protected by placement in tunnels in the grass, in deep crevices, or in mammal burrows. The nest is usually adjacent to salt water on sparsely vegetated sandy islands, sand dunes, sand spits, barrier islands, or pebble beaches. On clay or rocky islands the nesting colony site selected is likely to be more heavily vegetated, with 80% cover 75 cm (30 in) in height. Most colonies are adjacent to protected inshore waters of bays and estuaries. They often nest in subcolonies with Common Terns or with other terns in the genus *Sterna*.

Eggs The brown to greenish-gray eggs with black dots and freckles are 44 by 30 mm (1.7 by 1.2 in) and weigh 20 g (.7 oz). The clutch is 1 or 2 eggs with the proportion variable between populations. Second eggs average about 5% smaller than first eggs.

Incubation Both parents share incubation shifts of up to 6 hours for the 23-day incubation period. Nocturnal disturbance by predators may allow the eggs to cool and may extend the incubation time to as long as 30 days. The 2nd egg hatches 2 to 5 days after the 1st.

Fledging The buff chicks with brown to black speckles are precocial and may be led away from an exposed nest by the parents, while those in or adja-cent to cover may stay in place until 15 or 20 days of age. Parents may fish within 5 km (3 mi) of the colony or in other instances travel 19 to 22 km (12 to 14 mi) to feeding grounds when feeding chicks. The younger chick may starve in times of food scarcity, but there is little overt competition and hostility between siblings. Nest success is increased for nests placed in or against beach flotsam or under over-hanging vegetation. The rate of weight gain of chicks may be reduced by half in windy weather that reduces aquatic visibility and makes precision flying more difficult. When the larger of the chicks fledges, one parent stays with it while the other parent continues to feed the smaller chick. Juveniles continue to be fed by the parents for at least 8 weeks after fledging.

Age at First Breeding Most juveniles remain in the wintering area their 1st and 2nd summer, but some may visit the breeding grounds. Most do not reproduce successfully until their 3rd year.

BEHAVIOR Individual distance in roosting groups may be as close as 10 cm (4 in).

MIGRATION American Roseate Terns from the Northeast migrate directly south across the ocean to winter on the north coast of South America and apparently do not stop in the Antilles en route. Caribbean Roseate Terns also migrate south to the coast of the South American mainland. European Roseate Terns migrate south; most band recoveries indicate that they spend the winter off the coast of Ghana. Nonbreeding birds usually stay on the wintering grounds.

PREDATORS Black-crowned Night Herons eat the eggs and hatchlings. Great-horned Owls hunt adult Roseate Terns in breeding colonies and may cause the entire colony to desert for the night, resulting in chilling of eggs and chicks. Foxes and skunks eat the eggs in colonies accessible from the mainland. Egg-eating Ruddy Turnstones have devastated entire colonies of Roseate Terns. Eggs and adults are still collected by humans for food.

LONGEVITY Survival to breeding age of 3 years is estimated to be 16%. The oldest, recovered banded Roseate Tern was 14 years of age and still breeding. Wear and loss of bands on marked birds probably limits the detection of older birds.

CONSERVATION ISSUES Gull predation has had significant influence on the North American population, causing them to nest in more terrestrial sites that expose them to more avian and mammalian predators. Human predation on adult terns continues in the wintering areas of West Africa and in the Caribbean. There is a loss of breeding habitat due to increased coastal use and development by humans.

NOTES The genus name is from the old English name *starn* used for this group of birds. The species name honors Peter McDougall (1798–1834), a British botanist and scientific collector who worked in North America. Other English common names include gullie, davie, and carite. In Spanish it is called *dougall* or *charrán rosado*, and in French *sterne de dougal* or *petite mauve*.

SUGGESTED ADDITIONAL READING

Burger, J., I.C.T. Nisbet, C. Safina and M. Gochfeld. 1996. Temporal Patterns in reproductive success in the endangered Roseate Tern *(Sterna dougallii)* nesting on Long Island, New York, and Bird Island, Massachusetts. Auk, 13:131–142.

Gochfeld, M., J. Burger and I.C.T. Nisbet. 1998. Roseate Tern *(Sterna dougallii)*. In A. Poole and F. Gill (eds.), *Birds of North America. No. 370.* Philadelphia: The Birds of North America, Inc.

Shealer, D.A. 1998. Size selective predation by a specialist forager, the Roseate Tern. *Auk,* 115:519–525.

Least Tern

Sterna antillarum | **Laridae Charadriiformes** | **p. 66**

DISTRIBUTION This genus with 30 species is found worldwide. The Least Tern breeds from Maine to Texas and has many colonies in the interior of the country in the Mississippi drainage. They nest on both coasts of Mexico south to Honduras and Belize as well as on most of the Caribbean islands. The Least Terns found on the East Coast of North America are classified as *S. a. antillarum*; in the Mississippi watershed they are *S. a. athalassos*; and *S. a. browni* are from the coast of California south along the Pacific coast. The Least Tern has recently been separated as a distinct species from the very similar Little Tern *(S. albifrons)* found in Europe, Asia, Africa, Australia, and islands in the Indian and Pacific Oceans.

FOOD AND FEEDING HABITS

Least Terns hunt for prey by flying 1 to 10 m (3 to 33 ft) over calm water, looking down and hovering when prey is sighted, then plunging to grasp the prey in the bill. Only rarely is the body fully submerged. The prey is manipulated and swallowed in flight. The primary prey are cylindrical, surface-swimming fish 2 to 9 cm (0.8 to 3.5 in) long including herring, dwarf herring, anchovy, menhaden, killifish, and mosquitofish. Shrimp and other aquatic invertebrates are captured when near the surface. Flying insects are captured and eaten after aerial pursuit. Prey capture is impeded by silty water and choppy conditions produced by high-speed operation of powerboats and jet skis.

REPRODUCTION Least Terns raise a single brood per year but will renest if the eggs or young chicks are lost early in the season.

Seasonality The spring migration north is quite rapid, with the birds arriving on nesting sites from March to May depending on weather and latitude. Most eggs are laid in April, but renesting efforts may produce eggs as late as July. In the late summer and fall, breeding birds on the East Coast of the United States and the Caribbean islands gradually move south in small, loose groups to South America.

Courtship The first courtship displays are by a male flying in a stereotyped manner with a fish conspicuously crosswise in his bill. The following ground phase of the courtship involves the feeding of the female along with distinctive parading and posturing leading to copulation. Courtship feeding continues through incubation. The pair forms a monogamous relationship that often lasts into succeeding breeding seasons.

Territoriality The defended nesting territory extends less than 1 m (40 in) from the nest. The normal internest distance is 3 to 14 m (10 to 46 ft) with some nests packed more tightly and others dispersed more than 100 m (320 ft) from the nearest neighbor. The entire colony may mobilize to dive at, defecate on, and mob mammalian intruders in the nesting colony. The nesting colony may be abandoned after repeated predator attacks, particularly if the attack is at night. Least Terns in nesting colonies destroyed by high water may gather at another area to attempt to renest or may abandon breeding attempts for the balance of the season. They often nest on the same site the following year.

Nest and Nest Site The pair make several scrapes, then select one to receive the eggs. During incubation the scrape is often supplemented with bits of light-colored shells, stones, plant material, or plastic. The nest site is selected in a very open area without vegetation, such as a beach, sandspit, or sparsely vegetated island with a sand, shell, or gravel substrate. An elevation to avoid flooding and the absence of mammalian predators are desired. Dredge spoil islands and barrier beaches are the most favored colony sites. The adjacent water may be open ocean, estuaries, rivers, or large lakes. The average distance from the nest to the nearest water is 41.5 m (136 ft). With the loss of habitat due to development and recreational use of nesting areas, Least Terns have turned to man-made nesting sites such as mine tailings, cleared construction sites, dredge spoil islands, and gravel rooftops. Least Terns show little site fidelity. Entire colonies may move to new sites within and between breeding seasons. Individuals commonly change colonies in subsequent breeding seasons. Decoys have been successfully employed to reestablish Least Tern nesting at prior colony sites.

Eggs The beige to olive-brown eggs with brown and black splotches measure 30 by 23 mm (1.2 by 0.9 in) and have an average weight of 8.1 g (3 oz). The normal clutch is 2 or 3 eggs, which are laid at intervals of 24 to 48 hours. Single lost eggs are not replaced, but renesting is common after a lost clutch early in the season.

Incubation The incubation is inconsistent after the 1st egg is laid but becomes very attentive after the complete clutch is in place. The male feeds the female on the nest, which allows her to incubate about 80% of the time over the incubation period of about 21 days. Flooding by storm tides and heavy rains may result in nest failure for the entire colony. With good weather and no disturbance by humans or predators, hatching success can exceed 90%.

Fledging The newly hatched downy chicks are streaked and spotted with black. They are brooded until they are capable of leaving the nest to seek shade at 2 days of age. The first flight is at about 20 days of age, but full independence is not achieved for several more weeks. Fledged young often stand at the edge of nearby water while they wait on adults returning with food. As the young mature they follow the adults to the feeding grounds to be fed, and eventually they begin to feed themselves. Most parental foraging is less than 5 k (3 mi) from the colony. Although it is little studied, it seems that nest success or young fledged per pair is about 0.2 per year. Fall migration sometimes begins while parents are still feeding fledged young, indicating that family units may migrate together.

Age at First Breeding Most Least Terns first nest successfully at age 3, but some birds nest late in the season with low success rates at age 2.

BEHAVIOR Least Terns are gregarious and roost, feed, and migrate in flocks of 5 to 25. The individual distance when loafing on sandbars is 1 m (40 in) or less. The flap rate in level flight is 3.7 flaps per second and 5.3 per second when hovering.

MIGRATION The full extent of the winter range is probably not recorded, but Least Terns are known to be regularly found on the north coast of South America from Venezuela to Brazil.

PREDATORS Avian predators reported to feed on the eggs, chicks, or adults include crows, ravens, grackles, gulls, Great Blue Herons, Black-crowned Night Herons, Ruddy Turnstones, hawks, and owls. Mammalian predators include red foxes, coyotes, striped skunks, opossums, mink, weasels, mongooses, feral hogs, rats, cats, and dogs. Ghost crabs and fire ants may attack pipped eggs and very young chicks. Domestic cats and dogs can severely disrupt nesting colonies without directly preying on the adults.

LONGEVITY The maximum-recorded longevity for a banded bird is 24 years. Least Terns have been recaptured at their natal colony up to 21 years after they were banded as chicks and have been recorded as nesting successfully at 20 years of age.

CONSERVATION ISSUES At the end of the 19th and early in the 20th centuries, huge numbers were killed for use in the millinery trade. The California population of Least Terns was listed as a federal endangered species in 1970, and the interior population in the Mississippi drainage was listed as threatened in 1985. The Least Tern is listed as an endangered species in Mexico. Least Terns are still killed in parts of Latin America for food or sport, and the eggs are openly collected and sold in some Caribbean markets. Nests of colonies on usually dry shorelines are regularly lost to flooding from storm or spring tides.

NOTES The genus name is from the old English name *starn* used for this group of birds. The species name records the Antilles as the source of the first specimens described. Other common names include little tern, kill'em polly, and sea swallow. In Spanish it is called *gaviota pequeña, gaviota chica, charrán mínimo* or *charrancito,* and in French *sterne naine* or *pigeon de la mer.*

SUGGESTED ADDITIONAL READING

Atwood, J.L. and P.R. Kelly. 1984. Fish dropped on breeding colonies as indicators of Least Tern food habits. *Wilson Bulletin,* 96:34–47.

Thompson, B.C., J.A. Jackson, J. Burger, L.A. Hill, E.M. and J.L. Atwood. 1997. Least Tern (*Sterna antillarum*). In A. Poole and F. Gill (eds.), *The Birds of North America. No. 290.* Philadelphia: The Birds of North America, Inc.

Wolk, R.G. 1974. Reproductive behavior of the Least Tern. *Proceedings of the Linnean Society of NY,* 72:44–62.

Bridled Tern
Sterna anaethetus | Laridae Charadriiformes | p. 67

DISTRIBUTION This genus with 30 species is found worldwide. *S. a. antarctica* is found in the Red Sea, Persian Gulf, and along the East Coast of Africa. *S. a. anaethetus* is found in the Eastern Indian Ocean and Western Pacific. *S. a. nelsoni* is found on the Pacific coast of Central America. *S. a. melanoptera* is found in the West Indies, northern coastal South America, and West Africa.

FOOD AND FEEDING HABITS
Feeding is generally solitary and offshore but on the continental shelf. They feed primarily by dipping and often search along mats and lines of sargasso weed for small creatures that venture away from their protective weedy labyrinth. The primary diet is squid, flying fish, halfbeaks, and anchovies but also includes larval clams, snails, and arthropods. A colony near Australia preyed predominately on pelagic larvae of goatfish. Bridled Terns rarely join the nearshore melee of terns, gulls, and pelicans mobbing shoals of baitfish but do join mixed flocks feeding offshore to plunge-dive on schools of anchovies forced to the surface by feeding tuna and other predators. Returns to nests at all hours of the night indicate they may also feed at night.

REPRODUCTION
Bridled Terns raise a single brood per year on small predator-free islands.
Seasonality Nesting grounds are first occupied at night only, but after several weeks of courtship, progressively more time is spent on or near the nest until it is occupied continuously before the eggs are laid. Caribbean populations breed on a precise annual cycle, with most laying in the first 2 weeks of May. Bridled Terns breed on a 220- to 240-day cycle in the Seychelles with the result that the month of peak breeding changes from year to year. Other populations seem to have protracted breeding seasons in which eggs are laid in every month.
Courtship The monogamous pair bond often lasts for 2 or more seasons, resulting in paired birds arriving at the nest site together.
Territoriality In a territorial display on the ground, the body is tipped forward 45 degrees, and the carpal joints of the wings are held away from the body as the bird rapidly nods its head. Combat with raised crown, grabbing with the beak, and beating of wings may accompany territorial disputes. Courtship leading to a pair bond involves both aerial and ground displays. Birds may spiral up to 300 m (1,000 ft) above the colony then glide downward while swaying side to side, with members of the pair overtaking each other. Nests may be solitary or clumped in open colonies and less than 1 m (3 ft) apart to more 30 m (100 ft) apart. Territorial displays seem to separate individual pairs so that nests are not in sight of each other.
Nest and Nest Site The nest is a bare scrape that is usually prepared under an object that provides shade and visual cover from above. The site may be a hollow in a cliff face or a gap

under slabs of broken coral or driftwood. The tern will also tuck under or form a tunnel in dense overhanging vegetation. The nest is usually near the periphery of an island. The same nest site is often used by the same pair in subsequent years. Changes of nest site are often related to divorce or loss of mate, and the new nest is likely to be near the prior nest site.

Eggs The single, smooth, slightly glossy cream-colored egg is marked with dark-brown or reddish spots and blotches. It measures about 46 by 33 mm (1.8 by 1.3 in) and weighs about 20 g (0.7 oz). Replacement eggs are laid, but only 1 chick is raised per season.

Incubation Both parents share the 29-day incubation period, with nest relief occurring at periods of less than an hour to as long as 24 hours. The incubating bird sometimes departs from the nest for short periods to dip the belly in the sea. Hatching success has been recorded as exceeding 90%.

Fledging The drab-gray to buff hatchling, mottled with dark-brown markings, remains in the nest for about the first 3 days, then hides nearby. After fledging at the age of 8 or 9 weeks the juveniles practice feeding by dipping while the parents continue to provide supplemental food in the vicinity of the nest site. The parents' advertising call summons the young to the vicinity of the nest for feeding. Chicks stay near the nest and do not join in crèches. After the chicks fledge, both parents continue to provide food for at least several weeks.

Age at First Breeding Bridled Terns develop adult plumage by the 2nd year. First-, 2nd-, and 3rd-year birds visit the breeding colony but usually do not successfully reproduce until 4 years of age.

BEHAVIOR Entire colonies or clusters of nesting birds within colonies often show panic reactions called "dreads" in which individual birds give a *mer-er-er* call and leave the colony with swift, violent, side-to-side evasive movements. The call and behavior incite nearby pairs and sometimes entire colonies to take flight in a similar manner.

MIGRATION When chicks fledge in the Caribbean, the adults and juveniles leave the breeding grounds and are not seen again until the following breeding season. Sightings of Bridled Terns off the southeastern U.S. only occur in the spring and summer while breeding is progressing in the Caribbean. The entire population seems to move south to the equator in the winter. In other locations, outside the breeding season, they are known to rest near shore on flotsam and small islands.

PREDATORS Bridled Terns do not generally nest in the presence of terrestrial predators. Gulls and night herons take unguarded eggs and inattentive chicks wandering in the open.

LONGEVITY Breeding Bridled Terns over 18 years old have been recaptured, but they probably live considerably longer than that.

CONSERVATION ISSUES Increased human use of the traditional nesting islands is reducing available nesting habitat. Harvest of eggs for human consumption continues to affect some Caribbean populations.

NOTES The genus name is from the old English name *starn* used for this group of birds. The species name is from the Greek *anaisthetos* (senseless or stupid) applied because the birds allowed seafarers to kill them on the nest. This tern has also been placed into the genus *Onychoprion* with the Sooty Tern. The Bridled Tern is also called bonito gull or egg bird in English, *charrán embridado* or *oscura* in Spanish, and *sterne bridée* in French.

SUGGESTED ADDITIONAL READING

Diamond, A.W. 1976. Sub-annual breeding and moult cycles in the Bridled Tern. *Sterna anaethetus. Ibis,* 118:414–419.

Dunlop, J.N. 1997. Foraging range, marine habitat and diet of Bridled Terns breeding in Western Australia. *Corella,* 21:77–82.

Hulsman, K. and N.P.E. Langham. 1985. Breeding biology of the Bridled Tern. *Emu,* 85:240–249.

Sooty Tern
Sterna fuscata | **Laridae Charadriiformes** | **p. 68**

DISTRIBUTION This genus with 30 species is found worldwide foraging over temperate and tropical ocean waters. The Sooty Tern has been divided into 7 subspecies, with 6 in the Pacific and Indian Oceans and 1 (*S. f. fuscata*) in the Atlantic. They are the world's most abundant tropical seabird and have nested on almost every small, isolated, nonforested island in the tropics. Most nesting colonies are within 30 degrees of the equator. In areas of cold currents flowing toward the equator, such as the Benguela in Africa and the Humboldt of western South America, nesting may extend only slightly south of the equator. The only known nesting colony in the contiguous United States is on Bush Key in the Dry Tortugas, but the terns nest on many islands in the Caribbean. Outside of the breeding season, Sooty Terns may fly for months over the open ocean without ever resting on land or sea.

FOOD AND FEEDING HABITS
Sooty Terns feed far from shore in deep, blue ocean, but when breeding they usually forage within 80 km (50 mi) of the nesting colony. They feed on small fish such as flying fish, jacks, and squid 2 to 8 cm (1 to 3 in) in length forced to the surface by pelagic fish such as tuna, dolphin and mackerel. Prey is captured by approaching and sometimes brushing the water surface while dipping the beak and head. Airborne fish are also caught. This is the only tern species that does not carry prey back to the young in its beak. They have been observed feeding on moonlit nights, and regurgitated fish recovered at the colony include species that only come to the surface at night.

REPRODUCTION Sooty Terns nest in large dense colonies on small islands isolated from predators and other disturbances.

Seasonality The laying dates for a colony of Sooty Terns are remarkably synchronous, with thousands of pairs laying in a 3- or 4-day period. In most of the Caribbean, eggs are laid in the first 10 days of May, but in the Dry Tortugas the colony has laid earlier each year until eggs are now present as early as February. In other parts of the world, Sooty Terns nest on a 6- to 10-month cycle.

Courtship Sooty Terns begin to congregate and fly about the nesting colony at night 2 or 3 months before nesting. Just before nesting, they begin to land in the colony at night for courting and copulation. Daytime landings in the colony are usually associated with egg laying. Pair bonds seldom last more than 1 year, but subsequent mates are often neighbors from previous years' nesting.

Territoriality Sooty Terns have territories defined by the reach of the beak of an incubating bird, with the result that nests may be as little as 30 cm (12 in) apart. They show considerable fidelity to territory in subsequent years, with many individuals nesting within 5 m (16 ft) of the previous year's nest. Individuals restrict their ground activities to an area of about 10 sq m (108 sq ft) near the nest. Nesting areas in colonies are sometimes abandoned after repeated egg collection by poachers. Interchange of terns between breeding colonies has been repeatedly recorded.

Nest and Nest Site Nesting habitat requirements for Sooty Terns are generally considered to be a site that is free of predators and has no dense vegetation at ground level and is near fishing grounds. They are very adaptable and willing to use atypical sites. They will nest on the ground in closed-canopy forest and between clumps of dense growths of overhanging grasses and sedges. On predator-free islands, nesting is often in the open, even when cover is available.

Eggs The single, buff egg with dark reddish-brown spots measures 51 by 40 mm (2 by 1.6 in) and weighs about 34 g (1.3 oz). Nests with more than 1 egg are considered to be an artifact of egg dumping or accidental rolling of an egg out of one nest and into a nearby nest. They never raise more than 1 chick to fledging. In nests with 2 chicks, the reduced food supply usually results in the death of both chicks. Sooty Terns renest and lay a new egg about 12 days after nest loss. They produce only 1 brood per season.

Incubation The average incubation period of 29 days is shared by both parents, who exchange nest duties about once a day.

Fledging Hatchlings are precocious and leave the nest to seek nearby cover soon after hatching. By the age of 3 weeks the chicks are often left untended for much of the day, with the adults returning to feed them at night. Intermittent, failed, and prebreeders may continuously attend a nest area and guard and feed the chicks. Fledging is usually accomplished in 6 to 10 weeks, depending in part on food availability. The fledglings remain in the colony for 2 or 3 weeks and continue to be fed by the parents. Juveniles depart the colony in the company of the male parent 2 or 3 weeks postfledging and do not seem to return to land until ready to breed many years later. Once juveniles are fully competent they migrate across the Atlantic and lead a pelagic existence in the Gulf of Guinea off western Africa.

Age at First Breeding Sooty Terns rarely breed before the age of 6, and some may be 10 years old before nesting.

BEHAVIOR The feathers of Sooty Terns are not waterproof, perhaps due to inadequate production of oils by the uropygial gland. While they dip briefly in water for bathing or cooling, they must take off from the sea surface promptly because they are unable to leave the water's surface when wet. They have never been seen to rest on the water and are believed to fly continuously (including while sleeping) when leading a pelagic existence away from the breeding colony.

MIGRATION Juveniles leave the nesting colony and migrate through the southern Caribbean following the intertropical convergence weather to the Gulf of Guinea. They remain off the African coast until they return to their natal colony as adults. Because individuals may take as long as 5 years to mature, they may stay continuously in the air from the time they leave the colony until they return as adults or prebreeders. Adults arrive at the nesting colony with predictable precision from a pelagic existence out of sight of land.

PREDATORS Gulls, night herons, Cattle Egrets, and Ruddy Turnstones take the eggs. The chicks are taken by gulls, night herons, frigatebirds, and Cattle Egrets. Adults are taken by hawks and owls. Rats and cats introduced to islands with nesting colonies can have devastating effects on nest success. Frigatebirds have been recorded eating all the chicks in a Sooty Tern colony.

LONGEVITY A Sooty Tern banded in the Dry Tortugas was recaptured at age 32 while sitting on eggs. The majority of birds at the breeding colony are 12 to 18 years of age.

CONSERVATION ISSUES Overfishing by man of pelagic fish stocks in the world's oceans may have a long-term negative impact on Sooty Terns through a reduced level of beaters to crowd prey to the surface. Large-scale harvest of eggs as human food was more widespread in the past but still continues in the Caribbean and other parts of the world in spite of legal protection.

NOTES The genus name is from the old English name *starn* used for this group of birds. The species name is from the Latin *fuscatus* (dark). The Sooty Tern has been grouped with the other oceanic dark-backed terns in the genera *Haliplana, Onychoprion,* and others. They are also called wideawake in English, *charrán sombrío* or *charrán oscuro* in Spanish, and *sterne fuligineuse* in French. Much of our information on Sooty Terns comes from the exemplary long-term population studies conducted by William B. Roberson Jr. and helpers in the Dry Tortugas.

SUGGESTED ADDITIONAL READING

Ashmole, N.P. 1963. The biology of the wideawake or Sooty Tern *Sterna fuscata* on Ascension Island. *Ibis,* 103b:297–364.

Brown, W.Y. 1976. Growth and fledging age of Sooty Tern chicks. *Auk,* 93:179–183.

Saliva, J.E. and J. Burger. 1989. Effect of experimental manipulation of vegetation density on nest-site selection in Sooty Terns. *Condor,* 91:689–698.

Brown Noddy

Anous stolidus | **Laridae Charadriiformes** | **p. 69**

DISTRIBUTION This genus with 3 species is found worldwide breeding on tropical oceanic islands. The Brown Noddy breeds in southern Florida in the Dry Tortugas, in the Bahamas, and on small islands throughout the Caribbean. On a world scale they are found on isolated islands and archipelagos in the tropical Atlantic, the Red Sea, Indian Ocean, Southeast Asia, and the tropical Pacific.

FOOD AND FEEDING HABITS

Although Brown Noddies may feed in protected waters such as lagoons or along reefs, they generally move offshore to deep, blue water to forage when they are nesting. When chicks are being fed in the nests, small groups of traveling noddies are regularly encountered 16 to 32 km (10 to 20 mi) offshore. Some authors have concluded that they feed as far as 80 km (50 mi) offshore. Feeding is often in mixed-species flocks on prey forced to the surface by schools of predatory fish such as jacks, tuna, and dolphin. Prey includes Spanish sardines, flying squid, flying fish, and many species of larval fish. Prey is captured at the water surface by dipping the beak while still flying, diving and impacting the water with the body without submerging, or thrusting at prey while floating.

REPRODUCTION Brown Noddies may breed as solitary pairs, as part of small groups, or in colonies of several thousand.

Seasonality Noddies return to the Caribbean breeding colonies only at night to reestablish pair bonds beginning 2 weeks before they are seen in the daytime. They arrive on the breeding grounds at night in April and lay in early May. Some nests with eggs as late as July are probably renesting attempts. The trickle of individuals leaving the nesting ground becomes a general departure when the sharp barometric drop associated with a hurricane is felt. The departure is before the arrival of tropical storm winds and occurs even when a hurricane track does not adversely influence the colony. A colony in the Dry Tortugas has gradually shifted the breeding season earlier and now lays in February. In Pacific and Indian Ocean colonies, the breeding is more dispersed over time, with eggs present in most months.

Courtship The male calls to flying birds while perched at the nest site. The female lands at the nest site of a displaying male and is initially attacked. With repeated landings, aggression subsides. The pair display, and several times a day the female solicits and the male provides courtship feeding. This extra food may help the female produce the egg. The pair often preen each other as a prelude to copulation. About 70% of pairs remain together in succeeding years. Of the pairs that do not mate in a succeeding year, 63% have lost a mate. In divorces, the male inherits the nest site 2/3 of the time. Adults show almost total fidelity to a colony site and very high fidelity to individual nest sites.

Territoriality Nests may be located as

near as 0.5 m (20 in) from each other if rocks or vegetation prevent visual contact between them. A nest site is typically used again by the same pair in subsequent years.

Nest and Nest Site The nest may consist of only a few shell fragments scattered on a rock ledge, a scrape in the soil with little added vegetation, or a depression in low herbaceous vegetation. Elevated nests are constructed of twigs and may be found low in bushes such as bay cedar at moderate height, in prickly pear cactus and fig, or in tall trees such as coconut and gumbo limbo. Twig nests often contain pebbles or shell fragments. Noddies seem to prefer to nest on cliff ledges if suitable nest sites are available. A maximum density of 1.7 nests per square m (1.2 nests per sq yd) has been reported.

Eggs The smooth, off-white eggs are lightly marked with brown, gray, and lilac splotches, spots and specks. A typical egg measures 5.2 by 3.5 cm (2 by 1.4 in) with a weight of 40 g (1.4 oz). The individual egg in the clutch makes up about 21% of the female's body mass. Replacement eggs are laid when an egg or young chick is lost, but multiple broods are not recorded.

Incubation The incubation period is 35 days. While incubating on hot days the adult may leave the nest for a few minutes and splash into the sea, returning with moistened breast feathers to cool the eggs. The incubation period ranges from 29 to 37 days. Among colonies, incubation shifts vary in duration from 2 hours to 24 hours. The duration of the shift is probably related to the distance an adult must fly to a feeding area.

Fledging The parents actively brood the chick or shade it from the sun for the first few days. The down of new chicks is usually either cream or dark gray-brown but may be intermediate. The proportions of the chicks with each color vary considerably among populations and may reflect advantages in different climatic regimes. The weight of the chick equals that of the parents by about day 35, and the chick may weigh more than the adult before fledging. Age at first flight is variable but averages 46 ± 5 days. The parents continue to provide food for several additional weeks but may provide supplemental feeding to 14 weeks while the young learn to feed themselves. Nest success at undisturbed colonies may exceed 90%.

Age at First Breeding Brown Noddies are 3 to 7 years of age before the first breeding attempt.

BEHAVIOR Brown Noddies are named for an agonistic behavior in which the white cap flashes as it is alternately hidden and exposed when the bird is facing an opponent—the bill is first pointed up, then down. The chicks have a harsh cheep when calling the adults for help, a screech in response to a perceived threat, and a cheep rising in pitch as a food-begging call. Outside the breeding season Brown Noddies roost and sometimes forage in flocks. The flight speed when traveling is as much as 32.8 km/hr (20 mph) and varies from 0 when hovering over prey to 51.5 km/hr (32 mph) when the noddy is in a hurry. The wingbeat averages 3.5 per second. The Brown Noddy walks with small dainty steps and does not hop, preferring to fly when moving any significant distance.

MIGRATION Brown Noddies do not seem to migrate in a seasonally directed group movement, but they all arrive at breeding grounds within a 2-week period. Departure is more gradual from August through November. After the breeding season they may disperse thousands of miles across the ocean from their breeding or natal island.

PREDATORS Fire ants sometimes attack and consume chicks in pipped eggs. Night herons, gulls, frigatebirds, and crabs take the eggs and newly hatched chicks. Red-tailed Hawks catch and eat the adults at nesting colonies. Rats, cats, and mongooses may attack the nestlings if they gain access to the breeding sites. It is likely that predatory fish catch some adults in feeding frenzies.

LONGEVITY The oldest-known banded bird was still breeding at 25 years of age.

CONSERVATION ISSUES Humans collect the eggs and more rarely the adults as food.

NOTES The genus is from the Greek, meaning "stupid." The species is from the Latin, meaning "dull" or "foolish." They are also called noddy terns and common noddies in English, relating to the brown color and a nodding display made conspicuous by the white cap. It is called *gaviota bobo, charrán bobo* and *charrán pardello* in Spanish, and *noddi niais* or *noddy brun* in French.

SUGGESTED ADDITIONAL READING

Chardine, J.W. and R.D. Morris. 1996. Brown Noddy *(Anous stolidus)*. In A. Poole and F. Gill (eds.), *Birds of North America. No. 220.* Philadelphia: Birds of North America, Inc.

Dorward, D.F. and N.P. Ashmole. 1963. Notes on the biology of the Brown Noddy *(Anous stolidus)* on Ascension. *Ibis,* 103:447–457.

Harrison, C.S. and D.L. Stoneburner. 1981. Radiotelemetry of the Brown Noddy in Hawaii. *J Wildl Manage,* 45:1021–1025.

Black Skimmer

Rynchops niger | Laridae Charadriiformes | p. 70

DISTRIBUTION This genus with 3 very similar species is found in large rivers and estuaries in Asia (*R. albicollis*), in large rivers and lakes in Africa (*R. flavirostris*), and in sandy marine coasts in North and South America (*R. niger*). The New World species is generally divided into 3 subspecies with *R. n. cinerascens* in northern South America, *R. n. intercedens* on the South Atlantic coast of South America, and *R. n. niger* in North America south to Panama in Central America and Guadeloupe in the Caribbean.

FOOD AND FEEDING HABITS

The normal, solitary feeding habit is to fly close to the surface of the sea, allowing the lower part of the beak to knife through the water. Skimming is usually within 2 m (6 ft) of a land-water interface, often adjacent to mudflats and oyster bars. Skimming is often focused on small surface disturbances produced by schools of fish. Studies have shown that ground effect greatly increases flight efficiency while the bird is skimming. The upper part of the beak is flexibly attached to the skull and hinges upward while the bird is skimming. When the lower mandible touches anything, the upper part of the beak (maxilla) snaps closed as the head swings backward under the breast. The highly muscularized upper end of the esophagus allows it to be constricted to prevent the swallowing of water while the bird is fishing. Main foods are killifish, anchovies, herring, silversides, young mullet, menhaden, flounder, ladyfish, pipefish, shrimp, and incidental catches of the young of various species that live as adults in deeper water. Captured fish range in size from 3 to 12 cm (1 to 5 in) and average about 8 cm (3 in) in length and 8 g (0.3 oz) in weight. Parents select very small fish to feed to newly hatched chicks. Chicks regurgitate pellets of difficult-to-digest prey remains. The fishing technique requires calm, protected water with little wave action, such as tidal estuaries and creeks in salt marshes. On days with little wind, the fishing may extend to the shoreline of more open bays or the seacoast. Fishing is almost always in shallow water so prey fish will be near enough to the surface that the slicing beak will encounter them. Feeding is most frequent on a rising tide about 2 hours after the low tide, but an intense bout of feeding may be triggered by a falling tide at dusk. The large pupil and feeding by touch allow the bird to fish effectively at night when fish cannot see its approach.

REPRODUCTION Skimmers nest in loose colonies in open sandy habitat on dredge spoil islands, isolated barrier beaches, shell berms in salt marshes, or similar areas not subject to disturbance. They usually nest in or near tern colonies, presumably for protection from predators.

Seasonality Skimmers are relatively late breeders, depositing eggs in May or June.

Courtship The pair is monogamous within a season, and many pairs remain together in succeeding years. Skimmers return to a nesting colony as a flock, but pairs begin to separate on territories after about a week.

Territoriality A small territory is maintained around the nest by the pair. The nearest neighbor is usually more than 1 m (3 ft) from the nest in dense colonies but may be several times that distance, depending on habitat. The territories are defended against terns as well as other skimmers. Threat displays used to defend the territory include barking, head tossing, displaying upright with the legs and neck fully extended upward and the beak slightly opened, walking toward an intruder, and even aerial chasing.

Nest and Nest Site The nest is a scrape in the sand in open habitat. In marshes, skimmers will nest in a depression on mats of dead marsh grass or seaweed. The nests are usually close to the water and only slightly above sea level and thus may be lost due to flooding by spring tides, strong onshore winds, or heavy rains. There is considerable fidelity to breeding colonies from year to year. Skimmers sometimes nest on gravel rooftops or cleared inland sites when no suitable coastal sites are available.

Eggs The smooth, cream to olive eggs are blotched and spotted with dark brown or black. Markings and background color are highly variable. The 1st egg of the clutch is usually darker and the last egg distinctly pale. Eggs measure 35 mm by 44 mm (1.4 by 1.7 in), weigh an average about 27 g (1 oz) and constitute about 8% to 10% of the female's weight. The average clutch size is 4, with a range of 1 to 5. In years with poor food supply or in colonies further south in the range, the average number is closer to 3. The clutch is deposited over 4 to 6 days.

Incubation Incubation begins when the 1st egg is laid, resulting in asynchronous hatching. Both parents incubate and provide shade for the eggs, trading places every 2 to 4 hours. As the nests are usually in the open and away from shade, the absence of parental shade can result in rapid death of eggs or chicks due to overheating. If the nest is flooded, the eggs remain viable after immersion for up to a day in fresh water and for a few hours in salt water. Hatching is after 22 to 24 days of incubation, with the chicks emerging at about 1-day intervals. Due to the mobility of the early-hatched chicks, incubation may cease or the nest site may be abandoned before the last egg is hatched.

Fledging At hatching, the chicks are completely covered with down (grayish buff with black speckles on top, and white on the underside). They walk easily after the 2nd day. Food is carried intact to the nest and not regurgitated. The parents closely brood very young chicks, but after 1 or 2 weeks the chicks are too big to brood and may be left to themselves for increasing periods. Cold rainy weather during this period may result in very high mortality. By the 2nd week, the chicks are very mobile and may run several hundred meters if pursued. They may also leave the territory to seek safer refuges if disturbed. By the age of 24 days, males usually exceed 320 g (11.3 oz), and females weigh less than 300 g (10.5 oz). By the 4th week, the young birds are jumping and flapping and a few are venturing on their 1st flight. By the 5th week most juveniles can fly. The 1st skimming flights are within a few days of the 1st flights but have a predictably low rate of success. Parents continue to feed the juveniles for at least 2 weeks while they perfect their fishing techniques. Due to flooding, bad weather, and predation, only half of the nesting pairs produce a fledged juvenile. The 1st chicks to hatch in a clutch have a higher probability of survival. Later chicks are likely to survive only if something happens to the older siblings.

Age at First Breeding Some birds breed at 2 years of age, but most probably first nest in their 3rd spring and some not until their 4th spring.

BEHAVIOR Skimmers almost never alight on the water but may drag their feet and belly in the water either to wash or cool them. Flight speed while skimming ranges from 16 to 32 kph (10 to 20 mph). The damp feet and belly also may be used to cool the eggs in hot weather. Cooling by gular fluttering is common on hot, still days. When sleeping, they may lie on the sand with neck and bill extended. They may rest in flocks of over 1,000 birds on sandbars where the individual distance between birds may be as close as 50 cm (20 in). These resting flocks inevitably face the direction of the prevailing wind with almost military precision.

MIGRATION The birds living along the northern and central Atlantic coast of the U.S. move south to Florida for the winter.

PREDATORS The eggs and chicks are the most vulnerable to predation, which may be significant even on islands. Gulls, Norway rats, and raccoons have all caused nesting failure of colonies on islands. On barrier beaches, humans, dogs, cats, foxes, skunks, mink, and weasels are regular mammalian predators of eggs, chicks, and more rarely adults. Hawks, owls, night herons, gulls, and crows may attack uncovered eggs or young chicks. Boat-tailed Grackles, Ruddy Turnstones, and American Oystercatchers sometimes consume significant numbers of eggs. Human disturbance of a colony may result in high rates of predation by gulls while the adult skimmers are in flight.

LONGEVITY Individual skimmers have been recovered 20 years after banding. It is probable that individual birds live beyond that age. Most known-age breeding adults are 5 to 9 years of age.

CONSERVATION ISSUES Tissues of Black Skimmers have been shown to contain organochlorine pesticides, heavy metals, and PCBs, but none of these at levels known to be toxic to adults or embryos. Human disturbance in various forms is probably the greatest single threat to colonies of skimmers. Collection of eggs as a human food item, a conservation problem with colonial nesting seabirds, has reappeared as a cultural tradition among some Asian immigrants who harvest skimmer eggs along the Atlantic coastline.

NOTES The skimmer is sometimes placed in a family of its own, *Rynchopidae*. The genus is named from the Greek *rhunkhos* (bill) and *ops* (face). The species name is from the Latin *niger* (black). Other common names include cutwater, scissorbill, razorbill, and shearwater, all in obvious reference to the very narrow bill and its use in fishing. In Spanish it is called *pico de tijera, arador* or *rayador,* and in French *bec-en-ciseaux noirs.*

SUGGESTED ADDITIONAL READING

Blake, R.W. 1985. A model of foraging efficiency and daily energy budget in the Black Skimmers (*Rhynchops niger*). *Canadian Journal of Zoology,* 63:42–48.

Erwin, R.M. 1977. Black Skimmer breeding ecology and behavior. *Auk,* 94:709–717.

Gochfeld, M. and J. Burger. 1994. Black Skimmer. In A. Poole and F. Gill (eds.), *The Birds of North America. No. 108.* Philadelphia: The Birds of North America, Inc.

Mangrove Cuckoo
Coccyzus minor | **Cuculidae Cuculiformes** | **p. 71**

DISTRIBUTION This genus with 8 species is found from Canada to Argentina. The Mangrove Cuckoo breeds in southern tropical Florida, the Bahamas, most Caribbean islands, Central America, and sporadically in northern South America. At least 13 subspecies have been named, but individual variation of color and size within populations is quite extensive and leaves subspecific taxonomy in doubt.

FOOD AND FEEDING HABITS

The mangrove cuckoo moves slowly and silently through the branches with frequent periods of stillness. The primary food is caterpillars when they are available. Otherwise it gleans grasshoppers, moths, butterflies, flies, beetles, walking sticks, preying mantises, tree frogs, and lizards by meticulous examination of the vegetation in thick brush or forest. When opportunity presents, cuckoos eat the eggs and chicks of small songbirds. As the name would suggest, it is found along the coast in stands of red or black mangrove, but it also ventures into adjacent dry lands with dense and often thorny scrub, coastal forest, hardwood hammocks, and low-elevation forest partially cleared for coffee plantations. They are generally absent from open, cleared or early successional areas.

REPRODUCTION The Mangrove Cuckoo is even more secretive in its nesting habits than it is in its feeding habits.

Seasonality Nest building has been observed as early as March and as late as October, but most eggs are probably laid in May. The nests observed in late summer may be replacement or 2nd-brood nests.

Courtship The male cuckoo initiates courtship by repeating a single guttural call 4 or 5 times. A receptive female responds with a similar call repeated 6 or 7 times. The male approaches the female while holding food such as a spider in his beak and perches on her back. She twists and tilts her head to accept the gift. In an observation of copulation, the female pumps her tail vigorously and utters soft calls before the male approaches and mounts her while holding her beak.

Territoriality The daily behavior of the Mangrove Cuckoo makes it very difficult to study. Banded birds have been recovered in subsequent years at almost the same spot of original banding. An incubating bird was seen to swoop aggressively without vocalization at a house cat in the vicinity of the nest.

Nest and Nest Site The flat, flimsy stick nest about 20 cm (8 in) in diameter is built over or near water in a thicket of mangroves or thorn scrub, 1.5 to 5 m (5 to 16 ft) above ground.

Eggs The eggs in the typical 2- or 3-egg clutch each measure 31 by 23 mm (1.2 by 0.9) and weigh about 9 g (0.3 oz). The eggs are a uniform bluish-green color with no gloss.

Incubation Other species in the genus begin shared incubation after the 1st egg is laid. Incubation is 10 to 12 days.

Fledging Both parents bring insects to

feed the young in the nest. The young of other species in the genus develop rapidly, fledging at 6 to 10 days.

Age at First Breeding First breeding is probably at the age of 1 year as with other cuckoos.

BEHAVIOR The attractive, cryptic plumage and the habit of motionlessness or silent sneaking through the brush makes the cuckoos difficult to discern even when close by. They are usually heard rather than seen. Mangrove Cuckoos are unusually tolerant of a still, silent observer and often go on about their business while being watched from a distance of less than 2 m (6.7 ft).

MIGRATION If Florida Mangrove Cuckoos do migrate south, a few sedentary individuals stay behind to winter in the southern part of the state. The population in Florida seems to decline in winter, but Mangrove Cuckoos seldom call outside the breeding season and thus are very difficult to locate in the winter.

PREDATORS The normal habits of Mangrove Cuckoos seldom expose the adults to natural predation, but they are commonly killed when hit by automobiles or when flying against large glass doors. The nest with eggs or young chicks is subject to random discovery by snakes and mammalian predators.

LONGEVITY Very few birds have been banded and even fewer recovered. The oldest recovered bird was 1 year 3 months of age. The data probably do not yield a realistic estimate of the age structure of a population that does not develop adult plumage until the 2nd year.

CONSERVATION ISSUES A breeding-bird survey with a small sample size in Florida shows significant decreases in population size in the last 30 years. These data may represent the loss of habitat due to the removal of mangroves and the loss of coastal lowland forest, along with the development and increasing recreational use of the coastal zone. The Mangrove Cuckoo seems to be very sensitive to habitat fragmentation and was found only in forested study plots larger than 12.8 ha (32 acres). Suitable habitat blocks are becoming increasingly rare in Florida and throughout the range of the Mangrove Cuckoo. The fringes of mangroves sometimes left between developments and the sea are inadequate to support Mangrove Cuckoos unless accompanied by adjacent tropical woodlands. Houses dispersed in a woodland that is more than 50% undisturbed do not seem to eliminate cuckoos.

NOTES The genus name is from the Greek *kokkuzo* (a call), in reference to the conspicuous and distinctive calls of these birds. The species name is from the Latin meaning "smaller." Other common names are rain bird, cat bird, four o'clock bird, coffin bird, and dumb bird. In Spanish it is *pájaro bobo menor, cuclillo manglero, cuco orejinegro,* or *gogo*. In French it is called *coucou manioc gris* or *coulicou des palétuviers*. Folk tradition has it that the call is a prediction of rainfall, and indeed rain often falls after the call. Perhaps the bird can detect the transient low barometric pressure associated with a passing squall or the sharp temperature drop ahead of the rain.

SUGGESTED ADDITIONAL READING

Hughes, J.M. 1997. Mangrove Cuckoo *(Coccyzus minor)*. In A. Poole and F. Gill (eds.), *Birds of North America. No. 299.* Philadelphia: Birds of North America, Inc.

Langridge, H. 1990. Courtship feeding behavior in the Mangrove Cuckoo *(Coccyzus minor)*. *Florida Field Nat,* 18:55–56.

McNair, D.B. 1991. Copulation in the Mangrove Cuckoo. *Florida Field Nat,* 19:84–85.

Boat-tailed Grackle
Quiscalus major | **Icteridae Passeriformes** | **p. 72**

DISTRIBUTION This genus with 5 species is found from the U.S. south to Peru. The Common Grackle *(Q. quiscula)* breeds from Canada to Mexico. The Greater Antillean Grackle *(Q. niger)* is found from Cuba and the Cayman Islands to Puerto Rico. The Carib Grackle *(Q. lugubris)* is found in the Lesser Antilles from Anguilla to Grenada. The Great-tailed Grackle *(Q. mexicanus)* is found from Texas and Arizona south to Peru and the Caribbean coast of Colombia. The Boat-tailed Grackle is found near the coast and along estuaries from New York through Florida to Texas. When the latter 2 species live in the same area, the females are able to select sexual partners of their own species due to distinctive differences between the displays and vocalizations of the males of the 2 species.

FOOD AND FEEDING HABITS
Grackles are opportunistic omnivores that eat fruits, seeds, insects, crustaceans, fish, frogs, eggs and hatchlings of other birds, and agricultural grain crops. When water is available, some foods such as bread and kibbled pet food are dunked and softened before they are eaten. Grackles feed on marshes, mudflats, beaches, shallow water, open grasslands, and in urban settings. Foraging behavior is a slow walk while closely examining the surroundings and often turning over leaves, shells, and stones to expose invertebrates. In soft substrates they may insert the beak in the soil and open it to expose prey. When foraging in shallow water they often tilt the head to one side while scanning for prey, then fixate with both eyes before plunging the head into the water for capture. They forage for mollusks and arthropods by standing on one lily pad while lifting an adjacent pad and examining its underside. They adapt readily to take advantage of food provided in landfills, garbage bins, and picnic areas and even pick insects off automobile radiators.

REPRODUCTION Boat-tailed Grackles practice harem polygeny in which females gather in colonies of up to 100 and attract males. Multiyear linear dominance hierarchies are formed among males, with older males holding the dominant positions and accomplishing most of the copulation. When the ruff-out dominance display is given by individuals in groups of males, the head and body feathers are erected, the bill is pointed upward, the tail is fanned, the wings are quivered, and a characteristic rattling call is produced. The ruff-out is often followed by a bill-up display in which the neck is extended upward while the feathers of the head, neck, and body are sleeked. Dominance disputes may be resolved by physical combat including bill-fencing, pecking, and clawing.

Seasonality Both sexes begin to regularly visit nesting areas in February or March and begin egg laying about 30 days later. Most 2-year-old females nest in a 2nd peak about 2 weeks after the more experienced females. Successful nesting may continue into the fall in Florida.

Courtship High-ranking males sing from elevated exposed perches, while other males sing from more concealed locations. Male solicitation displays are similar to the ruff-out, but the beak is pointed downward and the body contours are smooth. In female solicitation, the tail and beak are raised, the back is bowed, and wings are drooped and quivered. Lower-ranked males use the exposed perches and attempt to copulate with females when high-ranked males are absent. When a precopulatory call is given, a higher-ranking male may fly to the site and disrupt proceedings. The dominant male accomplishes most of the copulations in a colony on the female nest site, but genetic studies of offspring show that over half of the chicks in a colony are sired by males other than the ones attendant at the colony. Subordinate males may wait in foraging areas to attempt copulations away from the colony. Two broods per season are common.

Territoriality Flocks of grackles roost communally in a general area of marsh but show no fidelity to a specific site. In the evening they gather in single-sex flocks near the roost, then travel together to the communal roost. In the breeding season individual males defend small groups of nesting females.

Nest and Nest Site Females choose nest sites such as islands that are secure from most ground predators, often over water inhabited by alligators. Terrestrial colonies in trees are frequently surrounded by open terrain. Saw grass, palmetto, oak, willow, wax myrtle, mangroves, and cattails are the usual substrates. Females build a shallow platform of coarse stems, then an outer cup of grass stems, and an inner cup of mud and vegetation. The nest is lined with fine material. A great variety of materials, including many man-made products, may be incorporated into the nest. The female is sexually receptive only in the final stage of nest building. Nests average 3.5 m (11.5 ft) apart in colonies in cattails, but nest platforms may be in contact. In oak trees the nests average 1.5 m (5 ft) apart. Males and females frequently return to the same colony site in succeeding years.

Eggs The light-blue eggs with darker scrawls average 32 by 22 mm (1.3 by 0.9 in) and weigh about 8 g (0.3 oz). Each egg weighs about 8% of the female body weight. The proportion of yolk in the egg increases as the egg size increases. The average clutch size is 2.7 eggs with a range of 1 to 5. One egg is laid daily, and each is slightly smaller than its predecessor. Renesting occurs if a clutch is destroyed, but only 1 brood per year is raised.

Incubation Incubation usually begins after the 2nd egg is laid but may not begin until the clutch is complete. Late in the season or in the northern part of the range, incubation may begin as soon as the 1st egg is laid. Females incubate exclusively for the 13-day incubation period. In the sun, incubating females often ruffle the feathers and pant with the beak open or stand over the nest with wings open to shade the eggs. Hatching may be synchronous or spaced over several days, depending on incubation regime.

Fledging The newly hatched chicks are partly covered with a tan down. In nests with asynchronous hatching, the 1st-hatched young are larger and able to compete more effectively for food, with the result that later hatchlings have a considerably reduced rate of survival. The nestlings peep at first, then produce begging calls that continue for 3 or 4 weeks after fledging. Only the female feeds the chicks. Male chicks gain weight faster than females, and by 13 days weigh 50% more than females. Female chicks attain internal temperature control by the 6th day and males by the 10th. Fledging is at 14 to 16 days of age, but full feather growth is not attained until about 2 weeks later. About 60% of nests produce a fledgling.

Age at First Breeding Females usually breed at the age of 1 year, but their peak of nesting is 2 weeks after that of the older females. Second-year males are physiologically capable of breeding but seldom do so due to low ranking in the dominance hierarchy.

BEHAVIOR Flap speed is 3.8 flaps per second when the grackle is traveling in a continuous flap mode. Flight speed has been reported up to 62 kph (39 mph). They regularly bathe by wading into the water until the abdomen is submerged, then ruffle the plumage, dip the head, and use the wings to throw water onto the back. Both sexes intermingle in night roosts but form single-sex flocks when leaving the roost for the day's foraging. Males begin singing in the roost before dawn, are less boisterous at midday, and resume singing in the evening until after sunset. When disturbed at night, both sexes give *chack* alarm calls. Individual distance between perched males is 22 cm (8.6 in), between males and females 14 cm (5.5 in), and between females 6.7 cm (2.6 in). Boat-tailed Grackle roosts are sometimes joined by small groups of blackbirds or starlings. Both sexes give mobbing calls and dive at potential nest predators and at predators with a captured grackle.

MIGRATION The population in the northern part of the range moves south in the winter to avoid snow and ice in feeding habitat.

PREDATORS Yellow rat snakes, various rats, crows, Great Blue Herons, Purple Gallinules, and alligators take eggs and young from the nests. If predation is severe, the colony may abandon the nesting area and move to another one nearby.

LONGEVITY Banded birds have been recovered at 12 years 9 months of age, but they probably exceed this considerably, as Common Grackles have been recovered 20 years 11 months after banding.

CONSERVATION ISSUES Coastal development continues to eliminate nesting and feeding habitat. Predators are the major sources of mortality of eggs and chicks. Starvation is the primary source of mortality from hatching to fledging.

NOTES The genus name is probably from the Latin *quiscalis* (quail). An alternative source of the name has been suggested as *quisquilla* (a trifling dispute), in reference to the often continuous calling between members of a flock. The species name is the Latin *major* (greater or larger). The common name "boat tailed" is in reference to the keel-shaped tail and the word "grackle" (a jackdaw), an Old World blackbird. It is also called crow blackbird or jackdaw in English, *tordo* *cola ancha* in Spanish, and *quiscale des marais* in French.

SUGGESTED ADDITIONAL READING

Bancroft, G.T. 1984. Growth and sexual dimorphism of the Boat-tailed Grackle. *Condor,* 86:423–432.

Bancroft, G.T. 1986. Nesting success and mortality of the Boat-tailed Grackle *Quiscalus major. Auk,* 103:86–89.

Post, W. 1995. Reproduction of female Boat-tailed Grackles: Comparisons between South Carolina and Florida. *J Field Ornithol,* 66:221–230.

Cave Swallow
Hirundo fulva | **Hirundinidae Passeriformes | p. 73**

DISTRIBUTION This genus with 25 species is found worldwide. The Cave Swallow expanded its range to Texas, New Mexico, and south Florida during the 20th century. The species has been divided into 5 subspecies in which *H. f. pallida* occurs in the southwest U.S. and nearby Mexico, *H. f. citata* on the Yucatan Peninsula, *H. f. aequatorialis* in Ecuador, and *H. f. ruficollaris* in Peru. *H. f. fulva* is found in southern Florida and the Greater Antilles. There are widespread reports of vagrants. Their habit of nesting in caves and the walls of sinkholes previously isolated them from other swallows, but a range expansion due to the use of highway culverts has brought them into regular contact with Barn Swallows, leading to some hybridization.

FOOD AND FEEDING HABITS
While in flight, Cave Swallows feed on insects up to 100 m (320 ft) over open areas or bodies of water. They may fly through dense vegetation with strong wingbeats to flush insects into the air for capture. Insects are eaten in flight or carried in the beak to nestlings. The particular prey varies geographically and includes bees, ants, wasps, butterflies, moths, aphids, lacewings, bugs, flies, grasshoppers, and beetles. They usually drink water in flight by skimming the surface with the beak open. Cold or rainy weather that reduces the numbers of flying insects can lead to famine, emaciation, and death.

REPRODUCTION Cave Swallows raise 2 or 3 broods per year in mud nests stuck to vertical rock or masonry walls.

Seasonality Most nests are built from late April to mid-June in temperate areas and may be seasonally dispersed from May to October in the tropics.

Courtship After in-flight courtship displays, a monogamous pair bond is formed, with most copulations taking place on the nest. Males spend considerable time defending their mates against copulations with other males. Both sexes frequent mud-gathering spots, where they almost continuously flap their wings. When a female interrupts her fluttering, often a male with which she is not mated will land on her back and attempt to copulate. At mud-gathering spots a male may copulate with several females

Territoriality Cave swallows often nest in colonies. Nests may be situated close together, but due to irregularities of the substrate a nest usually cannot be seen by its neighbor. The nest site is defended by the perched bird, which chatters at intruders while spreading the wings and extending the head. Cave Swallows are quite tolerant of other swifts and swallows and often feed and nest in mixed-species groups.

Nest and Nest site The nest is often built in caves but may also be built under overhanging cliffs, in pockets in the sides of sinkholes, and under man-made structures such as bridges and large culverts. The South American subspecies may nest on more-exposed cliff faces or even the sides of buildings. The nest is composed of saliva mixed with mud or bat guano cemented to a rock or concrete wall. It is lined with soft plant material such as the down from thistles, dandelions, cottonwood, or other trees with silk on their seeds in the tropics. The nest may be a simple quarter-sphere open cup or may be almost an enclosed hemisphere. The location is usually chosen to be above the reach of climbing terrestrial predators and out of sight of most avian predators. They are able to nest far back in the twilight zone of caves. In box culverts, the nest is often near the joint of walls and roof in low-light conditions. A pair may raise several broods in the same nest within a breeding season. Nests are often used again by the same pair in succeeding years.

Eggs The white eggs measuring 20.5 by 14.6 mm (0.8 by 0.6) and weighing about 2 g (0.07 oz) are marked with light- and dark-brown spots and may also have dark-purple markings. A clutch usually has 3 or 4 eggs with a recorded range 1 to 6. As with many birds, 2nd clutches have fewer eggs.

Incubation The 15- to 18-day incubation period is accomplished primarily by the female. Males may sit on the eggs, but they do not develop brood patches. A hatch success of 78% has been recorded.

Fledging When 1st hatched, the chicks are blind and naked but soon are covered with a buff-tinted white down and are able hold their heads up with a bright-yellow gape. Both parents participate in bringing insects to the nestlings. Most chicks are able to fly short distances at 3 weeks of age, but some may stay in the nest a few days longer. After leaving the nest, the young birds in crevices or on cave or culvert floors are still fed by the parents. Fledging success has been recorded at 37% to 65% in caves with significantly greater success in culverts. **Age at First Breeding** Limited data indicate that Cave Swallows breed at 1 year of age. Average life span is 2.7 years in 1 studied population with no banded birds.

BEHAVIOR Cave swallows seldom walk more than 10 cm (4 in), but they are able to cling to rough limestone walls while building nests. Feeding, nest defense, drinking, and bathing are usually accomplished in flocks. They bathe by immersing themselves in shallow pools while fluttering wings and tail. In deeper water the belly is dunked while in flight. Individual distance in neutral territory is about 10 cm (4 in). Cave Swallows mob, pursue, and strike Great Horned Owls near nesting caves. Flight speed has been measured up to 25 kph (15.5 mph).

MIGRATION Populations in warm climates are sedentary, while those in the northern part of the range must move south for the winter to find flying insects. Hatching-year birds leave the colony first and disperse widely. In recent years a small population has wintered in south Texas.

PREDATORS Great Horned Owls, Barn Owls, and Peregrine Falcons have been recorded feeding on adult Cave Swallows. West Indian boas (*Epicrates*) have been observed lurking at cave mouths to catch bats and probably take Cave Swallows that venture near. Remains have been found in scat from raccoons and ringtails. Grackles take eggs and hatchlings.

LONGEVITY A Cave Swallow was recaptured 9 years 4 months after banding.

CONSERVATION ISSUES Free-tailed bats, which often share caves and diets with Cave Swallows, have been found to have high levels of DDT and DDE, suggesting that Cave Swallows may be similarly poisoned.

NOTES The genus name is the original Latin name for a swallow. The species name is from the Latin meaning "yellowish brown" or "tawny." It has also been placed in the genus *Petrochelidon*. It is also known in the British Caribbean as rain bird. In Spanish it is known as *golondrina de cuevas ,* and in French as *hirondelle.*

SUGGESTED ADDITIONAL READING

Martin, R.F. 1981. Reproductive correlates of environmental variation and niche expansion in the Cave Swallow in Texas. *Wilson Bulletin,* 93:506–518.

Smith, P.W., W.B. Robertson Jr. and H. M. Stevenson. 1988. West Indian Cave Swallows nesting in Florida, with comments on the taxonomy of *Hirundo fulva. Florida Field Nat,* 16:86–90.

West, S. 1995. Cave Swallow (*Hirundo fulva*). In A. Poole and F. Gill (eds.), *The Birds of North America. No. 141.* Philadelphia: The Birds of North America, Inc.

Fish Crow
Corvus ossifragus | **Corvidae Passeriformes** | **p. 74**

DISTRIBUTION This genus with 40 species is found worldwide except for South America. The Fish Crow is found from New York to Texas along the coast and inland along large rivers. The American Crow *(C. brachyrhynchos)* is found throughout southern Canada and the U.S. Several similar endemic species of crows inhabit the Greater Antilles.

FOOD AND FEEDING HABITS
The main foods are carrion on roadsides and shorelines, crabs, shrimp, snails, clams, crayfish, frogs, mice, beetles, grasshoppers, scorpions, spiders, caterpillars, grains, fruits, nuts, and many types of wild berries. They have been seen grabbing minnows from the water with the feet. They are notorious as robbers of eggs and chicks from the nests of songbirds and are particularly adept at flying into heron rookeries and snatching eggs and chicks while the herons are disturbed by humans or other predators. Crow predation may disrupt entire colonies of nesting gulls, terns, and shorebirds. They are sometimes significant predators of freshwater turtle eggs and attack hatchling gopher and box turtles.

REPRODUCTION Fish Crows nest singly or in small groups in the tops of tall trees near water.

Seasonality Eggs may be laid as early as the 1st week in April in the South, but most are laid in May, with a few late nests in the North having eggs until mid-June.

Courtship The courting pair engage in joint aerial maneuvers in which they may touch wings and heads. Sometimes 2 males compete for the attentions of a single female. The mated pair alight nearby, preen each other, and vocalize in a quiet and melodic warble very different from the normal call. Duration of pair bonds in the wild has not been determined.

Territoriality No records have been published of a defended territory.

Nest and Nest Site Both sexes carry sticks, grass, small roots, bark, string, hair, and feathers to build the nest at elevations from 3 to 45 m (10 to 150 ft) above the ground. Nests are usually placed in a fork near the trunk of a tree. Tall pines are a favored site for the 40 cm diameter (16 in) nest. Nests are in loose, open groups near water, sometimes with several nests in the same tree. Old hawk nests are sometimes taken over and refurbished.

Eggs The clutch is 3 to 5 greenish-blue eggs with brown spots. Eggs measure 37 by 27 mm (1.5 by 1 in). Replacement clutches are laid, but only 1 brood is raised per season.

Incubation Both sexes share nest-sitting duties for the 19-day incubation period.

Fledging The chick is naked at hatching but soon acquires a grayish-brown down. Fledging is at about 22 days with a dull brownish-black juvenile plumage that is molted by September to a winter plumage that is similar to but less glossy than that of the adult.

Age at First Breeding Fish Crows usually breed at the age of 1 year.

BEHAVIOR Fish Crows are gregarious and are usually found in small flocks. Outside the breeding season they may gather in night roosts of several thousand. Flight speed is 40 to 50 kph (25 to 32 mph). The flap rate is recorded as 2 flaps per second but increases considerably when the crow is in haste. Crows are inclined to mob raptors and cause a huge commotion when they find a sleeping owl in the daytime.

MIGRATION Fish Crow and American Crow populations in Florida are increased in the fall by winter migrants from freezing climates.

PREDATORS Raccoons, opossums, and snakes eat the eggs. Hawks and owls eat the chicks and sometimes catch the adults.

LONGEVITY A Fish Crow was recorded as killed 8 years after banding.

CONSERVATION ISSUES Crows are very adaptable and seem to be maintaining their populations by taking advantage of the activities of man.

NOTES The genus name is from the Latin *corvus* (raven). The Fish Crow species name is from the Latin *os* (bone), and *frag* (to break), probably in reference to dropping bones on rocks in order to break them and gain access to the marrow. The species name for the American Crow is from the Greek *brachys* (short) and *rynchos* (beak). The American Crow is also called common crow or southern crow. Nesting blackbirds and other songbirds often show a particular animosity to crows, attacking them furiously when the crows are perched or flying near the nest. Crows are called *cao* or *cuervo* in Spanish and *corneille* in French.

SUGGESTED ADDITIONAL READING

Chamberlain, D.A. and G.W. Cornwell. 1971. Selected vocalizations of the common crow. *Auk,* 88:613–34.

Frings, H. and M. Frings. 1959. The language of crows. *Scientific American,* 20:119–131.

Hardy, J.W. 1990. The Fish Crow (*Corvus ossifragus*) and its Mexican relatives: Vocal clues to evolutionary relationships. *Florida Field Nat,* 18:74–80.

General References

Allen, R.B.1956, *The Flamingos: Their Life and Survival. Research Report 5.* New York: National Audubon Society.

American Ornithologists Union. 1983. *Check List of North American Birds.* Washington, DC: AOU.

Angel, T. 1978. *Ravens, Crows, Magpies, and Jays.* Seattle: University of Washington Press.

Ashmole, N.P. 1963. The regulation of numbers of tropical oceanic birds. *Ibis,* 103b:458–473.

Bannerman, D.A. 1960. *Birds of the British Isles.* London: Oliver and Boyd.

——— 1963. *Birds of the Atlantic Islands.* London: Oliver and Boyd.

Bellrose, F.C. 1976. *Ducks, Geese and Swans of North America.* Harrisburg, PA: Stackpole.

Bennett, L.J. 1938. *The Blue-winged Teal, Its Ecology and Management.* Ames, IA: Collegiate Press.

Bildstein, K. 1993. *White Ibis: Wetlands Wanderer.* Washington, DC: Smithsonian Press.

Bird, D.M. 1983. *Biology and Management of Bald Eagles and Ospreys.* Quebec: Harpel Press.

Brown L.H. 1976. *Birds of Prey: Their Biology and Ecology.* London: Hamlyn.

Burger, J. 1978. Competition between Cattle Egrets and native North American herons, egrets, and ibises. *Condor,* 80:15–23.

Butler, R.W. 1997. *The Great Blue Heron.* Vancouver: University of British Columbia Press.

Cade, T.J. 1982. *The Falcons of the World.* Ithaca: Comstock-Cornell University Press.

Cade, T.J., J.H. Enderson, C.G. Thelander and C.M. White (eds.). 1988. *Peregrine Falcon Populations.* Boise: Peregrine Fund.

Carson, R. 1962. *Silent Spring.* Greenwich, CT: Fawcett.

Cramp, S. and K.E.L. Simmons. 1985. *Handbook of the Birds of Europe, the Middle East, and North Africa: The Birds of the Western Palearctic.* New York: Oxford University Press.

Croxall, J.P. (ed.). 1987. *Seabirds, Feeding Biology and Role in Marine Ecosystems.* U.K.: Cambridge University Press.

del Hoyo, J., A. Elliot and J. Stargatal (eds.). 1992. *Handbook of the Birds of the World. Vol. 1.* Barcelona: Lynx Edicions.

Eckert, A.W. 1981. *The Wading Birds of North America.* New York: Doubleday.

Edwards, E.P. 1972. *Field Guide to Birds of Mexico.* Sweet Briar, VA: E.P. Edwards.

Erwin, R.M. 1989. Responses to human intruders by birds nesting in colonies: Experimental results and management guidelines. *Colonial Waterbirds,* 12:104–108.

Farrand, J. (ed.). 1983. *The Audubon Society Master Field Guide to Birding.* New York: Alfred Knopf. Gooders, J. and T. Boyer. 1986. *Ducks of North America.* New York: Facts on File.

Goss-Custard, J.D. (ed). 1996. *The Oystercatcher: From Individuals to Populations.* New York: Oxford University Press.

Hancock, J. and H. Elliot. 1978. *Herons of the World.* New York: Harper and Row.

Hancock, J. and D. Goodwin. 1976. *Crows of the World.* Ithaca: Cornell University Press.

Hancock, J., J. Kushlan. 1984. *The Herons Handbook.* New York: Harper and Row.

Hancock, J.A., J. Kushlan and M. Kahl. 1992. *Storks, Ibises and Spoonbills.* San Diego: Academic Press.

Harrison, C.S. 1990. *Seabirds of Hawaii: Natural History and Conservation.* Ithaca, NY: Cornell University Press.

Harrison, H.H. 1975. *A Field Guide to Birds Nests.* Boston: Houghton Mifflin.

Jenni, D.A. 1969. A study of the ecology of four species of herons during the breeding season at Lake Alice, Alachua County, Florida. *Ecological Monographs,* 39:245–270.

Johnsgard, P.A. 1975. *Waterfowl of North America.* Lincoln: University of Nebraska.

——— 1978. *Ducks, Geese and Swans of North America.* Lincoln: University of Nebraska.

——— 1978. *Ducks, Geese and Swans of the World.* Lincoln: University of Nebraska.

——— 1981. *The Plovers, Sandpipers and Snipes of the World.* Lincoln: University of Nebraska.

——— 1987. *Diving Birds of North America.* Lincoln: University of Nebraska.

——— 1990. *Hawks, Eagles and Falcons of North America.* Washington, DC: Smithsonian Institute Press.

——— 1993 *Cormorants, Darters and Pelicans of the World.* Washington, DC: Smithsonian Institution Press.

Johnston, D.W. 1961. *The Biosystematics of American Crows.* Seattle: University of Washington Press.

Kale, H. (ed). 1978. *Rare and Endangered Biota of Florida.* Gainesville: University Press of Florida.

Kear, J. and N. Duplaix-Hall. 1975. *Flamingo* . Berkhamsted, England: T. and A.D. Poyser.

Kent, D.M. 1986. Behavior, habitat use and food of three egrets in a marine habitat. *Colonial Waterbirds,* 9:25–30.

——— 1987. Effects of varying behavior and habitat on the striking efficiency of egrets. *Colonial Waterbirds,* 10:115–119.

Klein, M.L., S.R. Humphrey and H.F. Percival. 1995. Effects of ecotourism on distribution of waterbirds in a wildlife refuge. *Conservation Biology,* 9:1454–1456.

Kushlan, J. 1984. *The Herons Handbook.* New York: Harper and Row.

Kushlan, J. and M. Kahl. 1992. *Storks, Ibises and Spoonbills of the World.* San Diego: Academic Press.

Maxwell, G.R. II, and H.W. Kale II. 1977. Breeding biology of five species of herons in coastal Florida. *Auk,* 94:689–700.

Meyerriecks, A.J. 1962. Diversity typifies heron feeding. Natural History. 72:48–59.

Nelson, J.B. 1978. *The Sulidae.* Oxford: Oxford University Press.

——— 1979. *Seabirds, Their Biology and Ecology*. New York: A and W Publishers.

Olsen, K.M. and H. Larsen. 1995. *Terns of Europe and North America*. Princeton: Princeton University Press.

Orians, G.H. 1985. *Blackbirds of the Americas*. Seattle: University of Washington Press.

Owre, O.T. 1967. *Adaptations for Loco-motion and Feeding in the Anhinga and Double-crested Cormorant. Ornithology Monograph No. 6.* Lawrence, Kansas: American Ornithologists Union.

Palmer, R.S. 1962. *Handbook of North American Birds*. New Haven, CT: Yale University Press.

Pennycuick, C.J. 1989. *Bird Flight Performance*. New York: Oxford University Press.

Poole, A.F. 1989. *Ospreys, a Natural and Unnatural History*. New York: Cambridge University Press.

Ratcliffe, D. 1993. *The Peregrine Falcon*. San Diego: Academic Press.

Ripley, S.D. 1977. *Rails of the World*. Boston: David R. Goodine.

Robertson, W.B. Jr. and G.E. Woolfenden. 1992. *Florida Bird Species: An Annotated List*. Gainesville: Florida Ornithogical Society.

Rogers, J.A. Jr. and H.T. Smith. 1995. Set-back distances to protect nesting bird colonies from human disturbance in Florida. *Conservation Biology*, 9:89–99.

Serventy, D.L., V. Serventy and J. Warham. 1971. *The Handbook of Australian Sea-birds*. Sydney: A.W. and A.H. Reed.

Sibley, C.G. and B.L. Monroe Jr. 1990. *Distribution and Taxonomy of Birds of the World*. New Haven, CT: Yale University Press.

Sowls, L.K. 1955. *Prairie Ducks, a Study of Their Behavior, Ecology and Management*. Harrisburg, PA: Stacpole.

Sprunt, A. IV, J.C. Ogden and S. Winckler (eds.). 1978. *Wading Birds*. New York: National Audubon Society.

Stevenson, H.M. and B.H. Anderson. 1994. *The Birdlife of Florida*. Gainesville: University Press of Florida.

Tacha ,T.C. and C.E. Braun. 1994. *Migratory Shore and Upland Game Bird Management in North America*. Washington: International Association of Fish and Wildlife Agencies.

Todd, F.S. 1996. *Natural History of the Waterfowl*. Vista CA: Ibis Publishing.

Turner, A. and C. Rose. 1989. *Swallows and Martins*. Boston: Houghton Mifflin.

Index

NOTE:

Bold page numbers refer to entry in Part I (General Descriptions and Photographs). *Italic* page numbers refer to entry in Part II (Species Accounts).

A

Actitus macularia, **52**, *231*
Ajaia ajaja, **28**, *158*
American Anhinga, **13**, *108*
American Avocet, **48**, *220*
American Coot, **40**, *198*
American darter, **13**, *110*
American Egret, **16**, *119*
American flamingo, **29**, *163*
American gallinule, **41**, *203*
American Kestrel, **38**, *190*
American Oystercatcher, **46**, *214*
American White Pelican, **11**, *101*
Anas
　　bahamensis, **32**, *172*
　　discors, **31**, *169*
Anhinga anhinga, **13**, *108*
Anhinga, American, **13**, *108*
Anous stolidus, **69**, *283*
Ardea herodius, **15**, *114*
Arenaria interpres, **53**, *234*
Atlantic booby, **7**, *91*
Audubon's Shearwater, **4**, *80*
Avocet, American, **48**, *220*
Aythya affinis, **30**, *165*

B

Bahama duck, **32**, *173*
Bahama pintail, **32**, *173*
banjo-bill flamingo, **28**, *160*
Barbary falcon, **39**, *196*
bastard hawk, **38**, *192*
bastard yellowlegs, **58**, *251*
beach plover, **54**, *239*

bead bird, **53**, *236*
big cucu, **49**, *224*
big yellow-legged plover, **49**, *224*
big-footed falcon, **39**, *196*
bishop plover, **53**, *236*
black curlew, **27**, *157*
black jack, **30**, *167*
Black Skimmer, **70**, *286*
Black-bellied Plover, **42**, *204*
black-capped night heron, **23**, *144*
Black-crowned Night Heron, **23**, *142*
black-legged peep, **55**, *242*
Black-necked Stilt, **47**, *217*
blue crane, **15**, *116*
blue gaulin, **15**, *116*
blue gauling, **17**, *122*
blue shanks, **48**, *222*
blue stocking, **48**, *222*
bluebill, **30**, *167*
blue-faced booby, **9**, *98*
blue-wing, **31**, *171*
Blue-winged Teal, **31**, *169*
boatswain bird, **6**, *88*
Boat-tailed Grackle, **72**, *293*
bonito gull, **67**, *279*
bonnet martyr, **20**, *133*
Booby
　　Brown, **7**, *89*
　　Masked, **9**, *95*
　　Red-footed, **8**, *92*
bosun-bird, **5**, *85*
brasswing, **32**, *173*
Bridled Tern, **67**, *277*
Brown Booby, **7**, *89*
brown gannet, **7**, *91*
brown ibis, **26**, *154*
Brown Noddy, **69**, *283*
Brown Pelican, **10**, *98*
brown snipe, **59**, *253*
Bubulcus ibis, **21**, *134*
buff-backed heron, **21**, *137*

bull peep, **54**, *239*
bush gannet, **8**, *94*
Buteo
    jamaicensis, **36**, *184*
    lineatus, **37**, *187*
Butorides virescens, **22**, *138*

C
Cabot's tern, **64**, *269*
calico bird, **17**, *122*
calico-bird, **53**, *236*
Calidris
    alba, **54**, *237*
    himantopus, **58**, *249*
    mauri, **56**, *243*
    minutilla, **57**, *246*
    pusilla, **55**, *240*
carite, **65**, *273*
Casmerodius albus, **16**, *117*
Caspian Tern, **62**, *261*
cat bird, **71**, *291*
Catoptrophorus semipalmatus, **51**, *228*
Cattle Egret, **21**, *134*
cattle gaulin, **21**, *137*
Cave Swallow, **73**, *297*
chalk-line, **22**, *140*
Charadrius
    semipalmatus, **44**, *209*
    vociferus, **45**, *211*
    wilsoni, **43**, *207*
chicken hawk, **36**, *186*
chicken plover, **53**, *236*
chicken-foot coot, **41**, *203*
cobbler, **14**, *113*
Coccyzus minor, **71**, *290*
coffin bird, **71**, *291*
common booby, **7**, *91*
common crow, **74**, *301*
common dowitcher, **59**, *253*
common egret, **20**, *133*
common gallinule, **41**, *203*
common gull, **61**, *260*
Common Moorhen, **41**, *201*
common noddies, **69**, *285*
common oystercatcher, **46**, *216*

common yellowlegs, **50**, *227*
Coot, **40**, *198*
Cormorant, Double-crested, **12**, *104*
Corvus ossifragus, **74**, *300*
cow heron, **21**, *137*
crabcatcher, **24**, *147*
crabcracker, **24**, *147*
crabeater, **24**, *147*
crane, **15**, *116*
creek broadbill, **30**, *167*
crow blackbird, **72**, *295*
Crow, Fish, **74**, *300*
crow-duck, **12**, *107*
Cuckoo, Mangrove, **71**, *290*
cutwater, **70**, *288*

D
davie, **65**, *273*
diablotin, **4**, *82*
didapter, **3**, *79*
Double-crested Cormorant, **12**, *104*
Dowitcher, Short-billed, **59**, *252*
Duck
    Blue-winged Teal, **31**, *169*
    Lesser Scaup, **30**, *165*
    Red-breasted Merganser, **33**, *174*
    White-cheeked Pintail, **32**, *172*
duck hawk, **39**, *196*
duck snipe, **51**, *230*
dumb bird, **71**, *291*
dusky shearwater, **4**, *82*

E
eastern dowitcher, **59**, *253*
egg bird, **67**, *279*
Egret
    Cattle, **21**, *134*
    Great, **16**, *117*
    Reddish, **19**, *128*
    Snowy, **20**, *131*
Egretta
    caerulea, **17**, *120*
    rufescens, **19**, *128*
    thula, **20**, *131*
    tricolor, **18**, *124*

Elanoides forficatus, **35**, *181*
Eudocimus albus, **26**, *151*

F
Falco
    peregrinus, **39**, *194*
    sparverius, **38**, *190*
Falcon, Peregrine, **39**, *194*
field plover, **45**, *212*
Fish Crow, **74**, *300*
fish duck, **33**, *176*
fish eagle, **34**, *179*
fish hawk, **34**, *179*
Flamingo, Greater, **29**, *161*
flinthead, **25**, *150*
forked tail kite, **35**, *183*
four o'clock bird, **71**, *291*
Fregata magnificens, **14**, *111*
Frigatebird, Magnificent, **14**, *111*
frost snipe, **58**, *251*
Fulica americana, **40**, *198*

G
Gallinula chlorops, **41**, *201*
gaulin, **18**, **19**, *127*, *130*
Glossy Ibis, **27**, *155*
gourdhead, **25**, *150*
Grackle, Boat-tailed, **72**, *293*
gray plover, **42**, *206*
Great Blue Heron, **15**, *114*
Great Egret, **16**, *117*
great white heron, **16**, *119*
Greater Flamingo, **29**, *161*
Greater Yellowlegs, **49**, *223*
greater yellowshank, **49**, *224*
Grebe, Pied-billed, **3**, *77*
Green Heron, **22**, *138*
green ibis, **27**, *157*
green-backed heron, **22**, *140*
grey gaulin, **15**, *116*
Gull
    Laughing, **60**, *254*
    Ring-billed, **61**, *258*
gullie, **65**, *273*
gullie bird, **64**, *269*

H
Haematopus palliatus, **46**, *214*
Hawk
    Red-shouldered, **37**, *187*
    Red-tailed, **36**, *184*
hell diver, **3**, *79*
hen hawk, **37**, *189*
Heron
    Black-crowned Night, **23**, *142*
    Great Blue, **15**, *114*
    Green, **22**, *138*
    Little Blue, **17**, *120*
    Tricolored, **18**, *124*
    Yellow-crowned Night, **24**, *145*
Himantopus mexicanus, **47**, *217*
Hirundo fulva, **73**, *297*
hurricane bird, **14**, *113*

I
Ibis
    Glossy, **27**, *155*
    White, **26**, *151*
Irish snipe, **48**, *222*
ironhead, **25**, *150*

J
jackdaw, **72**, *295*

K
Kentish tern, **64**, *269*
Kestrel, American, **38**, *190*
kill'em polly, **66**, *276*
Killdeer, **45**, *211*
killi killi hawk, **38**, *192*
Kite, Swallow-tailed, **35**, *181*

L
lake gull, **61**, *260*
lapwing, **42**, *206*
lark, **9**, *98*
Larus
    atricilla, **60**, *254*
    delawarensis, **61**, *258*
Laughing Gull, **60**, *254*
Least Sandpiper, **57**, *246*

least stint, **57**, **58**, *247*
Least Tern, **66**, *274*
Lesser Scaup, **30**, *165*
Lesser Yellowlegs, **50**, *225*
lesser yellowshanks, **50**, *227*
Limnodromus griseus, **59**, *252*
Little Blue Heron, **17**, *120*
little gaulin, **22**, *140*
little green heron, **22**, *140*
little stonebird, **50**, *227*
little tell-tale, **50**, *227*
little tern, **66**, *276*
little white heron, **20**, *133*
long white, **16**, *119*
long-legged sandpiper, **58**, *251*
longshank, **47**, *219*
longtail, **5**, **6**, *85*, *88*
Louisiana gaulin, **18**, *127*

M
Magnificent Frigatebird, **14**, *111*
man o' war bird, **14**, *113*
Mangrove Cuckoo, **71**, *290*
mangrove heron, **22**, *140*
marlinspike, **5**, *85*
Masked Booby, **9**, *95*
Merganser, Red-breasted, **33**, *174*
Mexican duck, **31**, *171*
Moorhen, Common, **41**, *201*
mud hen, **40**, **41**, *200*, *203*
mud peep, **57**, *247*
Mycteria americana, **25**, *148*

N
night gaulin, **24**, *147*
Noddy, Brown, **69**, *283*
noddy terns, **69**, *285*
Nyctanassa violaceus, **24**, *145*
Nycticorax nycticorax, **23**, *142*

O
Osprey, **34**, *177*
Oystercatcher, American, **46**, *214*
ox-eye, **57**, *247*

P
paddlebeak, **28**, *160*
Pandion haliaetus, **34**, *177*
pasture bird, **45**, *212*
peep, **54**, **55**, **56**, **58**, *239*, *242*, *245*, *251*
peet-weet, **52**, *233*
Pelecanus
    erythrorynchos, **11**, *101*
    occidentalis, **10**, *98*
Pelican
    American White, **11**, *101*
    Brown, **10**, *98*
Peregrine Falcon, **39**, *194*
Phaethon
    aethereus, **5**, *83*
    lepturus, **6**, *86*
Phalacrocorax auritus, **12**, *104*
Phenicopterus ruber, **29**, *161*
pied heron, **17**, *122*
pied oystercatcher, **46**, *216*
Pied-billed Grebe, **3**, *77*
pied-winged curlew, **51**, *230*
pill-will-willet, **51**, *230*
pimlico, **4**, *82*
pink curlew, **28**, *160*
Plegadis falcinellus, **27**, *155*
Plover
    Black-bellied, **42**, *204*
    Semipalmated, **44**, *209*
    Wilson's, **43**, *207*
Pluvialis squatarola, **42**, *204*
Podilymbus podiceps, **3**, *77*
pond bird, **56**, *245*
pond gaulin, **22**, *140*
preacher, **25**, *150*
Puffinus lherminieri, **4**, *80*

Q
Quiscalus major, **72**, *293*

R
rain bird, **71**, **73**, *291*, *299*
razorbill, **70**, *288*
Recurvirostra americana, **48**, *220*
red-bellied hawk, **37**, *189*

red-bill, **46**, *216*
red-billed mud hen, **41**, *203*
Red-billed Tropicbird, **5**, *83*
Red-breasted Merganser, **33**, *174*
red-breasted snipe, **59**, *253*
Reddish Egret, **19**, *128*
Red-footed Booby, **8**, *92*
red-legged gannet, **8**, *94*
redshank, **47**, *219*
Red-shouldered Hawk, **37**, *187*
Red-tailed Hawk, **36**, *184*
Ring-billed Gull, **61**, *258*
rock peregrine, **39**, *196*
Roseate Spoonbill, **28**, *158*
Roseate Tern, **65**, *271*
rosy flamingo, **29**, *163*
rough-billed pelican, **11**, *103*
Royal Tern, **63**, *265*
Ruddy Turnstone, **53**, *234*
Rynchops niger, **70**, *286*

S
sand ox-eye, **55**, *242*
sand peep, **55**, **57**, *242, 247*
sand snipe, **52**, *233*
Sanderling, **54**, *237*
Sandpiper
    Least, **57**, *246*
    Semipalmated, **55**, *240*
    Spotted, **52**, *231*
Stilt, **58**, *249*
    Western, **56**, *243*
Sandwich Tern, **64**, *268*
sawbill, **33**, *176*
scarlet flamingo, **29**, *163*
scissor tail kite, **35**, *183*
scissorbill, **70**, *288*
scissors tail, **14**, *113*
scissortail, **6**, *88*
sea dotterel, **53**, *236*
sea swallow, **66**, *276*
see-saw, **52**, *233*
Semipalmated Plover, **44**, *209*
semipalmated ringed plover, **44**, *210*

Semipalmated Sandpiper, **55**, *240*
shag, **12**, *107*
shearwater, **70**, *288*
shite-poke, **22**, *140*
Short-billed Dowitcher, **59**, *252*
Skimmer, Black, **70**, *286*
snake bird, **13**, *110*
snake hawk, **35**, *183*
Snowy Egret, **20**, *131*
soldier, **47**, *219*
soldier bird, **42**, *206*
Sooty Tern, **68**, *280*
southern crow, **74**, *301*
Spanish curlew, **26**, **27**, *154, 157*
Spanish plover, **51**, *230*
sparrow hawk, **38**, *192*
splatterer, **40**, *200*
Spoonbill, Roseate, **28**, *158*
spotted heron, **17**, *122*
Spotted Sandpiper, **52**, *231*
sprat bird, **63**, *267*
Sterna
    anaethetus, **67**, *277*
    antillarum, **66**, *274*
    caspia, **62**, *261*
    dougallii, **65**, *271*
    fuscata, **68**, *280*
    maxima, **63**, *265*
    sandvicensis, **64**, *268*
Stilt, Black-necked, **47**, *217*
Stilt Sandpiper, **58**, *249*
stint, **54**, **55**, **56**, **58**, *239, 242, 245, 251*
stonehead, **25**, *150*
stone-pecker, **53**, *236*
Stork, Wood, **25**, *148*
streaked-back, **53**, *236*
striated heron, **22**, *140*
Sula
    dactylatra, **9**, *95*
    leucogaster, **7**, *89*
    sula, **8**, *92*
Swallow, Cave, **73**, *297*
Swallow-tailed Kite, **35**, *181*

T

tattler, **49**, **50**, *224*, *227*
teal, **31**, *171*
teeter-peep, **52**, *233*
teeter-tail, **52**, *233*
telltale, **47**, *219*
Tern
    Bridled, **67**, *277*
    Caspian, **62**, *261*
    Least, **66**, *274*
    Roseate, **65**, *271*
    Royal, **63**, *265*
    Sandwich, **64**, *268*
    Sooty, **68**, *280*
thick-billed plover, **43**, *208*
tick bird, **21**, *137*
tip-up, **52**, *233*
tree booby, **8**, *94*
Tricolored Heron, **18**, *124*
Tringa
    flavipes, **50**, *225*
    melanoleuca, **49**, *223*
Tropicbird
    Red-billed, **5**, *83*
    White-tailed, **6**, *86*
Turnstone, Ruddy, **53**, *234*

W

water hen, **40**, **41**, *200*, *203*
water turkey, **13**, *110*
water witch, **3**, *79*
waterfowl, **40**, *200*
wedrego, **4**, *82*

West Indian flamingo, **29**, *163*
Western Sandpiper, **56**, *243*
whelk-cracker, **46**, *216*
whistling booby, **9**, *98*
white booby, **8**, **9**, *94*, *98*
white crane, **16**, *119*
white curlew, **26**, *154*
white gaulin, **16**, **20**, *119*, *133*
white heron, **16**, *119*
White Ibis, **26**, *151*
white-bellied booby, **7**, *91*
White-cheeked Pintail, **32**, *172*
white-faced teal, **31**, *171*
whitehead, **32**, *173*
white-tailed booby, **8**, *94*
White-tailed Tropicbird, **6**, *86*
wideawake, **68**, *282*
will willet, **51**, *230*
Willet, **51**, *228*
Wilson's Plover, **43**, *207*
winter hawk, **37**, *189*
wood ibis, **25**, *150*
Wood Stork, **25**, *148*

Y

yellow-billed tropicbird, **6**, *88*
Yellow-crowned Night Heron, **24**, *145*
yellow-legged plover, **50**, *227*
Yellowlegs
    Greater, **49**, *223*
    Lesser, **50**, *225*
yelper, **47**, *219*

Here are some other books from Pineapple Press on related topics. For a complete catalog, write to Pineapple Press, P.O. Box 3889, Sarasota, Florida 34230-3889, or call (800) PINEAPL (746-3275). Or visit our website at www.pineapplepress.com.

The Climate and Weather of Florida by James A. Henry, Kenneth M. Portier, and Jan Coyne. This comprehensive book offers in-depth, clear explanations of the entire range of Florida's weather, from sunny skies to hurricanes. ISBN 1-56164-036-0 (hb); 1-56164-037-9 (pb)

The Everglades: River of Grass, 50th Anniversary Edition by Marjory Stoneman Douglas. This is the treasured classic of nature writing, first published fifty years ago, that captured attention all over the world and launched the fight to save the Everglades. The 50th Anniversary Edition includes an update on the events in the Glades in the last decade. ISBN 1-56164-135-9 (hb)

The Exploring Wild Florida series: A series of field guides, each with information on all the parks, preserves, and natural areas in its region, including wildlife to look for and best time of year to visit.

Exploring Wild Central Florida by Susan D. Jewell. From New Smyrna and Crystal River in the north to Hobe Sound and Punta Gorda in the south, including Lake Okeechobee. ISBN 1-56164-082-4 (pb)

Exploring Wild North Florida by Gil Nelson. From the Suwannee River to the Atlantic shore, and south to include the Ocala National Forest. ISBN 1-56164-091-3 (pb)

Exploring Wild Northwest Florida by Gil Nelson. The Florida Panhandle, from the Perdido River in the west to the Suwannee River in the east. ISBN 1-56164-086-7 (pb)

Exploring Wild South Florida Second Edition by Susan D. Jewell. From Hobe Sound and Punta Gorda south to include the Keys and the Dry Tortugas. This new expanded edition includes more than 40 new natural areas and covers Broward, Hendry, Lee, and Palm Beach Counties as well as Dade, Collier, and Monroe. With this edition, the entire state of Florida is covered in the four-volume Exploring Wild Florida set. ISBN 1-56164-125-1 (pb)

Florida's Birds: A Handbook and Reference by Herbert W. Kale II and David S. Maehr. Illustrated by Karl Karalus. This fully illustrated guide to identification, enjoyment, and protection of Florida's varied and beautiful population of birds identifies and discusses more than 325 species, with information on distinguishing marks, habitat, season, and distribution. ISBN 0-910923-67-1 (hb); 0-910923-68-X (pb)

Poisonous Plants and Animals of Florida and the Caribbean by David W. Nellis. An illustrated guide to the characteristics, symptoms, and treatments for more than 300 species of poisonous plants and toxic animals. ISBN 1-56164-111-1 (hb); 1-56164-113-8 (pb)

Sea Kayaking in Florida by David Gluckman. This guide to sea kayaking in Florida for novices and experienced paddlers alike includes information on wildlife, camping, and gear; maps of the Big Bend Sea Grasses Saltwater Paddling Trail; tips on kayaking the Everglades; lists of liveries and outfitters; and much more. ISBN 1-56164-071-9 (pb)

Sea Kayaking in the Florida Keys by Bruce Wachob. Florida's lower Keys can be best experienced in a kayak. Including insider information such as directions to remote launch sites, tips for trip planning, and listings of nearby campsites, dining, and lodging, this guide lists thirteen detailed trip descriptions for kayakers of every skill level. ISBN 1-56164-142-1 (pb)

Seashore Plants of South Florida and the Caribbean by David W. Nellis. A full-color guide to the flora of nearshore environments, including complete characteristics of each plant as well as ornamental, medicinal, ecological, and other aspects. Suitable for both backyard gardeners and serious naturalists. ISBN 1-56164-026-3 (hb); 1-56164-056-5 (pb)

The Shrubs and Woody Vines of Florida by Gil Nelson. A companion to *The Trees of Florida,* this field guide covers more than 550 species of native and naturalized woody shrubs and vines. ISBN 1-56164-106-5 (hb); 1-56164-110-3 (pb)

The Springs of Florida by Doug Stamm. Take a guided tour of Florida's fascinating springs in this beautiful book featuring detailed descriptions, maps, and rare underwater photography. Learn how to enjoy these natural wonders while swimming, diving, canoeing, and tubing. ISBN 1-56164-054-9 (hb); 1-56164-048-4 (pb)

The Trees of Florida by Gil Nelson. The first comprehensive guide to Florida's amazing variety of tree species, this book serves as both a reference and a field guide. ISBN 1-56164-053-0 (hb); 1-56164-055-7 (pb)